Jonathon G ... s the world's leading lexicographer of dictionaries of anglophone slang. His first dictionary appeared in 1984 and since then he has written and broa cast widely on the subject. *The Cassell Dictionary of Slang* appe red in 1998, the *Chambers Dictionary of Slang* in 2008 and the t ree-volume *Green's Dictionary of Slang* in 2010. The material, hich deals with the slang of every English-speaking country, es from approximately 1400 and continues as far as possible t he present day. As of 2016, this has been available online and expanded and revised in quarterly updates. At present it off approximately 140,000 slang words and phrases, underpi l by around 635,000 citations or illustrative examples.

en has also written a history of lexicography (*Chasing the Dictionary-Makers and the Dictionary They Made*, 1996), a y of slang (*Language! 500 Years of the Vulgar Tongue*, 2014) 'lexico-biography' (*Odd Job Man*, 2014). Other slang- titles include *The Slang Thesaurus* (1988), *Slang Down the* 1993), *Getting Off at Gateshead* (2008), *Crooked Talk*) and *The Stories of Slang* (2016). His ongoing collection of imelines of Slang* (the chronological ordering of the slang ularies of the counter-language's favourite topics) is avail- nline.

e links:

en's Dictionary of Slang: https://greensdictofslang.com
imelines of Slang: the timelines of slang.tumblr.com
Website: jonathongreen.co.uk
Twitter: @misterslang

Sounds & Furies

JONATHON GREEN

ROBINSON

ROBINSON

First published in Great Britain in 2019 by Robinson

1 3 5 7 9 10 8 6 4 2

A CIP catalogue record for this book
is available from the British Library.

ISBN: 978-1-47214-192-7

Typeset in Adobe Garamond by Hewer Text UK Ltd, Edinburgh
Printed and bound in Great Britain by Clays Ltd, Elcograf S.p.A.

Papers used by Robinson are from well-managed forests and other responsible sources.

Robinson
An imprint of
Little, Brown Book Group
Carmelite House
50 Victoria Embankment
London EC4Y 0DZ

An Hachette UK Company
www.hachette.co.uk

www.littlebrown.co.uk

For Etta Lucky Green

Contents

Foreword

In 1770, an anonymous pamphlet titled *The New Art and Mystery of Gossiping* was printed in Stone-cutter-Street, London. The author, whoever they were, claimed it was 'a genuine account of all the women's clubs in and about the city and suburbs of London'. Of course, it's a work of satire intended to send up how women talk to one another, what they talk about, and, by extension, what they think about. Though the work was written over 250 years ago, the stereotypes employed throughout remain ugly comedic tropes today; women talk too much, gossip endlessly, can't keep secrets, and will bitch about everyone and everything. The text features characters such as 'Mrs Chit-Chat', 'Madam Prate-a-Pace', 'Ms Pritle-Prattle', and 'Mrs All-Talk', who swap stories about everything from clothes and hair, to the sex lives of their neighbours and who has fallen out with whom – all while quaffing tea, gin, and wine. As these chattering women drink 'as much gin as will scald a pig', their language becomes decidedly 'unfeminine', and the author has tremendous fun detailing the slaps and scratches of the ensuing cat fight and the cries of 'you brazen fac'd whore', 'bitch', and threats to 'maul' one another.

The narrator of *The New Art and Mystery of Gossiping* is a man, and the author is almost certainly a man, and therein lies the irony; this is not a text about how women speak, it is a text about how men think of how women speak. This captures the challenges facing any researcher who attempts to record women's linguistic history, in a nutshell. While there is an abundance of male-authored works all throughout history that lay claim to understanding language, women are conspicuous by their absence. Of course, men have always written about women – we are surely one of their favourite subjects. Virginia Woolf once claimed that women are 'the most discussed animal in the universe' but finding the voice of everyday women in historical studies is notoriously difficult. Power resides with the penholder, and the penholders were overwhelmingly men. But, the study of slang can reveal a great deal about women's history.

As Jonathon notes, slang is not kind, but it is, at least, an ugly kind of honest. While we can never know who spoke or created various slang words, slang can show us how women were socially constructed, defamed and defended at various points in history. It can tell us much of historical attitudes and cultural biases around women's bodies and their sexuality. An absence of evidence is not evidence of absence when it comes to slang – far from it. Take the clitoris, for example. In his wonderful *Green's Dictionary of Slang*, Jonathon records some 1,350 slang words for the penis, dating back to the mid fifteenth century. By comparison, there are only 27 recorded slang words for the clitoris and the clear majority crop up in the twentieth and twenty-first century. Slang words for the vulva, however, comes in at 1,122 entries. What can this tell us about women's history? The clitoris has only one function, to bring pleasure to its owner, and yet it is almost entirely ignored by slang. Vulval slang frequently codes the vulva as a receptacle for the penis ('cock-alley', 'love-hole', 'pintle-case', etc.), or as missing a penis ('wound', 'gash', 'flat-cock', etc.), rather than an organ in its own right. It seems ignoring women's sexual pleasure is woven into the very register of sexual slang.

Linguists have historically viewed slang as being 'man-made', and given the linguistic gender gap apparent, there are good grounds for such claims. Not only have women been historically disadvantaged in terms of voice, narrative and agency, but women's use of language has been heavily policed in terms of what is and what is not 'ladylike'. Men have always enjoyed greater freedom to swear and use course language than women have. On 3rd December 1897, an article was published in *Daily Telegraph & Courier* that lamented the 'bad language among girls' that characterised the 'vast proportion of young working womanhood at the present time'. These 'naughty and precocious minxes' are derided as being 'hateful and unfeminine', and their use of coarse language is considered evidence of 'a widespread character of evil' that thrives among working class women. Opinions like this are far from unique and a cursory search of any historical newspaper database brings up page after page of articles fretting about women using 'unladylike' language. From the Scottish town of Kirtentilloch introducing heavy fines to stop an 'epidemic of bad language' among women in 1892, to the Liverpudlian school mistress who forced her female students to scrub their tongues with carbolic soap to 'cure' them of 'bad language' in 1941, a lot has been said about how women should speak. Language is a powerful agent of social control, and dictates the acceptable, the feminine, and the well behaved. As Jonathon notes, slang is not well-behaved – 'slang is funny. It is fun'. It is also highly subversive and empowering. Language has long been a battleground for feminists in the fight for gender equality and continues to shape the debate today.

The 2017, the #MeToo movement allowed women around

the world to collectively speak out about the sexual abuse and sexual harassment they have experienced. It is the most significant feminist event of recent years and began as a viral hashtag on social media. If anything can show us the power of language and its impact on women's rights, its #MeToo. Just two words became a rallying cry around the world, facilitated important debates, and became a byword for a new wave of feminism. Women are now speaking for themselves, creating their own slang, and answering back. There is no #MeToo equivalent in the history of slang, but Jonathon has captured a linguistic history of the struggle for women's emancipation. The register of slang here shows us how patriarchal cultures have understood women, controlled women, and marginalised women. However, this book also reveals that it is the rebellious women who used slang; the fishwives, the scolds, the whores, and the harridans. Long may they continue to do so.

Dr Kate Lister, sex historian and curator of
the online research project Whores of Yore

Introduction

Stephen considered for a moment and then said, 'So *roger* joins *bugger* and that even coarser word; and they are used in defiance and contempt, as though to an enemy; which seems to show a curious light on the lover's subjacent emotions. Conquest, rape, subjugation: have women a private language of the same nature, I wonder?'
　　　　Patrick O'Brian, *The Wine-Dark Sea* (1993) p.106.

THE PURPOSE OF this book is to consider what I and others 'in the trade' see as the great missing piece of slang's jigsaw: the relationship of women to what I term the counter-language. In shorthand, women *and* slang. Not the topic of woman *in* slang. Anyone who has looked at my 'Timelines of Slang', especially those that deal with the vocabularies of heterosexual intercourse, commercial sex, men, women and their respective genitals, will have absolutely no illusions. This – arguably slang's overriding obsession – will be addressed and only a misogynist could really rejoice at what we shall find, but that is not our objective.

What this book represents, like many others, is a quest. Quest, meaning a search and thus redolent of the Knights of the Round Table and the Holy Grail, and also linked to inquest or inquiry

I

and both finding roots in the synonymous Anglo-Norman *queste* and beyond that the Latin *quaestus*. For my purposes the grail is to see what if any links there are or have been between women and slang. Obviously slang is filled with women-focused terms, usually pertaining to her sexuality or making judgements regarding her physical appeal or social activity. All these – is she sexy or prudish, is she pretty or plain, is she complaisant or argumentative – are seen through what is widely accepted (typically by the male lexicographers noted below) as lying at the heart of slang: a pervasive male gaze.

The quest is to determine the extent to which what is widely accepted is also what is correct. The grail is the evidence for what may or may not be a revised verdict. I have done what I can to find examples of relevant material. What I have not done and could not do is find what, at least in recorded terms, was never there. This is not a dictionary but a narrative yet it remains a lexicographer's book (rather than a linguist's, sociologist's or historian's) and draws extensively on the evidence that this lexicographer has unearthed. The aim is to use this evidence to show and tell what is, not what might or ought to be. Like the dictionary-maker, we must work with what we have.

It may be useful, however briefly, to name our primary parts. First, women. I shall be looking through slang's eyes and on many occasions through those of earlier centuries. Whatever may have emerged in the last few years as regards trans-sexuality, the nuances of its attribution and its much-expanded visibility, slang offers a more simplistic, monochrome and ultimately traditional arena. It demands above all breasts and a vagina that came at birth and not via surgical or chemical skill. Nor is it open to self-identification. Slang notes alternatives, but its nature being conservative, merely sneers. One might wish otherwise; the choice is not on offer.*

Second, slang itself. Perhaps it should be stated at the outset: slang is not 'woke'. Slang, indeed, has remained unimpressed by five hundred years of whatever form that monosyllable of the month has currently taken. For slang the burning-eyed zealotry of some newly minted creed is no more than the sanctimonious nagging and gloating triumphalism that are the necessary spawn of every witch-hunt. Slang, after all, requires humour: it is in short supply at the barricades. On the other hand, one might say, and many will find this cynical, that slang is all too woke: its take on humanity skewers the hypocrisies, the fantasies, the rivalrous varieties of 'true' belief (secular as much as spiritual) and those who espouse them. It is all too human, too human for humanity when that word is, surely naively, defined as a synonym of compassionate. The themes that underpin it are indomitable. Slang is aggressive, negative, cruel and when approaching those topics that give it the opportunity, sexist. We ought, surely to have learned, to have moved on, but of course we never do. Technology moves on, humanity lacks the skills.

Yet slang ought to be a woman's ally. If what is seen as 'women's language' is also seen as weak within the overall power structure, then so too is slang. If, again as stereotyped, women are seen as less competitive than men, then slang's role as a bonding agent, a language that underpins group identification, should appeal: affirmation of the group over the proclamation of individual ego is seen as a major characteristic of female speech. To denote 51 per cent of the population as 'marginal' seems counter-intuitive,

---

* I would also suggest that such terms as the trans debate has created are far more jargon – 'interest-specific' terminology – than slang as such. *TERF* or *dead-naming* can only exist in a single context.

but many activist women claim just that. Quality rather than quantity is what matters. Slang, the voice of the marginal, ought to be theirs too. If slang is seen as subversive and oppositional, are those qualities anywhere limited to men? It is the language of rebellion; in the era of #metoo, it seems an ideal vehicle. If, as the historian Mary Beard suggested in her *London Review of Books* Winter lecture of 2014,[*] becoming part of the male elite means claiming the right to speak, rebellious, impertinent slang might offer a way to break down traditional boundaries.

The term slang has existed in print and in the context of language (initially criminal, subsequently 'low') since 1756,[†] and many words and phrases that, while uncategorised at the time of their coinage (or at least first recorded use), would unarguably qualify for inclusion in any slang dictionary, long pre-dated it. Thus we find 'slang' in Chaucer, Shakespeare and a number of other canonical writers. Qualifying a word as slang has never been simple. There are dozens, even scores of definitions, from academics, amateurs of varying degrees of expertise, and of course the makers of slang dictionaries. Some suggest that a slang term needs to register positive for certain characteristics (the list of which can be as few as four and as many as twenty-one); others see slang as the equivalent (doubtless fittingly) of pornography, something that is hard to define, but which one knows when one meets it.

As the author-in-place, I must opt for my own interpretation and make no excuses for seeing it as the evocation of a state of mind and the lexical representation of a style of life rather than something the qualifies via a list. Slang for me is first and foremost a counter-language, a term that deliberately mimics the

[*] M. Beard, 'The Public Voice of Women', *LRB* (20 March 2014).
[†] Senses meaning 'nonsense' and 'a job or line of work' existed slightly earlier.

'counter-culture' of the 1960s and holds the same deflatory sedition at its heart. It also remains part of the greater English language (and of any other language group of which it is a sub-set).

Slang does not do ideology, of whatever hue. It is voyeuristic, amoral, libertarian and libertine. It is vicious. It is cruel. It is self-indulgent. It treats all theologies – secular as well as spiritual – with the contempt that they deserve. It is funny. It is fun. Slang is the lexical reification of the comedian Lenny Bruce's dictum: 'Everybody wants what should be. But there is no what should be, there is only what is.' Slang, as the cultural critic Jonathan Meades has noted, is 'a depiction of the actual, of what we think rather than what we are enjoined to think.' Slang as I see it, is us at our most human. This should not be confused with admirable. We are living in an era when 'what should be' (not to mention 'what should have been') appears to be the base requirement of acceptability. Slang, less susceptible, is quite unimpressed.

Its lexis is older but the acknowledgement of slang as a specific linguistic register is relatively new. If it turns up in this sense in 1756, it remained fluid for some time afterwards. A century on George Augustus Sala, writing in Dickens' *Household Words*, ranged so widely over language that one could see that to him slang meant simply the special vocabulary of any given group, from nobs to yobs and artists to engineers. The idea of slang as the gutter tongue was far from fully established. For some, including George Eliot who mocked 'the slang of prigs', it was no more than a synonym for affectation. Only the slang lexicographers tended to showcase working-class and criminal language. In all cases, though the rule was not laid down but presumably so common as to need no introduction, it was associated with men.

That association is not merely linked to slang, though it is generally seen as the most uncompromisingly 'man-made' of languages, to borrow the term coined by the Australian feminist scholar Dale Spender who in 1980 published her study *Man Made Language*. It noted and dissected what she perceived as a male bias in the formation of language which in turn under-pinned the dominance of the patriarchy as a social force.

Spender was not the first to overlay language with gender. The founding mother, as it were, is acknowledged to be the American academic Robin Lakoff, in her essay 'Language and Women's Place'* (1973), but the idea that men and women have different modes of speech has further antecedents, both in popular belief and in academic discourse.

Rather than attempt a detailed overview, I offer an outline. I am grateful to Dr Sarah Hoem Iversen, Associate Professor of English Language at Western Norway University of Applied Sciences, for providing me with the necessary information on which to base what is by necessity the most simplified of over-views. (If I have misconstrued her advice the fault is wholly mine.)

The initial assumption, pioneered inevitably by influential men, was that women's use of language is 'deficient' compared to a male 'norm'. Writing in the London journal *The World* in December 1754, Lord Chesterfield, regulator of social accepta-bility, upheld the common stereotype of women's talkativeness, describing their use of language as 'promiscuous' and without regard for grammatical propriety. They talked too much and, seemingly worst of all, the words they used were often of their own invention. Many were adverbs: *vastly, horridly, amazingly,*

---

* *Language in Society*, Vol. 2, No. 1 (April 1973), pp.45–80.

abominably . . . all deemed too excessively emotional. As for such a term as *flirtation*, defined asexually in Johnson's *Dictionary* of 1755 as 'a quick sprightly motion,' it was merely a 'cant [i.e. in-group jargon] word among women' (even if his sole example came from Pope, a man). In his book *Language* (1922), the linguist Otto Jespersen claimed in a chapter devoted to 'The Woman' that women's vocabulary was poorer than men's, and that female speakers 'instinctively' shrank from using 'coarse and gross expressions' opting instead for refined, euphemistic and hyperbolic expression. At the same time he saw female speech as too emotional, not just those adverbs but adjectives – *divine, charming, cute* – as well. One thing remained paramount: women's speech deviated from a male 'norm'.

This idea of 'abnormality', it might be noted, also under-pinned a sustained view of black, originally slave speech in America. Any debt to African origins was ignored; slaves spoke a garbled version of the tongue of their white masters, and such 'illiteracy' underlined their perceived inferiority. This self-serv-ing argument further informs attacks on African-America's Ebonics, which is seen, in its deviations from a white norm and again a negative image as 'illiterate', as symbolic of racial powerlessness.

With the second-wave feminism of the mid-twentieth century, women joined the debate. In 1975 Robin Lakoff presented her theory on 'Women's Language', based on personal observation and what she gleaned from her conversations with female friends. The features of 'women's language' included politeness, hesita-tion and hedging, plus a richer vocabulary to describe typically 'female' fields (e.g. colours). As noted later by Ann Weatherall, 'Lakoff . . . thought women's language [was] hesitant, ingratiat-ing and weak . . . that women are socialised to hedge meaning, in order to avoid offending men."[*] In retrospect Lakoff's primary role was as a pioneer in the field: what followed was an upsurge in research into her topic. In time, Lakoff would modify her opinions, and the focused research of fellow-academics has questioned her beliefs, for instance the equation of tag questions ('it's a nice day isn't it?') with feminine hesitancy and by extension, weakness in the face of masculine assertiveness.

The 'linguistic gender gap' is a powerful myth. Wide-ranging and continuing research has never backed it up, but the idea of distinct 'men's' and 'women's languages', and the sense that, as the US author and former acolyte of the Maharishi Mahesh Yogi John Gray put it, 'Men are from Mars, Women are from Venus', continues to flourish in popular media. To steal from LGBT+ slang, men are 'butch' and women 'femme' even if the language and gender myths thus proposed have been exploded, notably by the linguist Deborah Cameron in her book *The Myth of Mars and Venus* (2007). That language has increasingly come to be seen as part of a person's identity, including their gender and sexuality, is not denied, but as writers such as Judith Butler in *Gender Trouble* (1990) have made clear, this cannot be asserted in such black-and-white ways.

Academic nuance, even reduced to the most broad-brush of descriptions, is still a minority pursuit. Learned journals make poor competition to tabloid conviction. For the majority of those who pause to consider it, the topic remains a matter of 'folk-linguistic stereotypes', the gender debate's fake news which, like the many popular etymologies that bedevil slang, defies all contradiction. These tried-and-tested beliefs steadfastly proclaim that: 'women talk more than men', 'women gossip, nag, and

* A. Weatherall, *Gender, Language and Discourse* (2002), p.57.

scold', 'women are better communicators', 'women are more polite', 'women are more hesitant and careful', and, as the logical extension of politeness and hesitancy, 'women don't swear or use slang'. They are also the source of proverbs ('A woman's tongue wags like a lamb's tail', 'A woman's tongue: the last thing about her that dies'), and similar folk 'wisdom'. Paradoxically, of slang's 120 terms that are defined as 'gossip', none seem especially linked to femininity, though simple verbosity does offer the comparison 'like old molls at a christening'. Some stereotypes, perhaps, are so inescapable that even mentioning them is unnecessary.

Beyond such behavioural stereotyping, women were considered simply ignorant and when they attempted to display some intellectual skills, embarrassing. The *echt* form of 'women's language' was often cited as the error-strewn declarations of the deliberately absurd 'Mrs Malaprop', created for Richard Brinsley Sheridan's play *The Rivals* (1775). Her response to the question 'what would you have a woman know?' ran thus:

I would by no means wish a daughter of mine to be a progeny of learning; I don't think so much learning becomes a young woman; for instance, I would never let her meddle with Greek, or Hebrew, or algebra, or simony, or fluxions, or paradoxes, or such inflammatory branches of learning— neither would it be necessary for her to handle any of your mathematical, astronomical, diabolical instruments.— But . . . I would send her, at nine years old, to a boarding-school, in order to learn a little ingenuity and artifice. Then, sir, she should have a supercilious knowledge in accounts;— and as she grew up, I would have her instructed in geometry, that she might know something of the contagious countries;—but above all ... she should be mistress of orthodoxy, that she might not mis-spell, and mis-pronounce words so shamefully as girls usually do; and likewise that she might reprehend the true meaning of what she is saying. This ... is what I would have a woman know;—and I don't think there is a superstitious article in it.

As we shall find, notably in discussing the *scold* (woman-to-man abuse) and *Billingsgate* (inter-women abuse), slang is keen to embrace the negative stereotypes. As ever with the register, such abstracts as humourlessness or politeness are ignored, but slang is keen to identify women with excessive, aggressive verbosity. Women are automatically slapped down for entering 'male' domains. Even 'mother', traditionally played in counterpoint to woman's alternative role as 'whore', falls prey to slang's cruelties: the counter-linguistic mother is usually a brothel-keeper or, more recently, an abbreviation of *motherfucker*.

Such a brief tour barely flickers across the substantial horizon of debates over whether or not men's language differs from that of women. Let us attempt to fine things down. To look from here on in at slang.

Herewith slang's taxonomy, based, with no excuses for its lack of internal detail, in descending order of frequency of those topics most often referenced in my own work:

Crime and Criminals; Drink, Drinks, Drinking and Drunks; Drugs; Money; Women; Fools and Foolish; Men; Sexual Intercourse; the Penis; Homosexuals/-ity; Prostitute/-ion; the Vagina; Policeman / Policing; Masturbate/-ion; Die, Death, Dead; Beat or Hit; Mad; Anus or Buttocks; Terms of Racial or National abuse; Defecate/-ion and Urinate/-ion; Kill or

*Murder; Promiscuous / Promiscuity; Unattractive; Fat; Oral
Sex; Vomiting; Anal Sex; STDs.*

That women are almost invariably considered negatively or at
best sexually, and men, while falling under many descriptions,
are not invariably, but often aggrandising their self-image,
emphasises slang's alleged 'male gaze', but the list is intended
simply to illumine rather than critique slang's obsessions.

It is a brutal list, filled with coarse and unbridled excess, of
self-indulgence, of vulgarity, of crudity, of impudence and sheer,
irrepressible *loudness*. If there are no positives (outside the charms
of sex, drink and drugs and various forms of 'rock 'n' roll') then
it is because slang does not offer them. It offers a vocabulary and
a voice to all our negatives. Our inner realities: lusts, fears and
hatreds. Wilfully shucking off every vestige of self-restraint it
subscribes to nothing but itself – no belief systems, no true
believers, no faith, no religion, no politics, no party. It is the
linguistic version of Freud's *id*, a concept that is laid out in the
New Introductory Lectures on Psychoanalysis of 1933:

> is the dark, inaccessible part of our personality, [. . .]most of
> this is of a negative character [. . .]. We all approach the id
> with analogies: we call it a chaos, a cauldron full of seething
> excitations . . . It is filled with energy reaching it from the
> instincts, but it has no organization, produces no collective
> will, but only a striving to bring about the satisfaction of the
> instinctual needs subject to the observance of the pleasure
> principle.

To remain in the Thirties, it is King Kong, it is definitely not
Fay Wray.

Gendering Slang

If gender does have a role to play in slang then it is less in practice and far more in theory. In the belief, long-held, that the register is a man-made phenomenon. That slang's vocabulary springs from the verbalising of the 'male gaze': that it is brutally and shamelessly sexist. That men are oppressors and aggressors and women's role is no more than that of victims. It is a belief that slang users bear out, slang studies encourage and slang dictionaries, having no choice but to base the material they list on the evidence that has been made available, underpin. This last, at least, is hard to contradict. If slang itself, especially as one retreats through time, is increasingly hard to find – a marginal language used by marginal people it was last in queue for elevation into printed books and the memorialisation that came with that process – then slang as used by women, on the margins of the margins, is even more elusive.

The words of English, lacking the structure of French and other Romance languages (and of course that of all others that qualify, e.g. Hebrew, Hindi or Russian) have no stated gender. English words, like those, may well find their origins in Latin and/or Greek, which do offer gender, but English does not add a defining particle (*la, il*) or a suffix (*-a, -o*) to flag it up. This ensures that we have no female penises nor masculine vaginas (*la bite, le vagin* of French). If this makes learning English easier, then such simplicity is far outweighed by its spelling and pronunciation. But as these French examples should show, the gender assigned by language (at least at this late date when coinage is so far away) is not a social/sexual construct. The French table (*la table*) or railway station (*la gare*) are both female: why?* These are

---

* *Table* may well descend from a 'female' Latin word, but *gare* links to terms meaning 'self-defence' and never claimed a gender.

not, surely, the equivalent of the feminised familiarity that is allotted, for instance, to a British ship or Australia's non-specific *she*, as in 'she'll be apples': everything will be fine. There is no implicit association of gender to word. This is equally true of slang's etymologies, the stories that lie behind the vocabulary. It is on the rarest of occasions that we can unarguably attribute the creation of a word or phrase to a woman or to a man. Some etymology is indeed anecdotal – it is based on a known, if often embellished story, for instance *Lady Dacre's wine* (gin, tipping the hat to a presumably drunken aristocrat) or *Mrs Phillips' ware* (a condom, and in this case supposedly referencing a well-known madame) – but of slang's 135,000 words and phrases, these are rare examples. Even the briefly celebrated *on fleek* turned out, for all its much-vaunted attribution to Ms Kayla Newman ('Peaches Monroe'), to be no more than a personal use of a term that was already available.

Maybe 80 per cent of the slang lexis is based on playing with standard English (for instance the single word *dog* – which itself lacks any concrete etymology – has well over one hundred slang meanings), and what remains has various sources. It is perhaps only in rhyming slang, which often depends on personalities, that we can definitely link origin to gender, but that link is based simply on what rhymes, rather than anything truly linguistic.

As with so much of slang everything depends on context (and of course author, though women can write male characters and vice versa. It should be noted that for the bulk, if not all of the material referenced, the concept of cultural appropriation had yet to attempt to force its ideological straitjacket on creativity).

As the linguist Deborah Cameron puts it, 'Sociolinguists have long since accepted that we can't solve what's called the "actuation problem". Who exactly invented a word. Very rarely we can.

So you're really talking about transmission. Transmission and use. And I don't think that there is any reason to think that this was all men. Even if we're talking about thieves' cant; it's not like women were never thieves, or that they didn't hang around with thieves. A lot of specialised slang must actually have been unisex.'

As this book proceeds, and research follows along its quest, the idea of slang as unisex – a term invented in the 'swinging Sixties' and first applied to fashion, hairdressers and other show-cases of the era's cultural symbols – becomes harder to resist. Slang cheerfully puts itself up for grabs: it has a job to do and plays no favourites when it comes to those who pluck it from the linguistic repository.

So, with the exception of certain etymologies, those rare instances when it can be proved that a given word or phrase is created by a male or female individual, there is no way to gender slang. We can ascribe certain terms to a gender: words for women that are only used by men, words for men that are the sole property of women, but that is all. And given the innately fluid nature of slang, the dominance of context in assessing and defining it, then this too is slippery and inconstant. The original use may point to one gender, its development may err elsewhere. It may be subjected to ironic or humorous reinterpretation whereby the whole point is to change the term's gender. It may be, as with *bitch*, that what begins as the description of one gender, is turned upside down, as is so often slang's way in its ludic adoption of standard English, and used to describe the other, although the innate inference – an insult – remains. In the end we are talking female dog, and seeing that, when applied to any human, as a put-down. In *bitch's* case the insult, for a man, being that he is called by a woman's name. For the woman it is being called that of a different, supposedly inferior species. In other words, to insult a man one may demean his prized male-ness, but he remains a human being; to insult a woman, one places her beyond the human pale.

The current status quo, at least as dictated by liberal orthodoxy, demands that women are en-pedestalled, irrespective of case-by-case reality, while men – especially as that bugaboo the 'centrist dad' – are automatically made objects of vilification. The whiter, the more middle-aged and middle-class, the less 'woke', the more inexcusable that vileness is and the more zealously the mob brandish their pitchforks and wave their torches.

Those who disagree, irrespective of gender, are instantly mobbed and condemned. Nuance is dead. The centre, that place of intelligent and necessary compromise that Yeats told us so percipiently would not hold, is apparently for none but cowards. If we extend this theory to language, slang or otherwise, then it would suggest that since derision and its kindred verbal assaults are seen as 'bad', then they must be male prerogatives. Shouty, mansplaining, arrogant, unable to listen. It may be that my own opinions are considered as such. Again I note, I deal as best I may in the evidence that can be found.

The assumption that women avoid (or should avoid) slang and taboo language further reinforces the notion that slang is male-generated. Yet one cannot take refuge in the idea that gender A is more extreme in the use of such terminology than gender B. In other words, men do not abuse women more than women abuse men. Five minutes on, say, Twitter makes this wholly clear. They use different stereotypes as the bases for abuse – certainly – but as will be found throughout this book, one must not confuse quantity with quality or form with content.

The more one looks at the relationship of women to slang and of slang's reciprocal role regarding women, the more one finds the term 'ventriloquy'.* Not in a derogatory sense, there is no suggestion that the creator views his/her creation as a dummy, but in the sense of linguistic role reversal: the gender-bending use by a creator of the language of the other. Men write women, women write men. It would not be possible to proceed with this story without acknowledging the centrality of the form. It flies, of course, in the face of identity politics, wherein no-one may comment, let alone create other than that of which they have hands-on, personal experience. Women to write women, BAME individuals BAME characters, gays gays and so on. No more blacked-up Othellos, though there seems to be no equivalent demand for equally race-legitimate Shylocks or Fagins. This may work for the future, it was not the case in the past. The problem with such a diktat – combining a self-righteous refusal to learn history with a desperate desire to rewrite it – is that yet again, the facts mock all such pretensions.

Thus, when it comes to assessing a cross-section of creative work, a woman playwright will be found using slang to delineate swashbuckling, macho males just as a male author will borrow from the counter-language to bring to life a sassy chorus girl. The thread runs through this book as it does through the history of the wider definition of 'creative' writing and we have no alternative but to acknowledge it. For this author it underlines yet again the essential greyness of reality.

What seems to be the first attempt to see whether or not slang use divides by gender came in 1903. Writing in the *Pedagogical Seminary*, a journal of child psychology, Edward Conradi,

---

* As Jennifer Lyndsay Grant noted in the preface to her doctoral dissertation on 'Prostitution in the Parisian Literary Market, 1830–1923' (2016) 'Like my predecessors, I began my study in a good faith effort to *chercher la femme*; what I found revealed men.'

President of the Florida State College for Women, offered a selection of data on 'Children's Interests in Words, Slang, Stories, etc.' The piece dealt with various aspects of the language enjoyed by those under eighteen, and its centrepiece was a list of some 850 slang terms, gleaned from 295 answers to a questionnaire circulated by high school teachers. These were divided by the gender of those who offered them – 'Boys', 'Girls' and 'Sex Not Specified' – and broken down into various sub-sections: 'Rebuke to Pride', 'Negatives', 'Shock', 'Exaggerations', 'Exclamations', 'Mild oaths', and a substantial section entitled 'Unclassified' and which included the majority of nouns and verbs. 'Unclassified' themes show terms for 'boasting and loquacity, hypocrisy, [. . .] attending to one's own business and not meddling or interfering, names for money, absurdity, neurotic effects of surprise or shock, honesty and lying, getting confused, fine appearance and dress, words for intoxication, [. . .] for anger [. . .] crudeness or innocent naiveté, love and sentimentality.'* The interviewees included their opinions on slang: '60 thought slang more emphatic' [. . .] '90 considered slang vulgar' [. . .] '53 considered boy's slang rougher than girl's', etc. A graph was compiled which suggested that slang use peaked between the ages of thirteen and sixteen.

Other than the perceived 'roughness' of 'boy's slang', and the acknowledgement that all of these young people fully understood the necessity of code-switching between school, the parental home and adult-free conversations between themselves, there was no suggestion that either gender was 'slangier'.

The still relatively modern focus on the concepts of male and female language has naturally included the slang sub-set. There

---

* G. S. Hall, *Youth: Its Education, Regimen, and Hygiene* (1906), p.164.

have been a number of studies. For examples, I offer the outlines of a couple.

In 1990, writing in the journal *Sex Roles*, the South African academic Vivian de Klerk pondered *Slang: A Male Domain?* Noting the statement by Stuart Flexner, co-editor of the *Dictionary of American Slang* (1960, 1975) that ascribed all slang to men, both as sources and users, she focused on the idea of slang as the product of social peer groups, which used it as a form of self-identification. Men, she acknowledged, 'belong to more sub-groups than do women' and added that there were differences between male and female peer groups: men were more hierarchical and competitive; women's groups were smaller, more intimate, and exhibited less verbal posturing. However, based on her research statistics, 'an assumption that males typically use more slang because they are male is a risky one, to say the least.' Her conclusion: males are not conspicuously heavier slang users, but females are socialised into believing this is the case, even though they themselves actually use it, Females using slang are 'guilty, self-condemnatory, narrow-minded.' Free and creative use of slang was part of an initiation to power, enjoyed by older boys. Females were excluded from this and she equated females with another 'out-of-power' group who therefore exhibited less slang: junior boys. She also looked ahead: 'As society changes and gender roles change in society, so language is likely to change concomitantly ... an increase in the female use of slang, indicative of subtle shifts in the social status of females generally.'

Five years later Deborah James of the University of Toronto published her study 'Gender-Linked Derogatory Terms and Their Use by Women and Men'.* She resisted extremes, and laid

---

* D. James, 'Gender-Linked Derogatory Terms and Their Use by Women and Men', *American Speech*, Vol. 73, No. 4 (Winter, 1998), pp.399–420.

out her conclusions on the basis of what she found. The aim, based on material offered by some ninety female and thirty-five male students, sought to see how derogatory terms illuminated the way ideas of femininity and masculinity are constructed. It all, unsurprisingly, came down to stereotypes. Among those used by men to describe women were Promiscuous/prostitute/sexually aggressive (sixty-two terms), unattractive (thirty-three terms), non-specific but perceived to be demeaning (forty terms), anti-male (twenty-eight), stupid (twenty terms), masculine, i.e. lesbian (eleven terms) and frigid or sexually frustrating (eleven terms). When the focus turned to the denigration of men, the list included 'mistreats others' – a cover-all for 'unpleasant'(108 terms), stupid (ninety-one terms), weak (twenty-eight terms), possibly or actually homosexual (thirty-eight terms), sexist (thirty-eight terms), socially inept (eighteen terms), unsuccessful (sixteen terms) and physically inadequate (ten terms).

Each gender seemed equally capable of attacking the other, but the overriding paradigm remained that set up by a male viewpoint. 'Males are evaluated primarily in terms of the extent to which they can function as competent masters of every situation, which in turn has much to do with gaining and maintaining status in the eyes of other males. Females, on the other hand, are evaluated primarily in terms of how well they conform to heterosexual male needs and desires, including being attractive, faithful to one man, of average intelligence, and docile and supportive.'*

James assessed what, for instance 'unintelligent' might mean in gender contexts. To lack intelligence was 'something to be disparaged in anyone, female or male.

---

* James op.cit. p.406.

However, the two sets of terms carry rather different connotations. The female-referential terms tend to imply that there is nothing in the referent's head (e.g., *airhead, fluff, bubblebrain*), while the male-referential terms are more likely to imply that there is something in the referent's head which should not be there (e.g., *shit-for-brains, farthead, butthead*). This implies that it is seen as more typical for women than for men to be empty-headed – that is, arguably, truly unintelligent.[*]

She also suggests that the insults used imply that it is 'a more serious flaw for a man to lack intelligence than for a woman to lack intelligence, which is in turn consistent with gender role expectations that men, but not women, should be competent, successful achievers.'[†] There is a vicious circle: if a woman is assertive, then this is bad and 'unfeminine'; at the same time, by simply being a woman, she is seen as weak by nature.[‡] It is also much worse for a man to be accused of femininity than its reverse. Thus to imply that a man is gay, is far worse than suggesting a woman might be lesbian. The equivalent terms are based on sex rather than gender, i.e. they suggest that a woman is either a nag or a whore.

James also listed a few terms that for once reflected a woman's point of view: 'ways in which women are evaluating men in terms of the extent to which MEN conform to WOMEN's needs and desires . . . They included terms for a boring man (*Mr. Dry Guy, fatiguer*); a few terms for unattractive men or fat men (e.g., *craterface, doughboy*); a few terms for attractive men parallel to terms such as *babe* for women (e.g., *hunk, hotty*); and a term, *sperm donor*, defined as a 'worthless man, no use other than sex'.[§]

* James op.cit. p.404.
† Ibid. p.405.
‡ Ibid. p.406.
§ Ibid. p.409.

Her conclusion suggested that on the whole, whoever was offering the insult, the overriding picture was painted by male values and assumptions. Nonetheless, this was changing. 'There are indications that some terms are coming to be used by both sexes in a more gender-neutral way than has been the case in the past, and that it is women who are leading in this direction.'*

If gender-neutral means that women can cheerfully appropriate and use the slang of their male peers then the regular lists of college-age slang published bi-annually by Professor Connie Eble from 1972 to 2018, and assembled by her students at the University of North Carolina, suggest otherwise. The bulk of those who respond to her appeal for words are young women. They may ignore most of the primary obscenities (an exception being the dismissive *go fuck a duck!*), but that is possibly because they feel them to be so common that they are not worth noting as neologisms. What they offer are a number of exclamations, all meaning, whether literally or figuratively 'go away!': *bite me! bite moose! blow off! bump that! bye, Felicia! crud! in your face! pickle it! sit on this and rotate! stick it in your ear!* and *get out of town!* There are also a couple of negative phrases: *isn't that special* (i.e. it isn't special at all) and *talk to the hand* (*because the face don't understand*). Other insults include *douchebag, jerk, poopbutt, scumbag, stooge* and *weenie.*

Finally, and with the focus four-square on lexicography, the opinions of Katherine Connor Martin Head of Content Creation at Oxford Dictionaries. Her essay on 'Gendered Aspects of Lexicographic Labeling' appeared in the journal *Dictionaries* in 2005.†

---

* Ibid. p.413.
† K. Connor Martin, 'Gendered Aspects of Lexicographic Labeling', *Dictionaries: Journal of the Dictionary Society of North America*, Number 26 (2005), pp.160–173.

Like de Klerk she posited Flexner's declaration that 'most American slang is created and used by males' (1960, xli) and referencing Dale Spender noted that the accuracy of his diktat – like others in the context of gendering language – is 'complicated by the subjective nature of the slang category, which has historically excluded speech associated with women. Since a sense of masculinity permeates the slang concept, the conclusion that women use slang less than men is circular.'

The idea that slang equates with masculine pursuits and by doing so automatically and perfectly happily excludes women from a role in its creation or use, is common to those who originally commented on the phenomenon: mostly men, mostly compilers of slang dictionaries. For instance Hewson Clarke, in the preface to his *Lexicon Balatronicum* (the 'Fools' Dictionary') an 1811 collection of 'Buckish slang, University Wit and Pickpocket Eloquence'. Dr Clarke saw slang in its primary guise: a secret language, in this case not of criminals (as had been its earliest, sixteenth-century incarnation) but of a whole gender: men. It insulated male society from women's supposedly prim censoriousness just as via their use of *cant* (the technical name of slang's early terminology) did the *ruffler*, the *upright ma*n and other varieties of villainous mendicant protect themselves from the eavesdropping of the *harman-beck* (the constable) and the bailiff.

'Improper topics can with our assistance be discussed, even before the ladies, without raising a blush to the cheek of modesty. It is impossible that a female should understand the meaning of *twiddle diddles*,* or rise from the table at the mention of *Buckinger's boot*.†

---

* *Twiddle-diddles*: the testicles; standard English *twiddle*, to play with.
† *Buckinger's boot*: the vagina; the proper name of Matthew *Buchinger*, b.1674 in Germany and known as 'The Little man of Nuremberg'. He was only 29" tall and born limbless. He was also a master dice manipulator. For him, a boot could fit only his *third leg*, i.e. his penis.

Modern commentators, again all male, have perpetuated the theory, if slightly less directly than Clarke. Slang comes from 'masculine' occupations – pleasurable or recreational – and as such excludes women.

The linguist James Sledd followed suit: 'Slang flourishes in the areas of sex, drinking, narcotics, racing, athletics, popular music, and other crime—a "liberal" language of things done in themselves by gentlemen who are not gentlemen and dislike gentility.' No women there, or so ran the implication. Similarly David Maurer, who specialised in the 'professional' vocabularies of a wide spectrum of criminals, was adamant in his dismissal of the one female group whom most people might see as regular slang users: prostitutes. While he was happy to attribute independent slang creation to other criminal groups, whores missed the cut. He termed their speech 'colorless' and claimed that 'they lack the sophistication to make and acquire an artificial language for themselves,' and did nothing more than parrot 'discarded argot words from other criminal professions.' We shall see in chapter 8 to what extent this was truth or prejudice. If nothing else, as Connor notes, 'It is also worth considering whether a male researcher, especially one with these preconceptions, would have been likely to find open and sympathetic informants among this group of women."*

Deborah Cameron, Murdoch Professor at Oxford, is equally pessimistic as to male researchers gaining access to women's closed societies. 'Slang is favoured by certain kinds of institutions . . . Those sort of groups existed for women but they were not studied. Who's done a study of the slang of nuns? It would certainly have been something in the middle ages. But people

* Martin op. cit. p.165; all quotes from Clarke, Sledd, Maurer and Flexner taken from her article.

didn't go into those totally female institutions. Prisons. Women's armed services where you'd have found the lesbians. But men couldn't collect it. The access wasn't available."*

Finally Flexner, aping James Murray, who prefaces the original edition of the *OED* with a visual representation of the way English breaks down into sub-species, offers his own diagram for slang. As Martin notes, Flexner's sub-groups are almost entirely 'masculine', certainly as envisaged when his Dictionary appeared in 1960: army, baseball, railroads and the like (all of which, I would suggest are more occupational jargons than slang). There are college students and teenagers, both of which might refer to either gender, but there are no labels that could indicate a 'women-only' lexis.

There is a sense, attested by anyone who has looked more than superficially at the possibilities, that again like the larger slang lexis, women's use of slang is drastically under-reported. It is the same under-reporting that may lie behind the long absence of slang of almost any sort from the standard lexicons. That its earliest glossaries – not yet dictionaries in the sixteenth century when they appeared – exist because they are associated with that ever-sexy topic: crime. Read this pamphlet, absorb the words it offers, and you may escape that dubious figure sneaking across the tavern to pick your pocket or con you at dice or cards. Such glossaries explore the exotic. They start by offering the entirety of slang as then recorded; in time they would be displaced and replaced by a far less specific style of counter-language.

The arrival of 'civilian' slang, of working-class language that rivalled the standard speech of those who ruled them, or at least made more money than they did, would not appear in

---

* D. Cameron, interview (12 February 2018).

lists for another century. Yet sixteenth-century London, and its earlier incarnations, was surely large and powerful enough to boast a working class, and that working class, as did its successors, would have used a vocabulary that was other than that of the ruling classes. Standard English had developed from that spoken by the royal court, the law courts, the universities and the city. This was what was used by elite speakers in south-east England, but they – and their language – were hardly representative of the entirety of the population. But proof is almost impossible to pin down. One sees hints in authors such as Chaucer, whose characters are not invariably criminals and whose speech is far from standard, but such records are limited. Women's use of slang remained even less accessible. Slang was positioned as a brutish, masculine speech, verbalised willy-waving, lexical pissing contexts. This was acceptable in men, it was not in women.

Yet just as one senses a whole absentee world of working-class, non-criminal slang users prior to 1698, when such *ur*-slang began to appear in printed glossaries, so too the absence of women. Katherine Connor Martin wonders 'whether we are missing, somewhere, a vein of historical usages associated with femininity that might yet qualify as slang by our current understanding of the concept.'* She suggests factory girls, and notes that women undoubtedly held the monopoly on what we might call 'family slang', those terms that the *OED* labels as 'nursery'. Euphemistic terms for the genitals, for defecation; ultra-local words that spring from the infant's (mis-)pronunciation of a given term, e.g. my own family's *geffy* for spaghetti. A dictionary of such terms has been attempted, Paul Dickson's *Family Words*

* Martin op. cit. p.166.

(2007), but there is no possible way in which it could even approach exhaustiveness.

Slang, ever omnivorous, has some 1,400 terms that qualify as euphemisms. We might feel that this should in fact *dis*-qualify them, since slang usually spares no feelings. They include a number of otherwise obscene or blasphemous exclamations and oaths, and a variety of terms, just as in family language, for defecation and parts of the body. What we do not find within the family, is of course the world of sex, especially intercourse, although the thousands of such terms are rarely marked as 'euph.' Nonetheless many such are effectively euphemistic. The simple fact that slang seems to have been driven to coin so many synonyms – they appear in the earliest glossaries, they are on offer in the most current – suggests as much. After all the supposed core lexis of 'dirty words', as laid down by US lawmakers, is barely a dozen terms. Yet slang, allegedly male and macho, is seen as spoiling for a fight; euphemism, soft-pedalling and ameliorative, is seen as quintessentially female. The soft word that turneth away wrath.

As noted, women's use of slang is frustratingly under-reported. Fortunately there are exceptions: for those who would like to look beyond the stereotype – whether of women's voluntary rejection of slang or respectability's demand that they sidestep it – we do have some examples. Writing in a special 'Women's Studies' issue of *The Radical Teacher* (December 1977) Rayna Green offered 'Magnolias Grow in Dirt: The Bawdy Lore of Southern Women.' Focusing on the language to which her own grandmother (born 1900) confessed to knowing and unrestrainedly using, and the bawdy story-telling that it helped put over, Green avowed that 'Women everywhere talk about sex — sex with young boys, old men and handsome strangers — and sexual errors both good and bad." The words themselves, such as Green offers examples, are not especially 'female', and she notes that while women might use *twat* for their own genitals they resist the overly masculine *gash, slash, pussy, cunt, cock* and so on. However they do come up with *chore girl* (a play on the US steel wool cleaning product *Chore Boy*) and *wooly booger*. But the general – the volume of bawdy talk – outweighs the lexical specific. To these Southern women, says Green, all this bawdy offered a women-only participation in 'fun, rebellion and knowledge-giving'[†] (just as such talk had always done for men). And, albeit somewhat folksily, she concludes: 'Next time you see a group of women . . . don't assume they're sharing the latest recipe for peach cobbler. The subject may be other delights.'[‡]

Socio-linguistics

If – rightly or otherwise – women were seen as avoiding slang we must ask why. Talking to a sex worker for this book it was suggested that prostitutes eschew the coinage of slang because slang is so devotedly, viciously misogynistic, especially as regards her occupation: why arm the enemy? Katherine Connor Martin echoes this on a more general level, adding that the wider, male-ordained society has always seen a woman using slang as 'unfeminine'. Slang's concerns, as noted, are seen as stereotypically 'male'. Aggression and competition dominate the lexis. There is, for instance, no word that is defined simply as 'love' and precious few for the emotions, other than *anger* and its synonyms, which

---

[*] R. Green, 'Magnolias Grow in Dirt: The Bawdy Lore of Southern Women', *The Radical Teacher* (December 1977) p.28/1.
[†] Green op. cit. p. 30/1.
[‡] Green op. cit. p. 30/2.

amass over four hundred variations. The assumption of 'women's language' is that it is far more focused on such 'soft' topics. The artificial language Láadan produced by linguist Suzette Haden Elgin for her novel *Native Tongue* (1984), whose plot 'revolved around a group of women, all linguists, engaged in constructing a language specifically designed to express the perceptions of human women.' Among its terms were these:

Ashon love for one who is not related by blood but is heart-kin

Azháadin to menopause uneventfully

Dólhorado to dominate with evil intent

Eeme love for one neither liked nor respected

Héena sibling of the heart

Lewidan to be pregnant for the first time

Loláad to perceive internally, to feel

Móna compassion for foolish reasons

Núháam to feel oneself cherished, cared for, nurtured by someone

Radena unfriendliness for good reasons

Wonewith to be socially dyslexic; uncomprehending of signals of others

If one wished to create a lexis that represents preoccupations that are the absolute opposite to slang's, Láadan is surely it.

It is, however, a fictional creation, as artificial as Star Trek's Klingon.

To see an attempt to assess 'real' women's language it is worth pausing to consider *The Feminist Dictionary*, published in 1986 by Cheris Kramarae and Paula A. Treichler and categorised by its authors as 'a dictionary of feminist thinking and word-making;

a conceptual guide to that subset of the lexicon concerned with feminism; a documentation of feminist perspectives, interpretations of words, and contributions to linguistic creativity and scholarship; and a dictionary itself made by feminists.' There had been a number of early reference works created by women. The first of such being the *Hortus deliciarum* (the 'Garden of Delights') which was an encyclopedia combining classical and Arabic works of philosophy, literature and theology among other themes (including songs) created by Abbess Herrad of Lansberg (Germany) in the twelfth century. The first in English appears to have been the creation of Samuel Johnson's friend Mrs Hester Thrale or Piozzi, whose *British Synonymy* appeared in 1794. James Murray employed his daughters in a variety of jobs on the *OED*, and in its unrivalled historian slang can boast Professor Julie Coleman of Leicester University.*

None of whose work even marginally suggests the *Feminist Dictionary*. There is no attempt to recreate another Láadan, but neither do Kramarae and Treichler fall into the constrictions of what they consider male-dominated mainstream lexicography.

Picking up on Dale Spender's man-made language, they state that

> For women . . . the ultimate outcome is the same: whether descriptive or prescriptive, authoritarian or democratic, massive or minimal, systematic or quixotic . . . dictionaries have systematically excluded any notion of women as speakers, as linguistic innovators, or as definers of words. Women

---

* It may be kinder to pass over *The New Dictionary of Americanisms* (1903) by the Quebecois linguist Sylva Clapin. The sole review to be found is a savage piece in *Modern Language Notes* which relishes every error, flags up every omission and generally trashes the book. On the other hand, the reviewer appears to think Ms Clapin is in fact 'Mr'.

in their pages have been rendered invisible, reduced to stereotypes, ridiculed, trivialised or demeaned. Whatever their intentions, then, dictionaries have functioned as linguistic legislators which perpetrate the stereotypes and prejudices of their writers and editors, who are almost exclusively male.

Nor was what they chose to attempt a traditional dictionary but a volume that fell, as its editors noted, into the area occupied by such quasi-'dictionaries' as Flaubert's *Dictionary of Received Ideas* and Bierce's *Devil's Dictionary* – although it lacks the irony of the one and the cynicism of the other.

It is not a dictionary in which one looks up words in the expected way. For instance those who search for a definition of 'ABILITY' find only this: 'ability "Is sexless" (Christabel Pankhurst *Calling All Women* February 2, 1957)'. Nor would the traditional dictionary offer 'ABOMINABLE SNOWMEN OF ANDROCRATIC ACADEMIA Scholars dominated by male-centred traditions'. Spelling may be standard English, but headwords are very much drawn from an alternative lexicon; definitions are consciously oppositional to what is dismissed as the 'male' norm, they are also more encyclopedic, even discursive, than would usually be expected; the tone is hortatory and to the jaundiced reader somewhat martyred as regards its consideration of traditional lexicography: those who are not positively with me, runs the subtext, must be aggressively against me.

By the standards that inform the traditional dictionary, this one fails as a lexicographical work, but those standards are indisputably 'male standards', restricting lexicography to the world of 'patriarchal authoritarianism'. Indeed, the rejection of such standards is wholly deliberate: as the editors point out, using 'a flexible format is a conscious effort to honor the words and arguments of women, to liberate our thinking about what can be said about language and to guard against lexicographical ownership of words and definitions.' They want quite specifically to produce something that is not the traditional 'dick-tionary'.

> We are also aware of the need to pay close attention to the words of disabled women, some of whom call others TABS— 'temporarily able-bodied.' One question is whether we make an effort to expunge phrases from our language like 'stand up for what you believe' or 'blind as a bat.'

The user must also make her or his decision as to the need for justifying the use of alphabetical order (which of course puts men before women, although housework before war) as not being 'a value judgement'.

Jane Mills, whose *Womanwords* (1989) is more an explanatory thesaurus of anti-female stereotyping than a dictionary as such, suggested that, 'Lexicographers deserve much of the criticism levelled against them. But not all of it . . . the basic source material of a lexicographer has been the written word, and most books have been, and still are, written and published by men. Dictionaries which chronicle usage are not necessarily prescriptive. If in the past a dictionary failed to refer to a young woman as a "girl" the lexicographer would have been failing in his job had he not used the term which the rest of society used and understood.'

Things were of course changing even as these books appeared. Especially so in works aimed at children, where short contextual sentences are used to back up the primary definition (and can also be found in dictionaries, such as Merriam Webster, where rather than 'live' citations, usage examples are created to achieve the most telling effect). Comparing such sentences in two editions of the same dictionary, published respectively in 1968 and 1983 Sidney Landau offered these examples. 'Cherish: A mother cherishes her baby' (1968) becomes 'Parents cherish their children' (1983), while 'Seize: In fright she seized his arm' (1968) becomes 'In fright I seized her arm' (1983).

Writing in my own *Chasing the Sun* (1996), a history of dictionary-making, I asked this:

> How much this influences the young reader is debatable. The larger world must conspire with the dictionary, however rigorously non-sexist, to effect that level of social revolution . . . All of this cultural prejudice, conscious or otherwise, may well be reprehensible; likewise a perfect world might well have been a very different place — experience, unfortunately, indicates a harsher reality. The problem for the advocates of PC, in lexicography as elsewhere, is that they demand 'what should be' in a world where there is only 'what is'. Such fantasies failed to work for the prescriptivist critics of *W3* [*Webster's Third International*, 1961], it is unlikely that it will gain any greater advances for those who would impose what is seen as a far more alien ideology on the dictionary. The grim truth that underlies dictionary reform, as much as any other, is that so much preaches only to the converted.

I would be hard put to let this pass unamended. Reading it nearly twenty-five years later demonstrates as well as anything the way what might once have been dismissed as that well-honed *cri de coeur* 'political correctness gone mad' is now par for many courses. Identity politics – can its determination to avoid all possible linguistic offense be termed a 'feminisation' of language? – would claim itself beholden to such mutual respect. Such for many is now the status quo. Alice Roosevelt, daughter of US President Teddy and embroiderer of a pillow stating 'If You Can't Say Something Good About Someone, Sit Right Here by Me,' would have been swept away in a Twitter tsunami.

At the same time, the male bias in dictionary-making is being overturned, or at least revised, but like every aspect of lexicography it remains slow work. It is perhaps in self-defence that women seem to have corralled for their own intellectual discussions a substantial chunk of the meta-lexicographical world, especially where it impinges on gender. No scholar of the craft will go far without encountering the work of Charlotte Brewer, Linda Mugglestone, Sarah Ogilvy and Kory Stamper.

If slang represents male rebellion, how do women rebel linguistically?

Female language innovation is not necessarily linked to vocabulary. There are other forms of linguistic innovation than slang. Notable are those pioneered by young women. In parallel to slang these are not welcome innovations: the speaking style of young women seems to alarm purists. Such innovations, notably *uptalk* (properly *high rising terminal*), *vocal fry* or *creaky voice* (produced by vibrations in the larynx) and the use of such interjections, or vocal fillers as *like*, are seen as problems and young women are regularly told that if they wish to be taken seriously or make a positive impression when interviewing for a job, they must avoid them. Yet as the computational linguist Chi Luu noted in JSTOR Daily,* the condemnation of such usage only seems to apply to young women; when powerful men use uptalk, as was suggested of former president George W. Bush, it is seen as a wholly acceptable adjunct of the assertion of that power. As young women age, they take their speaking style with them. More important perhaps, as mothers and other care-givers, they also pass on such style to new generations. What seemed marginal becomes mainstream.

Suzanne Grégoire of the University of Toronto noted this in 2006:†

Early dialectologists were among the first to recognize that gender plays a role in language innovation. [. . .] For example, in 1946 August Brun, a specialist in the Provençal dialect, observed that older members of the [Provençal] community over fifty spoke mainly Provençal, as did younger men, but *women* under forty-five spoke mainly French. [. . .] Brun suggested that women play a crucial role by adopting language change and using it to bring up the next generation.

In other words, husbands remained faithful to tradition, but wives were pushing out to create and embrace newer developments. She found the same thing in a 1905 study of a Swiss village which showed that 'younger members of the village were beginning to use newer phonetic variants, and further, among the younger generation, *women* used the newer forms more frequently'. Its author suggested that 'women welcome every linguistic novelty

* C. Luu, 'Young Women's Language Patterns at the Forefront of Linguistic Change', *Lingua Obscura* JSTOR Daily (2 February 2015).
† S. Grégoire, 'Gender and Language Change: The Case of Early Modern Women' (2006) passim.

with open arms.' Subsequent research has found that this may be over-simplistic – men too play a role in language change – but it certainly added a new dimension to concepts of motherhood.

Girls, adds Deborah Cameron, 'have sub-cultural style'[*] and the way they speak and the lexis they use is all part of it. As the slang lexicologist Michael Adams puts it, 'where the style goes, so goes the slang.'[†] However, being girls, they have to push the sub-culture's excesses further than do boys. For Cameron, 'Any subculture a woman belongs to – whether she wants to be one of the nerds, or she wants to be one of the Goths, or whatever – women and girls have to go over the top to be accepted as a legitimate member of the community.' Given that they come to these sub-cultures as interlopers, she notes, they must work that much harder on 'how they appeared, whether they were popular, those kinds of things. So they put a lot more into dressing right and talking right [and that] propels them to take whatever the subcultural style is to an extreme . . . In general they're a genera-tion ahead of boys.'

If girls led the way, they set the scene, rather than monopolise it.

What happened later was that all those things, those iconic things like uptalk, boys do that now just as much as girls. Middle-aged men do it now. Vocal fry, same thing. Boys do it, but girls do it more extremely, so they've become en-regis-tered. All this leads to a popular discourse which assumes that it [innovation] must be something to do with feminin-ity, that it's a thing girls do, whereas actually what it is, as time will tell, is a thing that everyone does, but girls got to

[*] D. Cameron, Interview (12 February 2018).
[†] M. Adams *Slang: The People's Poetry*, (2009).

1. Women *in* Slang

THIS IS NOT an exposition of slang's tried-and-tested stereo-types, but if we are to posit an alternative, there is no choice other than to assess the status quo. Like the Black Power leader Stokely Carmichael, who announced in 1968 that as far as the revolution was concerned, the only position for women was 'prone', slang's treatment of women is far from admirable. There may be the occasional outlier, but the weight of evidence, based on half a millennium of lexical invention, shows that as in its dealings with LGBT+ people, people of colour, Jews and other social minorities, slang's go-to treatment of women was as object, not subject. Showing little in the way of its usual subversive take on the world, the 'counter-language' proved itself depressingly conservative in its adoption of the usual stereotypes. Looking at the relevant words and phrases we find the whore/mother dichotomy (though whore terms outweigh those for mothers by several hundred to one); the sex object; the child and as such devoid of agency; the equation of the loved one with food ('good enough to eat' and parallel endearments) or less flattering, an animal; the scold; the agent of emasculation and of course, the *bitch* who combines pretty much every negative adjective.*

---

* As listed in my database bitch holds twenty-seven senses when used as a simple noun; there are forty-seven sub-entries; the verb gives nine plus fifteen.

Writing in *Womanwords* (1989), her invaluable lexicon of terms used to describe women, the majority of which have been coined in a less than complimentary manner by men, Jane Mills notes that so substantial is the slang vocabulary, especially that which equates 'woman' with 'slut' or its synonyms, that she 'had to draw an arbitrary line lest [the book] turned into a dictionary of slang.' Slang, it is widely believed, is the essence of 'man-made language', created by man and largely spoken by him too. A further breakdown works through physical appearance (attractive or unattractive), physical size (large or simply fat), sex (sexy and/or what is condemned as promiscuous and both judged by male opinion), speech (either gossips or nags), character (unpleasant, stupid or lazy) and dress (badly dressed, slovenly or overdressed).

We need go no further than the current outpourings of a variety of political extremists, both right and left, whether voiced in person or via the gutless anonymity of social media. In the UK alone, such female politicians as Diane Abbott, Luciana Berger, Mhairi Black, Jess Phillips and Anna Soubry as well as campaigners such as Gina Miller continue to face the scatalogical, sexist even homicidal rantings of what the net calls 'haters'. Abbott is regularly named 'bitch' and as woman of colour, 'nigger'; Mhairi Black of the SNP, an out lesbian, is a 'dyke,' a 'rug-muncher' and a 'slut' and required to 'eat shit and die'; Phillips's detractors sent her six hundred-plus rape and or death threats in a single evening in 2016. Then there is the flood of anti-semitism, which offers slang's tried-and-tested terminology for the Christ-killer.

If the slang lexis offers over two thousand hits in response to the search 'woman' (plus 'girl' and allied variations), one can be sure that 90 per cent will be negative; those that can be ranked as congratulatory are thus listed only in terms of sexual appeal. Sex aside, slang's point of view accords to male stereotypes, the linguistic equivalent of an unremitting 'male gaze'. And subversion, elsewhere so central to slang's opinion? We must contort that description pretty hard: if one wishes to justify it in this context. The only possible subversion here was of courtesy/politeness/treating women as in some way 'special'. One might see this as proto-feminist, the correct term, once one assesses the lexis, eye as ever on such evidence as can be adduced, is viciously misogynistic.

The aim of *Sounds and Furies* is to study woman *and* slang, and not women as portrayed within in it. It seems, nonetheless, worth offering a tasting menu of at least some of the vocabulary with which slang, in all its patriarchal confidence, typifies 'the gentler sex'.

The Sex Object

Of the various slang terms for woman a large number, no doubt unsurprisingly, see the woman as no more than a sex object and as such derive purely and simply from terms that otherwise mean the vagina. Though sometimes the sex, as it were, is muted and the object takes centre stage. This construction lies behind one of the oldest such terms, *piece*, which entered the language during the fourteenth century, and remained standard English for the next three to four hundred years, after which, in such combinations as *piece of stuff* (seventeenth century), *piece of ass*, *piece of tail* and *piece of stray* (all twentieth century), it became a staple of such dismissive descriptions. And if not a piece, then the equally dismissive *bit* which is first used to mean a woman in 1665, where a butcher's wife is punningly equated with 'a nice plump bit'. The full-out *bit of meat* means vagina from 1842, the woman in 1975 and intercourse in 1984.

Additional 'bits' include a *bit of muslin* (nineteenth century), a *bit of ebony* (a black girl) and a *bit of crackling* (a mix of *cracker*, *crack*: vagina, and roast pork skin). Most 'bits' implied an attractive woman, although a *bit of mutton* or a *piece of mutton* (from *mutton*: vagina or prostitute, especially as in *laced mutton*, where the *lace* is that of stays or corsets, embellishing a young, or disguising an ageing, figure) implied in this context a woman dressing younger than her years. As well as the well-known *mutton dressed as lamb*, such a self-deluding figure was also known as a *peg puff*, a *phizgig* (possibly related to its alternative definition: a pile of moistened gunpowder which when lit fails to flash) and a *mutton cove*.

Other early description include *pussy* (seventeenth century), *flat-cock* (eighteenth century) which also describes girl-to-girl frottage, *gusset* and *placket* (both seventeenth century), the latter duo metonymising aspects of clothing, all of which are purely anatomical. However the point of view was not wholly masculine: *gobble-prick* (eighteenth century) a 'rampant, lustful' woman,' as defined by lexicographer Francis Grose – the 'gobbling' is performed by the vagina, not the mouth, *staff breaker* and *staff climber* (nineteenth century, from *staff of life*: penis), were somewhat back-handed compliments, but did admit to some degree of female sexuality. The nineteenth century added *fish* and *oyster* (both nodding to the popular vagina as fish metaphor, and perhaps at least part of the imagery behind *Billingsgate* [see chapter 6]) plus *fluff* (otherwise pubic hair). The twentieth century *tuna* provides another 'fishy' image.

Just as in slang his penis can stand for the whole man, usually a stupid one (e.g. *dick*, *prick*, *putz*), so can her vagina (and sometimes her buttocks) represent the entire woman. Examples include the Afro-American *booty* and *butter* (both from *butt*:

40

posterior), *cock* (usually found as the masculine penis, but meaning vagina in the Caribbean and the Southern States of the US; possibly from seventeenth-century *cockles*: labia minora but more likely from French *coquille*, a cockleshell or cowrie, which supposedly looks similar), *coño* (from Spanish), *cookie*, *coot* and *cooze* (all euphemisms of *cunt, crack, crotch, gash* – as simple anatomy in the eighteenth century, but the derogatory use is twentieth and possibly adds a secondary use of *gash*: spare, waste, to the obvious physical description); other additions include *quiff, slit, snatch, hair* (thus *get one's hair cut*: to visit a woman for sex), *kitty-cat* (a variant of *pussy*) and *minge bag* (from *minge*, borrowed from the synonymous Romani *mingra*). Finally, definitively, comes *cunt* itself. Germaine Greer, writing in *Suck* magazine in 1971, demanded 'Lady, love your cunt' and the word features in Eve Ensler's *Vagina Monologues* (1996) but slang proved resistant: only when used between men, does the word claim a positive interpretation.

Promiscuity

Given the nature of this area of slang, the line between a 'neutral', i.e. a woman unscourged by slang's male moralists, and one who is deemed promiscuous is at times almost invisible. Of slang's 1,250 terms primarily meaning prostitute many can be used derogatively of women who while (immorally) enjoying sex do not charge for their favours. The terms that follow, some of which overlap with other sections, may be presumed to have a higher 'promiscuity' content than their peers. Virtually all are twentieth-century coinages, although on occasion their origins may lie somewhat earlier.

Perhaps the great modern put-down has been *bimbo*, which

with its less common abbreviation *bim*, has become (and to a great extent remains) the ultimate description of a certain type of contemporary young woman. Partially overtaken by the all-English *Essex girl*, such a figure is often seen as something of a *gold-digger* (her 1930s equivalent) and indulged as such by rich and/or powerful older men and the media to whom she tells or sells her tale. The earliest use of *bimbo* is found c.1900 in America, where it was synonymous with *bozo* to mean a tough guy. A parallel use was that to mean 'baby', abbreviated from the Italian *bambino*. By the 1920s the word meant young woman, often a prostitute. The current use stems from the revelations of a 'model', of her relationship with a millionaire businessman.

A number of terms simply equate sexually active women with dirt: thus *dirty leg, dirt-bag* and *shagbag* (from *shag* although the *bag* probably means a repository, i.e. for semen, rather than old woman), *grubber, scab, scuzz, sleaze, snot* (nineteenth century, usually nasal mucus, although nineteenth-century Scots cant defined *snot* as 'a gentleman'), *sweat hog, pig, scrubber* (a military coinage of the 1920s, but obviously linked to the eighteenth-century *scrub*: a cheap whore), *slag* (from standard English *slack*; its earlier, eighteenth-century use meant coward; Robin Cook's novel *The Crust On Its Uppers* [1962] defines *the slag* as 'young third-rate grafters, male or female, unwashed, useless') and *whore* (but with no commercial overtones) itself.

Predictable, easy availability underlines *dead cert, easy lay* (from *lay*, either intercourse or the woman who shares in it) or *easy ride, free for all, pushover* and the cognate *Little Miss Roundheels* (cf. nineteenth-century *lift the heels*: to copulate). The image of physical instability – unable to stand up straight, the woman is forever falling on her back and ready/eager for sex – is old: *light*, meaning promiscuous and suggesting one who is 'light upon her heels', is found in 1468 and soon followed by the *light housewife*, the *light lady*, *light skirts*, the *light woman* and *lightness*, promiscuity.

Ride means to have sex, which offers such mechanicals as the *bike*, the *motorcycle*, the *town bicycle*, and *ride* itself. Town gives *town pump* and *town punch*, while a *carpenter's dream* is 'flat as a board and easy to screw'. *Paraffin lamp* is rhyming slang for *tramp* and its cognate *bum*. *Knock* and *leg* both come from earlier terms meaning sexual intercourse, respectively *knock* (sixteenth century) and *leg business* (nineteenth century). Sexual enthusiasm in a woman is de facto impermissible: *goer* (originally nineteenth-century racing use: a good runner) allows a smidgeon of approval ('a right goer') as does *right sort* (from Australian *sort*, a woman) but *hot-bot* (cf. seventeenth-century *hot-arsed*, *hot-backed*), *screamer and creamer*, *lust dog* are all negatives (if pandering to male desire). Male dreams also underpin *nympho* and *nymph* (both from standard English *nymphomaniac*) although the use of nymph for prostitute, e.g. *nymph of the pave*, *nymph of darkness*, *nymph of delight* link to a mythical, even ethereal sense of the standard term. Ethereal or otherwise, such enthusiasts *bang like the shithouse door* (*in a gale*).

A *shack job*, *shack-up* (from *shack up*, to live with) or *sleepy-time girl* are good for a brief relationship. The *floosie* or *floozie* comes from the dialect *floosy*: flossy, thus soft, while *punch* originates in the eighteenth-century standard English verb *punch*: to pierce. *Broad* (possibly from a woman's physique, though most contexts ignore such a possibility) remains primarily US, while the sexually generous *charity girl* and *chippie* usually mean prostitute. Those who, from the viewpoint of various 'male' pursuits, are seen as parasites include the *groupie* or *band rat* and the *snow bunny* (specialising respectively in rock groups and skiers); a *splash* is a victim of gang rape, while a *buttered bun* (*butter*: semen, *buns*: buttocks) is one who has sex with several men in succession. The term was first coined to describe the sixteenth-century courtesan Louise de Quérouaille; the current use dates from the seventeenth century. Finally, the girl who is 'no better than she should be' is one who has had *more pricks than a second-hand dart-board*.

Animals and Food

A less aggressive, but barely more complimentary group of terms positions women as animals, or even food. *Bitch* had moved on from its fourteenth-century standard English origins as meaning a female dog to becoming a prostitute by the fifteenth century; that aspect vanished but the term has remained generally derogative since the eighteenth century, both for women and for men seen as literally or figuratively 'effeminate'. *Bird*, still extant today, appeared over a century ago; other birds include *biddy* which began life in the sixteenth-century meaning a chicken, became a young girl in the eighteenth century and has meant any woman since the nineteenth century; if anything the twentieth-century meaning, often with the adjective 'old' has made the logical last leap and means an old woman. *Hen* is an early seventeenth-century term, while *chick*, a byword for the politically incorrect, is twentieth century, although it has been used as an affectionate description of a child since the Middle Ages, as has the synonymous *chickabiddy*, which was coined by London costermongers during the nineteenth century. *Quail*, *pheasant* and *plover* all started life in the seventeenth century, when they generally meant prostitute, but became generalised terms by the nineteenth century; of the three *quail* (supposedly amorous bird) is the survivor – still widely used in the US – and the *San Quentin quail* is a synonym for *jailbait*, i.e. such a youngster can send a man to the San Quentin (or any other) prison. The link between them is that presumably all are *game*. *Poultry* (nineteenth century) meant women in general and *wool*, like *fluff*, also means pubic hair while *dish* invariably implies good looks.

Like *pussy*, *cat* has a lengthy pedigree: whore in the sixteenth century, argumentative termagant in the nineteenth century and gossip since the 1920s. *Mare* is a twentieth-century term, and like the similar *moo* gained wide currency during the successful 1960's television series, *Till Death Us Do Part*. Either term is open to affectionate as well as derogatory use. Moo of course references *cow* (seventeenth century) which may have begun life without prejudice but its modern use is strictly negative. *Filly* is seventeenth century, as is the male pursuit of *filly-hunting* and links, again, to *ride*. *Fox* is an exception: it is wholly approving although in the case of Amanda Knox, found innocent of murder after a convoluted Italian prosecution, her nickname 'Foxy Knoxy' surely signposted her 'bad' sexuality.

In the context of food, *trout* (eighteenth century) is another play on the 'fish' image, but originally *trout* = truth = honest, and, however much against slang's usual grain, implied the trustiness of the woman, rather than anything offensive. The *jelly* (nineteenth century) was a buxom and pretty girl, the *cherry*, with its image of ripeness, or *cherry ripe* (nineteenth century) and the *cherry pie* (twentieth century) are all virgins; a *potato* (a term much beloved of Damon Runyon's fictional Broadway hustlers), is in fact Australian rhyming slang: *potato peeler: sheila*.

The girl who is 'sweet' is good enough to eat and none of the terms that equate her to some form of sweetmeat is remotely negative. Even *tart*, long associated with promiscuity and thus disdained, has toothsome origins. As found in Hotten's dictionary of 1864, the term suggested tastiness (in slang as well as standard senses) and gay colours.

Such terms include *cookie* (US: biscuit), *banana* (possibly for a 'yellow' girl), *butter baby, poundcake, sweet potato pie, tootsie roll* (from a well-known US sweet), and *candy* (a sexually desirable person of either sex; cf. *sweetmeat*). *Cheesecake* (while commonly used as a synonym for pinup or *Page Three girl*, is also a richer version of the commonplace *tart*); similar are *creamie, crumpet, cupcake, dish, honey, jam* (also meaning semen), *pancake, peach, pie, sweetie* (although this is generally the abbreviation of sweetheart), *tomato* and the all-encompassing *yummy* and *yum-yum*, which also stood for the vagina and for intercourse.

The Attractive Woman

That its meaning is ostensibly positive does not render a term any more palatable. Nowhere is the male-orientated dimension of this particular area of slang so prevalent than in the terms to describe women or girls deemed attractive or, in the following section, those who are considered less physically favoured. A mix of lasciviousness and patronage infuses virtually every term. Once again some words overlap with more general uses, meaning simply 'woman'.

Among the most popular of today's terms is *stunner* or *stunnah* (as spelt by tabloid sub-editors). It is, in fact, a nineteenth-century coinage and can be found in *The Swell's Night Guide*, of 1846, where it applied to 'Slippery Sal, the Oakley-street stunner'. The *stunner's* peer, the *Page Three girl*, is all twentieth century, an invention of the *Sun* newspaper of the late 1970s, which started featuring scantily clad pin-ups on page three.

Other popular terms include *lovely*, *dreamboat* (equally common as a description of an attractive male), *eyeful*, *glamour puss*, *charmer* (usually as *little charmer*), *classy chassis*, and *cracker* or *little cracker*. Slightly more exciting are *scorcher*, *sexpot* and *hot number*. America offers *babe* and *real babe*, *cutes*, *cutesie-pie* and *cutie* (plus *cute chick*), *looker*, *nifty* and *nifty piece*, *patootie* (possibly from *potato*), *toots*, *little pretty* and *star*. A *ten* is a girl who rates at ten out of ten on any scale of male appreciation, the term comes from the eponymously titled film of 1979, starring Bo Derek. Back in Britain *doll* is compounded as *doll city*, *dollface* and *dolly*, an *angel* was originally a prostitute working near the Angel public house in Islington; the *talent* is a general term for pretty girls, e.g. 'Any talent about?' *Donah* is virtually defunct, but was a classic nineteenth-century term, a Parlyaree word that came from the Italian *donna*: a woman, and is enshrined in the music hall couplet (usually attributed to Gus Elen): 'Never introduce your donah to a pal / For the odds is ten to one he nicks your gal.'

Australia adds *beaut* and *grouse gear* (both of which can simply mean good) and the surfers' *ginch*. Afro-American terms have included *poodle* (an unusually complimentary twist on the negative *dog*), *Porsche* and *Mercedes* (both luxury motorcars), *melted butter* (a light-skinned girl), *mink*, *brickhouse*, *fleshpot*, *hamma* or *hammer*, *sleek lady*, *thoroughbred black* and the sexually paradoxical *stallion* (she gives a good ride?). Finally a *Barbie Doll* (from the trade-marked toy) is pretty but ultra-conventional and *all tits and teeth* describes a girl who is blatantly sexual, if less than notably bright.

The Unattractive Woman

Cow meant simply woman in the eighteenth century, but acquired the image of prostitution in the nineteenth century; modern uses tend to be as combinations – typically *stupid cow*, *ugly cow* and Nell Dunn's 1967 book title: *Poor Cow*. *Crow* comes from *chromo*, both of which can also mean whore (the term abbreviates standard English *chromolithograph*, a picture printed in colours from stone; the image equates an over-dressed, over-made-up woman, e.g. a prostitute, with a chromolithograph – both are colourful and flashy, but neither resembles natural beauty); *dog*, *dogface* (also a soldier) and *doggie* are common US pejoratives, all of which are presumably rooted in the earlier *bitch*, although *dog* (found as slang in 1508) is a general negative, as often found in non-sexual contexts. Other terms include *cull bird* (possibly from eighteenth-century farming use, *cull*: an animal too old for breeding), *bat* (often as *old bat* and originally, eighteenth century, a prostitute), *buzzard* (an ignorant and gullible person since the fourteenth century), *hedgehog*, *heifer* (nineteenth century), *hog* (from twentieth-century *hog*: to copulate) and *mule* (which can also mean an impotent male).

Other putdowns include *bad news*, *bag*, *double-bagger* (the need for both participants to place bags over their heads during intercourse) and *douchebag* (US; Australian has *Douche Can Alley*: Palmer Street, the red-light area of Sydney), *drack* (Australian, possibly from Dracula), *hairbag*, *pitch* and *skank*. Black America has its share: *bear*, *chicken* and *thunder chicken* represent the animal kingdom, while *B.B. head*, *nailhead*, *ragmop* and *tackhead* all equate ill-kempt or unfashionable hair with an unappetising person. A *welfare mother* extends the condemnation to poverty, while a *skeeza* (from *skeeze*: to have sex and

48

beloved of *rap* lyricists) is not merely ugly but promiscuous with it. The acronym *PTA* stands for *pussy, tits* and armpits – all of which allegedly smell.

Finally a fat woman is variously a *Bahama mama* (contrasting supposedly overweight West Indians with sleek US girls), a *butterball, Judy with the big booty* (from *judy*: a woman, and *booty*: the behind), a *pig, pigger* or *pigmouth*, a *shuttlebutt*, or a *teddybear*; the nineteenth century, slightly less cruel, opts for *feather-bed and pillows*.

General Terms

Sometimes a woman is simply a woman, for all that such general terminology in no way saves her. Of general terms for women, *mot* or *mort, blowse* or *blouse* and *gixie* (sixteenth century) have also been stolen to mean prostitute and the seventeenth-century *blowen* has had a similar treatment. Other seventeenth-century terms include *apron* (and *white apron* a whore), *smock* (cf. *skirt*) and *cooler* (from the assumption that passion cools after sex; a *wife in water colours* is cognate: unlike the harsh colouring of the oil-painted wife, the kinder mistress appears in softer watercolours). Like the generic *smock*, which can be used to mean woman in a variety of contexts, usually those injurious to her reputation, *petticoat* appears in a number of combinations: *petticoat government* (female rule in the home, a precursor of the twentieth-century *pussy-whipped*), a *petticoat merchant* (a whoremonger), *petticoat pet*, a lover, a *squire of the petticoat* (a pimp), and *petticoat led* (one who is infatuated). A *gig* is a flighty woman while a *crackish* one (from *crack*: vagina) is a 'wanton'; a *faggot* is synonymous with a *baggage* (which has strong overtones of promiscuity): both are something to be borne or carried. (Whether this

49

link of *faggot* and femininity underpins the use of *faggot* for a male homosexual remains debated.) *Moll* is yet another term that serves equally as whore, while a *catamaran* is a play on *cat*, or possibly puns on the nineteenth-century standard English use of catamaran: a *fireship*, which in slang is a poxed female. The suffix *-widow*, meaning any woman whose husband is occupied elsewhere, emerged in the eighteenth century, typically as *grass widow* or *widow bewitched*; such combinations as *golf widow* or *cricket widow* are twentieth-century coinages.

Doll, the ancestor of the 1960s *dolly* and *dollybird* appears in the mid-nineteenth century, while *hairy* ('a hatless slum girl in Glasgow') and its adverbial form *hairy* (sexually alluring) is a contemporary. *Judy*, possibly from Punch and Judy shows, appears c.1810; other nineteenth-century terms include *mivvy* (possibly from *mivey*: a landlady), *polone* (a Parlyaree term that echoes the older *blowen*), the generic *skirt* (often as in a *bit of skirt*), *totty* (from the proper name Dorothy or from *titty*; originally a high-class whore, by the twentieth century it was used without pejorative overtones) and *crumb* or *crummy* (a pretty, plumpish woman; the term comes from the crumb of a risen loaf), *sister* and the *echt* Australian feminine: *sheila*. *Sheila*, usually spelt *shaler* until c.1900, has no easy etymology. As a name it is all-purpose for an Irish girl, the female equivalent of *paddy*, which has come to mean any Irishman; both terms appear in that context in nineteenth-century Australia. Hotten suggests that it is the 'corrupt form of Gaelic, *caille*, a young woman.' The drift from Irish girl to any girl approximately parallels the *shaler/ sheila* spelling change; by 1919 the writer W. H. Downing defines it simply as 'a girl' in his *Digger Dialects*.

Modern terms include *babe*, *frail* (now US, although the 'frail sisterhood' was used in the UK c.1830 to mean prostitutes, albeit smart ones) and *jane*, all primarily US and all still smack-ing of the pulp novels wherein they first saw the lexical light. More recent Americanisms are the Afro-American *band* (used in Australia to mean a whore), *rag baby*, *real woman* and *one good woman*. The UK has *tart* (with its implication of promiscuity), *nammo* or *nemmo* (both backslang), and the rhyming slang *twist* (*twist and twirl*: girl) and *cuddle and kiss* (miss), *sort* (coined in Australia c.1910 it appeared in the 'old country' thirty years later); the term was briefly popularised c.1970 as the invariable name of the girls who associated with skinhead boys. *Mystery* describes young girls who had run away to London; thus *mystery mad* or *mystery punter*: a man who specialises in the pursuit of such girls. Among the most recent terms are the frankly vicious *come-dump*, *jezzy* (from the Bible's *Jezebel*), *yat* and *sket*.

Finally a party of women can be a *fool's wedding* (nineteenth century), a *hen party* (nineteenth century), *bitch-party*, *cat-party* or *tabby-party*.

2. All Our Own Work

LOOKING AT THE relationship of women and slang what emerges from these researches is twofold. One aspect concerns use and one creativity. Even discounting a persistent strain of gender ventriloquy (and acknowledging that this can work in both directions, with women mimicking men just as men ape women), there is no reason to pretend that women have not always used slang. It is true that such use has not always been noted down, an omission that has usually been the responsibility of men, in practice (and until relatively recently) the gatekeepers of the publishing process, and in depressingly persistent theory those who were and remain happy to assume that what women have to say, whatever the medium, simply doesn't count. In the case of slang the blind eye is proffered even more obdurately.

And if women's speech is noted, what happens if they choose, seeing its creative potential and ignoring the social prohibitions that accompany it, to use slang? The users – whether in speech or print – are immediately pilloried (once more by men, though far from invariably) as displaying unacceptable signs of social betrayal.

The positive potential of the content vanishes beneath the terror of the form. All this naturally muddies the water, but it does not empty the bath. The baby remains, bawling and in every sense lusty. The bottom line remains whoever may be the user, slang is used when it's found to be useful. Among such uses being the expression of emotions that mere standard English cannot properly encapsulate, the demonstration of a degree of shared involvement in some form of institution, whether licit or otherwise, that can best be achieved by a shared and restricted language, and, as a writer of some form of fiction, the conferring of authenticity upon the story and the characters with which one populates it. Whether, as is usually believed, all such slang is initially generated by men is hard to prove. We cannot, other than in the rarest of instances, where the etymology can be timed, dated and identified with a specific individual, lay down a moment of birth, nor can we ascribe that moment of lexical parturition to a man or woman.

Slang has its functions and even if its originators could be proved to be mainly men, then women, as they have with other male inventions, have co-opted and developed the words and their use. Sometimes they have modified it. We all use slang when we so require and sometimes it just provides services – typically in its unrivalled span of synonyms – that standard English simply cannot offer. Obvious? Of course, but somehow the idea that women and slang are in some way divided, one each side of a *cordon sanitaire*, persists. I would hope that in the chapters that follow it should be possible to lay this fantasy to rest.

This is not to deprive slang of its themes as laid down in chapter 1. These have not changed. There has not suddenly emerged a hidden cache of terms that, created by women, are devoted – as hitherto has never been the case – to the subjects that are exclusively associated with them. Caring, sharing and compassion, philosophising in place of concrete cruelties, dreams over what we accept as realities, all so alien it seems to the slang mindset, being the obvious contenders. However, when women do enter the game, as we shall see with the website Mumsnet, those exclusions are no longer an absolute. Still, if slang does not generally go there, it has other jobs to do. And does them very well. Yes, it is largely abusive – whether in traditional terms: blunt insult, or in the infinity of new areas of potential offence generated by concern with diversity, identity politics, the demand for positive role models, and every other category of the auto-bowdlerising Mrs Joyful Prize for Raffia with which we are currently living – but in the end it is no more than one more set of words. Neither sticks nor stones, fists nor feet. It is open to suggestions, available to all. Think of it as the free bike of communication; you may take it when and where you wish. You may not even bother.

Considered figuratively slang resembles some kind of lost entity, turned away from the standard lexicons and wandering, friendless, in a limitless desert. As noted by Jennifer Lyndsay Grant, the nineteenth-century French lexicographer Alfred Delvau took this a step further: not only was slang shunned by respectable dictionaries, it was, in effect, a linguistic prostitute, walking the streets, flaunting its flashy charms and hoping to 'pick up' writers who needed the sort of racy, 'seductive' language that was not on offer 'at home' in the orthodox dictionaries. Slang, to use its own term for a mistress, was 'a wife in water colours.' Or for modernity: the MILF. A complaisant and alluring alternative to demanding, critical standard English. Taken to a logical conclusion this made a slang dictionary language's version of a *maison close* and as such, Ms Grant suggests, subject to the male novelists who exploited it.[*]

There is an extra dimension. If slang of its essential nature comes bottom of the list for 'respectable' acceptability no matter who may be the speaker, then when it is ascribed to women it tends, as seen in the judgemental opinions not only of such as the late US slang collector David Maurer (see chapter 8) but also of scores of male critics beside, to be a badge not of creativity, however arse-about-face, but of wholesale failure. If one needs a synonym, let us suggest 'immorality'. A woman using slang is probably criminal, certainly in some way *declassé*. Dr Johnson, who equated female preaching with 'a dog's walking on his hinder legs. It's not done well; but you are surprised to find it done at all,' could not have permitted himself to acknowledge that such speakers existed. The earliest examples of such ran with gangs of criminal beggars or, tiring of the essentially subservient roles they were often forced to play, set themselves up as criminals in their own right, whether as gang leaders or independents. For a middle-class woman to use slang was, or so believed both intimates and critics, no more than an adolescent phase, born of an excess association with her brothers and their friends or from a fanciful desire to break away from their destined, domestic role in society. She might enjoy a few years as a 'fast girl' or 'new woman' but such aberrations with their concomitant interest in tobacco, horseflesh and even gambling, would, it was fondly hoped, soon pass. If she came from further down the social scale, then she was a scold or nag or purveyor of the eponymous 'Billingsgate'. In all cases she failed to fulfil that first of all commandments as issued by men:

[*] Grant op. cit. pp.27–29.

shut up. That the accusation often came with an inference of sexual 'incontinence'; should hardly need explanation. In a patriarchal world, its strictures backed up by the superstitions of those whose lives are delineated by the diktats of one or another old man living celibate in the sky, all female sins cohabit with a taste for forbidden fruit. Slang, born of sin and wilfully offering it a vocabulary, fitted the bill. That prostitutes were so imbued with slang merely spiced the dish. It is a literally vicious circle: the sinful whore uses slang; slang, since it is used by whores, is sinful. Language as Schnitzler's *La Ronde*. Nor was actually using it necessary: the briefest of encounters was enough. After all, as the prosecution counsel put it in the trial of the allegedly 'obscene' *Lady Chatterley's Lover* in 1960, 'Is it a book that you would even wish your wife or your servants to read?'

And if they did encounter such language? In 1921 Edith Swan, of the seaside town of Littlehampton, was tried for libel. A series of anonymous letters had plagued the town and while an initial prosecution had focused on the stereotypically 'working-class' (poor, argumentative, known to use 'bad' language) Rose Gooding, deeper investigation turned to Swan, a former servant but seen as scrupulously 'middle-class'. Many letters went to her neighbours Violet and George May. For instance (14 September 1921): 'You bloody fucking flaming piss country whores go and fuck your cunt. Its your drain that stinks not our fish box. You fucking dirty sods. You are as bad as your whore neybor.' Or soon afterwards: 'To the old bastards May. You can talk about us as much as you like you dirty cows. You bloody fucking sods, you think you are big but we are as good as you. You are bloody dirty or you would clean the yard sometimes you bloody rotten buggers.' As Christopher Hilliard, author of a study of the trial* put it, 'This was swearing as a foreign language by someone who had the vocab but was not sure of how to fit the words together,' and many saw Swan as mad rather than bad. Still, she went down, even if the judge, wholly swayed by her bourgeois affectations, made it clear that this was not his verdict. Middle-class female respectability could not swear.

Except that it can and these days class comes into the equation no more than it does for slang's male users. Vulgar, brazen, flaunting, whorish slang is used and exploited by women and on occasion, as much as we can hazard such guesses, coined by them too. I have chosen within this book to embrace all such activities. That said, it is vital that we ask: if 'female slang' exists, 'what are its preoccupations? Are these the same as those found throughout male slang or do they develop "female" centred' themes.

Looking at the bulk of women's slang use, let us say prior to the twentieth century and in particular before the girl-focused vocabulary of the flappers, the slang seems to be shared between the genders. If Chaucer can ventriloquise the rich and often misandrist vocabulary of that female role model the Wife of Bath, then so too can Aphra Behn offer swaggering Restoration rakes, effing, blinding and blaspheming, all mouth and voluminous trousers. Paradoxically John Cleland, voicing his eighteenth-century 'lady of pleasure' Fanny Hill, is at pains to exclude any 'dirty words' though his topic, commercial copulation and its hinterland, plays a leading role in counter-linguistic coinage. Women continue with slang in the nineteenth century, but it remains, seemingly, that of men. That is, when they are permitted such breaches in the high walls of self-censorship that

* C. Hilliard, *The Littlehampton Libels: A Miscarriage of Justice and a Mystery about Words in 1920s England* (2017).

surround the era's fantasies of female chastity and respectability. Surtees' nineteenth-century actress Lucy Glitters is both 'beautiful and tolerably virtuous', not to mention maintaining a first-class seat on a hunter (the subtext of slang's version of 'riding' can surely not be too far away), and as such is permitted slang, but Dickens' sanctimonious Esther Summerson, luxuriating in her own martyrdom, is standard English only. But, as we shall see, so too is that lowest of street girls, Bill Sykes's unfortunate girlfriend Nancy. The American linguist and slang lexicologist Michael Adams quotes *The Memoirs of a Highland Lady*, published in 1845 by Elizabeth Grant of Rothiemurchus. *The Memoirs* include such slang as 'A No 1', 'crack' (first-rate) and 'in the moon' (confused). This is hardly 'domestic' slang, but like her fictional contemporary Lucy, Ms Grant socialised with raffish, gaming, drinking and of course slanging males.

For Adams, women's slang has 'been there all along'. He takes Louisa M. Alcott's classic *Little Women* (1868–9) as a founding text, though the terms we find make Alcott a user rather than a coiner. Fifteen-year-old Josephine 'Jo' March, positioned as the tomboy of the group, is the slang user, and duly criticised by baby sister Amy as being thus 'boyish'. She defends herself, decrying in what were already dated terms' affected, niminy-piminy chits'. And her slang lexis is indeed mainly 'boyish': *camp down*, *blunderbuss* (a blunderer), *hey!*, *highty-tighty!*, *Sancho* (a slightly euphemistic substitute for *dago*, a Hispanic), *dig* and *peg away* (both to work hard); only *pop* (a poplin dress), might be termed 'girl talk'. She can also be uncannily modern: for instance *do the pretty*, which might have stepped from Adams' other speciality, the language of TV's *Buffy the Vampire Slayer*, and the suffix *-age*, in this case as *grubbage* (here meaning work). No room, however, for Buffy's trademark *much?*

It is, as Adams stresses, 'soft' slang; no hint of anything obscene and he suggests that if girls like Jo might regularly use some form of slang (perhaps as critics sneered, picked up from a loose-lipped brother, though there are none such in the March family) then 'they socialised one another out of its use by the time they became adults.'

A century and a half beyond *Little Women* and such socialisation has long since disappeared. Modern peer pressure operates in reverse. The birth of the teenager demanded a language pitched as rebelliously as were the group's clothes, movies, music and the rest of its avowedly non-standard culture. The specifics have and continue to change, notably the technology, and the ever-moving lexis, but the phenomenon is fixed. Slang is part of the game. The sole bar on slang usage is age: nothing so grotesque as a linguistic equivalent of mutton dressed as lamb. Slang's terms for the old are rightly never kind.

It is also a game that is played irrespective of gender. If the first step was usage, then the second is origination. If the coinage of slang has hitherto seemed to be a male preserve, that is no longer the case. Dr Jack Grieve, of Aston University, is researching the development of language in a number of on-line communities. He is seeing the growth of female-coined language, typically among Twitter users. Terms like *bae* and *on fleek* which originated in the US south east can be traced as colonising a wider world and thence moving into general slang use. It is a movement that seems to be gathering strength.

Yet slang still demands, irrespective of gender, a degree of self-censorship. When the US politician Nancy Pelosi, commenting in December 2018 in the aftermath of a more than usually narcissistic display by her President, tells us 'It goes to show you: You get into a tinkle contest with a skunk, you get tinkle all over you' surely that nursery term 'tinkle', in its attempt to euphemise the usual 'pissing contest' with its 'big swinging dick' subtext is far more painful than the actual term. Ms Pelosi claimed she wanted to act as 'mom' but this auto-bowdlerisation – however necessary in the context of speaking to the media – sends her back to kindergarten, albeit as the teacher. Like the asterisks employed by many newspapers, the attempt to avoid slang merely attracts the reader's attention. Still in Congress, the use a month later by freshman Representative Rashida Tlaib of a promise to 'impeach that motherfucker' brought the predictable howls; especially from those who had seemingly felt no qualms about 'that motherfucker's' cheerful use of phrases such as 'grab that pussy' to characterise his own activities. The double standard is not mandatory, but seemingly it is forever.

Like slang, there is of course no restriction of euphemism to gender. For whatever reason it can be necessary. My own dictionary of slang defines nearly eight hundred terms as 'euph.' with a further 650 references within the etymologies. There is no sense that men or women predominate as users. In her essay 'Gendered Aspects of Lexicographic Labeling'[*] in which she assesses the traditional belief that slang 'has historically excluded speech associated with women' the Oxford lexicographer Katherine Connor Martin notes that while taboo language is seen as male, sidestepping it with euphemism is 'regarded as emblematic of female discourse'. Slang-brandishing men are happy to offend, women, more concerned with linguistic politeness, prefer emollience. She then deals in detail with terms for menstruation which are classified as 'euphemisms' but which also qualify for inclusion in slang dictionaries.[†]

[*] In *Dictionaries* 26 (2005) pp.160–173.
[†] See my list of such terms below.

Other than in such relatively rare and purpose-built volumes as Kramarae and Treichler's *Feminist Dictionary* gender labelling is almost never attempted in dictionaries, of whatever genre of language. Or certainly not in the blanket way of 'drugs' or 'und.[erworld]' or 'Aus.[tralian]'. Certain slang terms, typically as regards sexual intercourse, are noted as being coined 'from a female point of view', but such notations remain the exceptions. Sex, at least in slang, is something men do to women, and the bulk of the terminology makes this wholly clear. In a 'historical principles dictionary', such as the *OED*, the only way to implement such differentiation would be by expanding the citations and labelling them *M* or *F* (though even that elementary bifurcation might now be insufficient). The disappearance of traditional space restrictions that has accompanied the move of lexicography from paper to screen means the job could be done; the human effort required may still make it more fantasy than fact.

We are also brought back to the problem that runs through much of this inquiry: where's the evidence. Of course women use slang, of course women are as capable as men of swearing, voicing misanthropy (not to mention misandry and misogyny) and whatever else lies at its negative, cynical heart, but the collectors have been badly served. Then, as noted, one faces the on-going problem of ventriloquy. On the other hand some topics, perhaps since no man would volunteer to participate, have been turned over to women alone. The slang that they have generated may be presumed, at least for the most part, to represent female agency.

Menstruation

If we wish to take a slang subset that, surely, is unarguably women generated, then the obvious selection must be menstruation. Given men's historical (and continuing) squeamishness as regards the non-sexual aspects of a female's 'down there', which is only intensified to a state of terror-cum-horror when one extends this to the fluids therein involved, it might be safe to say that when slang comes to dealing with the topic of menstruation, we are on women-only turf. Ventriloquy does not throw its voice that far. The sole exceptions being dismissive variations on 'got the rag on?' – since it is an article of male faith that menstruation, rather than anything external, will cause ill temper – to question the reason for a woman's lack of cheeriness.* And if the dismissive 'on the rag' (abbreviated to *on*) is one male acknowledgement of menstruation, slang does offer – in what for the register is something of rarity – a trio of phrases that, macho definitely aforethought, might be termed philosophy: *when the red is over the pink, go for the brown* and its synonym *if the river runs red, hit the dirt track*; and *if they're old enough to bleed, they're old enough to butcher*.

Women manage to resist such adjurations as the opting for anal sex when vaginal is deemed temporarily off-limits, nor do they advocate paedophilia as a companion to the onset of the menses, but they too profess a degree of squeamishness when it comes to simple description.† There is an argument that a substantial percentage of the slang lexis, especially as regards sex,

* Examples of this figurative use, found from the 1960s onwards, are refreshingly un-gendered: indeed, most seem to be used of males.
† These terms have been collected in the general run of slang research; those that show an asterisk have also been put forward by users of Mumsnet.

is also euphemistic; so be it, and menstruation is certainly up there on the leader-board.

The first thing about menstruation is its regularity: thus one finds *period* (the earliest sense of which was the time an illness took to run its course and the earliest use in this context, properly *monthly period*, dated by the *OED* to 1690), *mother nature, old faithful* and *time of the month** and *monthly bill*; there are also *woman's week**, the jocular *holy week* and *time for an oil change**; the proper name *monica* presumably plays on month.

It is also seen as a visitor, especially a grandmother – *granny, granny grunts* or *grandma George*, thus 'George called' and 'Grandma is here' – or a *friend*, thus the query 'have you got your friends?*' The *country cousin* and *little sister* may also pop in. Above all, there is one's *aunt: Aunt(ie) Flo** (with its pun on *flow*), *Aunty Frieda**, *Aunt Jane, Aunt Lilian, Aunt Rose, Aunt Susie, Auntie Jane* and 'Aunt Mabel's come for a visit'*. Other proper names, though undignified by a family honorific, are *charlie, jenny* and *tommy*.

A final 'visitor' is *Rita red pants** which moves into the second most popular menstrual image: blood and its colour, red. Terms include *blood sports, bloody mary, the blob* and 'on the blob'* or *OTB**, *have the painters in**, *have the rag on, on a streak* and the unapologetically graphic *twatsplat**. *Flowers*, one of the oldest terms and recorded around 1400, may suggest red petals, but the *OED* (albeit as yet unrevised for the term) notes a probable evolution from French *flueurs*, i.e. flows).

Red is the great stimulus of puns. There is *red-letter day* (originally a saint's day or other festival marked in red on a calendar) and *red sails in the sunset* (a 1935 hit for Bing Crosby and reprised by many others, including, bizarrely, the Beatles), *surfing the crimson tide** or *wave**, *paddling in scarlet waters** (and while in a watery zone, *breaching the beaver dam** where beaver means the vagina). We find another relation: *red-headed aunt* (from *Red Bank*) and a small detour behind the Iron Curtain: *fallen to the communists**, *have communists are in the summerhouse**, *surrendering to the red army** and *in the red tent**. Sport gives *the reds are playing at home*, which can also be used of *united . . .* and, apparently, any team who play in red (e.g. Benfica). A further couture-based subset draws on the colour of a uniform: two from the military, the *captain is at home,* and *entertaining the general* and one from the church, the *cardinal* (red-capped and vested) *is at home.*

If the *rag* plays a role here, then it is, inevitably *red* and often brandished as a *flag.* The link to communism is coincidental but slang gives several alternatives: *the flag is up* or *out,* one *flies* or *flashes the red flag* or simply *the flag. Flying baker* plays on the nautical alphabet where *baker* = B and the flag that signifies the second letter of the alphabet is red and in turns warns viewers: 'Beware, keep off'.

All of which comes under the rubric of 'ill': *poorly* (menstruation is *poorliness*), *out of order, up on (the) blocks** (usually of cars), *so* (which was a 1930s term for gay) or *so-so, squiffy* (usually drunk), *off games** and returning to blood with *dropping clots**. One can be *caught short, come crook* (Australian for ill), *have one's moons**, or *fall off the roof.* Menstruation can be the evasive *lady problems** or *mooncup time** and perhaps best-known, *the curse** (for some *of Eve*, for others *of Tom**, i.e. the *t*ime *o*f the *m*onth). The result is a *p.m.s. monste*r, which strictly refers to pre-menstrual syndrome, otherwise known as *coming on.* Couples vary, but for those who choose to eschew sex the period is known as a *beno* ('there'll be no sex'), *blow-job week** or *wallflower week.*

Then there is equipment: the tampon or sanitary towel. The

64

prophylactic role of either gives the *window-blind* and *saddle blanket* (and thus one is *back in the saddle*). The *manhole cover*, cited by Katharine Connor Martin as 'cringe-inducing' albeit available via the *OED* is, she suggests, probably a male invention. *Cover the waterfront* tips its hat to noir fiction. *Hammock* and *mouse mattress* are based on the towel's shape, though *little red mouse time** plays on 'hole'. Other terms include *ammunition, brillo pad, bunny, G-string, sling shot, spark plug* and the rhyming slang *little brown jug* (i.e. plug), *submarine, teddy bear* and the juvenile *Theresa* ('the tampon'). New Zealand's *sark* possibly comes from Scottish *sark*, a woman's undergarment, Australia's *gam*, for many years slang for a leg (not to mention, as an abbreviation for *gamahuche*, a term for fellatio), presumably refers to the vagina's position adjacent to the legs while the *Japanese flag week** – the flag's colours being red and white – evokes the blood streaked tampon or towel. Riding, usually reserved by slang for sex, is used in *ride a cotton horse** or *pony** and *ride the red horse**. The theme of cotton at least partially inspires *pack the pillow* (*pack* in its sense of 'carry'). *Clout*, which began life as fourteenth-century standard English meaning a (cotton) handkerchief, has also been borrowed. *There's a letter in the post office* offers yet another image (British post boxes are of course red, but this may be coincident) and a Mumsnet user offers the phrase *cram a tam**.

Rag has been mentioned; it recurs in *cunt-rag, fanny rag*, and the declaration 'it's rag week'*. There is also a brief deviation into 'food': *jamrag** (thus one is *jamming*), *jam sponge**, *jelly donut* and *jelly sandwich* (*jelly* being jam in the US), *coyote sandwich* and *vampire's teabag**. The unabashed coarseness with which these are relished again suggests male coinage, but several turn up on the predominantly woman-authored Mumsnet lists, and in any case, is such a belief not betraying this writer's kneejerk assumptions about female 'niceness'?

Finally, in what has been largely a parade of euphemisms, the quintessential example: *you know what**, even if hearers of the term may quickly have to assess which of its slang meanings is being used – the alternatives include the penis, the vagina, the buttocks, sexual intercourse and beyond sex, anything else seen as too embarrassing or otherwise problematic to spell out.

Not everyone, however, feels the need for euphemism. Perhaps we should leave the last word to the comedian Jo Brand. Complaining about such roundabout descriptions as 'I've got the painters and decorators in' or 'Arsenal are playing at home' she puts it succinctly (albeit transcribed via Mumsnet censorship) thus: 'I prefer "I've got a vast amount of blood squirting out of my c***, Vicar".'

If menstruation is a women-only topic, then pregnancy too – however sympathetic and involved the father-to-be – may also be seen as 'woman's work'. Slang offers around 120 terms, which, as ever, fall into a variety of themes.*

The group that starts with 'up the . . .' (*spout, chute* or *shoot, stick, stump, flue, kite, pole, way* and *wop*) might seem more male than female, depending on whether the user/hearer interprets the 'up' imagery as suggesting penis-in-vagina or embryo-in-womb. Whereas the various terms that might be bracketed as the 'p-words' (*preggers, preggo, preggy, pee-gee* and *p.g.* and perhaps *in pod* and *in pig*) are usually used by the woman herself. Euphemisms (*so, that way, like that* – all three once used to indicate homosexual males – *coming, expecting, fixed, gone,*

---

* Mumsnet, wherein one might expect many such terms is disappointingly limited, though it offers *Keith Cheggers*, rhyming with *preggers* (from the TV personality Keith Chegwin) and *upduffed.*

how-came-you-so, awkward, embarrassed and *on*) are available to all-comers.

A variety of terms – all implying either (negative) male agency or female error – which might be seen as 'wounded' or 'hit' suggest an involuntary pregnancy, conception out of wedlock. They include *shot in the tail, ruin't* (i.e. the moralist's 'ruined'), *banged-up, break* or *sprain one's ankle* (*break a leg* suggests seduction; the unwanted pregnancy is optional), *burn one's foot, fall/ fallen on, in for it, jacked up, knocked up, get a lap-clap* (the *clap* being a blow rather than an STD), *cut one's leg, hit on the master-vein, poisoned, sewed up, in trouble, cut in the back* or *the leg, caught* (*out*), *knapped* (a cant term for 'caught' or 'arrested'), *spoiled* (i.e. a woman's shape, though the underlying morality cannot be ignored).

Other terms are driven by the obvious physical changes: the growing foetus making itself obvious as the woman's stomach grows larger. Thus there is the simple *big* or *fat*, and with those *loaded, full of it, lumpy, showing, filled in* and *on the hill*. To *have one's apron up* recalls an earlier style of dress. The belly itself is featured in *have a belly, belly-up* and a *bellyful of marrow-pudding*, which lies behind the more recent *pudding club, in the club* and *in the pud*. The Caribbean *belly-woman* is a single mother-to-be. The stomach can be a *bay window* (more traditionally used of a portly, well-fed gentleman) and Australia offers *have a joey* (usually a baby kangaroo) *in the pouch*. This group also claims the seventeenth-century's *two-legged tympany* (from standard English *tympany*, a morbid swelling or tumour) which combines the woman's swollen stomach and the embryo it holds. Variations include the *two-legged tumour, two-heeled tympany* and *tympany with two heels* and thus *to be cured of a two-legged tympany* is to give birth.

The expanded belly also brought the eighteenth-century's *belly plea*, a legal plea, offered by a female criminal facing the death sentence, that since she is pregnant, the law should spare her unborn child's life and by extension her own; thus *plead one's belly*, to make such an entreaty. This might be counterfeited by a *belly cheat*, strategically placed padding, though this subterfuge could not have lasted long after the court enforced a necessary scrutiny. More practical, according to Captain Grose's dictionary of 1785 was a dependable stud: 'every gaol having, as the *Beggar's Opera* informs us, one or more child getters, who qualify the ladies for that expedient to procure a respite.'

The food imagery underpinning *pudding* extends to *have a bun in the oven* (also *have a bun in the club, a cookie in the oven, a bun in one's tin, a scone in the oven, bread in the oven* and *one in the oven*). One may also have *an egg in the nest*, thus the popular state of being *on the nest* and the word *clucky*, all of which suggest the farmyard's maternal hen. Final food imagery is more elaborate: in America a marriage that takes place when the bride is already pregnant is a *buckwheat crop*, since buckwheat ripens faster than other grains and, again from the US, to become pregnant is to *eat dried apples* or *pumpkin seeds*, noting the way in which dried fruit swells up when placed in water.

The eighteenth century also offered the *knobstick wedding*: this was a wedding forced on a couple when the woman became pregnant out of wedlock (itself more recently described as *beating the gun* or the *starter*). The background was an act of George II which stated that any woman not married but already pregnant could be arrested and compelled to name the father. The same act empowered the parish officers to arrest the father and imprison him unless he married the mother or gave bail to appear when the child was born.

Other terms include Ulster's seemingly incomprehensible *spitting at the tongs*, the punning *Egyptian flu* ('you're going to become a mummy'), *making feet for children's shoes* (also used for sexual intercourse) which sounds as if plucked from a riddle, the stereotyped *Irish toothache* (and with it the *Irish way*, i.e. hetero-sexual anal intercourse, based on the belief that pious Catholics used anal sex as their sole means of contraception) and *have a trout in the well.*

To what extent these can be attributed to a given gender is debatable. One can only assess the examples to hand and while the nature of slang research has emphasised the male, there are still examples from both. For all the woman described in such terms, there are plenty who use them of their own condition. As in other topics, those who use slang, whether women or men, will use the terms available, irrespective of possible origin.

Abortion

If menstruation tends to render men queasy, then the process of abortion, other than casting the father as the possible (and possi-bly reluctant) provider of the funds it may require, tends to be left to the woman. The concept of being pregnant and unmar-ried was recorded since the late nineteenth century as being 'in trouble' but must surely have been in spoken use long before. There are also such phrases as 'missing a month' or failing to 'come on' or whatever euphemism the bearer of bad tidings wishes to use. These are not slang.

It is the abortion itself, and the individual who makes it happen, that have earned the synonyms. To what extent these are woman-created is unknown, but it is surely likely. Nor is the abortion the sole means of getting rid of an unwanted infant.

The earliest terms deal in simple murder: the otherwise anonymous B.E.'s canting dictionary of c.1698 gives *Mother Midnight*,
defined as 'a Midwife (often a Bawd)' but known as one who
would, for a fee, dispose of the newborn in a convenient privy.
The same text has *stifle a/the squeaker*, to murder a child 'and
throw it into a House of Office [i.e. a privy]'. Two centuries later
we encounter the black humour of the *angel-maker*, a term that
doubled as a 'baby-farmer', a woman who took in (usually illegitimate) babies on the pretext of bringing them up in return for
a fee, and an abortionist. Given that the difference between her
roles was only the matter of whether the children died over the
long-term, of starvation and ill treatment, or immediately
through an abortion, the jobs – both labelled *angel-making* –
naturally overlapped. In either case the child had gone to 'join
the angels'.

There was animal imagery: to abort could be to *slink* or to *cast
a calf* or *the wanes* (i.e. *wean*, a child), both 'officially' used in the
farmyard. Australia offered *crack an egg*, one could also *have a
shot*, presumably an abortifacient injection (legally or
otherwise).

The mid-twentieth century's abortionists included the *lock-
picker*, *pin artist* and *rabbit snatcher* (a *rabbit catcher* was a legitimate midwife), all focusing in one way or another on the process.
Hoovering, a modern equivalent, does the same. Perhaps the
most brutal, was *scrape* (with its shades of the back alley and the
coat hanger), used as verb and noun and accomplished by the
scrape doctor who worked in a *scrape clinic*.

Some terms were deliberately vague: One could *bring it away*,
i.e. the foetus, or *make someone one*, where the image was that of
the woman and the embryo being 'two' people. Finally, a small
group from the Caribbean where the abortionist was a *chemist*, to

procure an abortion was *throw-away belly* and the woman who has had (or is suspected of having had) an abortion is a *cemetery*.

Menstruation, pregnancy and abortion are specifics; swearing, better defined as the use of words and phrases that have been categorised as obscenities of one level or another, general. And if the former seems almost wholly 'women talk' then the theory maintains that the latter is boys-only. In 2007 the British academic Mike Thelwall published 'Fk yea I swear: Cursing and gender in a corpus of MySpace pages', the results of his researches into teen users on of the online 'chatroom' MySpace, at the time a popular predecessor of Facebook. The aim was to test the traditional belief.

Thelwall looked at four levels of 'dirty words' and at both British and American teen users. He divided them thus (I have paraphrased his examples):

[very strong] *cunt, mutherfucker* and its variations, and the racist terms *jew, nigger* and *paki*

[strong] *fuck* and its various mutations

[moderate] terms referring to bodily parts, e.g. *arsehole/ asshole* and *cock/dick*; terms for masturbation, e.g. *wanking*; derogatory terms for male homosexuals, e.g. *gay, poof*; plus *piss* and *shag* and their derivatives

[mild] primarily terms for fools, e.g. *dickhead, dipshit, retard, tosser*; *shit* and its derivatives; body parts, e.g. *arse, fanny, tits*; derogatory terms for girls, e.g. *bitch, cow, slag*

[very mild] primarily terms of abuse, e.g. *butthead, pillock, dork, wuss*; also dismissive terms for girls, e.g. *bimbo, bird, tart*

What Thelwall found was that while there were subtle differences between the UK and the US, and between older and younger users, the genders, especially in the UK, were far from dissimilar. Some categories did reveal a 'swearing gender gap' but in no way could one maintain the fantasy that girls were 'cleaner' speakers than boys. In the UK very strong and strong terms were used equally by both genders. In the US the very strong stuff seemed to be reserved for boys, but other categories were pretty much undifferentiated.[*]

The evidence might not have been perfect, Thelwall notes that MySpace use may differ from conversational speech, and that certain racial terms, notably nigger, had been reappropriated and could be used other than as slurs, but the gender evidence seemed valid. What might be more debatable was the paper's attribution of swearing by UK girls to the *ladette* culture of the 1990s. Finally, there was a note of comfort: swearing was what adolescents do: 'swearing amongst youth is normal rather than deviant behaviour, parents should not be shocked or concerned if their daughter or son has a MySpace containing strong swearing.'

A decade later *Metro*, the London-based freesheet, asked its readers 'Do men find women who swear unattractive?' The answers, coming thick and fast via Twitter[†] made the female point of view absolutely clear; turning theory to practice and employing all the creative armoury of Twitter invention – gifs, photo-shopped and captioned pictures, in-your-face denunciation and much besides – they announced with a single voice: *we don't give a fuck.*

---

[*] However Michael Adams notes a US survey of similar date that showed that girls of seventeen to nineteen were in fact 'dirtier' than equivalent age boys.
[†] https://twitter.com/MetroUK/status/953280711888375810

All of which seems to underline the opinions voiced by Michael Adams in his study *Slang: The People's Poetry* (2009): in short, 'Twenty-first century slang belongs equally to men and women.' While accepting that soccer moms and guys on the corner won't be using the same slang, that in no way disqualifies the moms from coming up with their own lexis. Women, after all, 'can be just as vulgar as men' and 'if you get stoned and engage . . . in "illicit" sex . . . you're going to use slang to talk about it' [p.84] and that slang is not bound by gender, only by the topic under discussion. He also notes that a slang vocabulary is a piece of luggage that tends to accompany us through life. The 'hip, young millennials' of yesterday are today's soccer moms, and by implication they bring their slang with them. And on the way, come up with more.

The website Mumsnet (www.mumsnet.com) self-billed as 'by parents for parents' but as its name suggests, primarily a stage for mothers to express their opinions, ask for and offer advice and generally meditate on the ups and downs of parenting, was founded in 2000 by Justine Roberts. It has grown to become highly influential – spearheading a variety of campaigns, hosting a substantial blogging network and as an inescapable concomitant of digital life, attracting a good deal of hostility, typically in accusations targeting 'pushy middle-class mothers' – and is among those way-stations to which politicians now feel they must drop in when canvassing the national mood.

Given the inevitable 'but what about the kiddies' outcry that accompanies any discussion of the 'dirty words' that many see as slang's entirety, Mumsnet has cast its collective eye on that side of language. Its forums have dealt with such questions as 'would-you-call-someone-a-cunt-to-their-face?', 'What-is-the-Worst-Thing-You-Can-Call-a-Woman?' and 'teen-slang-especially-used-by-girls.'

The language of such Q&A strings – sexual or otherwise – varies from wholly standard English to out-and-out obscenity, although that, as ever, is not 'mum-created'.

The role of home-schooling sex educator naturally bulks large. It is a well-trodden path. In 2008 the commentator 'PortAndStilton' noted wearily (and wittily) that

You'll find that the standard pattern is

Poster A: We use the proper term and call it a vagina

Poster B: Actually, the proper term for what you're talking about is a vulva, not a vagina

[cue discussion on the difference between vulva and vagina. This sub-discussion alone can get heated, and the vulval and vaginal camps will end up coming to blows]

Poster C: We call it a [minnie/foo foo/zazette/etc.]

Poster D: NOOOOOOOOOOO! You can't call it a [minnie/foo foo/zazette] because that's my DD's name

Poster C: Oh, sorry

[The vulval and foo foo camps will now also come to blows over whether vulva is an ugly clinical word that they couldn't possibly use]

[Then a few revered posters of long standing will admit what they call it and you will never be able to look at them the same way again grin]

[Eventually there will also be suggestions of 'front bottom', 'bits' and 'privates'. Generally these posters don't come to blows with anyone, but there's always hope if you ply them with wine]

Possibly so, but that hasn't stopped the conversation.

In 2009, the correspondent 'cheesy charlie' asked 'What are you calling your daughter's fanjo?' and explained 'I was brought up with "fanny" but that grosses people out these days. Lots of friends use "nunny" which grosses me out.

What is the girl equivalent of the word "willy" – what are you all using with your DDs?'

Among the answers were:

bejingo, binga-binga-jing, bits/girly bits/girl's bits, bum, china, daisy, doo-da, down there, fairy, fanjo, fanny, flower, foof/fou-fou, foo-oo, front bit, front bottom, genis ('girl-penis'), *'gina, inbetweenoes, kimininunu, lady's area, looby-lou, lulu, mary, memy, miff miff, minge, minky, minnie/mini, nippy, noo-noo, nunny, pisshole, poonani, privates, quim, toot-toot, tuppence, twinkle, va-jay-jay, vulva, weehole, wincie, wink, woo-woo.*

Missing from the list but not from the website is *lady garden* ('What is expected of your lady garden?' asks a contributor wondering on 22 July 2017 whether to shave or not to shave), standing for pubic hair or the genitals which, judging by its popularity, may have established itself as the current go-to synonym.*†

---

* The same discussion offers *downstairs*; for those who might dismiss these as overly euphemistic/genteel, one respondent notes that as regards male opinions, 'I don't give a shiny shit'.

† For instance *The Lady Garden Foundation*, campaigning to raise awareness and funding for research into gynaecological cancers: 'We challenge taboos and do away with the "private" in our "private parts".'

A similar question referred to boys. *Willy* seems to have been the middle-class default for several decades, but other terms included:

> *bobby, winky, wee-wee, tidgy-widgy, tiddles, wanger, nob, little sausage, winkle, peepee, willy wonk/winky wonky, tail.*

Both questions also met the accurate (some might say po-faced) responses: 'vagina' (though that might be abbreviated as ''gina') and 'penis'.

What the lexicographer notes is how few, relatively, of these have been captured in slang dictionaries. There are around 1,500 terms for each gender's genitals but the bulk of these have not been included. *Fanjo*, which may be assumed, from its position in a question, to be generally understood, is one of them (though it must come from *fanny*, which is widely listed)*. Some too are surprisingly adult: are little girls and their mothers really using the undeniably coarse *pisshole* or *poonani*? Or *va-jay-jay*, which would usually be associated with an older sister. To borrow once again from Michael Adams, there is plenty of women's slang on offer, but it comes from different sources than does 'male slang'; those sources can often be termed 'domestic' and the nursery ranks high among them.

Thus a number of these terms come under the rubric of what qualifies as 'family slang'. 'Genis' for instance. Someone thought that up, 'girl-penis', but it sounds very local. So too *inbetweenoes* and *looby-lou*, neither of which achieve that broadest of

---

* In-house at least: of Google's five *fanjo* as vagina hits four are from Mumsnet, one from Urban Dictionary.

assessments, any other mentions online.* Whether this indicates a male bias, a refusal to acknowledge women's slang coinages, or whether these simply are one-offs, coined and used at a specific address and going no further, is very much the reader's choice.

Mumsnet has also evolved a substantial in-house vocabulary, sufficient to offer 'a list of the most common abbreviations and acronyms' used on the site. Some are well-known, e.g. *ADHD* (attention deficit & hyperactivity disorder), *FWIW* (for what it's worth) and the earthier *FFS* ('for f**k's sake'), *PITA* ('pain in the a**e') and *WTF?* ('what the f**k'). Others appear purpose-built.

Mumsnet slang, while happy to include the occasional obscenity (albeit spattered with the inevitably attention-grabbing asterisks) and giving space to such 'women-only' topics as menstruation, often falls under the name of what Michael Adams calls 'clean' slang. The terminology might not focus exclusively on the qualities of caring, sharing and compassion that are seen as slang's antitheses, but it permits them a space. The list of acronyms compiled by the site's members, the self-titled *Mumsnetters*, acknowledges feelings in a way that most slang cannot. Abbreviations such as *DA* or *EA* (domestic or emotional abuse) may not be slang, but they acknowledge in a non-standard manner topics that are otherwise beyond slang's chosen compass. So too are other domestic abbreviations, typically *NAK* (nursing at keyboard, i.e. typing while breast-feeding) or *SAHM* (stay-at-home mother).

Familial felicity is well represented and all, it appears, are beloved: *DD* (darling/dear daughter), *DC* (darling/dear child),

---

* *Genis*, on the other hand, does. *Urban Dictionary* grabs it for the boys, and defines it as 'The bulge of pant material that sticks up right on top of your crotch when you sit down' or, blending *gut* and *penis*, as a roll of fat that hides a view of the penis, the equivalent of the female *gunt*, i.e. *gut* plus *cunt*.

DF/DD (darling/dear father/dad), *DGS/DGD* (darling/dear grandson/granddaughter), *DFIL* (darling/dear father-in-law) and *DH* (darling/dear husband) and *DW* (darling/dear wife). There is room for *DTD/DTS* (darling/dear twin daughter/son) and *DSS/DSD* (darling/dear stepson/stepdaughter). The cynic might say that *DMIL* (darling/dear mother-in-law) suggests that politeness can stretch too far.

There is what some might term the considerate (and others the passive-aggressive) *AIBU* (am I being unreasonable?) which creates a number of answers: *YABU* (you are being unreasonable); *YANBU* (you are not being unreasonable); *YABOS* (you are being over-sensitive); *YWBU* (you were being unreasonable/you would be unreasonable, depending on context). Is it stereotyping to suggest that men would not come up with anything equivalent.

Finally a few that cut to the chase: *LTB* ('leave the bas**rd'); *MMTI* ('makes my teeth itch'); *POAS* ('pee on a stick' – take a pregnancy test); *STBXH* ('soon-to-be-ex-husband'); *DTD* (doing the deed/doing the dance: having sex); *SWI* ('shagging with intent': trying to conceive) and *SWOI* ('shagging without intent': not trying to conceive).

Arguing further for the ubiquity of women-created slang, Michael Adams turns to America's *Jane* magazine (now defunct), the August 2006 edition of which offered a 'dating diary'. As he points out, dating traditionally tends to suggest the encounter of two heterosexual genders and its vocabulary cannot be restricted to one or the other. Yet magazines like *Jane*, with their conscious focus on late teen and twenties girls and women, as well as the older 'soccer mom', must incorporate a good deal of the language they don't just use but also coin.*

* Material from M. Adams *Slang: the People's Poetry* (2009), p.82.

Words and phrases include *flirt buddies* ('friends or acquaintances who, though not romantically involved, flirt'), *fuck buddies* ('friends or acquaintances who, though not romantically involved, copulate'), *booty call* ('request, by telephone or otherwise, for sex with a reliable friend; what you give your fuck buddy, when you feel the need'), *perma-laid* ('constantly engaged in sexual relations,' a condition of the ridiculously hot), *mage double whammy* ('absolute winner' in which there are no wizards, but mage respells maj, clipped from major, *fella* ['fellow'] and *gent* ['gentleman'; a gentleman, that is, who is not a gentleman and dislikes gentility]), *hook up* ('copulate') *the shizzy* ('the shit, i.e., stuff, thing') and *sack* ('bed', where you have 'a garden variety' screw with your fuck buddy).

There are around twenty terms in all and as Adams notes, if you take it as a whole, it's a very 'suspicious' aggregation. It ranges from the seriously old-fashioned ('tripping the light fantastic' for dancing) to *shizzy* (which was then cutting-edge rap language). Terms like *blah* (nonsense), *hot* (attractive) and *ridiculous* (extremely) exist within memory, but of an older, if still juvenile generation. As for *fuck buddy*, this is definitely not 'domestic'. In the end it is slang that reflects the soccer mom's social position: she is educated, picks up lyrics from old songs in martini bars, knows gamers (her husband maybe one), likes some hip-hop (she was born, let's say, in 1974); she's old enough to say things that sound weird to young people and young enough still to absorb language of the moment. Her slang is mixed because her experience is mixed [. . .] Assessing the slang that identifies a (fairly large) social group, like 'soccer moms' or readers of *Jane*, can't proceed item by item: in Jane's 'dating diary,' slang is situated in a feminine discourse partly constructed by the slang itself.

The lexis of *Jane's* 'dating diary' has – naturally – moved on. Returning online we have Tinder, founded in 2012 as the first 'hook-up' app, aimed at facilitating dating and, as a knock-on effect, commitment-free sex. (The primary target was college kids; it has doubtless expanded but the necessity of photos must surely set certain impassable bars.*) Its tagline 'Swipe life' refers to the process whereby users choose or reject potential partners by swiping a picture on the screen of their smartphone: swipe right for yes, and left for no.† Whether the language generated by digital dating apps can be gendered is open to argument. It seems cheerfully omnisexual. Given its 3.7 million paid subscribers,‡ while compiling the stats might be feasible, the site has other purposes that doubtless take precedence.

The hook-up lexis falls, whomever the coiners, into the category of fun stuff. There are a range of online guides. The list that follows draws on a variety, accessed in late 2018.§

Benching: keeping a potential partner 'in reserve', i.e. dating occasionally but promising nothing permanent (from US football imagery).

Breadcrumbing: sending flirtatious, but ultimately non-committal texts (from the use of a trail of breadcrumbs to lure a possible prey).

---

* Which can be challenged: in November 2018 the Dutch 'positivity guru' and ex-MP Mr Emile Ratelband, born 1949, petitioned to have his age officially re-registered as forty-five, claiming that such was his 'biological age'. The aim, he explained, was to improve his Tinder profile. His petition was rejected.
† A 'handy glossary' to the slang of the reality TV show *Love Island* (in *Times* (London) Times 2 3 June 3/1) includes '*Swipe right* to find someone attractive' and references the app.
‡ Wikipedia, accessed 15 December 2018.
§ https://uk.askmen.com/dating/dating_advice/internet-dating-slang-terms.html; https://www.liveabout.com/slang-used-in-online-dating-profiles-1022066; https://www.thesun.co.uk/fabulous/3520762/dating-guide-modern-day-romance-slang-ghosting-breadcrumbing-terms/

Catfishing: innocently sending out messages to someone who is in fact pretending to be someone else (popularised by TV show of same name); a subset is Kitten-fishing: the subject of the messages identifies themself honestly, but presents as a far more alluring individual than is the case.

Cuffing: establishing a long-term relationship (from hand-cuffing); this usually happens in cuffing season (autumn/winter) and terminates at uncuffing season (spring).

Curving: to be rejected, usually indirectly but always cruelly (from the idea that a subtle curve is 'better' than the straight line of a simple 'no').

Cushioning: ensuring against the possibility of one's main relationship collapsing by staying in touch with a number of potential partners.

Dicksand: the emotional 'quicksand' in which a girl gets stuck when she becomes obsessed with a single boy (from *dick*: the penis).

Ghosting: the cruellest form of ending a relationship: one abruptly breaks all and any form of communication, reducing the erstwhile partner to a 'ghost'.

Haunting: the refusal to accept being 'ghosted': the jilted partner starts following and liking the rejector; also known as zombieing.

Kray Bae: an unstable individual with whom one would be extremely foolish to hook up.

Monkeying: the speedy movement from one relationship to the next (the image is of a monkey swinging from tree to tree).

Peacocking: creating an elaborate look for the photo that is presented on an app.

Penguin: 'Mr or Ms Right'. 'The one and only'. The lifetime partner. (Penguins mate for life.)

Roaching: cheating with multiple partners but claiming, if one complains, that you never committed to monogamy (from roaches, i.e. cockroaches, of which it is said that if one sees one there are inevitably many others nearby).

Sliding into someone's DMs: sending a direct message to the object of one's affections; since this is only possible after both parties have 'followed' each other, there has to have been some previous interaction.

Situationship: a status somewhere between a friendship and a full-on relationship. Similar to Friendship with Benefits (i.e. sex).

3. In the Beginning:
A Problem of Evidence

WE HAVE COME up to date. It's time to return to square one. The first slang collection of any sort – properly a small vocabulary of *cant*, the jargon of criminality – appeared around 1532, with gradually expanding follow-ups published as the sixteenth century proceeded. A marginal language that, when printing was still a relative novelty, rarely earned a place on a page, a rejection that was intensified by a generalised disdain towards its speakers, the poor and criminal and thus occupiers of the social margins. If their lexis was noted it was simply the better to avoid their tricks. So these glossaries – part of the pan-European category of such publications known as 'beggar books' – are pretty much all we have and if we remove these lists and pamphlets from our research it is very hard to find evidence of the counter-language so early in its life. Prior to that, virtually nothing. Factor in the big question that strikes at the root of slang's existence: can we even think of 'slang' when that register in the context of language (criminal or 'civilian') is not even named until 1756? A big question for linguists but in the spoken reality, and alongside that what is plucked from the street and thence into the slang dictionaries, most would dismiss it as needless nit-picking: the words are there, they are not about to join standard English; they need a name and that is slang. Is *fuck*, we may suggest, any less slangy when we first encounter it in 1508 than when it has been slotted into a newly acknowledged linguistic register nearly 250 years later?

Now add an extra ingredient: the use of slang by women, a marginal group in cultural terms. Criminals are at least titillating, these early glossaries a proxy walk on the wild side. But women? Women are simply 'not men', and everything that that implies. So: margins upon margins and the mist of time frustratingly obscures both.

But even before the glossaries began appearing there is evidence of something that has to be termed slang. Langland's *Piers Plowman* (written in the mid-late fourteenth century) has a sample: *arse*, *wench*, *maw* (the mouth, later the vagina) and *malkin* (a promiscuous girl). Lanfranc, writing of surgery around 1400, uses *cunt* for vagina and the word, without comment, is to be found in a variety of street names (e.g. various 'red light' streets known as *Gropecuntlane*) and human nicknames (*Fillecunte*, *Twychecunt*). It is hard to position such language, perhaps the simplest response is that these terms represent the way the average person spoke: not in the high-flown Norman French of the court or the Latin of the universities, but in the early Modern English of the street. And among those who spoke it was Chaucer's Wife of Bath, created for his *Canterbury Tales* around 1386.

Immediately, yet another stumbling-block: Chaucer, whatever else he may have been, was not a woman. If a woman speaks in the tales, then it is with the language that he has placed in her mouth. We are going to encounter this question throughout this book, it can as well be considered here as elsewhere. Does male authorship disqualify a female character from consideration. It is my belief – one might term it self-serving, but I hope to show examples that bear me out – that such women are not disqualified. The problem is, again, one of chronology and representation. Five-and-a-half centuries on and we need have no such problems with Mary Anne Duignan, better known as 'Chicago May' and one of the many villainesses revelling, however self-aggrandisingly, in the title of 'Queen of Crooks'. She lived from 1871 to 1930 and two years before her death and now calling herself 'May Sharpe' (a surname that presumably nodded to slang's favourite word for perspicacious, especially as regards exploiting the gullibility of others) penned her autobiography, a 'human documentary' as she termed it (see chapter 7). The book contains three hundred slang terms; in that context, and accepting that any analysis of a slang text must set aside the (surely unknowable) gender of the original coiner of a lexis, there is no need to question their validity as 'hers'.

But the past is trickier. The seventeenth century's Moll Frith, nicknamed for her job description 'Moll Cutpurse' (i.e. a pickpocket in a world where the modern pocket was yet to appear and purses were secured outside the garment) or the eighteenth's Moll King, accredited creator of that slang sub-set known as 'flash', were also real-life figures and in their day were as valid pretenders to the distaff side of villainy's throne as was May. Both are exemplars of slang-smart women and will be dealt with properly in chapter X. What we lack, however, are their own words. Moll Cutpurse is vocalised on stage by playwrights Dekker and Middleton as *The Roaring Girl* (1611); Moll King is given a lengthy and near-impenetrable 'flash' conversation (the pamphlet that carried it offered a 'translation' into standard English) which makes no pretence to have been taken down verbatim. Yet these two women are, *inter alia*, personified by their use of this outlandish, alluring language: slang. If we do not have chapter and verse, then we have reportage, and I am willing to accept it.

The late fourteenth century is even more elusive. The two Molls, of course, were real individuals, we even have pictures. The Wife of Bath is not.* Still, we are fortunate in the Wife, considered to be among Chaucer's most three-dimensional creations (her autobiographical prologue is among the longest), not to mention unashamedly mouthy: a 'verray jangleresse' (a mighty chatterbox) as she calls herself. With her checklist of disposable husbands, none of whom have remotely controlled her, her mockery of contemporary morality (she quotes religious dictates only the better to undermine them), and her generally hard-nosed take on life, she is surely an early feminist heroine.

The Wife is also a mistress of bawdy, although this is as much in the style of telling as in the terminology. In this she has been linked to the performers within the French *fabliaux*, a form of popular short story of which 150 have been found dated between 1159 and 1340. Such tales are explained by Amanda Hopkins as 'always intended to be humorous, and frequently cruel and mocking. [. . .] Tricks, ruses and cleverly-engineered love affairs are staple fare of the fabliau [. . .] The plots often revolve around base instincts, such as greed, avarice and/or sexual lust, and are driven by the desires of largely stereotyped characters: stupid peasants, randy clerks, avaricious friars, nagging women.'† There may be morals, but the greatest is that physical pleasure comes first.

---

* Successive illustrators have given us many pictures of her too. The earliest is in the Ellesmere Ms. of c.1410. She appears in the margins of her tale: black hat, red dress, what looks like a blanket wrapping her bottom half, holding a whip and mounted on what was probably a palfrey.
† A. Hopkins 'Chaucer and the Fabliau'. Lecture for the Medieval to Renaissance English Literature module, University of Warwick (2010).

Not all fabliaux were obscene, but some undoubtedly were. These titles give a flavour: 'The Maiden Who Couldn't Hear Fuck' (without heartburn), 'Berangier of the Long Arsehole' (a foolish knight who believed the anus and vagina to be a single, lengthy-mouthed orifice), and 'The Knight who made Cunts Speak' (though unfortunately, we are never told what these loquacious vaginas said).

If the Wife's origins were a little older than herself, then she has also been claimed for the then distant future. Margaret Rogerson, writing in 1998, sees her quite simply as the ancestress of female stand-ups. Not only is the 'autobiography' no more than one more made-up story for her fellow pilgrims to enjoy, but a complete 'comedy act'. Citing feminist film and TV critic Kathleen Rowe, and writing before Ms Barr's fall from grace, Ms Rogerson sees the Wife as in some ways a Roseanne Barr of the Middle Ages, who exploits the comedy inherent in the figure of the unruly 'woman on top', who is 'too fat, too mouthy, too old . . . too sexual . . . for the norms of conventional gender representation'. The stand-up routine, she notes, would probably have been performed 'live' and by a man. (She does not say whether that man would have been dragged up but it is surely possible.) Not only does the Wife prefigure Roseanne, she may also be a forerunner of Barry Humphries' housewife superstar Edna Everage of Moonee Ponds.[*]

Alisoun of Bath is a star in her own right and like Edna's ever-silent punch-bag Madge, it is pleasing that her *gossib* or close friend, also Alisoun, has no lines to speak.

---

[*] M. Rogerson 'The Wife of Bath: Standup Comic'. https://openjournals.library. sydney.edu.au/index.php/SSE/article/viewFile/526/498

Chaucer comes across, at least when dealing with such sex-focused tales as that of the Reeve or Miller, as no more biased towards male enjoyment than he is critical of female. Sex is fun – authors of the *fabliaux* would agree – and to be enjoyed. If that sex happened to be adulterous, or otherwise unsanctified by the marital bed, no matter; perhaps as such it was even better. The Wife is similarly positive, and there is no criticism, even implied, of her female perspective, unimpressed, as one would expect from a stand-up, by either the physical, emotional or indeed economic aspects of 'the wo[e] that is in mariage.'

She is, of course, a sexual sophisticate. She appreciates its centrality, is well-versed in its intricacies, both physical and in the context of controlling a relationship; five husbands and a variety of lovers have given her good practice. As Chaucer explains in the General Prologue to the *Tales*: 'Of remedies of love she knew parchaunce, / For she coude of that art the olde daunce.' This is possibly the oldest known use of *dance* as a synonym for intercourse. As a verb it dates, at least as currently recorded, to 1607, and develops a mass of phrases – e.g. *dance the buttock jig, dance the blanket hornpipe, dance the matrimonial polka* – all playing on the theme, sometimes even giving naughty nods to actual country dances, e.g. *dance Barnaby* or *dance Sallenger's* [St Leger's] *round*.

So how does the Wife speak? She is not, we must acknowledge, a fount of slang but it is there. She has her share, albeit minimal, of what Chaucer termed 'cherles termes', in other words 'bad' language as characterising churls or peasants. Slang, I would suggest, before its time. Chaucer, or at least his tale-tellers, has no problems with such language: in the prologue to his tale the Reeve declares that in recounting the cuckolding of the drunken miller, 'Right in his cherles termes wol I speke.'

(The *MED* quotes the phrase to illustrate the use of term as 'the diction associated with a particular class of people, level of education, etc.') In some episodes one might even see him approaching pornography:

Withinne a while this John the clerk up leep,
And on this goode wyf he leith on soore.
So myrie a fit ne hadde she natfulyoore;
He priketh harde and depe as he were mad.
[Reeve's Prologue lines 4228–31]*

But if the Miller's wife hadn't had such good sex for years ('myrie a fit', where 'fit' may even suggest an orgasm; the Wife uses it in the context of King Solomon's wedding night, where he had to satisfy all his many wives: 'The firste nyght had many a myrie fit / With ech of hem' [42–3]), she sadly for us keeps such feelings to herself. (And while Chaucer's use of *prick* as a verb obviously means to fuck, the image is still primarily of stabbing rather than using the penis, which would not be defined as a *prick* until the mid-sixteenth century.)

Mars and Venus may supposedly embody the male and female principles, but the Wife will not be shoehorned into other's fancies: and if 'Venus me yaf my lust, my likerousnesse [lecherousness] then Mars yaf me my sturdy hardynesse [boldness] [lines 609–12]. She boasts of her *colt's foot* character [youthful wantonness, desire] and points out the gap between her front teeth, always equated with randiness. All in all, 'as help me God, I was a lusty oon.' [605] No-one should be surprised that her

---

* 'Within a moment this John the clerk leaped up, /And on this good wife he lays on vigorously./ She had not had so merry an experience for a long time; / He stabs hard and deep as if he were mad.'

share of cherles termes focuses on sex. Or as she puts it, with a sexual frankness that would rarely appear outside porn for several hundred years 'And trewely, as myne housbondes tolde me, /I hadde the beste quoniam myghte be.' [607–8]*. *Quoniam* being the vagina and one of a variety of q— words that have no role but to euphemise their mutual origin: *cunt*, among them *queynte*, as used in the Miller's Tale. The Wife uses *queynte* as well, telling her husband 'For, certeyn, olde dotard, by youre leve, / Ye shul have queynte right ynogh at eve.' Queynte also occurs when she asks her husband:

> What eyleth yow to grucche thus and grone?
> Is it for ye wolde have my queynte allone?
> Wy, taak it al! Lo, have it every deel!
> Peter! I shrewe yow, but ye love it weel[†] [443–6]

Queynte appears in both its senses – used to mean 'odd' ('a queynte fantasye') but equally referring to the vagina, here metonymised to mean sexual desire and shown as such in the lines that follow where the Wife lays out this 'fantasye': 'Wayte what thyng we may nat lightly have,/Therafter wol we crie al day and crave.' And she adds a possible pun on *thing* as penis or intercourse in the next line: 'Forbede us thyng, and that desiren we'.

She also offers *belle-chose*, on two occasions, from French, a 'beautiful thing' (English slang but not found in French *argot*). Chaucer may have put the term into her mouth, but surely he deserves acknowledgement for coining one of slang's very rare

---

* 'And truly, as all my husbands told me, I had the best cunt in the world'
† 'What ails you to grouch thus and groan? / Is it because you want to have my vagina all to yourself? / Why, take it all! Lo, have it every bit! / By Saint Peter! I would curse you, if you did not love it well.'

positive terms for the female genitals and giving it to a female speaker. She also, obliquely, claims to have 'Martes [Mars'] mark' both on her face and also 'in another privee [i.e. private] place'. The modern privy means a lavatory, especially an outhouse, but *privy*, *privy-hole* or *privy paradise* have all meant vagina. She admits to the dual appetites: sex and food, noting that 'A likerous [lecherous] mouth moste han a likerous tail' where the initial lecherous suggests greed and the second lust; *tail*, the vagina, had already been used in *Piers Plowman*: it had meant the buttocks since at least 1303. Finally there are the references to 'oure bothe thynges smale', where *thing*, meaning both vagina and penis, plays the euphemistic role it has done in slang since the late sixteenth century. *Instrument*, i.e. 'of generation', first used for vagina here and for penis from 1505, is equally euphemistic. Given the frequency of vagina words, we can add *chamber of Venus*, even if slang's incorporation of the goddess of love and sex to render the female genitals is not recorded until around 1590 and a chamber is not mentioned, although *Venus's anvil, court, cradle, cup, field, hall, honeypot* and *mark* are all in the lexis (the Wife has only the *mark of Mars*, denoting courage), as are the *garden of Venus*, plus the *grove*, the *gulf*, the *hill*, the *mount*, the *mouth*, the *shrine* and the *temple*.

She also admits that, 'As help me God, I laughe when I thynke / How pitously a-nyght I made hem swynke!' Whether *swynke*, Middle English for 'work' is linked to slang's *work*, to have sex, currently recorded around 1600, is down to the reader. Her laughter suggests that it was so. The Wife also uses the verb *dight*, literally 'order' or 'deal with' (originally from Latin *dictare*, set in order) to mean copulate. The word never entered slang, though the idea of 'seeing to', usually as a noun and 'given' to a woman, remains.

It may be argued that these lines too are underpinned by double entendre,

> As, seistow, wol been withoute make.
> And seyst it is an hard thyng for to welde
> Athyng that no man wole, his thankes, helde.
> Thus seistow, lorel, whan thow goost to bedde* [270–3]

with their references to a man going to bed without a wife and finding that 'it' is a 'hard thing' to control, and one that no man 'would willingly hold'. But the stretch – suggesting the frustrated man resorts to masturbation – may be too far, even if it does fit with what we known of the Wife's somewhat 'Carry On' movie sense of humour. We can also note her mocking promise to the 'old dotard' of 'queynte right ynogh at eve' with its play on a man who both lights a literal 'candle' at a 'lantern' and the sniggering image of the male's 'candle' and perhaps also on 'firing' as ejaculation; the *lantern*, here a possible vagina, was never claimed by slang, although the *candlestick*, into which it fits and thus the vagina, is a mid-seventeenth-century coinage.

There need be no doubt about the flesh-and-blood *nether purs*. This, which figuratively means the scrotum and thus the genitals, is deliberately set against a husband's iron *cheste* (i.e. safe or strongbox) with the implication that a man's sexual performance at least equals economic success when it comes to selecting a mate. *Purse*, without qualification, would enter slang, meaning the vagina (from 1538) and the scrotum (from 1682). The appearance, almost immediately afterwards, of *workman*

* 'That, thou sayest, will be without a mate. / And thou sayest it is a hard thing to control /A thing that no man will, willingly, hold. / Thus sayest thou, scoundrel, when thou goest to bed.'

and *work*, and the dictum that practice makes perfect, would seem to keep the sexual imagery going.

Other terms move away from sex. There is *piss*, twice, once notably in the context of Xantippe, the classical epitome of female nags, pouring urine over her hapless husband Socrates. There is also *drunk as a mouse* (the comparison, equally unlikely, is usually with a *rat*), and such oaths as *pardee* (*par dieu*: by God), and *Jhesu shorte thy lyf!* She is less than complimentary to the husbands. They are variously a 'verray knave', an 'olde dotard shrewe' (1. 291) or 'sire shrewe'* (1. 355), an 'olde barelful of lyes' (1. 302), an 'olde dotard' (1. 331), a 'Sire olde fool' (1. 357), an 'old lecchour' and an 'old kaynard.'

None of these are slang, and *kaynard*, once meaning coward, seems to have completely vanished. One other is of interest. She uses the word *lorel*, otherwise *losel*, and defined as a worthless rogue, a profligate. The word would become part of the criminal vocabulary, usually in the proper name *Cock Lorel*, who may possibly have been a genuine person and who features largely in the literature of Elizabethan villainy, originally as the eponymous anti-hero of *Cock Lorel's Bote* (c.1515), a shipmaster, whose 'crew' is a group of rogues drawn from the workshops and gutters of London. Together they 'sail' the country, engaging in a variety of villainies. He appears in a number of works, as well as in the glossaries compiled by John Awdelay (whose *Fraternity of Vagabonds* [c.1561] was 'confirmed by Cock Lorel') and Samuel Rowlands, sometimes surnamed Rid (in *Martin-Mark-all*, 1610), who suggests that rather than a shipmaster he was a tinker. In all he remains at the head of his marauding beggars,

---

* Modern use of *shrew* invariably references a female; the unrevised *OED* (1912) shows that its use for a 'wicked, evil-disposed, or malignant man . . . a rascal' was 130 years older (and that Chaucer is recorded as the first person to use the female sense).

sometimes plotting against the state, on one occasion even entertaining the Devil to dinner, and pitching camp in a Derbyshire cave known as the Devil's Arse-peak. According to Rowlands' generally fictitious 'history' of the canting crew, Cock Lorel's rule supposedly lasted c.1511–1533.

Chaucer's Wife of Bath rides off down the road to Canterbury as the fourteenth century fades away with her. It is not, however, the last we shall see of this admirably independent figure. Fiction she may be but she has the style of some tutelary goddess, at least as representative of women who, whatever might be assumed for them, resolutely refused to know their place. Like some bawdy, sexy, golden-hearted and indomitable landlady (the only missing stereotype is motherly), whose regulars transcend the pub sign to substitute her own name in its place, one can envisage her appearances in the tales not as Chaucer's mouthpiece but as voicing the trash-talk of some women-only enclave: 'Alisoun's'.

As time passed there would be a variety of ballads and similar celebrations in which she played some kind of role, full-strength or cameo. Typical was the poet John Lydgate's *Disguising at Hertford* (ante 1427), which was explained in its preface: '*Nowe folowethe here the maner of a bille by wey of supplicacion putte to the Kyng holding his noble feest of Cristmasse in the Castel of Hertford as in a disguysing of the rude upplandisshe people [i.e. uneducated peasantry] compleyning on hir [their] wyves, with the boystous aunswere of hir wyves.*' In this brief piece of mummery, the husbands complain that their wives are tyrants and not partners, embodied in their nagging, overlooking of domestic duties, excessive drinking and physical violence aimed at the unfortunate men. As the Wife had once lamented 'the wo[e] that is in mar[r]iage', these supposedly put-upon husbands saw matrimony as a 'bonde of sorrow'.

There are no 'roles' as such, but a line suggests that among the six representative wives is 'the worthy Wyf of Bathe' who:

Cane shewe statutes moo [more] than six or seven,
Howe wyves make hir [their] housbandes wynne heven,
Maugré [despite] the feonde [the fiend, i.,e. Devil] and al his
   violence.

The men beg for the restoration of the patriarchal status quo; the women for royal support of their over-turning it. Far from following the original Wife's pioneering revisions of marital relations female sovereignty is dismissed as 'a thing uncouth'; there will be no gender reversals here.

In 1713 the still fledgling playwright John Gay (he of *The Beggar's Opera*, the hit of 1728) wrote his own take, *The Wife of Bath*. It drew a figure who maintained the original's feisty attitude but, along with the rest of the cast, who included 'Chaucer', held back from the cherles termes. She is also younger and less cynical than her originator. Where the original Alisoun had played with a society's fondly held beliefs – especially in the field of marriage and the respective roles of man and wife – her eighteenth-century 'reincarnation' (Alison) preferred to regale the audience with the safe assurances of well-honed proverbs and the comforting banalities of folk wisdom.

Her image and influence seem more substantial in a poem of c.1500: William Dunbar's *Tretis of the Tua Mariit Wemen and the Wedo* ('The Two Married Women and the Widow'). Dunbar, best known for his 'Flyting' verses (ritualised and often obscene vilifying of a named individual) has carved out a position in slang, notably for his role in 1508 as the first author to use the verb *fuck*. The Wife is name-checked only once, but she is seen as a role-model to whom the primary characters should pay attention. Laying down her laws, the Wedo charges her two dissatisfied Wives to note 'the good Wif of biside Bathe' in their management of their unsatisfactory husbands, notably by saying one thing – which he wishes to hear – and doing another – which is her will.

The bulk of the *Tretis* features direct speech either by the Wedo or one of the two Married Women. The Wedo is relatively restrained, but her companions are ruthless and use language that fits. Whether, as suggested in Grierson and Smith's *Critical History of English Poetry* (1944) that language is 'coldly obscene' [59] and 'nakedly sexual and lascivious' [182] is debatable. It is certainly to the point. Unlike the Wife's original lines, men are not allowed a say, even if that say was only there to provide her with something to knock down. The Married Women disdain their husbands: dirty, sexually repellent, probably cursed with a less than impressive member and even when they can bring themselves to accept his advances, impotent. Marriage gets short shrift.

One wife wishes, 'God gif matrimony wer made to mell for aneyeir!' [56] ('If only matrimonial sex was only mandated for a single year') while she goes on to suggest 'We suld have feiris as fresche to fang quhen us likit, / And gif all larbaris their leveis, quhen thai lak curage.' [66–7] ('We should have fresh partners to embrace whenever it pleased us and be able to rid ourselves of impotent, literally 'worn out', ones whenever they lost their energy'). *Mell*, cognate with meld, means to mix, in this case flesh, and thus to copulate; *larbar*, origin obscure, means exhausted and worn out, thus in sexual terms, impotent. Later in the verse the wife assures her hearers that I never that larbar my leggis ga betueene, although we may assume that his efforts would, as slang would come to put it, be *firing blanks*.

Bot I may huke all this yer, or his yerd help. *itch; before; penis*
Ay quhen that caribald carl lwald clyme one my wambe,
   monstrous man; belly
Than am I dangerus and daine and dour of my will; *reluc-*
   tant; haughty; unwilling [130–5]

The penis makes several appearances, whether as *gear*, *lume* or
pené. Chaucer's seems to be the first use of *gear*, already meaning
things or objects, to mean the penis; it would soon mean vagina
too. A *lume* was a tool, implement, instrument or utensil of any
kind; *tool* itself is recorded as penis from 1553, and *instrument*
from 1505 (*implement* must await 1884).

The *thing*, much used by Chaucer's Alisoun, returns. 'Na leit
never enter in my thoght that he my thing persit,', i.e. she
couldn't believe that he had actually pierced, i.e. entered, her
vagina. And later, to her greater satisfaction, 'A stif standand
thing staiffis in my neiff' [486]: an erect penis thrusts into her
fist and fills her, one way or another, with 'wellfair and joye'; it is
not, need we say, her husband's.

That unfortunate has quite another role. The theme of impotence is gloatingly recounted, and Alisoun notes that while his
beard may be as stiff as a bear's bristles, his 'sary [sorry] lume' is
'soft and soupill as the silk.' She also disdains his fumblings
between the sheets, a use of *fumyll* that may be literal, i.e. he
lacks sexual technique, but may prefigure slang's mid-seventeenth-century coinage of *fumbler* to mean an impotent, old
man. Either way, Dunbar seems to be the first to set this sense of
'fumble' in print. Nor, it would appear, is the hapless husband's
penis large, even when it does work. No virgin, terrified of a 'real
man' and his weapon as, suggests the wife, she may well be, need
worry about this husband. Even if he did manage to achieve

97

entry, so tiny is his member that she wouldn't realise he had done so.

A second wife seems to have done better with her spouse, but he too has become useless, whatever his partner tries to encourage his interest. He is, as modernity would put it, quite literally fucked out:

> He has bene lychour [a lecher] so lang quhill lost is his natur
> His lume is waxit larbar and lyis into swonne:
> Wes never sugeorne wer set na one that snaill tyrit [174–6]

Her use of *nature*, libido, prefigures by more than four centuries its next recorded appearance, in 1933.

There are other images for spousal dysfunction. He may look as if there was plenty of lead in his pencil but the reality is otherwise; instead 'he be litill of valour'.

> He dois as dotit [a stupid old, literally 'dotard'] dog that
>   damys [pisses] on all bussis [bushes],
> And liftis his leg apone loft, thoght he nought list pische
> [185]

But sexuality, or its absence, is not the only source of insult. The wives vie to smear their useless partners. For instance here, where a litany of insults are flung about, even if not all qualify as slang:

> I have ane wallidrag ane worme, ane auld wobat carle,
> A waistit wolroun, na worth bot wourdis to clatter

> Ane bumbart, ane dron bee, and bag full of flewme,
> Ane skabbit skarth, ane scorpioun, ane scutarde behind;

To see him scart [scratch] his awin skyn grit scunner I think,
Quhen kissis me that carybald, than kyndillis all my sorow
[88–96]

The burden of the lines is that the worn out old fool, especially when making his fruitless approaches to intercourse, disgusts her. The *Dictionary of the Older Scottish Tongue** fills out the detail:

According to the *DOST wallidrag* is a miserable creature or slovenly fellow; the dictionary suggests roots in a compound of *wallie*; an exclamation of sorrow or dismay, i.e. woe! and *draggle*, to bedraggle. The dictionary defines *worm* (with this line) as a vile, unpleasant or venomous person; slang does not use worm for penis until 1593 but there may be an implication of softness and thus impotence. *Wobat* is literally a 'hairy caterpillar' (a 'woolly body'); the term suggests the slow-moving creature, but slang would pick up caterpillar to describe a ne'er-do-well, one who lives on his wits and others' gullibility. A *waistit wolroun* is a 'wasted' or worn-out and despicable creature; its origins either from wolverine or 'wild, undomesticated'. *Bumbart*, from Middle English *bum*, to hum can be a bumblebee, and human-ised, a lazy stupid person. *Skabbit* equals scabbed and *skarth* has been defined as a monster or hermaphrodite. The term may be linked to old Norse *skratte* wizard, goblin or monster thus slang's *Old Scratch*, one of many terms for the devil. A *scutarde behind* suggests a shit-spattered posterior, but the scutarde himself is a sufferer from diarrhoea; despite what might seem a link to *shit*, the origin is in fact in *shute*, to shoot, i.e. 'loose stools'. *Scunner* is a non-specific source of disgust 'perhaps cognate with Old

---

* *Dictionary of the Older Scottish Tongue* (12 vols. 2002); digital version accessed at http://www.dsl.ac.uk/

Norse *skirra-sk* to shrink from'. Finally even *DOST* admits defeat with *carybald*: 'an abusive term of doubtful origin and meaning'. All it is sure of is that proposed links to 'cannibal' simply don't hold up.

Chaucer's Wife and her later epigones may have been fiction and allegorical, even if her ur-portrait was drawn, as has been suggested, from life; there were other early slang-speaking women who were not. The late fifteenth-century Welsh woman poet Gwerful Mechain (fl. 1460–1502) is one of her nation's most celebrated versifiers. She wrote poetry that the scholar Professor Katie Gramich has termed erotic and provocative, never more so than in her best-known poem *I'rcedor* (c.1480), usually translated as 'To the Vagina' although a variant is 'To the Pubic Hair'. This witty text mocks male poets for their regular and much-verbalised adoration of every aspect of the female body – hair, face, eyes, breasts, arms, hands – while never, ever mentioning what Mechain sees as the best and most important bit: the vagina.

It may be that translation disqualifies a text, but Prof. Gramich's modern (2003) take on Mechain's original is filled with slang. The poet would not have seen it thus, but if we trust the translator, then that was the register she chose, at least in part, to use. Aside from rendering the self-adoring male poet as 'king of cool' and 'silly sod', we find *arse, balls, bum, bush* and of course *quim*. There is also the Welsh *pant*, which translates to *cwm*, which in turn means a valley. Quim is primarily another of those q— terms that find their ultimate maternity in cunt, but cwm has also been suggested as a possible origin, the vagina being, figuratively, a valley. It is all somewhat circular. Nor do the vagina synonyms need be obscene or proto-slang. As Prof. Gramich has explained,

Gwerful is unafraid to use indecent words such as 'cedor' and 'cont' – in fact she uses them both a few times in the poem (and also in another poem called 'To jealous wives'). But the point of this kind of Welsh 'blazon' poem is to show off your ingenuity in finding as many images for the object in question as possible, so the 'cedor' is called a circle, a palace, a centre, a court, a seam, a curtain, a bush, a forest, a frieze, a fur, a hollow, a hedge, etc in the poem.[*]

The current slang lexis offers nearly 1,500 synonyms for vagina. Mechlain's imagery still underpins part of them.

[*] KG: email to author 16 July 2018.

4. Quarrelsome Dames

'Tis not enough that Ladies drink, whiff, whore, / Except they swear God-dammes by the score.

Henry Neville Newes from the New Exchange,
or, The commonvvealth of ladies, drawn to the life,
in their severall characters and concernments.
Printed in the year, of women without grace, 1650.

T HE *QUERELLE DES dames*, known in English as the 'women question' emerged around 1400 and would last for four centuries. The formal *querelle* – the same word as quarrel but perhaps best translated as debate or argument – represents feminism's first moments, a movement spearheaded by literate, intellectual (and initially French) upper-class women who found themselves denied their rights by a newly secularised culture, but, as noted by Joan Kelly, 'empowered by it at the same time to speak in their defence'*. The German scholar Heinrich Agrippa had suggested that in a world where men systematically oppressed women the cause was not some natural inferiority of the latter, but male insecurity and the desire to hold on to their social status and the powers it

---

* J. Kelly, 'Early Feminist Theory and the "Querelle des Femmes"', *Signs*, 8:1 (Autumn, 1982), pp.4–28.

offered. The women who pioneered the *querelle* moved on from there.

This feminist self-assertion would take on three forms: 1. Educational polemics that adopted an outspoken stand against male defamation and mistreatment of women. 2. The promotion of what would come to be known as gender, and the argument that despite male assumptions, women were in no way a 'defective' second-rate social group. 3. An attack on male-dominated ideology and a campaign for equality.

The *querelle*, naturally, had no direct use for slang: the French aristocrats who set it in motion would have had no conception of the register, while their successors as early feminists would never have seen it as relevant. Yet some pamphleteering, primarily in seventeenth-century England, was happy to employ it in what were artificial but still heartfelt face-offs between representative men and women. If these were less intellectual debates and more knock-down-drag-out episodes of mutual abuse, then such was the tenor of the language they preferred to use. They represent what would become called the Battle of the Sexes (first recorded in 1723 but not yet found again until 1886) rather than the Frenchified and thus somewhat over-precious 'querelle des dames'.

So too the topics. Intellect and similar abstract concepts did not come into the picture and like slang itself, the themes looked to more concrete complaints. These pamphlets, sometimes in pairs – one from a man with an immediate response from a woman – focused on topics that laid themselves open to the use of slang. Those penned by men focused on a single topic: the woman as nag or scold; those penned by women or at least purportedly so, stressed parallel male failings: cuckoldry, impotence and drunkenness, which in turn might lead to violence.

All of which in turn sprang from man's assumption, much challenged by these women writers, of their innate, not to mention religiously sanctified superiority. On the other hand, such failings, it might be suggested by female writers, might justify a woman's critique, however harshly delivered.

Before passing to specifics, it is worth an overview of the background, at least as seen through the slang vocabulary.

The Scold

As far as women were concerned, that is as villainesses and targets, the word was *scold*. The scold, to scold. *Shrew*, 'a small insectivorous animal thought to be venomous and generally injurious to humans,' (*OED*) was synonymous, and Chaucer used it to indicate a nagging, unruly wife. So too was *nag* itself. Slang has come up with a hundred more terms, though not all are aimed specifically at women (perhaps surprising given women's role in the register) and most are transitive verbs rather than the simple, descriptive noun.

Scold itself is first recorded around 1200 CE, and defined by Oxford thus: 'In early use, a person (esp. a woman) of ribald speech; later, a woman (rarely a man) addicted to abusive language.' It is the latter sense that lasted. A suggested etymology links it to the Old Norse *skáld*, a poet, though there is no suggestion that such poets were invariably minatory. The *OED* does note, however, that 'the derivative *skáldskapr*, lit. 'skaldship', poetry, has in the Icelandic law-books the specific sense of libel in verse.'

The uber-scold was the philosopher Socrates' wife Xantippe, who had become an eponym by the time Shakespeare referred to her in *The Taming of the Shrew* in 1616. Their marriage spawned a well-known tale, featured in James Howell's allegory *Thērologia, The parly of beasts, or, Morphandra, queen of the inchanted iland* (1660), in which Prince Pererius tours the island's inhabitants, a variety of men and women currently living in the bodies of animals. Among them a Hind [a female deer] who in human form had been a courtesan in Venice. The Hind seems to have studied her *querelle*, complaining that despite women's role as mothers and co-creators of the human race, 'ther is no other species of cretures wherin the female is held to be so much inferiour to the male as we are amongst you, who use to sleight, misprize, and tyrannize over us so much.' Pererius is unmoved:

'The reson of this is, because ther are so many of you either shrews, or light and loose in the hilts . . .'* and goes to tell how Xantippe 'her husband comming one day in when she was in an ill humour, she scolded him out of doors, and at his going out she whipp'd up into an upper room, and poured down a potfull of piss upon his sconce, which made the poor patient husband shake his head, and break forth into this speech, *I thought that after so much thunder we should have rain*.' Or there was 'another damnable scold having revil'd and curs'd her husband a great while, all which time she had the Devill often in her mouth, to whom she bann'd him, at last he said, Hold thy toung wife, and threaten me no more with the Devil, for I know he will do me no hurt, because I have married his Kinswoman.'

The punchline: 'that cautious proverb, *Honest men do marry, but Wise men not.*'

The proclaimed necessity to control women's language, and the creation of the demonised figure of the scold both, according to M. C. Bodden, emphasised the fact that such social

---

* *Light,* and thus unable to stay upright, in slang means promiscuous; *loose in the hilt* usually refers to a bout of diarrhoea, but here presumably attacks an 'over-sexed' female.

engineering effectively outlawed 'any woman who verbally resisted and flouted authority publicly.'* Unfettered women's language was a threat. The theologian John Wyclif went so far as to etymologise the word blasphemy as '*blas–femina*: foolish and harmful women'). Next stop: speaking like a witch and all that might imply. As Kirilka Stavreva[†] suggests, 'To many popular writers . . . the witch was, quite simply, a particularly heinous variety of scold, a woman whose harsh words more than merited the verbal affronts she received.' And like the classic scold, the words she used were part of a woman 'getting the upper hand in a verbal strife [and] asserting oneself over one's superior in the social or gender hierarchy.' To paraphrase Professor Bodden, in her critics' eyes the scold could not control herself and in her malicious gossiping and nagging confused truth and tales and metaphorically pisses her falsehoods on the world. From a modern perspective, she disseminated fake news.

In practical terms, when for the first time she is acknowledged by the courts as one worthy of prosecution, the scold is a product of the mid-fourteenth century. The US academic Sandy Bardsley looked at her development in her study *Venomous Tongues: Speech and Gender in Late Medieval England* (2006). The concept of the shrewish, nagging woman, wife or other, was of course nothing new: popular culture had long since enshrined her on this dubious, misogynistic altar. Men might talk to excess, but that was acceptable; by the 1400s, as Bardsley puts it, 'women were to words as geese were to excrement.'[‡]

The move from gossiping housewives in some urban court-yard to defendants and prosecutors in an actual court seems to

---

* M. C. Bodden, *Language as the Site of Revolt* (2011) p.28.
† Quoted in Bodden op. cit. p.27.
‡ Sandy Bardsley, *Venemous Tongues* (2006) p. 25.

have been a product of the Black Death of 1351, a plague that turned the world upside down and in its swathe of corpses, attacked the upper levels of society as much as it did the rest. Such 'ruling classes' felt threatened, and especially so by the 'unruly' woman. The scold was threatening not just the other side of the garden fence, but the inner sanctum beyond the castle wall. Her words must be checked. If they were silenced (voluntarily or under compulsion) society could and would return to normality: i.e. dominated by males. Just as the state and its upholders claimed the sole power to carry and use deadly weapons, it was reserved to the powerful to 'name and shame', and thereafter punish; the scold, unofficial, self-motivated, was challenging for those roles and it was not to be permitted. The Church, as ever, backed the powers that be. Harping on what it termed 'sins of the tongue' it allied women's speech to 'blasphemy, hypocrisy, rumour, lying, flattery, mocking of good people, and sowing of discord.' The creation of women alone? Hardly – for instance one statistic showed that of those tried for gossiping in church some 80 per cent were men – but that was not the point. The tongue was not a man's weapon – that was the fist – but undeniably that of a woman.

One should not, however, elevate these arguments, even if they did end up in court, over-muchly. The slurs that Prof. Bernard Capp, an indefatigable truffler in the archives of a variety of Britain's urban Record Offices, found are as reminiscent of soap opera cat fights as of anything more heightened. Chapters 5 and 6 of his study *When Gossips Meet: Women, Family, and Neighbourhood in Early Modern England* (2003) deal with disputes between women and between women and men. (Those between men and men were different: there might be a bit of preliminary argy-bargy but men preferred physical violence to the verbal kind.) The primary insult was, predictably enough, *whore*, and we find 'burnt-arsed whore', 'pocky whore', 'hollow-tree whore' and 'hedge whore'. The first two qualifiers meaning venereally diseased, and the second couple implying the depths of rural poverty, forcing the girl to entertain a client against a tree or beneath a hedge.

But as Professor Capp notes, *whore* suffered from 'massive over-use' and 'speakers were able to draw on a rich lexicon of synonyms [. . .] jade, quean, baggage, harlot, drab, filth, flirt gill, trull, dirty heels, draggletail, flap, naughty pack, slut, squirt, and strumpet, generally heightened by adjectives such as arrant, base, brazen-faced or scurvy.' Most of these would enter the slang lexicons. There were also regular mentions of the term *tail*, which conveniently meant the genitals of either sex as well as the buttocks and offered multi-purpose uses. It was usually 'dirty'.

Thus he cites (all women targeting women): 'Look where the naughty pack standeth, for naught she was before she came to the town, and naught she is still'* (1574), 'lousy quean, filthy quean . . . stand off lest thou fill me full of lice, thou art fit to carry Jack an Apes and for nothing else' (1596) and 'Hang her, she is like a salted bitch and not like a woman . . . a woman would do as a woman should do, but she doth like a bitch and dogs fight for her'† (1616). Professor Capp immortalises various unfortunates: 'Joan Easton, a Sussex villager, was dubbed "the arrantest whore that ever had shoone of leather . . . an arrant whore as ever pissed"',‡ Alice Richardson was 'as common as the

---

* While *naughty* means immoral, *naught* is not an abbreviation but means wicked, i.e. morally zero.
† *Salt bitch*, used generally for 'a bitch in heat', was an early slang term for a gay man. Thus the poem 'Court Diversion' (1686): In France he was the Town and Court's salt-bitch; / Each page and footman knew him by his breech; / Till of both sides and tongue he was so free, / He was banished Sodom for debauchery.
‡ *As ever pissed* was flexible: by the nineteenth century it was a term of praise or at least an indication of extreme, often as . . . *as pissed between two feet/shoes.*

highway,' Alice North 'kept open shop and open hole'. Anne Gibbons was branded an insatiable 'jumping jade' and accused of a marathon session with 'a rogue that occupied thee nine times and bade thee lay still.' One Joan Webb apparently paid her lovers, bribing them with venison, cheeses and a shirt in return for their favours. She had a fiancé: he broke off the wedding. A last example was Isabel Yaxley of Barnewell in Cambridgeshire, informed by a neighbour that '*she* would scorn to be fucked for a pennyworth of fish, as thou wert.' The idea of fucking 'below oneself' seems to have been as much an insult as the act of adultery or promiscuity itself. One woman defended herself by riposting 'I never showed my arse in an alehouse, nor pawned my muff [i.e. vagina] for drink' (1637) and another told her assailant that '*she* had never lain on her back and broken her elbows'.

When it came to seeing off men, women could be equally outspoken. The defendant in a 1704 rape case testified how her attacker assaulted her in a stable, pulled up her clothes 'and did then spend his nature upon my thighs'. In 1597 the subject of the churchwardens' reproof for her supposed immorality replied simply 'Shit on the churchwardens'. A man might be pilloried as a 'drunken fuddling fool', a 'drunken pocky-faced rogue', a 'filthy pig', a 'stinking fool and ass', a 'horse-turd' and a 'town bull' (a boastful, unfettered womaniser).

The law could not see off scolds, but its implementation could. There is no suggestion that such cussing-matches experienced a time limit. The street theatre, if nothing else, was too enjoyable for the bystanders and perhaps for the performers too. However even if the woman-only variety of such combats cannot be seen as threatening the gendered order, the law was keen to act and women's speech was legally devalued. They lost what had once been equal powers, such as that of calling the hue and cry after thieves, and at the same time became the primary targets for 'speech crime'.

Cuckold

If the mouthy woman was seen as one source of social disruption, so too the sexually self-determined one, especially as a wife.

Some scolding women concerned themselves with their husband's work, especially when suggesting that their business methods were far from honest (peddling short measure as a grocer, underfilled pots as a publican, second-rate goods as a merchant), but slang does not really concern itself with business failure (other than in a variety of coincidental terms for theft, deception or other forms of malfeasance). Thus, aside from alcoholic excess, which generated thirty-three slang terms for drunkard and a further 135 for drunkard in the period, when it came to inter-gender abuse, cuckoldry – the cheating of the husband by his wife – plays the primary role.

Cuckoldry prompted detailed analysis. Early slang collectors liked to propose a taxonomy of villains and sex 'crimes' received similar treatment. *The Cobler of Canterburie* (1590) offered 'The eight orders of Cuckolds'. These were:

1. Cuckold *Machomite*, 'an ancient cuckold, who hath bene married some thirtie or fourtie yeres and hath continued content in that estate'
2. Cuckold *Hereticke*, 'hee that having a faire wife and an

---

* *Machomite*: i.e. Mohammedan and playing on twin stereotypes: the long-married cuckold has been cuckolded many times while the 'Machomite', with his numerous wives, will also have suffered similar problems.

honest, is so blinded with jealousie and suspicion, as he thinks her to be as dishonest as the best'

3. Cuckold *Lunaticke*, 'hee that being a Cuckold conceives such inward griefe, that he suffers his passions to take no rest, but as a man distrackt from his senses'

4. Cuckold *Innocent*, 'hee that being simple of himself suspecteth nothing'

5. Cuckold *Incontinent*, 'hee that marries himselfe to a wife of a light disposition, who makes him a Cuckold the very first day of their marriage'

6. Cuckold by *Consent*, 'hee that of all other cuckolds is most infamous [and] fostereth his wife up in hir follies, and is content to keep the doore to his wifes lascivious wantonnesse'*

7. Cuckold by *Act of Parliament*, 'such a one that when he takes his wife faulty is not content to secretly punish the offence, but goes to lawe with the man for recompence'

8. Cuckold *Quem Fecit Ecclesia*, 'hee whom the Church maketh a Cuckold and this is when a young man marrieth a maide [. . .] whome he supposes to be a maide, and yet hath plaid false before [. . .] In marrying him to such a one he is a Cuckold in the Church'

Cuckoldry is an active performance. The wife strays, the husband pays, but the era's social dictates ran contrary to the way modernity might attribute blame. The idea of the 'bolter', the runaway wife who is henceforth excluded from respectable society, is far away. The adulterous wife may have transgressed the seventh commandment, but down on earth she was

---

* *Keep the door.* i.e. to act as a brothel-keeper or madame.

essentially innocent (at least within her own marriage: others, often other women, might be less impressed), guilt lay with the husband who in the prevailing hierarchical sense of the world, had let down the side and betrayed what should be a male prerogative. If the domestic world might be thus turned upside down, how much more dangerous might such reverses be when challenging the order of the wider society.*

In the shaming rituals that were still regular, if, for the purposes of historians, badly recorded events (the researcher's suggestion being that they were indeed so regular that it was rarely thought necessary to describe them in detail) it was the husband who would be paraded amidst a procession of rough music (the banging and rattling of kitchen implements) and dragged-up actors seated backwards ('bum to bum') on horseback (symbolic of the family life reversed, thus the husband might often be holding a distaff, a 'female' object) at Horn Fair (the London version of which took place at the suitably named Cuckold's Haven or Cuckold's Point on the Thames near Deptford). Horn Fair, keeping up the primary image, was held on St Luke's Day, 18 October; St Luke being the patron saint of the ox, the quintessential 'horned beast'. The wife might face her own ritual, the skimmington or riding, more rough music, more symbolic figures, but that focused not on an errant vagina, but an over-used tongue.† Meanwhile

---

* *Cuckold* of course lies behind the contemporary *cuck*, used both in the sexual and political worlds. The former also pillories the husband, but the backdrop is his active participation – as voyeur, possibly with camera – in an arranged coupling between his unsatisfied wife and a compensatorily endowed black male; the seventeenth century would have termed him a *wittol*, or even *suffragan*; the latter, in act of auto-cannibalism, savages those who while grudgingly acknowledged as conservatives, are deemed insufficiently so.

† *Skimmington* comes from the large wooden spoon used to skim milk and thus a quintessential 'women's' tool. (It could also be seen as phallic, another reverse for the established order). The aim of the ritual was the shaming of men who had been beaten by

the husband wore the horns; there were, as yet, no scarlet letters for his wife.

One further public shaming, this for women-only, was cucking: the use of a special cucking stool on which a woman was seated then dipped into water until she promised to mend her verbose ways. The similarity to *cuckold* was pure coincidence. The term came from Latin *cathedra stercoris,* a shitting stool (probably rooted in *cacare,* to defecate), its earliest form *cokestole* is found in Scotland where it was used to punish alewives who tampered with the beer.* Such stools, which were regularly built and then rebuilt, given their proximity to water and its effects on wood, were essentially large-scale replicas of shop scales. They were initially used on bakers and brewers, many of the latter being women, who were suspected of short measure. It was this established link of ducking seat and woman that may have facilitated the transfer of the stool from crooked food and drink manufacturers to scolds.

By the late seventeenth century such women were the only victims. As noted by the legal scholar William Sheppard in his 'Grand Abridgement of the Common & Statute Law of England' 1675:

A common scold is a troublesome and angry woman, who, by her brawling and wrangling among her neighbors, doth break the publick peace, and beget, cherish and increase publick discord. And for this she is to be presented and

---

their wives: they should henceforth take back control. An alternative name was *riding the cowl-staff*: 'to be set astride a pole and carried in derision about the streets; a rough form of popular punishment, inflicted esp. on a husband who allowed himself to be beaten or abused by his wife' [*OED*].

* According to the Law Dictionary (1835) *cokestole* was derived from 'choaking stool'; other names include *tre-bucket, tymborella, castigatory stool,* and *goginstole.*

punished by being put in the Cucking or Ducking-stole, or Tumbrel, an Engine appointed for that purpose, which is in the fashion of a Chair, and herein she is to sit, and to be let in the water over her head and ears three or four times, so that no part of her be above the water.

This submerging was aimed at extinguishing the fire of her hot, unruly tongue. As a sermon on 'The Taming of the Tongue' (1616) put the problem: *It hath fired, and shall be fired* with such fire as is not to be quenched. But blessed is the sanctified tongue. God doth now choose it as an instrument of music to sing his praise; he doth water it with the saving dews of his mercy.' The Sandwich stool carried the motto: 'Of members ye tongue is worst or beste / An ylltonge oft doth breede unreste.' How many women drowned as a result of divine mercy is unknown. Some held out with admirable determination. The anti-heroine of the ballad 'The Cucking of a Scould' (1616)* was obviously a star of her type. As the introduction explained:

> She was a famous Scould
> A dainty Scould in graine,
> A stouter Scould was neuer bred
> Nor borne in Turne-gaine Lane.

The qualification 'in grain' denoted 'best of a type'; slang gives examples of a knave or rogue in grain, a saint in grain and, unsurprisingly, a cuckold and wittol (a sexually complaisant husband) in grain. Turne-again lane was an alleyway near Billingsgate, the London fishmarket which was home, as was

---

* https://bit.ly/2LYPFoX

well-known, of mouthy women. The scold in question was already generally unpopular when she hit the last straw: complaining against the constable 'that did / But pisse against her wall.' She called him 'beastly knave / And filthy jack' and complained he had turned her wall into a public privy. He in return and taking unfair advantage of his powers, vowed revenge: the cucking stool. She survived some seventeen duckings before, after the eighteenth and last, she finally promised to shut up.

Scolds also faced the *scold's bridle* or *branks*, a form of cage in which the head was imprisoned, and by inserting an iron 'bridle-bit' into the mouth speech was rendered impossible. The resemblance to a horse's bridle and bit was not coincidental, though the homonyms of *nag* for both scold and horse probably were. (Such versions as have been pictured look alarmingly similar to another, later means of suppressing women: various anti-masturbatory 'chastity belts' available in the nineteenth century). The bridle was by no means restricted to the British Isles. As noted by @Whores of Yore on Twitter (10 February 2019) the *shrew's fiddle* was used in medieval Germany and Austria, where it was known as a *Halsgeige*, meaning 'neck viola'. It could be used on a single woman, with holes to imprison her neck and both hands, or on a squabbling pair. A flat piece of wood, with two holes, would be locked onto their necks and they stayed thus attached until they were considered to have made sufficient peace. Both 'instruments' were sometimes accessorised by a bell.

The scold, the mother-in-law in embryo, was always available for a session in the literary if not literal pillory. Sometimes condemned, sometimes pleading her own case. A couple of examples are *Poor Robin's true character of a scold, or, The shrews looking-glass dedicated to all domineering dames, wives rampant, cuckolds couchant, and hen-peckt sneaks, in city or country* (1678)

given horns, you *wore* them. *Horns-to-sell* was both cuckold and cuckolder, the sexually generous wife; there were no 'sales' and any 'prostitution' was merely in the eyes of a censorious beholder. The cuckolder was also a *horn-maker* and her behaviour *horn-work*.

Slightly less obvious were *holy Moses* (contemporary paintings of the patriarch displayed him with a part-halo, the curves of which resemble horns protruding from his head), *hoddy-peak* or *hoddy-peel*, where the horns are those of a *hoddy*, a snail. *One of the livery* refers to *livery* companies, military or city bands distinguished by their uniforms and badges, in the cuckold's case the 'badge' he 'wears' is that of the *horns. Ninnyhammer* seems to compound *ninny*, a fool, and *hammer*, a clumsy person. It links to *nincompoop* (also *nickumpoop, nink-a-poop,* and *ninny-cum-poop*), which sees the cuckold as an effeminate weakling, as Francis Grose defined the term in 1785, 'one who never saw his wife's cunt', though he saw the root as *non compos*, 'not all there'. A *cotquean* was similar, a husband too interested in cooking and other 'feminine' duties. Cuckold itself comes from *cuckoo*, a bird that lays its eggs in another's nest; slang's *cuckoo's egg* is a child fathered by another man with the husband's knowledge. Strictly, there were three levels of cuckold: the *cuckold* itself, the complaisant, but passive *wittol* and the *suffragan*, who colludes in his own betrayal. Wittol supposedly comes from the *woodwale*, a bird that is often the target of the real-life cuckoo, who lays its egg in the woodwale's nest. Suffragan uses the then current meaning of suffer, to allow, and thus Christ's 'suffer the little children to come unto me'. Again we have the underlying theme: husbands allow their wives to find alternative sexual satisfaction; there's no-one else to blame but their own feeble self.

Slang does not acknowledge the word adultery, though an

adulterer could be a *horner* or a *trader* (which was better known as one of many terms for prostitute). One found more possibilities with a verb form, to cuckold. Again, horns were at the forefront: *cornute, horn* and *hornify*, with such images as *make a monster of, make someone a stag* or *wear the stag's crest.* To *put a bone in someone's hood* played on the standard English phrase *put a bone in someone's hood*, to break or cut off someone's head, while to *give someone's head the bastinado*, came from *bastinado*, to beat, to cudgel, and the phrases suggested that 'the lover's penis is the cudgel and the bumps that it "raises" on the unsuspecting husband's head are the cuckold's horns'* while *make* or *spin crooked spindles* referred to a woman who by sleeping around, had abandoned her 'proper' wifely tasks.

Men were not going through some uncharacteristic period of self-restraint. 'Cuckold' was not a synonym for 'husband'. As we shall see, a regular feature of women's slanging-matches was the throwing of an errant husband's extra-marital dalliances in his wife's face. Yet there seems to be only one word for a cuckolded woman: *cuckquean*, literally a 'woman cuckold'. There are forty-four for her more sexually indulgent sisters, including *tirliry-pufkin, smock rampant, marmuley madam*, and a number of plays on *light* (*light heels, light housewife, light lady*, etc), all of which suggested some form of imbalance within the female heel, which causes her to fall so regularly on her back. (The modern *round-heels* is a direct descendant.)

Male assumptions under threat, women increasingly unruly: if we are to believe the *Oxford Companion to Shakespeare's England*, the late sixteenth to mid-seventeenth

---

* J. T. Henke, *Gutter Life and Language* (1988), p.17.

centuries saw a major crisis of the patriarchy.* As the historian Roger Thompson has explained,† 'Much of the satire on marriage was of well-worn antiquity, but an important inno-vation of the Interregnum [i.e. mid-seventeenth century], perpetuated in the Restoration, was the literary reversal of traditional sex roles. Males tended to be depicted as sexually unsatisfying or as gigolos, obediently servicing their mistresses. Females are the huntresses, the sexual activists; it is their wanton urges which generate the plots.'

In the arena of pamphleteering there would be much evidence. In prize-fight terms, there would be an undercard, with a variety of preliminaries, but the major clash can be seen in 1640, with a dry run twelve months earlier. The launch examples were authored, albeit pseudonymously, by the same pen.

Written pseudonymously, or with fictional 'authors' these pamphlets may have claimed to present a range of female voices, but we must assume that readers were not fooled. As Elizabeth Harvey entitled her 1992 study of male writers appropriating female voices, these were no more than 'Ventriloquized Voices' and far from celebrating women's opinions at the expense of men, they served only to underline negative stereotypes, in the *Lectures*' case, of the woman, usually wife, as *ex officio* scold.

In 1639 John Taylor, the self-styled 'Water Poet' (he combined a popular writing career with a day job of ferrying passengers back and forth across the Thames), offered his audience: *A iuni-per lecture With the description of all sorts of women, good, and bad: from the modest to the maddest, from the most civil, to the scold*

---

* This book focuses on slang and inevitably bypasses a good deal of the era's prototype feminist campaigning. For examples of a wider view readers might consult James Grantham Turner *Libertines and Radicals in Early Modern London* (2002) and the many texts on which he draws.
† R. Thompson, *Unfit for Modest Ears* (1979), p.114.

rampant, their praise and dispraise compendiously related. Also the
authors advice how to tame a shrew, or vexe her.

With a blurb from the suitably named, if fictional, 'Margery
Quiet of Tame' (in Oxfordshire) who professed 'her ingenious
friend the Author' to be 'a well-wisher to all good women', the
pamphlet, some two hundred pages in all, offered thirteen wife-
to-husband lectures, a 'Dialogue between three Gossips, over a
cup of Sacke, tutering one another how to domineere over their
Husbands' and 'Lastly the Authors advise how to tame a Shrew,
with new Additions'.

The tone was set in the frontispiece. A bearded husband
starts up in bed, a shoe in one hand, what looks like a baluster
in the other; meanwhile his wife waves a wooden spoon
(presumably a skimmington) and tells him to 'Rise you
drunken slave.'

Writing 'to the reader', the author asks, 'Why is it called a
Juniper lecture?' And, setting it alongside a Crabtree lecture and
a Curtain lecture (the latter based on the curtains that still
surrounded the marital bed) answers, 'Marry for sundry small
reasons . . . It is said that Juniper being on fire is the most lasting
wood in the World, and that if the fire of it be rak'd up in the
Embers or Ashes it will not be extinguish'd in a year or more,
which may be alluded to some revengeful women who being
once offended, the fire of their malice will hardly be quenched in
their Ashes, or Graves.' In addition, 'Juniper is hot and drye in
the third Degree (as Galen saith) and the tongue of a scold is
altogether combustible. It is full of prickles, so are a curst womans
words very peircing to the eares and sharpe to the heart.' A few
ameliorative paragraphs on 'good', i.e. soft-spoken, complaisant
woman, are appended, but the point is made. As one wife
advises, 'It lyes with you [. . .] with the Clapper of your tongue

to ring him a perpetual peale',* and so they do, repeatedly, in the lectures that follow.

Their complaints follow the established pattern. There is drunkenness on the night before, when home he staggers, 'up and downe the streete, and making Indentures' [a reference to the zig-zag indentations along the top of documents]: 'You, you drunken sot, you pisse-pot, know not when you have sufficient; thus to come home reeling and staggering' . . . and in the morning after: 'What, are you awake, good man Foxe-catcher [to *catch a fox*, to be drunk]: are you in any better humour than you were last night.'

There is sex. Are there other women? 'I marvaile whither you went, or in what new hole you had entertainment'. Was she hot? 'Those young gill-flurts, who trick themselves up like a *Bartholmew-faire* Babie'† . . . or tawdry, some 'durty draggletail *Ioane*, that came with nothing to their husbands but the cloathes on their backes.' There is general abuse: 'You a Husband: you a Coxcombe, a mere Lubby, a Moon-calf, one that hath more haire than wit . . . Out you Slabber Choppes, go trudge with thy fellow *Hob*, and drive the cart. And the popular dismissal, 'Thou art [. . .] not worthy to carry guts to a bear.' 'Out you Dosser-head, shallow-brain'd companion.' It allows for self-pity: 'I am married to a grumbling [. . .] *Dunghill*, a *Cullion*, a common *Town Bull* . . . There's not a Bawd, Quean, Punk, Tib, Trash, Trull or Trully-bub, Oyster-wife, or Kitchen-stuffe Slut, but lives a merrier life than I doe.'

On the other hand, what's to lose. Like many such husbands, he manages both to philander and yet be impotent at home,

---

* All quotes from Taylor, *Juniper Lecture* (1639) passim.
† The 'baby' was a gaudily-clad doll sold at Bartholemew Fair, London's celebrated annual bacchanalia.

always a good excuse for a bit of double-entendre as she dreams of a replacement: 'I will have a Husband that shall alwayes be provided like a Souldier, never not with standing [. . .] with his Match lighted and cocked bolt upright, and ready to do execution.' And if he does perform elsewhere there's the clap: 'He got a pocky blow with a *French* Cowle-staffe' (a variation on the more common 'faggot-stick'). Fortunately (for her) he paid the price: he 'gave up the Ghost' and with him conveniently dead, 'the Marriage was ended and Giblets were joyn'd.' The fresh-cooked giblets, we may be sure, being those of a new innamorato.

Otherwise, still tied, still miserable, she fights back, in a way that all would recognise: 'I am no *Goose* to be *Crow-trodden* by such a Buzzardly Gull as thou art.' He is a 'beetleheaded cuckoe' [stupid cuckold] a 'foolish joltead' and she is ashamed to be seen with such a 'Lubberly Lout', 'Shee makes her husband a very Asse, an *Abram*, and a Ninnihammer [. . .] though shee be counted a Whoore or a light woman' and makes him wear 'an invisible Cuckooes Feather in his Cap.'

A year later and Taylor followed with a new assault, again posing as a variety of scolds: *Divers crabtree lectures Expressing the severall languages that shrews read to their husbands, either at morning, noone, or night* . . . The final section, *Also a lecture betweene a pedler and his wife in the canting language*, is the predictable contrivance, a supposed conversation between two villains and no more credible than any other animated glossary of its type.

Taylor does not explain the use of 'crabtree' but there are plays on slang's *crab*, to nag or criticise and the sour crab-apple and an illustration rubs the message in. Shadowed by an overhanging fruit tree (presumably crab-apples) a shame-faced husband, grinning in self-defence, is menaced by a wife, wielding the inevitable spoon. 'O good wife', he pleads, 'Sirrah, you are a drunkard' is her only response.

On this occasion the purported author(ess) is one Mary Makepeace, like Margery Quiet an ameliorative name, whose home is the Mannor of All-Well. Addressing her 'fellow spinster' she explains that 'the course carriage of some amongst our Sexe . . . has come to my hearing.' Such termagants have been 'publickly branded'. Among them are Tabitha Turbulent 'of a terrible tongue', Franke Froward . . . 'given more to pouting than to prating', plus Betrisse Bould-face, Ellen Ever-heard, who makes too much noise, Parnell Prate apace, Ursala Upseefreeze, i.e. a consumer of strong Dutch beer, Hannah Hit-him-home and Joan Jowle him well. Not that all such eponymous women are bad. On the other side Mark presents Grace grieve him not, Kate Kisse-well, Luce Lye-close, 'no wanton, but a willing wench', Dorothy Doe-little, Sisly Sweet-lips and, still in the country, Margery Quiet. 'If all the rest were of their simplicity, and modesty, men should not have such reason to cavell.'

Her task, she makes clear, is, as her name suggests, to make peace between the genders: 'let us seeke to please proper men, least they bring us down upon our Maribones [knees].'

Crabtree showcases twenty-five women haranguing husbands for their failings: deceitful in conducting business, spending excessive time in the tavern, useless between the sheets. A verse underlines the contemporary disdain for a world in which the social order seems threatened by weak men, and it is a woman, a glasier's wife, rather than a whingeing male, who promotes the status quo:

Ill fares the hapless family that shows
A Cock that's silent and a Hen that crows
I know not which live more unnatural lives,
Obedient Husbands or commanding wives.

Among the 'commanding wives' are those of an apothecary, a barber, a tailor, a poet, a horse-courser, an innkeeper, a lock-smith, a police informer and a broker. There is also a 'skimming-tons lecture to her husband'. As one husband, a farrier, punningly puts it, 'I dare warrant you [. . .] I shall have a dish of maunder-ing Broath [i.e. a scolding], thickened with a few small Reasons [and] I shall be constrained to sup it up scoulding hot."*

Once again, the main complaint is husbandly drunkenness.

'You may be ashamed [. . .] to bee such a common drunk-ard, a pisse-pot, a beast [. . .] every day foxed & at night brought home by a watchman', 'and next morning you are then a little crop-sick, and then to cure your squeezy stom-ach, you get a haire with the same dog [. . .] a cup of the same wine burnt or mild that you dranke raw over night', 'I would you had but a looking-glasse to see how you looke now you have been a foxing.' And perhaps most pertinent, 'You are never kind to mee, but when you are fuddled, and then you can cogge and dissemble with me, to have your own will, or what you want.'

Like his Juniper predecessor the Crabtree husband is another spouse torn between chasing other women (or so it is claimed: the sense, again, is that if these husbands ever pursued the practise, it

* All quotes from Taylor, *Divers crabtree lectures* passim.

has long turned empty theory) and disappointing his wife. 'Sirrah, I hear you are a Mutton monger [a womaniser] and run after laced Mutton [whores in fancy clothes]', 'Nay more, thou keepest thy hackny Whoors: They stand at the bottle (of Sacke and Clarret).' There are the inevitable double entendres: 'Thou [a butcher] art every day basting and basting, and yet canst afoord me no roaste-meat all the weeke long.' A 'Tayler [. . .] talks of nothing but his yard, his yard [both measure and slang for penis], and is not able to afoord his wife London measure. When he thinks do to his best it is but so so, and he cannot goe narrow stitch with any thing. So purblind a Coxcombe that cannot see in the darke to find the eye of his own needle which any other could doe blind folded [stitch-ing is intercourse, a needle the penis].' So: 'she must strike back, and It will be long enough before thou wilt set up thy Nagge [another slang penis, the standard English *nag* in this case being a horse] in my Stable, thou wall-ey'd wickednesse.'

Every lecture offers its share of abuse. Angry wives denounce 'a Bottle-nose, one whose nose turnes up againe like a Shooing-horn', 'You great Calfe' and 'Thou lousie nitty Tayler' [which may of course be an in-joke by the author]. The author addresses 'her' readers: 'call him Capon'; but said the other, 'never Cocke of the game [. . .] no I will see him in the pit first, which word may carry a double meaning', . . . 'I call him Owle, and Booby, and now and then saucer-ey'd slave and platter-fac'd rascall'. He is 'a meere Sheepeshead, or rather a Rams head in a Wolfes Skinne', a 'Mopus', a 'Grout-headed booby' and a 'knave in graine; indeede thou art as coarse as thy Bran'.

She is unrestrainedly coarse, with her accent on the posterior: 'I have put the breeze under your Taile, I think I have netled you', and noting her rival, suggests that while 'shee [. . .] kept her selfe sweete and cleane, he came home every night with a foule and stinking Pipe' [i.e. uncleaned anus]. In the end, she's had enough: 'I had as live thou kisst me where I sat [. . .] for to thee the cheekes with eies and the blind cheekes [i.e. buttocks] are all one'. His business failure seems to be as important as any sexual dalliance. She will grass him up for short measure and 'make you looke through a two inch boord on Market day' the 'two-inch board' being the wood of the pillory in which he is to be set. 'The name of Broker was well given to you: for you were Broak before you set up' but she scorns his larcenous efforts to improve their income: 'Hast thou outfac't him [a buyer] that he [a horse] had no other fault but that he took him when his feet were asleepe: and what was this better than Conicatching?' [i.e. confidence trickery].

The 'sour' imagery underpinning the crabtree re-emerged mid-century, when in 1673 one J. W. compounded condiments and the bitter flavouring agent wormwood to offer *Vinegar and mustard: or, Worm-wood-lectures for every day in the week Being exercised and delivered in several parishes both of town and city, on several dayes. A dish of tongues here's for a feast, sowre fawce for sweet meat is the best. Taken verbatim in short writing.*

Later in 1640 came what was advertised as the women's reply to Taylor's lectures: *The womens sharpe revenge: or an answer to Sir Seldome Sober that writ those railing pamphelets called the Iuniper and Crabtree lectures, &c. Being a sound reply and a full confutation of those bookes: with an apology in this case for the defence of us women. Performed by Mary Tattle-well, and Ioane Hit-him-home, spinsters.*

Mary and Joan celebrate the eponymic surnames that typify such pamphlets and many of those symbolic speakers who appear within them. The question remains: who were they, or was there but a single 'her' and, ultimately, was that her a 'him'. The theory, at least among a subset of scholars, is that John

Taylor, having made a few shillings from his earlier efforts for the prosecution, now compounded his profits by presenting himself for the defence.

This was hardly new. Within the world of slang, and fifty years earlier in 1591, the playwright and cant glossarist Robert Greene, after excoriating contemporary villains in several 'coney-catching' pamphlets, repurposed himself as 'Cuthbert Coneycatcher, Licentiate in Whittington College' (i.e. Newgate prison, refurbished in 1422 via a legacy from Richard 'Dick' Whittington and nicknamed in his honour) and published *The Defense of Conny-Catching, or A Confutation of Those two injurious Pamphlets published by R.G. against the practitioners of many nimble-witted and muysticall Sciences*. Cuthbert is furious, railing against this 'cursed book of Conycatching' and reviling 'this R.G. that had made a puyblike spoyle of so noble a science . . .'

Doubling down in this manner would certainly have been typical of Taylor, a man who would have been happily at home in the modern world of self-publishing and its attendant self-advertisement. Much of his work was based on taking subscriptions – for instance for the story of his proposed voyage around Britain in a boat made of brown paper (it sank) – and only then getting on with the necessary work. Returning to a successful theme and rewriting it from a contradictory point of view would not have been hard.

Yet while the theme may have been similar – how could it not since such was the point – the language, while slangy in all three pamphlets, does not in fact overlap. One might have expected Taylor to call on a vocabulary with which he was comfortable – his many works are filled with slang – but there are only two instances in which the *Lectures* overlap with the *Sharpe Revenge*: the use of *muff* for female genitals and that of *fox-catcher/*

fox-catching to mean drunkard and drunk. Mary also used eight further terms that can be found in Taylor, but these date back to writing in the 1620s, and the majority are common terms for drunk: *bewitched, blind, have a dirty nose, pot-shaken, scratched, see the lions* and *whip the cat*. Logically enough, since their nickname for the Lectures' author, Taylor or otherwise, is 'Sir Seldom (or never) Sober'. An outlier is *carpet knight*, whose chivalry concentrates on the boudoir rather than the battlefield.

Mary and Joan had no doubts that Taylor was the author of the lectures. Pondering the Crabtree author, and jabbing elbows into any adjacent ribs, they wonder 'if hee were a Tailer' and noting that if so 'most sure he was [not] a Womans Tailor or (if so) no good Artist, because not being able to take the measure of a woman's body, much less was he powerful to make a true dimension of her mind (and therein you are gone, Master tailor).' (Given slang's playing with sewing and needles, there might be an extra nudge towards impotence.) Later they ask the writer of this 'very passionate but most pittifull Poetry … whether you be a Land Laureate or Marine Muse; a land Poet or a Water Poet; a Scholler, or a Sculler; of *Parnassus* or puddle Dock'. All the waterly alternatives, of course, fitting Taylor's biography. Finally, in a direct assault, they recount an anecdote (was it as well-known as its target, or was Taylor venting a family secret?) in which his wife, having suffered a rope's-end beating from her husband, served him up a dish consisting of the same piece of rope, now carefully boiled and plated.

Mary sustained some degree of fame herself: in *The Parlament of Women* (also 1640) we find one 'Mistris Tattle-well'. This unruly figure appears in the House to tell her fellow members 'that it was not only fitting but necessary that every woman should have two husbands fore said she, was not every woman borne with two legges, two hands, two eyes, two eares and every deepe Well ought to have two Buckets etc.'

The *Sharpe Revenge* opens with a walk-on from that mythical, tutelary London figure, Long Meg of Westminster. Long Meg, so called from her height which was over the contemporary average, had been one of the owners of the celebrated brothel the Hollands Leaguer (situated by the Thames at Southwark, it featured a purpose-built moat, exceptionally beautiful girls and concomitantly high prices). She was also fêted as a kitchen maid-turned-military heroine, for her supposed role at the Battle of Boulogne (1544).

In *Peirce's Supererogation, or a New Praise of the Old Asse* (1600) Gabriel Harvey wrote as follows. 'Long Megg of Westminster would have bene ashamed to disgrace her Sonday bonet with her Satterday witt. She knew some rules of decorum: and although she were a lustie bounsing rampe, somewhat like Gallemella, or maide Marian, it was she not such a roinish rannell, or such a dissolute gillian-flurtes, as this wainscot-faced Tomboy.'

A Lancashire girl, she had come down to London around 1540 and after tricking the carrier out of his fare, took a job at a taphouse (possibly the same Eagle tavern that offered Marie Lloyd her first gig three centuries later). According to Frank Chandler she 'loved good company, especially affecting that of Dr. [John] Skelton, the jester Will Sommers, and the Spanish Knight, Sir James of Castille. She delighted to assume man's apparel, and at last went to the wars with King Henry and returned wedded to a soldier, and set up a public house at Islington.'* It was in masculine drag that she fought and defeated the notable braggart, Castille. Her life had already been the

---

* F. W. Chandler, *Literature of Roguery* (1907), pp.144–145

subject of a number of chapbooks, and Jonson mentioned her in *The Gypsies Metamorphosed* (1621) where he uses her name as generic for any exceptionally tall woman. In 1598 she appears in Thomas Deloney's *The Gentle Craft*, a form of broad-humoured jest-book otherwise focusing on the glory and importance of shoemakers. The 'definitive version' appeared in 1635: *The life of Long Meg of Westminster: containing the mad merry pranks she played in her life time, not onely in performing sundry quarrels with divers ruffians about London, but also how valiantly she behaued her selfe in the warres of Bolloingne* [i.e. Boulogne].

This last was presumably another occasion on which Meg dressed as a man. A French soldier came forward to challenge the English.

> After a long and desperate combate Meg ouerthrew him and pulling out her Scymeter cut off his head, then taking off her Burganet [a light steel cap, used by the infantry], her hair did fall about her ears, whereby the Frenchmen perceived that she was a Woman, and the English giving a great shout. Meg, by a drum sent to the Dolphin [i.e. the *Dauphin*, heir to the French throne] his Souldiers head, and said, an English woman sent it.[*]

Back from the wars, and by now married to a soldier, she became landlady of a tavern in Islington, north London. When one Huffing [i.e. boastful, thuggish] Dick attacked one of her maids, she first beat him with a staff, then informed him 'Thou shalt put my Maides Peticoates on, and follow me to day to dinner with a Sword and a Buckler, and I will be drest in mans apparell.' She duly put on her men's clothes, and paraded petticoated Dick

* *Life & Pranks* (1635) sig. B22.

through the streets, finally arriving at an inn where she displayed him to the amusement of an aristocratic friend and his guests.

Although in some stories she may have qualified as a villain, and thus added extra titillation for those who enjoyed reading of such immoral individuals, in this supposedly women-authored text she appears as a feminist saviour. Like King Arthur, who will allegedly rise from his grave when England calls, 'the famous Amazon Long Magdalena' emerges from hers after 'hearing the abuse of other women'. Appalled that 'any one who was a mother's son / Should thus affront our sex', she addresses Sir Seldom Sober and calls on him 'to confess thine error, fall upon thy knees, / From us to beg thy pardon by degrees.' As for males in general, she suggests they note her physical prowess and its previous male victims and warns future transgressors that 'Thou knowest thy doom, if farther thou offend.'*

If the Lectures have multiple targets – albeit every one a husband – the Revenge is a rebuttal and at the same time a justification. Once Long Meg has returned to the shades Mesdames Tattle-well and Hit-him-home start to bring Sir Seldom to boot.

'You Sir Seldome Sober . . . be founde guilty of Calumny, scandall and most palpable Contradiction'† and therefore . . . at best, they think he may have been drunk, that 'when you writ this bitter invective you were either in your holyday and hic-up healths, in your bouzing Cups, and bouncing Cans.'

---

* Meg, as rough, tough anti-heroine, had European sisters. Among them Dulle Griet, folk heroine among Flemish peasants (and painted by Pieter Brueghel the Elder). Her name was often Englished as Dull Gret, but there was an alternative: Mad Meg and she flourished around 1560, contemporary with Long Meg. Her moment of glory came with an assault on hell itself by an all-woman army, with Griet as its general.
† All quotes from *The Women's Sharpe Revenge* passim.

Echoing the Crabtree 'author' Mary Make-peace, they write 'from our Mannor of Make-peace' but there is not much molli-fying on offer. Noting [p.5] that the three lectures 'have laide most false aspersions upon all women generally, some they have texted with incontinency . . . incivility . . . scolding . . . drink-ing . . . backbiting . . . slandering . . . lying . . . gossiping' they accept that women are by no means perfect but that male double standards are unacceptable. A women's failings last a lifetime, a man's are soon forgotten: the 'shame or scandall of a whoremon-ger is a nine dayes wonder [. . .] a record written in sand . . . the faults of a weake woman . . . are ingraven in brasse.' As for Sir Seldom's accusations he is nothing but a 'scoffing fool' and it were 'better for a man to be born foolish than to use his wits unwisely'; 'he is guilty of detraction and slander . . . the super-fluity of a cankered heart overcome with choler' and 'it is the fashion of all these calumniating Coxecombs to bite those by the backe, whom they know not how to catch by the bellies'. Are women truly less intelligent and educated than men? If they are then the reason is because they are not allowed to be: they are allowed no education, just 'housewife stuff' (i.e. sewing/music/singing).

And lest Sir Seldom might come too near a mirror, they note his furrowed complexion and a horrid beard; they, meanwhile 'are a true representation of a delectable garden of intermixed Roses and Lillies . . . But sure Sir Seldome (or never) Sober, your Father was some Jakes-Farmer [privy-cleaner] and your Mother a Midwife, or hee some Rake-shame, or Ragg-gatherer, and shee the daughter of a Dung-hill'.

They deal with women's supposed verbosity – if women supposedly talk too much then men write too much (as, for instance, in the Crabtree lectures) and their alleged irrelevance to male society –'if wee were such toyes and trifles, or so vile and vitious . . . how comes this seeking, this suing, this Courting, this cogging, this prating, this protecting, this vowing, this swearing, but only to compasse a smile, a kinde look, a favour, or a good word from one of us?' If, in the end, 'men see such dangers in women, why doe they not let them alone?' They give their answer to the aspersion cast upon women for being Gossips. And note that Women after all, are not born to be men's slaves. All the tropes are refuted: why do women lie? To save their husbands' images; 'if we women bee addicted to pride it is because of you men' who tell women how beautiful they are. They are also less than impressed by male self-regard. 'Mighty men (for so you thinke your selves) when alas we know by proofe, that when you brave Masculines are at any time encountered by our FemineSexe, even in the first assault, you are as soonetam'd as talkt with.'

They also deplore the terminology of his language, even if they do rate him (perhaps proudly) with speakers of their own gender: his 'Tinkerly tearmes more foule-tongu'd than a Fishwife, and more open-mouth'd than any Oyster-wench.' Their own slang lexis, perhaps in rivalry with their Billingsgate sisters, is equally pungent. These terms may be aimed at Sir Seldom Sober, but it is our female authors who are using them.

Aside from those few terms that overlap with John Taylor, drink plays the largest role, especially at pp.173–175 where they delineate some thirteen synonyms, of which the first few are names for the toasts one drinks en route to excess: 'The first Health is call'd a *Whiffe*, the second a *Slash*, the third a *Hunch*, the fourth *Thrust*, the fifth is call'd *Pot-shaken*, the sixth is seeing the *Lions*, the seventh he is *scratch'd*, the eighth, his *Nose is dirty*, the ninth he hath *whipt the Catt*, the tenth, he is *fox'd*, the

eleventh, he is *Bewitch'd*, the twelfth, he is *Blinde*, and the thirteenth, and last, he is drunke.' Drunkenness also brings *tap-lash*,
the dregs of a barrel, and thus third-rate beer, the *maltworm* and
the *pot-leech* (drunkards)and the adjectives *pot-valiant, stewed as
a prune, mulled* and *pickled*. With drink comes tobacco, *mund-
unga*, and sex: the *town bull* (a rural womaniser and no congratulation), the *cock of the game* (probably self-appointed) and the
sword (a penis and one of many equations of that organ with
'boys' toys'). The poetic *play at wiley beguile me* is to have sex and
madame mackerell a bawd (not, as assumed from the fish, though
fish and femininity are often combined in slang, but from the
Dutch *makelaar*, a merchant). There is *roaring* (hooliganism)
and whoring, and a number of terms for physical assault: 'I have
heard some to brag, as he *payd one*, hee *pepperd* another, hee
sawced a third, he *anointed* a fourth, hee *scowred* a fifth.' To have
diarrhoea is to *squirt* (*the squirt* is contemporaneous), and the
dismissive exclamation *a turd in your teeth!* and the term *sir-
reverence*, excrement* keep up the latrinal feel. (The authors use
the term in a pun when they accuse the author of being 'ambi-
tious to purchase a Knight-hood & to adde a sir-reverence to
your name'.) To *wind up one's bottom*, however, refers to drink
and meant to leave a mouthful of alcohol in the glass; it was
considered rude to one's fellow-drinkers. Finally another phrase,
over the left shoulder, used to express distrust; the term is often

---

* A fourteenth-century formal phrase; Nares *Glossary* (1822), suggests originally *save
reverence*, meaning 'begging your pardon' and used as 'a kind of apologetical apostrophe,
when anything was said that might be thought filthy, or indecent'. By the late sixteenth
century it had taken on this euphemistic secondary meaning and is the basis of the
twentieth century+ euphemism to 'excuse oneself' and the schoolchild's cry of 'Can I be
excused?' Thus: 'Reverence, an ancient custom which obliges any person easing himself
near the highway or foot-path, on the Word Reverence being given to him by a
Passenger, to take his Hat between his Teeth, and without moving from his station to
throw it over his head, by which it frequently fell into the Excrement. This was considered as a Punishment for the Breach of Delicacy' (Grose, 1788).

accentuated by gesturing over the left shoulder with the thumb and may reflect the superstitious throwing of spilled salt over one's left shoulder, thus one takes such dubious information 'with a pinch of salt'.

They also quote Seldom Sober's introduction, through the mouth of a Country Farmers wife, of a range of insults that he, not they, aimed at men 'Wittall, Mopus and Moonecalf, Hobbinol and Hobnailes, Lurden and Looby, Francis Fill-gut and Furmity-pot, Booby and Blockhead, Dunce and Dotard Bull-beife, Barley pudding, Sim Slabber-chops and the like.'

This gendered call-and-response pattern continued through the period. Among the most interesting variations appeared in 1662, though it contained no slang, and both parts of the argument were created by a single author: the poet and philosopher Margaret Cavendish, the Duchess of Newcastle. Her *Orations of Divers Sorts* covered a wide variety of topics, with a pro followed almost invariably by a con. Thus 'An Oration against the Liberty of Women' is followed by 'An Oration for the Liberty of Women'. And in the 'Femal Orations' (pp.225–230) that follow, she uses women speakers to speak for and against what might be termed feminism, but finally and resoundingly, gives the last word to the status quo. However she puts up no defence of one 'Foolish Custom': the scapegoating (in a skimmington ride), of a neighbour in place of a husband who permits himself to be beaten by his wife. 'For the Foolish Husband of Such a Wife Rampant, should ride in Disgrace, Scorn, and Pain, by Reason he Suffers himself to be degraded of his Masculine Authority.' * Like the

* M. Cavendish, *Orations of Divers Sorts* (1662), pt X p.221; Cavendish also authored a pair of feminist fantasies – 'The Liberty of Women' and *Travelia* – whose protagonists represent *femmes fortes*, which one might translate as 'riot grrls'.

cuckold, who had no-one to blame but himself, the weak husband deserved his own punishment.

What Roger Thompson has specified as 'two Restoration contributions to the *querelle des femmes*' or 'this Restoration rugby match'* came as the century drew to its close. *The XV comforts of rash and inconsiderate marriage, or, Select animadversions upon the miscarriage of a wedded state* appeared in 1682. There was no stated author. Twelve months later came the fight-back: *The womens advocate, or, XV real comforts of matrimony, Written by a Person of Quality of the Female Sex.* If the initial volley had been supposedly 'done out the French', then the riposte offered a brief introduction signed by 'Votre Bonne Aime & Tres Humble Servante'.

Marriage, and not only that which is judged 'rash and inconsiderate', comes over as a mistake. Like slang's images of the vagina, it is a bad place, dangerous, illusory and ultimately a literal man-trap. Like some modern lad's mag or sodden stag-night orator, the preface stresses how nothing improves a man's life like unrestrained autonomy. To ignore such pleasure can only appeal to those who would 'hug their fetters and embrace their Chains'. Man, once free, is caught within 'the Net of Matrimony': 'The wild Beasts of the desert are ensnar'd and taken in Pitfals by the Craft and Cunning of the wary Hunstman.' Such pitfalls, conveniently mimicking the female reproductive system, 'are narrow at top, and broad at Bottom' and offer no possibility of escape. 'The same thing may be said of [. . .] Matrimony, a sad state [. . .] from whence there is no Redemption.' The so-called 'comforts' of matrimony are 'the greatest Misfortunes, Pains, Discontents and Torments'. The

---

* Thompson op. cit. p.112.

anonymous author is adamant: husbands deserve no sympathy, merely the 'Burial of an Ass'. Let them 'drop into the Grave without either Tears or pity'.*

The text, as advertised, offers detail on the non-existent 'comforts' of the hapless hubby. Once trapped at home he resembles no free man, but *John* Hold-my-staff [a servant]†. Whatever may have been hoped and promised, all goes downhill and while he stays in the house, she has other fish to fry: 'through her loose course of life the Candle burns at both ends, they lie at Rack and Manger [. . .] and all tends to Ruin and Destruction'. Like so many women in these diatribes she is branded as sluttish: she 'enjoys her stolen Amours undiscovered: grows at length as common as a Barber's Chair'. It is, supposedly, his own fault: like so many men in these stories, his sex drive is lacking: 'She wants due Benevolence, and requires more Milk than he can give her and is therefore resolved to Lap elsewhere'. 'Abroad she roams and picks up the first Stallion that comes to hand' though this is but the first of many, since 'Every one has a fling at his Jacket, and the Gallant many at his Wife's Placket' and 'He paces about the Town Actaeonniz'd'.‡

And so it goes. The wives – some scolds, some trollops – put their various husbands through all conceivable wringers. A dose of clap, wide-spectrum cuckolding (one wife attends a party with her husband and only he is unaware that she has had every

---

* Thompson op. cit. Preface.
† All quotes from *The XV comforts of rash and inconsiderate marriage, or, Select animadversions upon the miscarriage of a wedded state* passim.
‡ This is a succession of double entendres: *benevolence*, literally kindness to others was a popular synonym for intercourse; *milk* is semen, *lap*, a pun on *lap*, to drink and slang *lap*, the female genitals and thus intercourse, *stallion* a male lover, *placket* a garment metonymised as the vagina and *Actaeon* a mythological cuckold. *Jacket* is used for human skin in slang, and could thus work here, but it is not recorded until later (thus note West Indies *give someone a jacket*, for a married woman to conceive and bear a child by her lover and pass it off to her husband as his).

man in the room), a touch of prototypical *Belle de Jour* for pin-money, his demotion to little more than a useful servant (though with none of the sexual perks that the strapping, virile footman of such tales of marital disharmony invariably enjoys). It is all thoroughly misogynistic: in short, 'wife' if not synonymous with 'nag' is another word for 'whore'. As the modern French author Celine would say: 'It's hate that makes slang' and both are highly visible here.

The reply is perhaps less hateful, but definitely slangy. It does not, however, pretend to the 'make-peace' guise of earlier pamphlets. In a preface aimed at 'The Injur'd Ladies', while the author 'would not have you Massacre them all' she suggests firmly that the readership should learn up her treatise by heart 'so that you may be able to repay your murmering, repining, complaining ill-natur'd Husbands, your domineering, spend-thrifts, and by-hole-hunters in their own coyn.'

She also employs some interesting neologisms: *flipperous*, superficial and characteristic of he whom she calls a 'Flibergebit"; *Lacedemonians* (for whom she doesn't 'care a F—t') which despite its usual meaning of Spartans, seems to refer to whores, and this plays on *laced mutton*; *nooning*, the seventeenth-century equivalent to the modern *matinee* or *cinq-a-sept*, i.e. adulterous afternoon sex (in this anecdote the husband is locked in a large chest, with the randy couple bouncing on its top). *Scaperloytring* means wandering or hanging around, possibly in pursuit of (adulterous) sex; it can have negative consequence and she notes 'Fatal scaperloytring sometimes, that frequently brings the lascivious Prodigal more than Circumcis'd from the Surgeon, and sends him Noseless to the grave' the loss of a nose, of course, implying

---

* All quotes from *The Women's Advocate, or, XV Real Comforts of Matrimony, Written by a Person of Quality of the Female Sex* passim.

the acquisition of syphilis. Such venereal souvenirs as painful pustules feature as the *Nuts of Priapus* and if she sees them a woman would best 'careful of her husbands ware.' But then again, as she says, the clap is everywhere and there is 'so much work for the Surgeons and Pintle-smiths about this Town [. . .] such swarms of Charlatans and Knights of the Syringe in every corner of the City.' What she terms *light housewives* or *daughters of joy*, do not always produce happiness. 'But who can keep his mistris from gadding? [. . .] Where's your Empire and Dominion there Sir? She scorns the domineering Cully.' Talking of punks or mistresses, she offers another neologism – cowbaby – to fool which seems to play on *calf*, which applied to humans means a foolish male, and thus his escort treats him.

She offers advice: 'Surfeits are dangerous; and the surfeit of a long thing with one eye, may be as deadly as the surfeit of a long thing with nine eyes [i.e. a lamprey]. *Change your Cock*, was a piece of advice once given to a Lady, by a person of eminent gravity.'

Meanwhile her husband is off on his own 'unruly and wandring footsteps of scaperloytring Leachery', in this case visting 'the Taylors Wife, I see by your *hang-dog* countenance.' In which case, 'I'le spoil your swan-hopping' and sends the 'old fool . . . horn-mad'.

We also receive her disdainful assessment of the BDSM frolics that give a little life to otherwise enfeebled members: 'But what may we think of those decrepit half-pint Lechers [. . .] as sapless as a dry'd Fennel-stalk, yet you may dog them shuffling along with their crickling [creaking] hams, till they pop into one of their old haunts of inquity? Where they call for *Vice* to correct *Sin*, for forgetting their former lessons of Lasciviousness, while the sturdy Quean belabours their buttocks, till their impotent

wimbles peep out of their bellies to beg a reprieve for their Tayls.'
English culture, though the term was three hundred years into
the future, has a lengthy backstory.*

Then there are [. . .]

'some, that when their other Tackle fails them, love to forni-
cate with their eyes': 'Let a handsome draggletail [literally
one whose dress drags along the ground; effectively a prosti-
tute] come in sight, and they cry, *Fair and sluttish*' and others
who go for something more elaborate: along with a 'leash or
a leash and a half [i.e. three or four] of young Queans in his
pay [. . .] when they came to supper, they were to enter and
sit down as naked as they were born, and fall to merrily,
while he, as naked as they, crept under the Table, and there
lay *erring* and *snarling* like a Dog, and snapping sometimes
at their Shins, sometimes at their thighs, and crunching the
bones which they threw him.'

If he can go out drinking, so can she. After all, men use liquor as
an excuse for their bad behaviour 'flinging their Glasses over their
Shoulders, [. . .] burning their Coats, hats and Perriwigs, and then
running to Bawdihouses, mad as March-hares, their *Scowring*, as
they call it, [. . .] breaking peoples Windows, their quarrels with
the Watch.'† In which case, 'Let her toss off her Noggins by Wholesale; let the Brandy-Firkin stand by her bed-side.'

* For instance a throwaway line in the *Knavery of Astrology* by 'Tell-Troth' in 1680: 'Of
late years there's a neat *Invention*, called *Flogging*, invented on purpose to pleasure *Old
Fumblers*, or weak *Youngsters*: what it is, they may easily learn at *Betty B-'s School*, or
Moorfields.'
† A *scourer* was a dissolute young man who roamed the streets, usually as one of a gang,
beating up passers-by, breaking windows, attacking the watch and generally acting in a
hooligan manner. The type was notorious enough for Thomas Shadwell to write a play
The Scowrers in 1691.

All in all the *XV Real Comforts* uses thirty-five slang terms. Aside from those already listed there is *Bromigham-groat*, a counterfeit fourpenny coin (from Birmingham, the supposed origin of such debased coinage), *flams*, *shams* and *flim-flams*, all meaning lies and trickery; *old hunks*, a surly miser, perhaps tipping the feathered hat to *Hunks*, a well-known bear, kept in seventeenth-century London for baiting, though like bears, the miser hugs, in this case his money, and the surly individual is a *bear* (*with a sore head*). To *take pepper in the nose* is to become angry, as does a wife who sees 'a *Nickapoop* revealing the secrets of his wife to his own ignominy'; while a rampant male is *hot-codpiec'd*. The 'cunning *tongue-pad* Slut [who] undermines the very heart of a man' is one who persuades one to act foolishly or against one's will; the *crack rope*, one who might 'crack' or break a hangman's noose, is another con-man and the author cites a gang who persuade a 'credulous goose' that they can turn him invisible. Then there are the unfortunate consequences of adultery: Mrs *Betty* has been Moulding of Cockle-bread,*and her Mother discovers it.' Now 'The Daughter have got a By-blow [a bastard] in her Belly.' Finally, a proverb: 'A T[ur]d's as good for a Sow as a Pancake.'

There is no sense that in any such give-and-take one side actually 'won' or 'lost'. But they vented and perhaps that was the point. Certainly there were many such pamphlets, answered or simply declaratory. Like the French revolution, which included sexual scurrility in its propagandising, the Civil War tossed

---

* John Aubrey defined this around 1697: 'Young wenches have a wanton sport which they call moulding of cockle-bread, viz. they get upon a table-board, and then gather up their knees and their coates with their hands as high as they can, and then they wabble to and fro, as if they were kneading of dowgh, and say these words, viz. My dame is sick and gonne to bed, And I'le go mould my Cockle-bread.' Ostensibly linked to *cockle*, to wobble unsteadily, but very likely nodding to *cock*, the penis.

around smears and slurs. Women of both sides – puritan round-heads and hedonistic cavaliers – were pictured as either insatiable sluts or sex-starved spinsters (unusually in the absence of their war-making partners). In 1647 appeared *The City-Dames petition*, a complaint by female Cavaliers (or at least put in such mouths) of their frustration while husbands were at the front. The text is filled with double entendres:

> [*T*]*rading* [i.e. whoring] of all sorts have been mightily impeded, unless a little in the *Suburbs* [the red light zones], where your *French Commodities* [the vagina, possibly diseased] are so frequently vendible*. [W]hen our poore husbands have been hard at it all day, must bee forced (though may be disabled in the service) to *work* [to have sex] at night and the only solution seems to come in the form of [A] mouse-hair'd fellow, with a *long thing* God blesse us by his side, as rusty as himself.

If anyone still missed the point, they could check the authors: Mrs I Stradling, Obediah Placket, Mary Lecher, Sarah Lovesicke, P. Horne, Rachel Wantall, Dorothy Swiveall, Priscilla Tooly, Mrs E. Overdooe, Hannah Snatchall, K. Stretch, A. Troublesome, Jo. Scanted, Rebecca Dooling, &c.

Much the same themes came, the same year, with *The parliament of ladies. Or Divers remarkable passages of ladies in Spring-Garden* by Henry Neville. Another example of heavy-handed ventriloquising, Neville teased a variety of named and real Cavalier women. Among his sniggerings (starting with the title's *passages* which may well have been a coarse pun; *Spring garden*

---

* All quotes from *The City-Dames petition* passim.

was certainly the home of well-known brothels) were their vote that 'no round head should dare come into any of their quarters,' and that they gave themselves 'leave to sell, give away, or otherwise to dispose of their french commodities, without paying Excise or custome.' There were also the inevitable references to Ladies who 'negotiated, with members of both Houses' and, mocking males for once, the admission that 'divers weak persons have crept into places beyond their abilities.'

Neville also offered, *Newes from the New Exchange, or The commonvvealth of ladies, drawn to the life, in their severall characters and concernments*. Printed in the year, of women without grace, 1650. No ventriloquising was offered, but again the targets were all well-known. For instance Lady Carlisle 'being charged in the Fore-deck by Master Hollis, in the Poop by Master Pym, whilst she clapt my Lord of Holland under hatches [. . .]: [S]he was put in the Tower, where she now pines away for want of fresh-Cod, and [. . .] My L[ords] Londen, Lauderdale and Dumferling were clapt in her hole of Repentence.

Neville had no copyright on female parliaments. *The parlament of vvomen With the merry lawes by them newly enacted* appeared in 1640. Its subtitle promised a female point of view.

> *To live in more ease, pompe, pride, and wantonnesse: but especially that they might have superiority and domineere over their husbands: with a new way found out by them to cure any old or new cuckolds, and how both parties may recover their credit and honesty againe.*

And while there is no named author, the voice is certainly female. She bemoans the married woman's frustration, 'A Fools bolt (like my husbands) is soon shot' and she is left like so many wives,

'sighing and groaning, as if her very twatling-strings would break
[. . .] making her moan to the curtains, fumbling and biting or
tearing the Sheets'[. . .] and suggests a solution: 'Ought not, I
say, such women to have two or three Husbands.'

Or if not polygamy, then its short-term equivalent: adultery.
As ever, what's good for the gander . . . Says one Dorcas
Doe-Little (using at least eight double entendres on the theme of
'playing' and 'games') 'As hee games abroad, so I play at home: If
he be at Bowles and kisse the mistris, I can for recreation play at
rubbers with his man: when he hath been all the day at passage
and hazard, at night he comes home and playes with me at
Doublets, Baramel-ace and backegammon [. . .] when he with
his Sweet-hearts ventures his state at the Hole, I with his servant
can passe away the time at In and In.'

Other female members include *Mistris Rachel Rattle a pace*
[*rattle*: to have sex and reminiscent of the older *Mort Wap-apace*,
a sexually eager girl] who in one of bawdy's many tributes to
millers, hopes that when 'I bringing my Sacke to the Mill, it may
be grinded', but advocates less kindness to her actual husband:
'If he cog and offer to kisse you [. . .] bid them take you about
the middle and kisse the heaviest end.' In other words, 'tell him
to kiss my arse!' The moral, accepted by all the Parliament, is
simple: 'The chiefe heads of the womens Lawe [. . .] That women
may twang it as well as their husbands.'

In 1660, on the very cusp of restoration, came *Select city
quaeries discovering several cheats, abuses and subtilties of the city
bawds, whores, and trapanners*. This predates various similar
essays in faux-naive, quasi libellous nudge-nudgery e.g. the
short-lived 1840s 'newspaper' *Paul Pry*. Its heavy-handed, but
judiciously self-censored entries featured a variety of well-known
City merchants and their ladies.

Whether Diana his Mistris does not carry a Fiddle in her A—, because of the frequent fingering her Instrument.*

Whether P—at the Crown near Broadstreet did ever read Juvenals Description of a Wittal.

Whether the Comb-makers Complaint in Houndsditch be currant, that his wife hath no Commodity; and whether [. . .] Miles (the barber Chirurgion) could not clear her passage with his Womb-perspective Instrument.

Whether Mrs S—does not stop the Orifice of her C—with a Clout, to keep the old man her Husbands Rag out.

Instrument, wittal, commodity, arse and just plain *cunt*: we get the picture.

Finally, that ever-popular, if boneless, bone of contention: the impotent male. Like the Jews, who in anti-semitic fantasies combine world-domination with impoverished parasitism, the married man is simultaneously both rampant philanderer and literal *limp-dick*. No serving-girl may be safe; no wife is ever satisfied.

The theme runs through many contemporary pamphlets. In 1647 *A remonstrance of the shee-citizens of London. And of many thousands of other the free-borne women of England* who called for the many *grievances, and burdens they now lie under* linked politics and porn in an orgy of double entendres. Calling on the Puritan Col. Luttrell 'a stiff stander for the subjects Liberties' they went on to complain of their husbands 'defaults or debilities' and suggest that this being the case, 'we may our selves trade a broad in the country and utter our warres [wares, i.e. vaginas] to our best advantage.' What they need is for the King and his imbroidered Courtiers to return to town, bringing with them

* All quotes *Select city quaeries discovering several cheats, abuses and subtilties of the city bawds, whores, and trepanners* (1660) passim.

'the heavenly dew that they were wont daily to water us with, and to our infinite joy, jog us [. . .] stuffing our bellies with cakes, and creame.'*

The problem is perhaps best seen in a publication of 1675: *Fumblers-Hall, kept and holden in Feeble-Court, at the sign of the Labour-in-vain, in Doe-little-Lane, wherein divers complaints &agrievances, out of the feminines in* Cornucopia, *are presented to the grave wisdoms of the masters of that company: concerning non-performance, want of due benevolence, deficiencie and corporal disabilities in man-kind, whereby poor distressed females languish under a pressing weight of misery, not only to the great decay of their trade and occupations, but to the destruction of generation it self. Whereunto is added the second part, newly discovered and set forth for information of delinquents that are to answer to these interrogations that shall be objected against them.*

As the title suggests (the sign of Labour-in-Vain, Feeble Court, Doe-little Lane, the 'horn' pun of Cornucopia) it is all great fun. Like the female parliaments this has a formal setting, a trial conducted by the 'Master and Corporation' of the Hall, itself timbered in 'horn-beam' and with a roof of 'Unicorn-Horn richly guilded, Studded and Imbossed with lesser Horns, of all sorts of colours.'

Under the auspices of Sir Fernando Fumbler, clerk of the company and himself burdened, as the frontispiece reveals, with a substantial pair of horns, all 'artists of the horned trade' are called to witness the proceedings. Six female plaintiffs are pitted against six male defendants. As usual, they have tell-tale names; Allice All-cock, Joan Wou'd-have-more, Doll Hold-up, Kate Knock-well, Nan Tickle-tail, and Bess Bear-up-stiff take on their

* *A Remonstrance of the Shee-Citizens of London* (1647), pp. 3–4.

opposite numbers: Sir Nicholas Fribble, Daniel Doe-little, Fran. Fain-would, Will. Dry-bones, Pete Bad-cock and Simon Silly-P[rick]. Further plaintiffs and defendants include Winnie Wagtail, Susan Shrews-face, Jack Jolly-boy and Joseph Woodcock.

Aside from the 'proper names' which offer such slang as *tickle-tail* and *wagtail*, both whores, *fribble*, a sexually inadequate male, *dry-bones*, an emaciated individual (though here the inference is a lack of 'juice', i.e. semen) plus *cock* and *prick*, the text adds such staples as the *suburbs*, *John-hold-my-staff*, *play at in and in*, *fiddlestick* (a penis), *jack-pudding* and *sheep's-head*, both fools and *alley-bird*, a scold. There are also a trio of wife-to-husband insults: *pawn petticoat*, *smock*, *waistcoat*, all seeming to equate a (weak or effeminate) man with a female undergarment. *Fumbler* itself is first recorded in 1635; this remained the primary use, though the late seventeenth century has a couple of variations that mean a randy young man.

Joan-Wou'd-have-more's complaint is typical of the evidence: 'Hes but a meer Gut, a Chitterling, a fiddle-string that will make no music to a Womans Instrument; yet when I tell him on't, he pulls it out and shakes it, and puts up his fiddle-stick again.' To Allice All-cock, her husband is 'no more to me [. . .] than a straw in the Nostrils of a cow, a very slug, a meer fribble.' Doll Hold-up excoriates Frances Fain-would as a 'Liar, a Dog, a Toast of the foul pit, the froth and scum of hell.' Kate Knock-well bemoans a six-year marriage: 'he told me he was a Clerk, but the Devil of one drop of Ink have I found in his Pen.' Nan Tickle-tail and Peter bad-cock are well-named: she, it appears has borne out her trade and brought home a dose of pox.

And so it goes. The women complain of their husbands' inadequacy, their own frustration and the mockery they experience from their neighbours.

The men, as should perhaps be expected, are as vapid in their defence as they are flaccid between the sheets. 'Every Night she Farts in her sleep,' whinges Allice's husband Sir Nicolas Frible, which [. . .] 'is most hateful to me.' Neither the Master nor Frible's wife are remotely impressed and Sir Nicholas decides that he had best leave home. William Dry-bones accepts that 'horns are my fate'. Only Bess Bear-up-stiff seems to lose her case, and is ordered to be given a yellow coat and banished to the West Indies.

The eighteenth century offers another Bess. This was Bess Weatherby, who in 1760 inspired the celebratory pamphlet 'Great news from hell; or, The devil foil'd by Bess Weatherby.' Bess seems to have been a woman of every part and an admiring poem delights in every one:

Who, like thee, can quaff the Bowl,
Or delight the drinking Soul?
Who can half thy merit boast,
At the luscious Health, or Toast?
Who can tell the wanton Tale
Or the letch'rous Ear regale?
Who, like Thee, the Cully smoak; [nose out a sucker]
Or indulge the looser Joke?

The pamphlet climaxes with Bess' appearance in Hell, there to marry the Devil himself. Here she has the 'Table in a Roar' at her wit and drinks the Devil (who is forced to pour the odd glass onto the floor) and all his guests beneath the table. Unfortunately for the Lord of the Underworld such excess affects him as it does many men and Bess is left frustrated on her wedding night. 'Grumbling and Mumbling' ensues, and after that, to everyone's relief, a divorce.

The scold rarely appeared in court beyond the seventeenth century. Though there were occasions. For instance the US papers of mid-September 1821 variously reported on one Catherine Fields 'indicted and convicted for being a common scold.' The trial, it was noted, was 'excessively amusing . . . from the deversified manner in which the Xantippe pursed her virulent propensities. "Ruder than March wind, she blew a hurricane;" and it was given in evidence that after having scolded the family individually, the bipeds and quadrupeds, the neighbours, hogs, poultry and geese, she would throw the window open at night to scold the watchmen. Her countenance was an index of her temper—sharp, peaked, sallow, and small eyes.'

The key word, however, is probably 'amusing'. No-one seems to have been frightened by Ms Field, no patriarchy felt itself tremble; irritation, perhaps, and a community that had simply run out of patience and used such tools as were available to silence an infuriating member. She lies en route to the scold's modern incarnation, the mother-in-law, drawn by Donald McGill for smutty seaside post-cards, the butt of Max Miller's 'blue-book' jokes, her imprecations usually reduced to smut's trope of choice, the double-entendre. Orwell, writing in 1941, noted how for Britain at least, 'Next to sex, the henpecked husband is the favourite joke. Typical caption: "Did they get an X-ray of your wife's jaw at the hospital?' — 'No, they got a moving picture".' Domestic life à la McGill had 'the drunken, red-nosed husbands roll[ing] home at four in the morning to meet linen-nightgowned wives who wait for them behind the front door, poker in hand.'

On that same route are a couple of popular humour books: *Mrs Caudle's Curtain Lectures* by Douglas Jerrold (later of *Punch*) which appeared in 1845 and *Mrs Rasher's Curtain Lectures* by the author of 'A bad boy's diary', i.e. Metta Victoria Fuller, published in New York in 1884. The curtains in question were those of a four-poster bed; behind them the wife was at liberty to scourge her unfortunate and allegedly peccant husband. The slang was unexceptional: *that beats the Dutch*, *moneybags*, a *whopper* (i.e. a lie), *little minx* and *pot-companion*. At least Mrs Rasher, perhaps deliberately, uses *save our bacon*.

Neither wife appears to draw breath, neither husband to reply. One of John Leech's illustrations for *Mrs Caudle* suggests that while Mrs C's mouth is open wide, Mr C's eyes are tight shut. Perhaps that was the only defence.

In the 1955 stage comedy (filmed in 1956) *Sailor Beware!* she was appositely surnamed Emma Hornett, played by newcomer Peggy Mount. The critic Ken Tynan told *Observer* readers how Mount/Hornett 'scorches the earth about her' and noted 'the savage impatience' of her acting. The first-nighters gave her a standing ovation, admiring the performance but perhaps hopeful of placating such demonic femininity. Soap operas would introduce such as Coronation Street's Ena Sharples (one of a trio of harpies who could have stepped un-modified from a McGill sketch). Later the show offered the wheelchair-bound harridan Maud Grimes, 'the mother-in-law from hell'. The word, much-used, was *battleaxe*, the first record of which came in 1896 with the amplifying note: 'She had a face on her that'd fade flowers.' Yet Orwell saw the upside: if humour gives us 'jokes about nagging wives and tyrannous mothers-in-law. They do at least imply a stable society in which marriage is indissoluble and family loyalty taken for granted.'

As 'A Smoky House & A Scolding Wife',*a ballad of 1818, had already put it, such eruptions were all part of life's rich

---

* *New Evergreen, Being a Select Collection of the Most Celebrated Songs* (1818).

pattern – wasn't this, after all, exactly what one expected from a woman – nothing that couldn't be cured with a foaming tankard:

My wife scolds – my houses smokes – an ev're thing goes wrong
So off I to the alehouse go, and chant a merry song

It is harder to see the prototype scold as a creature of comfort, whether of her own volition or through her neighbour's eyes and ears.

5. Billingsgate

Where is there more scolding than at Billingsgate? And yet where more love and friendship? Those very woman you saw engag'd tongues and nails just now, you shall see the next moment bubbing [drinking] together like sworn sisters.

XV Real Comforts of Marriage 1683

Billingsgate. As in fish. As in *Belin's Gate* which may memorialise one Belin, who, according to Charles Dickens Jr's *Dictionary of the Thames* (1881) which quoted Geoffrey of Monmouth, was a king and built the first water gate on the site around 400 CE. The gate, giving onto the Thames, was indeed a water one, and an original quay once existed, as perhaps did a southern section of the city wall erected to hold back the river; both have long vanished in the unequal battle of stolid land and energetic water. Belin, however, may have been less grand, and merely the owner of the riverine acreage.

Fish were one of the cargos landed there from the thirteenth century and earlier (the trade is mentioned in the laws of Ethelred), but the piscine link only became formal in 1699 when a statute declared the site as the city's single fish market; after that it's all open sheds and *bummarees* (etymology sadly unknown) bargaining over freshly unloaded catch until the

Victorians, as was their way, required something more splendid. That appeared mid-nineteenth century – the building is still there: a mix of offices and party space – and lasted till 1982 when the market packed up and relocated at Poplar.

Fish meant sailors but also fish wives, sometimes known as *fish fags* (defined by Hotten in 1873 as a generic for 'any scolding, vixenish foul-mouthed woman'; the *fag* perhaps an abbreviation of *faggot*, an unflattering synonym for 'woman'), and generally identified with language as foul as the guts or *puddings* they ripped from their ichthyoid stock-in-trade.* The three-dimensional form of the old term 'cry stinking fish'. The fishwife was often bracketed with her sister-in-trade, the oyster-woman, another whose tongue was considered over-ripe. The eponymy of the place name and the alleged foulness of the language used by those who worked there is first recorded in 1676 and flourished as a stereotype for three centuries. The fish fag's vocabulary could sometimes be loaned to men – such as he who in 1851 displayed a 'coarseness of language [that] emphatically betrays him as obscene slang does the fishfag' but actual evidence was still withheld.

It is also possible – consciously or otherwise – that the link of foul language and its female users reflects another of slang's adoptions of *fish*: as an image – misogynistic as ever – of the vagina (e.g. *bit of skate, bearded clam, old ling, oyster, cock* – as in *coquille*, a cockleshell – and of course *fish* itself). The seventeenth-century poet Wycherley termed oysters a 'juicy, salt commodity' in his poem *'To a Pretty* Young Woman, *who*

---

* France's equivalent, the *poissarde*, i.e. fish-wife, was also known for abuse ('marchande aux halles grossière et hardie dans ses manières et son langage' *TLiF*), and like Billingsgate, also meant 'bad' language (the *poissardes* also spearheaded many riots during the Revolution).

opening Oisters said, She wou'd open for Her, and me too; since 'twas for her Pleasure'. The poem is filled with sexual imagery and slang: *juicy*, sexy, *salt*, randy (of a woman), *commodity*, *old ling* and *oyster* itself, all the vagina. The poet also names '*Venus, that Fish-Wife*' and begs 'Open your Legs, not Shells for me.'

If one cannot gender slang then occasionally one can do so for its specifics. As 'bad' language created by an identifiable occupation, 'Billingsgate', product of London's fish-wives, can be seen as the female predecessor of 'bullocky', the notoriously lurid outpourings of Australia's male bullock-drivers. And if the latter tended to be aimed at the unfortunate draft-animals, especially when stuck in some clinging bog, rather than a fellow man, then Billingsgate was stereotyped as targeting other women.

As 'The Husband's speech to one of his Neighbours, out of his wives hearing' in the Juniper Lectures explained:

It is a schoole where shame-fac'd women may
Heare impudence anatomiz'd so right,
That she, who scarce i' the morn knows what to say
May learne the Art of scolding all by night
They jeere, they fight, they swear, & curse like Roisters,
I'de ne'er abide the place, were't not for Oysters*

Certainly the cartoonists' take was almost invariably woman-to-woman. There are illustrations by such as Rowlandson and Cruikshank: Fishwife A, large of breast, solid of buttock, arms akimbo, mouth agape, assails Fishwife B, similarly accoutred, though perhaps in contrasting colours. But Billingsgate is rarely detailed, any more than bullocky. The caption may offer

---

* *Juniper Lecture* (1639), pp.100–101.

suggestions but they are en-blanked and on occasion the fish-wives are neither female nor engaged with fish but such contemporary politicians as Pitt or Fox *en travesti* and the connoisseur of eponymy has nothing to latch onto.

Yet try to trace some authentic Billingsgate and where is it? The references are too frequent to deny the link but it is hard to go beyond. Fortunately one of the city's great chroniclers, Ned Ward, did pay a visit to the market in its linguistic prime, and recorded it in his *London Spy* (1703). For a change, the fish-fags' target was male. After making their way down

'a narrow Lane, as dark as a Burying Vault, which Stunk of *stale Sprats*, *Piss*, and *Sirreverence* [. . .] We e'en turn'd our selves into the Smoaky *Boozing Ken* [. . .] where round the Fire sat a tatter'd Assembly of Fat Motherly *Flat-caps*, with their *Fish-Baskets* hanging upon their Heads instead of *Riding-hoods*, with every one her *Nipperkin* of warm *Ale* and *Brandy*; and as many Rings upon their Thumbs as belongs to a suit of Bed-Curtains. Everyone as Slender in the Waste as a *Dutch* Skipper in the Buttocks; and look'd together, like a Litter of Squab Elephants. Their Noses were as sharp as the *Gnomon* of a *Dial*, and look'd as Blew as if they had been Frost-nip'd. Their Cheeks were as plump as an Infants Buttocks, but adorn'd with as many Crimson Carnossities as the Face of a Noblemans Butler, who has liv'd Forty Years in a Family; and plainly proved by the depth of their colour, That Brandy is a Nobler Die than Claret. Their Tongues were as loud as the *Temple-Horn*, that calls the *Cuckold-makers* to their Commons: And every word they spoke was at least in the Pitch of *double Gammut*.

Then one looking over her Shoulder, and spying me

behind her, accosts me after this manner; *God save you, honest Master, will you Pledge me? Ay, Dame*, said I, *with all my Heart. Why then, says she, here's a Health to mine A—s, and a Fart for those that owe no Money.*

Lord help my poor Masters, says another, *they look as if they had disoblige'd their Wives or their* Landladies, *and they would not rise, and let them in to Night.*

Ward's companion pulls him away: 'Let's seek another Apartment: These saucy Tongu'd old Whores will tease us to Death.' Bad move. 'Which unhappy words one of them over-heard; and starting up like a Fury, thus gave her Lungs a Breathing.'

You White-liver'd Son of a Fleet-street Bumsitter [prostitute], *begot upon a* [sedan] *Chair at Noonday, between* Ludgate *and* Temple-Bar. *You Puppily off-Spring of a* Mangy Nightwalker, *who was forc'd to Play the Whore an Hour before she cry'd out* [i.e. in childbirth], *to pay the* Bawd *her* Midwife, *for bringing you, you Bastard, into the World. Who is it that you call* Whore?

This time they do leave, 'thankful to Providence we escap'd so imminent a Danger, as if deliver'd from the Rage of so many *Wild-Cats.* And indeed if their Tallons were as sharp as their Tongues, they need not fear a Combat with all the Beasts of America.'

Nonetheless, he returns, and encounters

a Crowd of *Thumb-Ring'd Flat-caps*, from the Age of Seven to Seventy, who sat Snarling and Grunting at one another, over their *Sprats* and *Whitings*, like a pack of *Domestick Dogs* over the *Cook-maids* kindness, or a parcel of hungry *Sows* at a Trough of *Hogwash*; every one looking as sharp as a strolling *Fortune-teller*; that I fear'd they would have pickt my Pocket with their Eyes, or have brought me under an *ill-Tongue* before I could have shot this dangerous Gulph, where the Angry Surges of a Tempestuous Tittle Tattle run Mountain high, dashing into my Ears on every side, that I was as glad when I had weather'd this Storm of Verbosity, as an *Insolvent Creditor* who has slip'd the Villanous gripes of a gang of *Protection-Cursers.**

Nothing lasts and by 1914, a smug report could claim that OLD BILLINGSGATE VERNACULAR LOST. LONDON'S FISH MARKET HAS MENDED ITS MANNERS and stated that '"Aw, git orf, carn'tyer," [is] the most outrageous extent to which one "lady" will venture with another.' Cocks on this particular dunghill, the evangelicals: 'Our Sunday schools, Bands of Hope, temperance meetings, and home visits have done an everlasting amount of good among the people here. It is only the loafers who are responsible for keeping up the bad name of the neighbourhood.'

No matter. Eponymy had transcended geography early on. The play *King Leir* (c.1590 and still unattributed though the cant pamphleteer Robert Greene is one of its possible authors) condemns 'as bad a tongue . . . as any Oysterwife at Billinsgate hath'.[†] A century on and readers were tempted by a book that, among other contents, promised (but sadly failed to deliver) 'Billingsgate Raileries'. The sporting journalist and slang collector Jon Bee (real name John Badcock), in his 1821 rip-off of Egan's *Life in London*, took his Corinthians Bob Tally-ho and

---

* N. Ward, *London Spy*, pt II pp.38–40; pt III p.48.
† *King Leir* (1605) 12.1022L.

Tom Dashall there. An earlier ballad, 'The Bloody Battle at Billingsgate, Beginning with a Scolding bout between two young Fish-women, Doll and Kate', promises much but is conducted in standard English, with a few *trulls* and *punks* thrown in for good measure. There is some tearing of both gowns and hair but in the end all is love and peace, washed down with two quarts of hot ale and brandy. In 1825 Charles Westmacott, another of those who sought inspiration in Egan's best-seller, took his *English Spy* to the fish-market, but only for a slumming *grande dame* to mock the stall-holders by suggesting that their stock was not 'sweet'.* A 'volley of abuse fiery and appalling as the lava of a volcano followed,' concluding, 'Not *sweet*, you— ,' said the offended deity; 'how can I answer for its sweetness, when you have been tickling his gills with your stinking paws?' Teasing the fish-fags was once perhaps a regular form of class warfare, akin to young rakes tipping over the boxes in which stood early-nineteenth century watchmen or 'charlies'. According to Boswell, Johnson, on a bet, volunteered to reduce a fishwife to fury simply by using terms of which she was ignorant. He called her a succession of parts of speech – an 'article,' a 'noun,' a 'pronoun' and so on. The bet was duly won and the unfortunate woman threw herself into the market mud, unable to respond to terms she failed to understand, railing dejectedly against this unfair 'black-guarding'. Not that the fish-fags always lost. In 1747 no. 139 in the ninth edition of *Joe Miller's Jests* offers this encounter:

A Gentlewoman who thought her Servants always cheated her when they went to Billingsgate to buy Fish, was resolved to go thither one Day herself. Arriving at the stall, and

---

* C. Westmacott, *English Spy* (1825) I p.342.

considered the produce over-priced, she offered half its price. Lord, Madam, said the Woman, I must have stole it to sell it at that Price, but you shall have it if you tell me what you do to make your Hands look so white. Nothing, good Woman, answer'd the Gentlewoman, but wear *Dog Skin Gloves. D—n you for a lying B—ch*, reply'd the other, *my husband has worn* Dog-Skin Breeches *these ten Years, and his A—se is as brown as a Nutmeg.*

The term remains but seems wholly defanged. In 1933 the film *Britannia of Billingsgate* (based on a recent play) would be summed up by the BFI as 'this effervescent musical comedy that jaunts between the cloth caps of Billingsgate Fish Market and the top hats and heady glamour of the film world. Things have never looked so good for Billingsgate chippy owner Bessie Bolton (Violet Loraine) after she is presented with the opportunity of becoming the singing sensation of the silver screen – Shepherd's Bush style.' 'Flat-caps', once slang for 'citizens', may have made the trip, 'Billingsgate' railleries did not.

And were the railleries, or such as we can find, that exceptional? Is there a lost parcel of women-only coinages that rivalled the well-documented 'male' obscenities in their gross and gendered excess? We lack proof but perhaps in the end the whole notoriety of 'Billingsgate' was no more than a male's reaction to the simple idea of women's unrestrained effing and blinding, a supposed shock that reminds one of Johnson's affected surprise at the possibility of a female preacher. The form, rather than any special content, caused the ruckus.

Whether Billingsgate, fish-fags or oyster-women were cited or not, the idea of women cursing women regularly amused the composers of the seventeenth century's pamphlets. As all too often, it is hard to name an author, but the speakers, at least, were more than usually female.

The New Brawle, or Turnmill-street against Rosemary Lane appeared in 1654. It was essentially a face-off between top-ranking scolds, each 'team' recruited from a celebrated red-light area, where criminality and prostitution play major roles. Rosemary Lane,* near Tower Bridge, was, in the words of Ned Ward, 'A heathenish part of the Town . . . which in ridicule of fragrant fumes that arise from the musty rotten rags and burnt old shoes, is called by the sweet name of Rosemary Lane. Here such a numberless congregation of *ill-favoured sluts* were gathered together that we thought a fleet of French Protestants had just arrived . . . but upon a true inquisition into the meaning of this tattered multitude, we were informed . . . it was Rag Fair.'[†]

Or to quote the seventeenth-century clergyman Donald Lupton, the street was home to a population of women, who 'traded on their bottom'.[‡] Given its situation Rosemary Lane attracted the same sea-faring clients as frequented nearby Ratcliffe Highway, where as nowhere else in London 'Jack ashore' might be robbed and beaten, but also offered places to eat, drink and sleep not to mention a wide range of commercial sex. Damaris Page, known as 'The Great Bawd of the Seamen', kept two bawdy-houses: a somewhat down-market establishment on the Highway, and a classier place – it was nearer the city and further from the docks – on the Lane. Either way the zone was dangerous: drunken sailors and rampageous whores had no time

---

* All pertinent references taken from Janice Turner *An Anatomy of a 'Disorderly' Neighbourhood: Rosemary Lane and Rag Fair c.1690-1765*. PhD Thesis University of Hertfordshire, 23 June 2014.
† N. Ward, *London Spy* (1703), edited with notes by A. L. Hayward (1927), pp.248–249.
‡ D. Lupton, *London and Country Carbondated and Quartered into Several Characters*(1632), cited in McMullan, *The Canting Crew* (New Jersey, 1984).

for 'decent persons'. The social reformer Francis Place noted girls who 'had ragged dirty shoes and stockings and some no stockings at all . . . many of that time wore no stays, their gowns were low round the neck and open in the front . . . to expose their breasts, this was a fashion that the best dressed among them followed . . . drunken bold women, some with black eyes who could have easily been found fighting with men as with women.'* Such girls were roundly assessed as sexually insatiable and socially out of control. They epitomised contemporary fears of unruly women. There was a degree of circularity: women complained that they grew unruly and looked for new sexual partners because their husband had grown impotent. But as Janice Turner explains, 'Early modern men seemed terrified that women might gain the upper hand and overturn the patriarchal applecart rendering them impotent.' On either score 'the women of Rosemary Lane became symbolic of chaos and urban disorder.'†

Turnmill, or Turnbull Street, another centre of social and sexual squalor, lay on the banks of the increasingly foul and stinking Fleet River near Farringdon. Clerkenwell, just beyond the city walls, was among the original suburbs, where, unrestrained by intra-mural regulations, a variety of 'stink industries', tanning, slaughterhouses and the like, might flourish, as well as bawdyhouses and street prostitution. Turnmill was at one extreme of an area that ran east to Whitecross Street, one of the nineteenth century's 'worst streets in London' and which now sports a blue plaque, an item usually memorialising of the ultra-respectable, but in this case commemorating (and placed there informally) the much-celebrated Priss Fotheringham and her

* BL. Place Papers, BL. Add. MS, 27, 828, Place Papers. Vol. XL, Manners and Morals, Vol. IV, [fol.119].
† Turner op.cit. p.266.

'half-crown chuck-office'. [see chapter 8] *A List of the Parliament of Women* (1679) gives *Turmill-street* [sic] four supposed MPs: Mrs Knock-Ox, Mrs Tripe-wash (both references to the nearby meat market at Smithfield), Mrs Impudent and Mrs Lye-apace.'

Ships are 'she' and so are whores. Slang combines the imagery. In 1600 Thomas Haywood in his play *Edward IV* named a few, the *pinnaces, fly-boats* and *carvels* who cruised the grimy lanes of 'Turnbull and Spital': 'Commend me to blacke Luce, bouncing Bess, and lusty Kate, and the other pretty morsels of man's flesh.' They were also known as 'Venus' nuns' and slang offered a blasphemous subset of *abbesses* (madames) and *nunneries* and *convents* (brothels). Beaumont and Fletcher wrote about it, as did Jonson (his Bartholomew Fair was just up the road in Smithfield) and Dekker pitied the whores as 'The poor catamountains in Turnbull who venture upon the pikes of damnation for single [i.e. minimal] money.' Everyone knew it, including Falstaff who in *Henry IV* part II, mocks justice Shallow who 'hath done nothing but prate to me of the wildness of his youth, and the feats he hath done about Turnbull Street; and every third word a lie.' In its Turnbull-street guise, the road offered a pair of place-specific slang terms: the *Turnbull Street bee* and the *Turnbull Street flea* were, respectively, a venereally diseased prostitute and a crab-louse.

The New Brawle is a dialogue between Jack (representing Turnmill Street) and Doll (spokeswoman for Rosemary Lane) his 'bozzy Wife' (a seeming first recorded use of *bossy*, domineering, and not found again until 1882). Theirs is not a happy marriage, and 'Like Dogge and Catt, they always live at strife.' Fun for the on-lookers, however, and their arguments, suggests the author, 'Would break ones twatling-strings with laughter.'

Like some pantomime city merchant found on stage as the

curtain rises, Jack opens proceedings and, in a literary variation of breaking the fourth wall, lays out his miserable situation to the reading audience: 'Never was poor man so perplex'd with Wife as I am. If there be a destiny in Marriage and *hanging*, would I had wedded the *three-legg'd bride* at *Hidepark corner* [i.e. the three-cornered Tyburn gallows], for I never enjoy'd happy houre since; they say she was made of that cro[o]ked thing call'd a *rib*, but she hath ribb'd me with a vengeance.' And more of the same, including his resigned admission that 'I must wear the *Cuckold's Badge*.' Doll, it appears, is an unabashed scold who 'hath *oyld* her tongue with the Oyl of *Barley*' [i.e. strong beer] and attacks the neighbours, or 'comes home as *Bubby* [tipsy] as a *Tub-woman* [a woman who carries tubs, e.g. of milk] and rather than properly calling him 'Lord and master' prefers 'Roague and Rascall.' He cuts himself short: 'But *mum*, here she comes to speake for herself.'

And so she does. Jack, as contemporary spouses always seemed to be, is a second-rate husband, and second-rate man, 'good for nothing, but to be set in the Chimney-corner, to dry pist clothes on his horns.' Has she looked elsewhere? Well, no surprise with a such a 'suck-egg, a askall [. . .] one who would rob a Hen-roost, rather than pleasure a Wife. Such feeble do-littles makes so many honest Women goe astray.' In fact she can barely tolerate him. '[O]ut thou unnaturall Knave', she tells him, 'a feeble dick thou' but while it is tempting to link this *dick*, generic for 'man' (and thus cognate with *Tom, Dick and Harry*) with slang's penis/fool combination, chronology rules it out. *The New Brawle* seems to coin this link between dick and simpleton – perhaps stereotyping it as a 'peasant' name – but dick as penis must wait until the mid-nineteenth century and even then it appears initially only as a punning nickname, e.g. the rapaciously womanising 'Dick

Forcit". A few pages on and she repeats her dismissal: 'Go, go ye Bulking Roague you, go to your fellow Pick-pockets sirrah, go Pinch the Rum Culle [i.e. rich fool] again of the *Coale* [i.e. money, one of slang's many terms that equate money with one of life's staples]. Poor Jack, he is a 'Villaine, [a] *nitty* [louse-ridden] *Breech'd Knave.*' If he is not actually jeered in the street, it is because some wifely loyalty keeps her from betrayal: '[D]oth not the courtesy of the Wife many times utter her Husbands ill *Commoditie*, or unsaleable *Ware*.'†

'I have a Coltes-tooth in my head still,' she explains, and like the Wife of Bath who uses the same image – a colt's tooth is a horse's first tooth, and thus equated with youth and strength – she claims continuing sprightliness and an active sex-life: Doll is a bawd and her house is very popular. 'Not a *Lansprisado* [a foot-soldier, though slang uses it to mean informer] nor a *Tarpawling* [a sailor and abbreviated, the basis of *Jack Tar*] that furrowed over the rugged botom [*sic*] of *Neptune*, but paid *Custome* to my House. [They] found such sweet entertainment, that as long as one penny was left, they'd be hang'd ere go to sea again. [I] kept two Beds going, and had as much resort to my House, early and late as the best *trader* of them all.' She adheres, no surprises, to the first rule of brothel-keeping: 'No, no, *no money, no Coney*; if they would not be *packing*, I had a *Chamber-pot* to wash them out, or a *Winchester goose* for them to pull.' The pot is self-evident; a *Winchester goose* was a dose of clap and reminded sufferers that the brothels of Southwark, like Clerkenwell beyond the city walls, were owned by the diocese of Winchester. As a

---

* Noted in the *Satirist & Sporting Chronicle* (Sydney) 1 Apr. 1843 page 2/4: 'Here's to the Maiden of blushing fifteen' by Dick Forcit. [. . .] Dick was heard to say, that he was not particular; anything with a cap and a smock on would do for him.
† All quotes from *The New Brawle* (1654) passim.

saying of the era noted, referring to a well-known whore: 'No Goose bit so sore as Bess Broughton's.'

Jack is unimpressed. 'A worshipfull occupation indeed, to keep a *Bawdy-House*, and be as common as a *Barber's Chaire*' which as the contemporary proverb noted, specifically linking it to prostitutes, was 'fit for every one'. In any case, 'your honest house, and *trade* too, grew quickly too hott for you', a pun on *hot* meaning venereally diseased, and he reminds her of when her 'pocky Petrenells were sent to be [. . .] scour'd.' This may use *Petronel* as a generic female name for whore, but the term also meant a large pistol and thus the soldier who had one (and *pistol* in turn was of course open to double meaning); it may at least initially have been the clients, rather than the girls, who were 'pocky'.

Nor is he much a fan of her amatory wanderings: 'I was never *flogg'd* yet [. . .] for keeping a *Case* [a brothel], I was never [. . .] taken by the Watch with the *Bawdy Barber* [. . .] when you ask'd him, Whether he would ride a trott, or a gallop.' Others may like 'Thy nasty *Tap-hole*' and he reminds her of when 'the Cobler's Boy thrust his *Aule* in your *Buttocks*, [Y]e had been at *Mount-Mill* a *knocking* with the *Tinker*.' He mocks her seeming insatiability: 'You'll be in your *Dissembling Fitts* again anon, and none but *Ned* the *Butcher* must come and cure thee again with his lusty [. . .] *Diddle*.'

Doll is unabashed. If she puts it about, so does he: '[H]is wenches are mad for him [. . .] There you are lusty Laurence,* ready to run over them all.' And what of the pox? 'The best

---

* Lusty Lawrence came from a lost sixteenth-century ballad; the term came to mean 'womaniser', 'a stallion that neighs after every female Filly', and Lawrence variously 'got five hundred bastards in one town', 'robbed fifty wenches of their virginity' and fathered various breeds of children.

woman living, and the carefullest, may now and then get a clap, or a Disease from an unwholsom Knave.' Such perhaps as Jack himself who has also suffered 'That Disease made you to be roasted alive in Old *Cornelious* his Tub'.* Nor did the cure work that well, since 'Thy Nose is consum'd by the *Crinkums* [syphilis].' At least she isn't a *white-liver'd Roague*, a thief who knows 'the *Whit* [i.e. Newgate prison, from its patron, Richard 'Dick' Whittington], and the letter T [for 'thief'] well enough', a 'base *Pad*, thou *Prigger* [robber] of *Cullies*, thou *Shop-lift*.' And worse still a grass: 'Out, ye *Whidling Shammock* you, if you had not *peach'd* [i.e. informed] Sirrah, ye might have both been *nubb'd* [hanged] like two Roagues together, but the *Hemp* [i.e. the hangman's rope] was not ripe.'

In the end the victory is hers. 'Good devil, come out of the Woman,' implores Jack, but to no avail. Instead Doll threatens even worse: 'Ile be more terrible to thee than that Shee-Devil in Poppinjay Alley [. . .] she is my Kinswoman and I know she would teach me [. . .] how to torment a husband [and] thou shalt finde (like a Roague thou are) whether I am Devill or no.' And to round things off, the bowls and dishes start flying and we leave Jack begging, 'Oh my head, oh good wife hold your hands' and Doll, as might be expected, merely throwing more.

The tongue combatants, or A sharp dispute between a comical couragious country grasier, and a London bull-feather'd butchers

* The *Cornelian tub*, the contemporary form of treating STDs, presumed an actual *Mother Cornelius*, whether a nurse or a procuress; but note the masculine 'Cornelius' in Taylor, 'Travels to Bohemia' (1620): 'Or had Cornelius but this tub, to drench / His clients that had practis'd too much French' (i.e. venereal disease); other theories include the physician Henry Cornelius Agrippa (1496–1535) a leading advocate of hot baths for medicinal purposes; Henke, in *Gutter Life and Language* (1988), also notes the possible use of a hard dense wood, necessary to withstand the heavy salt brine used in 'pickling' patients, known as *cornel-wood*, 'the wood of *Cornusmascula*, celebrated for its hardness and toughness' (*OED*); also possible puns on *cornel* and the 'cornuted' cuckold or Latin *cornu*, a horn; one's current incapacity is the result of one's *horn*.

twitling, twatling, turbulent, thundering, tempestuous, terrifying, taunting, troublesome, talkative tongu'd wife. With The comical humours of the joviall London gossips, in a dialogue between a maid a wife and a widdow, over a cup of the creature is an all-woman conversation. Published in 1684 it is less a dispute than the schooling of the younger woman by her knowledgeable elders (a 'clean' version, as it were, of much contemporary porn). If there is a moral it is simple: women enjoy getting drunk and staying late at the tavern. Just like men.

The century closes with *An account of a great & famous scold-ling-match between four remarkable scolding fish-women of Rosemary-lane, and the like number of basket-women of Golden-lane, near Cripplegate, on Monday last, upon a wager for five guin-ea's,* published in 1699. This 'Tryal of their Skill at the *Tongue-Tallent-Art*' brings back the women of Rosemary Lane, and this time the harridans' face-off is with their sisters of Golden Lane, now part of the Barbican development and then (as now) one street down from the sordid indulgences of Whitecross Street, and like its neighbour a place where, as a ballad promised, 'do strapping lasses dwell.'

For the Rosemary-lane 'Disputants, alias, Scolders': Widow Webb, Nell Chadd, Dorothy Evans and Joan Boss; in the Golden-lane corner, Bess Pierce, Ann Williams, Barbary* [*sic*] Adams and Sarah Wyatt. The lack of the usual lubricious, pointed pseudonyms suggests that these may even have been real women, though whether the contest was too cannot be proved.

Golden-lane Bess goes first: calls her team 'disputants' but their rivals simply 'Noisemakers'. She's proud of her side, and 'ready to engage with the most obstinate *Mother Damnable*

---

* Presumably Barbara but Barbary was north Africa and perhaps she was black.

that Rosemary-Lane ever yet Spawn'd'. And we're off, Widow Webb comes back hard: 'An excellent rare Speech indeed; I believe you think you are as Cock-sure of the *Five Guinea's* as you was held up against the Butt of Beer by Mr. *R-l-*stapster.' Nor was that encounter – 2/6 the proposed fee – very profitable though 'if all be true as was reported, he made you amends afterwards by making you a fine present with a *French Alamode*— You know my meaning, Bess, I am sure.' And so do we: that 'French' gift may be fashionable, but it is not the oral sex variety.

Bess is fired up now. 'Aye . . . Mrs *Spit-Venom*, I won't give my *A—s* for a thousand such *Tatterdemallions* as you; Faith, better to have a Butt of Beer at my Back [. . .] than to be laid on a heap of Dung on Tower-Hill with a Pocky Tom Turd-man [a night-soil collector] a playing on my Dulcimer; and for my Reward have a damnable Kick on the britch for being sluggish and inactive. [. . .] Out upon you, you fulsom Punk you; your Breath stinks worse than the rank Piss of a hunted Bitch-Fox. For the poor fellow (whom I much pitty) affirm'd in my hearing [. . .] that had he not just before been emptying of a House of Office [a privy], you had certainly strangled him with your unsavoury Breath; but as it happen'd, prov'd at that time something Natural.'

And on they come, each taking a turn at the invective. The slang flows free and fast.

Joan Boss, *'raving and knitting her Fist* against Bess' notes how Nell 'served the Baker's Boy. I see him stand [. . .] cringing against a Wall' and Sarah Wyatt reminds 'Mrs. Joan' how 'the Taylor of *Spittle-fields* made you a Loose boddied Gown [synonymous for a whore], and when he brought it home, put in a Yard [in slang, the penis] more than your Husband allow'd of.' Speak for yourself, responds Dorothy Evans, and recalls how Sarah

– 'Mrs. *Wrigle-Tail* . . . a Cursed piece of Liquerish Damnation'
– 'receives all and deceives all', English, Dutch, Spanish and
both 'the back-door'd Italian', and 'the French Man' who 'brings
up the Rear with Fire and Faggot, Aye and Faith he sticks to
your Bumm with a vengeance.' [7]

The end, after all the melodrama, is strangely anti-climactic.
After a final burst from Barbary Adams, Dorothy throws in the
towel. Not because of her team's failure to produce the vituperative goods but because everyone, in their efforts to smear and
slander, is being far too honest. No shaming perhaps, but definitely naming, and that way professional reputations are lost.
'We'll loose the Wager [. . .] with all our Hearts, rather than
Spoil our Trade; for to be expos'd at this foul rate we shall be
ruin'd.' With a final 'Farewell, Elizabeth Damnable' ringing in
her ears it is left to Bess to offer the verdict to the audience.
'*Upon which the Company, Clapping hands unanimously Cry'd out*
Golden-lane, Golden-lane.'*

The idea of a bunch of potty-mouthed working-women
sounding off about illicit sex may have been titillatory for some
men. This has been the argument against the early slang analyst
Thomas Harman, who has been accused of voyeurism in his
inclusion of 'dells' and 'doxies' in his lists of sixteenth-century
criminal beggars. Perhaps, even if there was plenty of dedicated
porn available for those who wanted it. What can be noted here
is that other than the mutual recriminations conjured up for the
text, there is no sense of moralising. If the basket-women and
fish-wives wish to indulge their sexuality, if they are willing to go
on the game, what matter. Nor is the scold herself pilloried. This

---

* I am amused, 300-plus years after the event and living half-way between Golden Lane
and Turnmill Street (both brought sadly low, or in real-estate terms, 'gentrified') that I
find a personal delight in 'my girls' verbal victories.

is about verbal skill. Bess Pierce gets the good lines and thus her Golden-laners win. The readers can clap their hands as well.

In the end working-class women were meant to brawl. With their fists, perhaps; with their tongues, without a doubt. If Billingsgate was past its prime by the late nineteenth century, the river- side slums of Ratcliff (or Radcliffe) Highway, just east of the Tower of London, could always welcome the researcher to somewhere equally exciting.

> The female of the locality in question [Ratcliff Highway] is seldom seen dead drunk, as it is termed. Such a condition is almost impossible to her. She is far advanced beyond the weakness of succumbing easily to the influence of intoxicating fluids — if she was ever subject to it, which is doubtful-bred and suckled on gin, as she probably was, and weaned on gin and bitters. [. . .] It is marvellous that even spoony 'Jack ashore' can discover anything in the least attractive in her. In language and manner she is as coarse as a coal-whipper, and the guiding principle of her shameful existence seems to be to make known her contempt and abhorrence of all that is modest and womanly.

The sociologist James Greenwood, going 'Down Radcliffe Way' in 1875. He was censorious, such horrid revelations were the foundation of his 'made my excuses and left' career. Not everyone was so affrighted. George Augustus Sala, one of Dickens' 'young men' on *Household Words* and a dedicated bohemian journalist in his own right, was far more tolerant.

> You are not to suppose, gentle reader, that the population of Ratcliffe is destitute of an admixture of the fairer portion of

the creation. Jack has his Jill [. . .] Jill is inclined to corpulence; if it were not libellous, I could hint a suspicion that Jill is not unaddicted to the use of spirituous liquors. Jill wears a silk handkerchief round her neck, as Jack does; like him, too, she rolls, occasionally; I believe, smokes, frequently; I am afraid, swears, occasionally [. . .] Jill has her good points, though she does scold a little, and fight a little, and drink a little. [. . .] She takes care of Jack's tobacco-box; his trousers she washes, and his grog, too, she makes; and if he enacts occasionally the part of a maritime Giovanni, promising to walk in the Mall with Susan of Deptford, and likewise with Sal, she only upbraids him with a tear.[*]

Like the 'rings' of men and other onlookers who would gather round a pair of tussling women, whether throwing punches or insults, the media loved a good all-girl ruckus. In 1828, for an example, the *Morning Advertiser*[†] offered what it sniggeringly termed 'A Picture of "East End" Love' in its latest report from the Thames Police Office.

A woman, with both eyes blackened, was charged with assaulting another female in the same class of life herself. This was one of many desperate female fights which occur between the fair of the East end, all produced by the jealous fiend; and, strange say, the very men greatly prized by rival damsels are the respective callings, in the flash vocabulary, known as follows: "Peter-men" (coach robbers); "cracksmen" (house-breakers); "fogle-hunters" (pickpockets); "buz-men", also a term for pickpockets in crowds. Arc.— These ladies

[*] G. A. Sala, *Gaslight & Daylight* (1859).
[†] *Morning Advertiser* (2 October 1828), p.4.

had quarrelled about a swell buz-man," and, after beating each other for some time, the lady who had received the worst of the battle appealed to the Office for "a slang" (the flash term for an assault warrant) against the more successful combatant; and it also appeared that the subject of their quarrel, the swell buz-man," was so disgusted with the quarrel that he took himself off 'vith a vidow' who kept a chandler's shop.

As one sees in many contemporary reports of cases before the lower courts, however impoverished the principals, decorum was at a premium. It was doubtless why the press enjoyed them. Both ladies were keen to have their say.

Mrs. Miles said, at the same time elevating a hand covered with handsome rings, 'Why, your Worship, she took my man from me, and I whopped her for it.' Mrs. Rose Lambert, the complainant.—That's false, cause he has bolted with the vidow. Mrs. Miles.—Get out, you varmint—you lives with a coster monger. Mrs. Rose Lambert.—A costermonger, indeed ! I tell you never any sich rubbish—my fancy are of a higher horder of gentlemen. —A costermonger, indeed! Mrs, Miles, making significant motion of her finger, touching her neck, and pointing upwards—Yes, and you gets them all *scragged* and *lagged* (we believe the lady meant hanged and transported) when you tired on them.

Mr. Ballantine [the magistrate] said, they appeared a pretty pair; and doubted not but would send them both to the House Correction. Mrs. Miles.—Vy, your Worship, I never was in no trouble. Mrs. Rose Lambert.—Vy, you lying —!

you were nigh being 'lagged' once or twice. The ladies prepared for a battle royal, and eyed each other fiercely, that any body might see the recollection of 'swell Buzman' was not yet lost. At length the Magistrate sent for Wilton, an eccentric but valuable officer, to take peep of recognition at the ladies, and as entered politely made an acknowledgment of the head to each, at which signification of recollection of them the ladies seemed quite disconcerted. Mr. Ballantine. —Do you know them, Wilson? "Oh, yes, I do, indeed," said Wilson; "there's pretty Rose, an out-and-outer [a first-rate person] in her way, but the men never stops long with her; the last she had was a costermonger." Mrs. Miles (clapping her bands triumphantly).—There, your Worship, do you hear that? Wilson.—Well, as to Poll Miles, she has been in trouble or twice. Mrs. Miles.—La! Mr. Wilson how can you say so.

Wilson.—Why you know you have—don't you recollect Jack Burke, whose body you "waked" when [it] was brought from Newgate after being hanged—and your man George Brown, who after returning from a transportation of seven years, was sent again for life for robbing the people near Rag-fair. Mrs. Miles.—Well, that's nothing to me. Mrs. Rose Lambert here volunteered a long history of the unfortunate mishaps of 'Mrs. Miles's men,' but Wilson clenched it once by observing that one was bad as the other, and would have no 'compunctious visitings' in handing over to the law any of 'their men,' no matter how fondly caressed, if occasion required riddance him. The Magistrates held them both in sureties keep the peace.

There was always a good chance that the brawling women would be Irish, a synonym for the violent, noisy and wholly 'undeserving' poor. In 1847 'Mary Gavin appeared to an information charging her with assaulting Sarah Jarvis [. . .] the assault complained of took place after compliments in the true Irish slang had been exchanged.' Three years later we meet 'Mary Anne Armstrong, a powerful and forbidding-looking young Irishwoman, who spoke with that most repulsive of all pronunciations, the low Dublin slang' and in 1849 comes 'Biddy Moriarty [. . .] a virago of the first order, very able with her fist, and still more formidable with her tongue. From one end of Dublin to the other, she was notorious for her powers of abuse.' The reports kept coming: 'the scolding wife and the furious spinster each used all the low alley slang that they could think of', another loudmouth used 'the drunken slang of a prostitute of the lowest class' (an offered example: shindy, which suggests another Irish girl).

Australia was not immune, and a report of 1856 gives a brief reference to what must have been one of Tasmania's best-known, if squalid institutions.

'Mary M'Kinnon, who appeared before the Bench with one of her "optics" in mourning [i.e. a black eye], was charged [. . .] with making use of abusive and obscene language. The language being of that particular slang which is considered stunning at Gipsy Poll's, at Hobart Town.' The same year noted the activities of 'one of the Murray street gang from Hobart Town, and a friend of the well known "Gipsy Poll" of that interesting locality.' Gipsy Poll seems well enough known to have earned a role as a generic. *Bell's Life in Victoria** noted that:

* *Bell's Life in Victoria* (Melbourne) 7 June 1862, p.2/2.

Instead of wasting time in sifting evidence, and weighing the argument of counsel, the juries adopted an infallible martingale, which they called the alternate system. If John Brown wore convicted of horse-stealing, Giles Scroggins, who followed, was turned adrift whatever might be the charge against him, or the nature of the proof by which it was supported. If Gipsy Poll got off on a charge of robbery, poor Mary Jones, whose husband had fallen into the clutches of the press gang, was sure to be transported for stealing a loaf of bread for herself and her starving child.

In 1866 she was well enough known for an owner to borrow her name for one of his racehorses. The London essayist George Augustus Sala, on one of his hugely popular excursions to Australia, knew her, and averse to frightening his loyal middle-class readership, rendered a tavern known to be home to a regular clientele of 'thieves and vagabonds' as the safest of Victorian firesides. He wrote of 'Gipsy Poll in her noisy little hostelrie, redolent of rum and lemons, hot water and sugar, cutty pipes, and Barrett's twist, with its cosy fires and warm back parlors, in the venerable little Hobart Town-street of blessed memory." It also turned out that Arthur Orton, better known as the fraudulent Tichborne Claimant and actually a Hobart Town butcher, was usually to be found in Poll's concert room. By the end of the century with Poll and her criminals' retreat long gone, the place was wreathed in nostalgic reminiscences. The Hobart *Daily Telegraph* ran a series of 'memory lane' columns by their columnist 'The Vet'. He told how[†]:

* *Queenslander* (Brisbane) 19 June 1875, p.6/6.
† *Daily Telegraph* (Hobart) 20 April 1895 p. 6/5

6. Crime Says

You are all huddled together, and sit among yourselves, talking and hearing all manner of bad language, blackguard stuff and slang, and doing the worst kind of things. There was poor —; when she went in she was as modest a girl as possible for one of her sort to be, and she would blush when she heard any bad language, but when she came out she was as bad as any of us. She used often to say that she got her education finished there. We call it 'going to college'.

'The Spinning House' in
Morning Chronicle 2 January 1851[*]

L OVE AND MARRIAGE, horse and carriage . . . slang and criminality also offer one of the great indissoluble dualities. If the city is slang's home, then those who find their comfort zone on its mean streets remain the vocabulary's primary occupants. If we are to hunt down slang then this is where we must go. As we shall see, crime is an equal opportunity employer: women as well as men can transgress. But first, a little background.

While human thieves had presumably existed for as long as people declared that X was 'theirs' and Y disregarded the

---

[*] Slang *spinniken, spinning ken,* a workhouse; from Dutch *spinnhuis,* a women's house of correction; presumably the inmates were forced to spin thread.

exclusivity of such ownership, and person-to-person violence as long as that argument could not be resolved through persuasion or cunning alone, the language of anglophone crime was not recorded until the sixteenth century. The short glossaries that appeared through the century were not unique as regarded their style – there were a number of similar studies of what one might term niche occupations such as cooking and archery and a single specialist, Gervase Markham, whose son Lewknor would be rumoured as having married one of the succeeding century's great female thieves, Mary Frith, better known as 'Moll Cutpurse', looked at archery, cockfighting, agriculture, angling and a glossary of Anglo-Saxon words. All important vocabularies, but crime, it would turn out to no-one's great surprise, proved itself what modernity would call 'the sexiest'. The glossaries would evolve into canting dictionaries, i.e. collections of cant, the 'official' name for criminal slang (from Latin *cantare*, to sing and thus hinting at the sing-song patter of the various criminal vagabonds whose world originated such language).

The first such glossaries, not yet substantial enough to make a whole dictionary, were found in what were known as 'beggar books'. These represented a Europe-wide phenomenon. The format was pretty consistent: they offered a variety of anecdotes, the lowdown on a range of criminal tricks, a faked-up sample of criminal conversation and on occasion a list – real names – of a country's top villains. The first such book was Arabic and published in the eleventh century; thereafter was a gap till the late fifteenth (and the venue moved from the middle East to what would in time become Germany). It was interesting, for those who made the comparison, to see how many tricks had lasted, almost unchanged, though the one that claimed that a hapless mute had lost his tongue to the Crusaders now put the onus on 'the Moors'.

The stand-out English text appeared in 1567 (an earlier edition of 1566 has been lost). *The Caveat for Common Cursetours* (i.e. a guide or warning against wandering villains) was assembled by a Kentish magistrate, one Thomas Harman, who allegedly greeted those mendicants who appeared at his back door with a proposal: my food for your cant. Thus readers encountered such as the *upright man* (a leading villain), the *counterfeit crank* (one who pretended to foul diseases, augmented with self-created and wholly disgusting sores), the *clapperdogen* (a street-seller, summoning crowds by beating a pan), the *jarkman* (a forger of seals and other authorities) and the *fresh water mariner* (claiming to be the survivor of shipwreck, but rarely so). There were twenty-four in all, the foundation of a list that would rise to sixty-plus at its final appearance two centuries later. As a magistrate Harman himself was a *queer cuffin* or, it seems quite coincidentally, a *harman*.

Nor did he forget the women. Harman doubtless exposes his own predictable attitude to these criminal women: essentially seeing them all as potential if not actual whores and writing accordingly. He has been accused, in a feminist critique, of voyeurism: lining up the villainesses and listening (the implication suggests a hand beneath his breeches) as they 'talked dirty'. Reading his book it is hard to find passages that really qualify and reinterpreting a long-lost era via a modern filter is more of a stretch than this particular text will sustain.

The primary term was *mort*, and its basic meaning the female companion of a mendicant villain. Its etymology remains unknown, it may echo standard English *mort*, a salmon in its third year, i.e. the popular equation of women with fish; meanwhile Charles Ribton-Turner, in *A History of Vagrants* (1887), suggests Welsh *modryb*, a matron or *morwyn*, a virgin.

Co-habiting was more usual than marriage, and the *autem-mort*, literally a 'married woman' from *autem*, a church (itself perhaps from standard *altar*), was usually posing as such, and claiming that while she had had a husband, he had died 'eyther at Newhauen, Ireland, or in some seruice of the Prince'. She usually came with children who tramped alongside her and ideally excited the sympathies of those who might give her money. Harman was less than complimentary: such women, for all their protestations of matrimony were in fact 'as chaste as a Cowe I haue, that goeth to Bull euery moone, with what Bull she careth not.' The children were properly known as *kinchin morts*, from *kinchin* (i.e. German *kindchen*) children, specifically little girls. Harman continued condemnatory: 'A kinching Mort is a little Girle, the Morts their Mothers carries them at their backes in their slates, which is their sheetes, and bryngs them vp sauagely tyll they growe to be ripe, and soone ripe, soone rotten.' Not all morts were on the tramp, the *gentry mort* was an aristocrat or bourgeoise; the *Rome mort* (from *rum*, good) was Queen Elizabeth I.

Once the kinchin mort was sexually mature and had been deflowered she was rechristened a *doxy* (most likely from the Dutch *docke*, a doll, Lowland Scots *doxie*, lazy or from *dock*, a tail, and thus a coarse pun). Harman's predecessor John Awdelay explained in his *Fraternitye of Vacabondes* (1561) that once old enough she is 'brought at her full age to the Vpryght man to be broken, and so she is called a Doxy, vntil she come to ye honor of an Altham.' The *upright man* led a gang of beggars and presumably took virginities as some form of right; an *altham* was again a wandering villain's wife or companion. If Eric Partridge is right, the word is the root of *autem*.

Finally, Harman notes the *dell*. She was a younger version of the doxy, and still a virgin (though not for long); unless that is she was a *wild dell*, an orphan or a runaway servant, who is perhaps employed as a child prostitute.

The possible origin is the proper name *Doll* or, in the way that *cunt* can be linked to Welsh *cwm*, a valley, this represents a pun on standard English *dell*, also meaning valley; Ribton-Turner, again, notes Welsh *del*, pert, smart and Lowland Scots *dilp*, a trollop. Harman has her as a girl who is 'able for generation, and not yet knowen or broken by the vpright man. These go abroade yong, eyther by the death of their parentes, and no bodye to looke vnto them, or els by some sharpe mystres that they seme, do runne away out of seruice; eyther she is naturally borne one, and then she is a wyld Dell: these are broken verye yonge; when they haue beene lyen with all by the vpright man, then they be Doxes, and no Dels. These wylde dels, beinge traded vp with their monstrous mothers, must of necessytie be as euill, or worsse, then their parents.'

Like their male counterparts, these girls and women had specific jobs. There were the *bawdy baskets* who sold haberdash-ery – 'laces, pynnes, nedles, white ynkell [i.e. *inkle*, a form of linen tape], and round sylke gyrdles of al coulours.' They also bought and sold rabbit skins from local peasants and stole linen left to dry on a hedge. 'And for their trifles they wil procure of mayden seruaunts, when their mystres or dame is oute of the waye, either some good peece of beefe, taken, or cheese, that shal be worth xij. pens, for ii. pens of their toyes.'

Women – 'yonge harlots' in Harman's misogynistic taxonomy – also played the *counterfeit crank*, faking illness, especially 'the falling evil', i.e. epilepsy. They were also *demaunders for glymmar*, posing as the victim of a fire (complete with fake documents to prove it, supposedly signed by a local worthy) and begging alms so as to repurchase their lost possessions. A general-purpose beggar, working from house to house, was a *palliard* (from French *paille*, straw, upon which she or he slept) or *clapperdogen*.* The standard English palliard was 'a low or dissolute knave; a lewd fellow, a lecher, a debauchee' , but the term extended to a beggar-woman who uses a child, either her own or one borrowed for the purpose, to excite the pity of passers-by (this pity often increased by the child's piteous cries, promoted by judicious pinches and prods).

Finally there is the non-specific *pot*. It's use as 'vagina' is not recorded before 1632, but Harman uses it to mean the whole woman, which suggests that the equation came earlier in actual spoken use. His reference also accentuated the popular cliché of female talkativeness: 'O! how the pottes walke about! their talkinge tounges talke at large.'

Harman knew his visitors well enough to offer a list of names alongside the confected 'conversation' that ends the book. For instance, 'Harry Smith, hee dryveleth when he speaketh' and 'Richard Horwood, wel neer lxxx. yeare old, he will bite a vi. Peny nayle asunder with his teeth and a baudy dronkard.' There are, however, no women. He acknowledges the omission at the head of this list of men: 'Concerning the number of morts and doxies, it is superfluous to write of them. I could well have done it, but the number of them is great, and would ask a large volume.'

Harman's work was, ultimately, a sampler, a quick tour of mid-century villainy. The playwright and pamphleteer Robert Greene

---

* Standard English *clapper*, hitter + *dudgeon*, the hilt of a dagger. Origin unknown, but possibly from the beggar hitting his clapdish (a wooden dish with a lid, carried by a variety of mendicants to give warning of their approach and to hold alms) with a dudgeon.

attempted to put more flesh on the narrative bones. (Greene's plays have largely vanished from the stage; he remains best known as a critic of Shakespeare, labelling him 'that upstart crow' and 'an absolute Johannes fac-totum'.*) Around 1590–92 he wrote a number of what were termed 'coney-catching' pamphlets, studies of confidence trickery (the *coney*, literally 'rabbit', being the equivalent of the modern 'sucker'). The pertinent text was:

> A DISPVTATION, Betweene a Hee Conny-catcher, and a Shee Conny-catcher whether a Theefe or a Whoore, is most hurtfull in Cousonage, to the Common-wealth. DISCOUERING THE SECRET VILLANIES of alluring strumpets. With the Conuersion of an English Courtizen, reformed this present yeare, 1592. Reade, laugh, and learne.

It appeared in a revised and posthumous revision in 1615, now entitled:

> THEEUES FALLING OUT, True-men come by their Goods: or, The Bel-man wanted a Clapper A peale of new Villanies rung out; Being musicall to all Gentlemen, Lawyers, Farmers, and all sorts of people that come vp to the Tearme: shewing that the Villanies of lewd women, do, by many degrees, excell those of men.

The pamphlet took the form of a dialogue, between the thief, Laurence and the whore, Nan. While we have no choice but to accept Greene was ventriloquising both characters, Nan is still worth hearing. She has no illusions as to her job, nor its utility.

* R. Greene, *A Groatsworth of Wit* (1592).

'Where can such girls as myself be blemished with a thread-bare coat as long as country farmers have full purses, and wanton citizens pockets full of pence? [. . .] [M]ine eyes are stales [i.e. *stalls*, something that distracts from the active thief], & my hands lime-twigs [to which the property of others 'sticks'], else were I not worthy the name of a she cony-catcher.' She also notes that her prostitution is a good deal more profitable than his pick-pocketing: 'Alas, were not my wits and my wanton pranks more profitable than my husband's foisting [stealing], we might often go to bed supperless for want of surfeiting, and yet I dare swear my husband gets a hundred pounds a year by bungs [purses].'

And since it's a quiet day, and 'the conies in their burrows' she suggests a tavern meal 'and there for the price of our suppers I will prove that women, I mean of our faculty, a traffic, or as base knaves term us, strumpets, are more subtile, more dangerous in the commonwealth, and more full of wiles to get crowns than the cunningest foist, nip, lift, pragges [i.e. 'prigs'; all are terms for thieves, cutpurses, shoplifters], or whatsoever that lives at this day.'

She terms Laurence the 'king of cutpurses' but adds that patriarchal assumptions – men are the most skilful villains – act against those who hold them, 'for though they smoke [recognise] you, they will hardly mistrust us.' And what could equip her better for pickpocketing than acting the housewife in the marketplace: 'when every wife hath almost her hand on her bung [purse], and that they cry: Beware the cutpurse and cony-catchers, then I as fast as the best, with my handbasket as mannerly as if I were to buy great store of butter and eggs for provision of my house, do exclaim against them with my hand on my purse, and say the world is bad when a woman cannot walk safely to market for fear of these villainous cutpurses, when as the first bung I come to, I either nip or foist, or else stale another while he hath stroken, dispatched, and gone. Now, I pray you, gentle sir, wherein are we inferior to you in foisting?'

But for a woman picking pockets is no more than a hobby and its profits no more than pin-money. What counts, stresses Nan, is the brothel. First she persuades her client to have an overpriced meal, 'for he shall pay for a pippin pie that cost in the market four pence, at one of the trugging-houses* 18 pence.' She meanwhile eats nothing but plays with every dish, ensuring it cannot be sent back and the bill discounted. And when it comes to bed, Nan is an expert in what would be named the badger game and what was then known as *cross-biting* (i.e. deception, and used of many other criminal despoliations): 'Am I so simply acquainted or badly provided that I have not a friend which with a few terrible oaths, and countenance set as if he were the proudest soldado that ever bare arms against Don John of Austria, will face him quite out of his money and make him walk like a woodcock homeward by Weeping Cross [i.e. weeping like a fool over his empty pockets], and so buy repentance with all the crowns in his purse?'

And cross-biting is the one crime that no thief, however skilled, can achieve without a woman's help. 'You can foist, nip, prig, lift, curb [to use a form of hook to extract items from open shop windows] and use the black art [lock-picking], yet you cannot crossbite without the help of a woman, which crossbiting now-a-days is grown to a marvellous profitable exercise, for some cowardly knaves, that for fear of the gallows leave nipping and foisting, become crossbites, knowing there is no danger therein

* Italian *trucca*, 'a fustian or rogish word for a trull, a whore, or a wench' (Florio 1598). Possibly cognate with standard English *truck*, to barter or exchange commodities.

but a little punishment, at the most the pillory, and that is saved with a little unguantum [properly 'unguentum'] aureum [i.e. 'oil of gold', money].'

There is much more in this vein, and her slang continues, with term such as *hit on the master-vein* (make pregnant), *French marbles, French favours* and *morbus Gallicus* (all syphilis), *knight of the post* (a perjurer), *suburb* (a brothel zone) and *dine with Duke Humphrey* (to starve, and rooted in Duke Humphrey's Walk at Old St Paul's Cathedral, where the impoverished and hungry often walked in the hope of meeting someone who might offer them supper).

In the end Nan declares herself the winner. The thief has his skills, but the whore has even more: 'You men-thieves touch the body and wealth, but we ruin the soul, and endanger that which is more precious than the world's treasure. You make work only for the gallows, we both for the gallows and the devil, aye, and for the surgeon too.' And Laurence agrees: 'I confess it, Nan, for thou hast told me such wondrous villainies as I thought never could have been in women, I mean of your profession. Why, you are crocodiles when you weep, basilisks when you smile, serpents when you devise, and devils' chiefest brokers to bring the world to destruction. And so, Nan, let's sit down to our meat and be merry.'

Then, like so many other men Nan meets, the bill's on him.

If Nan is fictional, then villainy's next female celebrity is fact, though rendered fictional in most of her appearances: Mary Frith.

In 1651, Thomas Randolph's *Hey for Honesty* had this line: 'She is an Amashon [. . .] A Mall cutpurse, a Long Meg of Westminster.' If Long Meg had some celebrity [see chapter 4] then Moll Cutpurse, properly known as Mary Frith

(1584–1659), had even more. And like Long Meg she earned a biography: *The Life of Mrs Mary Frith Commonly Called Mal Cutpurse. Exactly Collected and now Published for the Delight and Recreation of all Merry disposed Persons* appeared in 1662. By then, however, Frith had come to symbolise everything that her male contemporaries saw as disturbing in a woman, and the 'facts' of her published life, a purported autobiography, are less than trustworthy.

Frith was born around 1584 and baptised at the London church of St Martin's Ludgate. Her first adult appearance was, fittingly, in a court record, accused with two other women of stealing a purse containing 2s. 11d. No verdict is recorded, but there were further court appearances, again for thefts, at all of which she managed to obtain a verdict of 'not guilty'. In 1612, however, her luck seems to have run out. Writing to his friend Sir Dudley Carleton on 12 February John Chamberlain told him how:

'Mall Cut-purse a notorious bagage (that used to go in mans apparell and challenged the feild of divers gallants) was brought to [Paul's Cross], where she wept bitterly and seemed very penitent, but yt is since doubted she was maudelin druncke, beeing discovered to have tipled of three quarts of sacke [i.e. a fortified white wine] before she came to her penaunce.'* The punishment was for wearing 'indecent dress': which as Chamberlain makes clear, referred to Frith's frequent sporting of male clothing.

By then she was a notorious figure, 'perhaps the most notorious Renaissance rogue on record.'† In a strictly male-dominated

* Quoted in A. B. Dawson, 'Mistris Hic & *Haec*', *Studies in English Literature, 1500-1900*, 33:2, p.388.
† P. Blank, *Broken English: Dialects and the Politics of Language in Renaissance Writings* (London 1996), p.59.

hierarchical society she had come to epitomise much that that world feared and thus condemned. Her cross-dressing was seen as undermining the established separation of genders, her frequenting of tobacco houses – the first woman recorded as so doing – and her boast that it was a lifetime's consumption of the weed that had ensured her longevity, was similarly subversive: women should not smoke, a belief that lasted well into the nineteenth century and for some even beyond. In these contexts, modern studies of her life have claimed her as a proto-feminist. In addition there was her image as a seventeenth-century 'Moriarty', controlling every aspect of contemporary crime. In her role as both receiver and broker of stolen goods she resembled her eighteenth-century successor Jonathan Wild. If one follows the sociologist John McMullan, who takes the picture of the contemporary underworld very much on its own merits:

She acquired some control over the organization of thieving in London in the 1620s and 1630s, and established a warehouse to handle stolen property. Her subordinates were paid higher rates and worked mainly for her; she in turn returned the stolen goods to their owners. Her influence as a receiver and thief-taker was institutionalized. Her informers and accomplices advised her about robbers and pickpockets, and advertised her reputation. She cultivated specific crimes, instigating a lucrative trade in stealing and returning shop-books and account ledgers that had specific value only to business owners. She established a market in high-value items such as personal jewels, rings, and watches. Her influence in the underworld stemmed from her power as defender of the public interest. After a theft, she guaranteed the recovery of the stolen property. [. . .] Commercial interests,

government, and the public at large recognized her authority, and the open trade in pardons and rewards linked the
judiciary to private retrieval and thief-taking schemes. As a
patron of crime, she provided shape and discipline to thieving gangs and she expanded the frontiers of theft.'*

In 1614 Frith married one Lewknor Markham, who may well
have been the son of the glossary-writing Gervase, a prolific poet
and playwright and apostrophised as 'the earliest English hackney writer'. As one might expect, she kept her maiden name and
it does not appear that the marriage lasted. She established a
fencing school, but this was probably a front for her criminal
dealings. In 1624 she was summoned before the Star Chamber
for an unpaid bill, and evidence emphasised her dissolute, non-
conformist life, as well as her criminality. Mary's last 'public
appearance' came in 1644, when she was listed among those
recently discharged from Bethlem Hospital, better known as
'Bedlam'; it appeared that at least for a while she had been
considered mad. She died on 26 July 1659.

Inevitably Frith became a symbol, and as such celebrated and/
or vilified in the contemporary media. In 1610 the writer John
Day composed, but it would appear did not publish a pamphlet,
*The Madde Pranckes of Mery Mall of the Banckside with her Walkes
in Mans Apparrell and to what Purpose*. Four years later Thomas
Freeman wrote that:

They say Mol's honest, and it may bee so,
But yet it is a shrewd presumption no;
To touch but pitch, 'tis knowne it will defile,

---

* J. McMullan, 'Criminal organization in London', *Social Problems*, 29:3, p.319.

Moll wears the breech, what may she be the while?
Sure shee that doth the shadow so much grace,
What will shee when the substance comes in place?*

And John Taylor, the Water-Poet, a few years later, praised her as
a contrast to those whose lives were dominated by ephemeral
fads and fashions:

Moll Frith doth teach them modesty,
For she doth keepe one fashion constantly,
And therefore she deserves a Matrons praise,
In these inconstant Moone-like changing dayes[†]

However it was not so much in prose and poetry that Mary Frith
was commemorated, but on stage. Her finest, if fictional, hour
came in 1611 as the star, albeit played by an actress, of Middleton
and Dekker's *The Roaring Girl, or Moll Cutpurse*. There was no
pretence about the heroine's identity and Frith, perhaps egged
on by the playwrights and actors for the purposes of publicity,
even appeared on stage at the Fortune Playhouse. She was dressed
as a man and closed the evening's performance with a jig.

Critics have argued over the play: some see it as an early
demonstration of feminism in action; others, given the final
scenes in which 'Moll' is re-absorbed into law-abiding society, as
a sell-out, a means of ensuring that the audience left the theatre
in the comforting knowledge that all was right in the larger
worlds and the underworld was no more real, let alone threatening, than a stage performance.

Moll's transvestism has greater weight. The idea of women

* Quoted A. B. Dawson op. cit. p.394.
† Ibid.

dressing in men's garments was not popular – among men. Religious conservatives saw it as near-blasphemy; social ones feared that a woman thus dressed would move from what could be dismissed as fancy dress into real revolution and having made herself look like a man, start tyrannising her adoptive gender peers. In John Reynolds' *Gods Revenge Against the Abominable Sin of Adultery* (1679) the adulteress Helda dresses as a man to run off with her lover. To Reynolds she 'forgets the modesty and pudicity that belongs to her Sex, she is without shame or blushing, and as if she had chang'd her nature with her cloathes she seems bold and impudent.'*

The Beaumont and Fletcher play *Love's Cure* (1606–13) used well-known double entendres (and thereby half a dozen slang terms) to showcase the sexual side of things:

What have you to doe with Armors, and Pistols, and Javelins, and swords, and such tooles? remember Mistresse: nature hath given you a sheath onely, to signifie women are to put up mens weapons, not to draw them.†

Such women were known as 'masculine-feminines' (a precursor of modernity's 'he-she') and seen as threat to the contemporary status quo. In 1620 *Hic Mulier; or, The Man-Woman: Being a Medecine to cure the Coltish Diseases of the Staggers in the Masculine-Feminines of our Times* complained that:

[S]ince the daies of Adam women were neuer so Masculine; Masculine in their genders and whole generations, from the

---

* Quoted in R. V. Lucas, 'The Female Transvestite in Early Modern England', *Renaissance and Reformation* (12:1 Winter 1988) p.70.
† Beaumont & Fletcher, *Love's Cure* II.ii.86-89; quoted in Lucas op. cit. p.74.

Mother, to the yongest daughter, Masculine in Number, from one to multitudes; Masculine in Case, euen from the head to the foot; Masculine in Moode, from bold speech, to impudent action; and Masculine in Tense: for (without redress) they were, are, and will be still most Masculine, most mankinde, and most monstrous.[*]

Hic mulier called for the traditional female role: 'Comeliness shall be our study: feare our Armour, and modestie our practice' but many women were not listening and as Valerie Lucas puts it 'the preachers' and pamphleteers' dream of subduing the female transvestite remained unrealized.'

Middleton was unphased by any such disapproval. In the introduction to the printed play he notes that 'Venus being a woman passes through the play in doublet and breeches, a brave disguise and a safe one if the statute [i.e. the law against excessive dress] untie not her codpiece point [i.e. the lace that secured it].'

The play as a whole and Moll in particular, are pleasingly en-slanged. The language works on two levels: the doubles entendres of what might be termed the 'Carry On' lexis, and the exhibition (and exposition) of criminal slang or cant.

For the first, there are a number of dialogues in which the seeming innocence of the words masks (though presumably not so to the original audiences) a good deal of smut. [The italics are added]

MOLL How now! What art thou?
TRAPDOOR A poor, ebbing gentleman that would gladly wait for the young flood of your service.

* Lucas op. cit. p.70.

MOLL My service! What should move you to offer your *service* to me, sir?

TRAPDOOR The love I bear to your heroic spirit and masculine womanhood.

MOLL So, sir, put case we should retain you to us, what *parts* are there in you for a gentlewoman's service?

TRAPDOOR Of two kinds, right worshipful, movable and immovable: movable to run of arrants, and immovable to *stand* when you have occasion to use me.

MOLL What strength have you?

TRAPDOOR Strength, Mistress Moll? I have gone up into a *steeple* and stayed the great bell as 't has been ringing, stopp'd a windmill going.

MOLL And never struck down yourself?

TRAPDOOR Stood as *upright* as I do at this present

Then there is the traditional play on the possibilities of an occupation. Often the tinker with his *hammer*, here the tailor with his *yard*:

MOLL There boy, there boy! What, dost thou go a-hawking after me with a red clout on thy finger?

TAILOR I forgot to take measure on you for your new breeches.

SIR ALEXANDER [Aside] Hoyda! Breeches! What, will he marry a monster with two *trinkets*? What age is this? If the wife go in breeches, the man must wear long coats like a fool.

MOLL What *fiddling's* here? Would not the old pattern have *serv'd* your turn?

TAILOR You change the fashion; you say you'll have the great Dutch slop, Mistress Mary.

MOLL Why, sir, I say so still.

TAILOR Your breeches then will take up a *yard* more.

MOLL Well, pray look it be put in then.

TAILOR It shall *stand* round and full, I warrant you.

MOLL Pray make 'em easy enough.

TAILOR I know my fault now: *t'other was somewhat stiff between the legs; I'll make these open enough*, I warrant you.

SIR ALEXANDER [Aside] Here's good *gear* towards! I have brought up my son to marry a Dutch slop and a French doublet, a codpiece-daughter!

TAILOR So, I have *gone as far as I can go*.

MOLL Why then, farewell.

And the simple pun:

SIR ALEXANDER I think you'll find an apt scholar of my son,

Especially for *prick-song*.

MOLL I have much hope of him.

What is equally important is Moll's cheerful revelation of the supposedly secret language of the underworld, its cant:

MOLL I hope then you can cant, for by your cudgels, you, sirrah, are an upright man.

TRAPDOOR As any walks the highway, I assure you.

MOLL And Tearcat, what are you? A wild rogue, an angler, or a ruffler?

TEARCAT Brother to this upright man, flesh and blood, ruffling Tearcat is my name, and a ruffler is my style, my title, my profession.

MOLL Sirrah, where's your doxy? Halt not with me.

OMNES Doxy, Moll? What's that?

MOLL His wench.

TRAPDOOR My doxy? I have, by the salomon, a doxy that carries a kinchin mort in her slate at her back, besides my dell and my dainty wild dell, with all whom I'll tumble this next darkmans in the strommel, and drink ben [booze], and eat a fat gruntling cheat, a cackling cheat, and a quacking cheat. [. . .] My doxy stays for me in a boozing ken, brave captain.

MOLL He says his wench stays for him in an alehouse. You are no pure rogues.

TEARCAT Pure rogues? No, we scorn to be pure rogues, but if you come to our lib ken, or our stalling ken, you shall find neither him nor me a queer cuffin.

MOLL So, sir, no churl of you.

TEARCAT No, but a ben cove, a brave cove, a gentry cuffin.

The nobs, who are listening, are confused – as cant demands that they should be.

LORD NOLAND Call you this canting?

JACK Zounds, I'll give a schoolmaster half a crown a week, and teach me this pedlar's French.

TRAPDOOR Do but stroll, sir, half a harvest with us, sir, and you shall gabble your bellyful.

MOLL Come, you rogue, cant with me. [. . .] Come on, sirrah.

TRAPDOOR Ben mort, shall you and I heave a booth, mill a ken, or nip a bung? And then we'll couch a hogshead under the ruffmans, and there you shall wap with me, and I'll niggle with you.

MOLL [*Slapping and kicking him*] Out, you damn'd, impudent rascal!

TRAPDOOR Cut benar whids, and hold your fambles and your stamps.

LORD NOLAND Nay, nay, Moll, why art thou angry?
  What was his gibberish?
MOLL Marry, this, my lord, says he: ben mort, good wench,
  shall you and I heave a booth, mill a ken, or nip a bung?
  Shall you and I rob a house or cut a purse? [. . .] And then
  we'll couch a hogshead under the ruffmans: and then we'll
  lie under a hedge. [. . .] And there you shall wap with me
  and I'll niggle with you, and that's all!
SIR BEAUTEOUS Nay, nay, Moll, what's that wap?
JACK Nay, teach me what niggling is; I'd fain be niggling.
MOLL Wapping and niggling is all one, the rogue my man
  can tell you.
TRAPDOOR 'Tis fadoodling, if it please you.
To show her skills, Moll and Tearcat duet on a canting song:
MOLL A gage of ben rom-booze
In a boozing ken of Romville
TEARCAT. Is benar than a caster,
Peck, pannam, [lap] or popler,
Which we mill in deuse a [vill].
[MOLL, TEARCAT]. Oh, I would lib all the lightmans,
Oh, I would lib all the darkmans,
By the salomon, under the ruffmans,
By the salomon, in the hartmans!
TEARCAT. And scour the queer cramp-ring,
And couch till a palliard docked my dell,
So my boozy nab might skew rom-booze well.
[MOLL, TEARCAT]. Avast to the pad, let us bing,
Avast to the pad, let us bing.

Their audience remains nonplussed, and not especially impressed.
Says one, 'The grating of ten new cartwheels and the gruntling

of five hundred hogs coming from Romford market cannot make a worse noise than this canting language does in my ears.' Nonetheless Lord Noland coughs up and Moll translates for her sidekicks – 'two boards and a half, that's two shillings sixpence' – and they leave, promising that 'We shall cut ben whids of your masters and mistress-ship wheresoever we come.'

Not that her fellow villains are that keen on Moll's revelations. When she mentions a foist, and the audience asks 'What's that?' she explains again:

MOLL Foist . . . A diver with two fingers, a pickpocket: all his train study the figging law, that's to say, cutting of purses and foisting. One of them is a nip; I took him once i' the twopenny gallery at the Fortune. Then there's a cloyer, or snap, that dogs any new brother in that trade, and snaps will have half in any booty. He with the wand is both a stale, whose office is to face a man i' the streets whilst shells are drawn by another, and then with his black conjuring rod in his hand, he, by the nimbleness of his eye and juggling-stick, will in cheaping a piece of plate at a goldsmith's stall, make four or five rings mount from the top of his caduceus, and, as if it were at leap-frog, they skip into his hand presently.

With which an attendant pair of cutpurses are far from happy.

SECOND CUTPURSE Zounds, we are smok'd!
OMNES [CUTPURSES] Ha?
SECOND CUTPURSE We are boil'd. Pox on her! See, Moll, the roaring drab.
FIRST CUTPURSE All the diseases of sixteen hospitals boil her! Away!

All good stuff no doubt, but it reads less like a feasible dialogue and more like a cursorily dramatised slang glossary, bereft only of alphabetical order and explanatory definitions. In parts it echoes Harman's canting dialogues, throwing in as many strange terms as possible into a supposedly spontaneous dialogue. Dekker, naturally, drew on what he knew: nearly three-quarters of the words can be found in his crime-based pamphlets *The Bellman of London* and *Lanthorne and Candlelight*. Several more are pre-dated by his play, *The Second Part of the Honest Whore* (1609). There are eleven first uses, none of them cant. To *make ducks and drakes*, to make a mess; *fadoodling*, used to mean sexual intercourse and offered as euphemistic explanation of *wapping* and *niggling*, both of which are spoken but not further explained, *fleshfly*, a whore, a *heap*, a good deal, e.g. of money; *hog-rubber*, a peasant; *muzzle-chops*, one who has a prominent mouth and nose; a *nipping Christian*, a cutpurse; *puggard* (from standard English *pug*, to pull or tug), a thief; *tearcat*, a thug; and *whisking*, brisk or smart. Finally the play is the first to use *moll* to mean a woman, usually with overtones of promiscuity. Moll, of course, has lived on, notably in the compound *gangster's moll*. The term was especially popular in the mid-nineteenth century when it was reclaimed by cant, stripped of any sexual overtones and used in such compounds as *moll-tooler*, *moll wire* or *moll whiz*, a female pickpocket, *square moll*, an honest woman and *moll-buzzer*, a street thief specialising in purse-snatching.

The Roaring Girl was not Frith's only on-stage representation. Later in 1611 Nathan Field staged his play *Amends for Ladies*. It was, as the title suggests, a response to the Middleton/Dekker play, and Moll appears in a much less kindly light. Nor does she play a central role, offering merely a cameo which may be seen as Field's attempt to profit from *The Roaring Girl's* success. Compared with the leading female roles, the Widow, the Wife and the Maid, and the story of their relations with their lovers,

Moll's subversive, transgressive personality, its parading of the sins of thieving and lust, has been clearly introduced only to provide a target for her vilification. Such subversive attitudes must be punished and Moll is duly pilloried as an emblem of everything seen as wrong with the over-independent female.

After one Moll, another: Moll King. And if the former paraded her skills in cant, then the latter showcased a successor: *flash*.

Hotten, in the first edition of his *Slang Dictionary* (1859), states that *flash* was coined in 1718 by Charles Hitchin in *The Conduct of Receivers and Thief-Takers*, but as he notes, ' "FLASH" is sometimes exchangeable with "fancy".' The ultimate etymology lies in a figurative use of *flash*, 'a sudden outburst or issuing forth of flame or light; a sudden, quick, transitory blaze' and beyond that 'gaudy, showy . . . ostentatious' (*OED*). Hitchin's senses were those of 'belonging to or connected with the underworld', thus the 'flash gaming house', or of being expert, 'knowing the ropes', specifically those of the underworld: 'The Cull is flash alias that is he Associates himself with Thieves'. In *The Regulator* (1718) Hitchin offers the *flash case*, a criminal pub, and the *flash cull*, a 'civilian' who hangs around with criminals; but he does not specify the language as such.

Flash ran through a number of definitions. Grose, from 1785, defined 'FLASH LINGO' as 'the canting or slang language'. By 1789 in George Parker's *Life's Painter*, it is lumped together with slang and cant: the reader is advised that 'The explanation of the Cant, Flash and Slang terms [. . .] gives at one view, a perfect knowledge of the artifices, combinations, modes and habits of those invaders of our property, our safety and our lives, who have a language quite unintelligible to any but themselves.' Finally, in its last incarnation, laid down in W.T. Moncrieff's 1821 play

Tom and Jerry (the dramatic version of Pierce Egan's *Life in London*) the man-about-town Corinthian Tom pronounces that, 'Flash, my young friend, or slang, as others call it, is the classical language of the Holy Land; in other words, St. Giles's Greek [. . .] a species of cant in which the knowing ones conceal their roguery from the flats.'

What is clear from the words themselves is that while as a vocabulary it is essentially the old cant made new, it has taken on an important new aspect: as Julie Coleman points out, 'What has happened is that cant has become stylish; it has become flash. Where the earlier glossaries presented the secret language of thieves and beggars , many of the later ones list the slick lingo of London's ultra-fashionable world.'* Flash dealt with some of the same topics as cant – typically money, drink, criminal types and their schemes – but its use did not automatically brand one as a criminal. To use flash was to be in the know; it was, logically, to be *flash to*.

Hitchin aside, if flash found a base from which it would spread, this was the celebrated Covent Garden coffee house run by Tom King and his wife Moll. Opening up after the taverns shut at midnight and staying open till dawn, the coffee house was a local fixture for customers both rich and poor. *Covent Garden in mourning, a mock heroick poem. Containing some memoirs of the late celebrated Moll King, and anecdotes of some of her sisters* (1747) noted 'Tom King's, a Shrine of Love, familiar known / To ev'ry Rake and *Fille de Joye* in Town'. In *The Life of the Woman of the Town*, serialised in 1762, it was cited as the resort of 'all the bucks, Bloods, Demi-reps and Choice Spirits in London. At Tom King's you might see every evening, women of the town, the most celebrated, and dressed as elegant as if to set

* J. Coleman, *History of Cant and Slang Dictionaries* vol. II (London, 2004), p.259.

in the stage box at an Opera. There you were sure also of meeting every species of humankind, that intemperance, idleness, necessity, or curiosity could assemble together." There is no mention of Moll, but her husband is 'rough as a Bridewell whipper, roaring down the long room, and rousing all the sleepers, thrusting them out of doors by the neck and shoulders, if they did not immediately call for something to drink.'†

It was never much more than a shack, though it appears to have boasted one room large enough to be termed 'long' and a couple of smaller ones. The same memoirist notes that 'riots , bowls breaking, shrieking, murder and such like amusements' were common, meanwhile in one small room a party might be drinking unperturbed, while in another 'it was common to have half a dozen ladies scratching one another for possession of a man whose person they cared no more for, than a sexton for a dead body, except for the perquisites.' The coffee house and its customers appear in a number of contemporary accounts, both fact and fiction. Thus, in Edward Kimber's *Life and adventures of Joe Thompson* (1751), its hero

strolled over to *Tom King's* [. . .] in one Corner two or three drunken Sleepers, snoaring away their Load of Liquor; here a group of Rakes in lascivious Discourse, and wanton Attitude, with half a Dozen Whores; others, of both Sexes, poaching after Game; Brawling and Wrangling at one Box; Cursing and Swearing at another; at this part of the Room a pair of Boxers dealt lusty Blows on each other's Chops, whilst some dirty Devil of a Prostitute remained the Prize of him who had the Fortune to overcome his Antagonist; at another

* In *The Beauties of all the magazines selected* vol. 3 (1762), p.49–50.
† In *The Beauties . . .* p.50.

Part, two or three Viragoes were demolishing each other's Coifs, and rooting up their Hair, inspired by some sudden Gust of Jealousy . . ."

Smollet mentioned the place in *Roderick Random* (1748) and *Peregrine Pickle* (1751). In 1732 Henry Fielding asked in his *Covent-Garden Tragedy* 'What Rake is ignorant of King's Coffee-House?'[†] *King's College*, as it was known, can be seen in Hogarth's engraving of 'Morning', the first of his series *Four Times of the Day* (1738). Outside a couple of rakes are pawing a pair of whores (or maybe market girls), while a cluster of waving sticks and a wig flying through the doorway show that one of the drink-inspired fights for which it was known had yet again broken out within.

In fact, and at least since 1739 when Tom had died, supposedly of alcoholism, his wife ran the place solo. *Covent Garden in Mourning* celebrated Moll's ascendancy in a final couplet: 'Pluto has turn'd his Proserpine aside / And Moll is Queen in her own Right, his Bride.'

King's had little in common with such respectable centres such Will's, popular with Dryden and other wits, or Lloyd's, the first home of what would become London's insurance centre, but it provided the perfect backdrop for the adoption, and alleged creation of a new variety of slang.

Moll's posthumous biography, *The Life and Character of Moll King* appeared in 1747. The new form of counter-language was sufficiently important for the author to note that, 'This Flash, as

* E. Kimber, *The life and adventures of Joe Thompson. A narrative founded on fact. Written by himself* (2 edn. 1751) vol. I pp.114–115.
† Quoted in H. Berry, 'Rethinking Politeness in Eighteenth-Century England', *Transactions of the Royal Historical Society,* Sixth Ser., Vol. 11 (2001), p.71.

it is called, is talking in Cant Terms, very much us'd among Rakes and Town Ladies.' It was never claimed that Moll had actually invented flash, but the sense of flash as a criminal language is not recorded before the *Life* and the suggestion is that 'This Lingua was very much in Vogue at King's Coffee-House, the better to conceal what was intended by those who spoke it.'[*]

The book used the traditionally popular form of a supposed dialogue – here between Moll and 'one of her best Customers, before her House was frequented by people of Fashion'. This was Harry Moythen, a man who was 'stabb'd some Time ago by *Dick Hodges*, the Distiller'.[†] According to *The Life* the dialogue had originally been published fifteen years earlier, in a lost pamphlet, *The Humours of the Flashy Boys at Moll King's* (a title that suggests that King's was known by either landlord or landlady well before the former died). It begins with Moythen asking Moll how much he owes for supper:

Harry. To pay, *Moll*, for I must hike.
Moll. Did you call me, Master?
Harry. Ay, to pay, in a Whiff.

Moll. Let me see. There's a Grunter's Gig, is a Si-Buxom; two Cat's Heads, a Win; a Double Gage of Rum Slobber, is Thrums; and a Quartern of Max, is three Megs: —That makes a Traveller all but a Meg.

Harry. Here, take your Traveller, and tip the Meg to the Kinchin.—But *Moll*, does *Jack* doss in your Pad now?

* *Life . . . of Moll King* (1747), p.11.
† Quoted in Berry op.cit. p. 75.

Moll. What *Jack* do you mean?

Harry. Why, *Jack* that gave you the little brindle Bull Puppy.

Moll. He doss in a Pad of mine! No, Boy, if I was to grapple him, he must shiver his Trotters at *Bilby's* Ball.

Harry. But who had you in your Ken last Darkee?

Moll. We had your Dudders and your Duffers, Files, Buffers and Slangers; we had ne'er a Queer Cull, a Buttock, or Porpus, amongst them, but all as Rum and as Quiddish as ever *Jonathan* sent to be great Merchants in *Virginia*.

Harry. But Moll, don't puff:—You must tip me your Clout before I derrick, for my Bloss has nailed me of mine; but I shall catch her at *Maddox's* Gin-Ken, sluicing her Gob by the Tinney; and if she has morric'd it, Knocks and Socks, Thumps and Plumps, shall attend the Froe-File Buttocking B[itc]h

Moll. I heard she made a Fam To-night, a Rum one, with Dainty Dasies, of a Flat from T'other Side; she flash'd half a Slat, a Bull's-Eye, and some other rum Slangs.

Harry. I'll derrick, my Blood, if I tout my Mort, I'll tip her a Snitch about the Peeps and Nasous. I shall see my jolly old Codger by the Tinney-side, I suppose with his Day-Lights dim, and his Trotters shivering under him.— As Oliver wheedles, I'll not touch this Darkee, I'll nap the

Pad, and see you in the Morning.[*]

All of which is explained in the 'KEY to the Flash Dialogue' which holds thirty-eight entries (with fifty-two terms in all). *To hike*, to go home.—*A Grunter's Gig*, a Hog's Cheek.—*Si-Buxom*, Six-pence.— *A Cat's Head*, a Half-penny Rowl.—A *Whyn*, a Penny.—*A Gage of Rum Slobber*, a Pot of Porter.—*Thrums*, Three-pence.—*Max*, Geneva.—*Meg*, a Half-penny.—*A Traveller*, a Shilling.—*Kinchin*, a little Child.—*Doss*, to sleep.— *Pad*, a Bed.—*Grapple*, to lay hold on.—*Trotters*, Legs.—*Bilby's Ball*, Tyburn-House.—*Ken*, a House.—*Darkee*, the Night.— *Dudders*, Fellows that sell Spital-fields Handkerchiefs for India ones.— *Duffers*, Those who sell British Spirituous Liquors for Foreign.—*Files*, Pick-pockets.—*Buffers*, Affidavit-Men.— *Slangers*, Thieves who hand on Goods from one to the other, after they are stole.—*A Buttock*, a Whore.—*Porpus* an ignorant swaggering Fellow.—*Rumor Quiddish*, Goodnatur'd.—*To puff*, to impeach.—*Clout*, a Handkerchief.—*Derrick*, to go away.— *Sluicing her Gob*, wetting her Mouth, or drinking.—*Tinney*, the Fire.—*Froe-File-Buttock*, a Woman Pick-pocket.—*A Fam*, a Ring.—*Dasies*, Diamonds.—*T'other Side*, Southwark.—*Half a Slat*, 10 s. 6. d.—*Bull's Eye*, 5 s.—*To tout the Mort*, to find out the Woman.—*Snitch about the Peeps and Nasous*, a Fillip on the Nose and Eyes.—*Old Codger*, an old Man.—*Day-lights*, Eyes.— *Oliver wheedles*, the Moon shines.—*To nap the Pad*, to go to Bed.[†]

Some of these terms are well established, others are more recent. As the anonymous editor explains, 'This was part of the cant that the gentry of King's College were mighty fond of; and

---

[*] *Life . . . of Moll King* (1747), pp.11–12.
[†] Ibid. pp.23–24.

which too many people now scandalously affect to practise; but by persons of modesty and understanding, those that are so ridiculous as to use it, are looked upon not to be very well bred: It is not a man's apparel or well furnished pocket that proclaim him a fit member for a sober company, but his discourse and behaviour; for it is notorious enough that we daily see highwaymen, house-breakers, pickpockets, money-droppers, &c. who make the appearance of gentlemen, and gild their vices with a gaudy coat, that they may be the less suspected.'*

Inventor or otherwise, Moll and her 'College' were undoubtedly linked to flash. The life claims to quote a popular question among rakes, 'Are you for *King's College* to have a dish of *Flash* with *Moll?*' Beyond the contrived conversation the memoir offers little. There is a reference to *bubbling*, i.e. fooling, a court, and the use of the terms *nymph*, *lady of pleasure* and *water wagtail* for a whore (with the pun on 'wagging her tail' first to attract men and then during intercourse), plus *bully* for a pimp. An infuriated Moll expresses the wish that an enemy will 'some Time or other, die of a Suffocation in the Road to Paddington', a reference, then well-understood, to the Tyburn gallows, upon which on *Paddington Fair day* one might 'dance the Paddington frisk' while wearing the *Paddington spectacles* (the hood that hid one's eyes from the audience) and which stood in what was still a village at the western end of modern Oxford Street.

Let us leave Moll, with the 'Elegy' that terminated the *Life & Character*:

Here lies my love, who often drove
Wheelbarrows in the street;

* Ibid. p.13.

From which low state, to Billingsgate,
With wickedness replete
She sold a dish of stinking fish
With oaths and imprecations;
And swore her wares were better far
Than any in the nation.
From thence she came to be in fame
Among the rogues and whores
But now she's gone to her long home
To settle all her scores.

We might have had hopes for John Gay's 1728 hit 'musical' *The Beggars' Opera*, with its cast of fences, whores and often female pickpockets but the reality is that the majority of the slang is to be found in his dramatis personae, the cast list. The chief villain Mr Peachum comes from *peach*, to inform; among his gang are Nimming Ned (*nim*, to rob), Ben Budge (*budg*, a housebreaker) and Harry Paddington (reminiscent of *padding*, highway robbery, though the then village of Paddington was synonymous with the Tyburn gallows). As for the female characters, the surnames *Trapes*, *Doxy*, *Slammekin* and *Trull* all signify whore and/or sloven. Mrs Coaxer, Molly Brazen and Sukey Tawdrey are self-evident, if in standard English. And Jenny Diver was the criminal pseudonym, literally 'Jenny Pickpocket', of the real-life Mary Young (born c.1700) who was hanged for street robbery in 1741.[*]

A little earlier, in 1707, John Shirley's *Triumph of Wit* produced what purported to be a woman's song: 'The Rum-Mort's Praise

---

[*] Jenny's specialty was her pair of fake arms: these would be on display, seemingly emerging from her sleeves and folded demurely in her lap; meanwhile her real ones would be hard at work with her fingers dipping into her neighbours' purses.

of her faithless Maunder'. That is, the good woman's praise of her faithless lover, a beggar. The eight four-line verses are dense with cant, but fall, like a fake 'villains' conversation' into the category of animated dictionary. A single verse, surprisingly sexy for the era, should be sufficient:

> Dimber-damber [the gang boss] fare thee well,
> Palliards [beggars] all thou didst excell
> And thy jockum [penis] bore the Bell [was unrivalled]
> Glimmer on it never fell. [glimmer = fire thus venereal disease]

In 1724 came 'Frisky Moll's Song', composed by John Harper and sung at the Drury Lane Theatre in the pantomime *Harlequin Sheppard*, an attempt (among many) to capitalise on the execution, twelve days earlier, of the popular hero but wholly criminal Jack Sheppard (1702–24). The panto flopped and closed after seven shows. Again the sense is that of a writer making their laborious way through a canting dictionary:

> A famble, a tattle, and two popps, [a ring; a watch; a pair of pistols]
> Had my *Boman* when he was ta'en; [lover, literally 'handsome man']
> But had he not bouz'd in the diddle shops, [drink in the gin-shops]
> He'd still been in Drury-Lane

Finally, though earliest, is 'A Mort's Drinking Song' from Richard Brome's play *A Jovial Crew* (1641). Nothing too elaborate, and plenty of respect for booze.

Enter Patrico with his old wife with a wooden bowle of drink.
She is drunk. She sings:—.

This is *bien bowse*, this is bien bowse, [strong ale]
Too little is my *Skew*. [cup, tankard]
I bowse no *lage*, but a whole *gage* [water; pot]
Of this I'll bowse to you.

This bowse is better than *rom-bowse*, [wine]
It sets the *gan* a-gigling, [mouth]
The *autum-mort* finds better sport [wife]
In bowsing than in *nigling*. [fucking]
This is bien bowse, etc.

[*She tosses off her bowle, falls back and is carried out.*]

The nineteenth century is frustratingly light on female criminals talking slang, even at the hands of male interpreters. While,
for instance, Stephen Crane's *Maggie: a Girl of the Streets* (1893)
showcases a good range of contemporary New York City's underworld vocabulary, it is Maggie's brother, not the eponymous
heroine who is using it. As we know, Dickens was only one
among those who felt that however fictional men might speak,
women, criminal and otherwise, were to be rendered in standard
English. To an extent this 'silence' is the result of the sort of
villainy that women pursued. On the whole they were involved
in so-called petty crimes, e.g. shoplifting or pick-pocketing.
These, unlike men's homicidal efforts and big-time robberies,
were far less likely to hit the headlines, and to gain, at least in the
earlier years of the century, some confected 'famous last words'
or gallows-side 'confession' to be touted in the street. Alternatively

they were found as stalls and sidekicks, working as distracting companions for confidence tricksters or those who robbed jewellers' shops with deception rather than violence. They might also be fences, typically New York's celebrated Frederica 'Marm' Mandelbaum, who also ran teams of blackmailers and con-men, and financed a number of major robberies all in parallel with posing as a leading member of legitimate society. Nonethleless, while Marm, once she had fled New York for Canada (taking a cool million with her), occasionally appeared in the press commenting on current criminal events, her ghosted tones were positively dowager-like.

Women did murder, and were hanged for it, but they do not seem to have been permitted that kind of memorial. Perhaps it was not seen as sensible to celebrate such attacks on male primacy. Perhaps it was the typical nature of the female killer's crimes – infanticide or polishing off a husband or lover; the *running patterer* who street-sold ballads and broadsides presumably found male villainy a better seller. Broadsides did appear for such as the Swiss ladies' maid Marie Manning, who in 1849 hanged with her husband Frederick on the gallows outside Horsemonger Lane prison (south of the Thames near Borough High Street) while Dickens, Thackeray and 30,000 others watched, but there was no attempt to put words, slang or others, into her mouth. The celebratory (if faux moralistic) 'flash songs' that spun off from such as Jack Shepherd were over. Dickens savaged the 'the atrocious bearing, looks and language, of the assembled spectators' and the 'thousands upon thousands of upturned faces, so inexpressibly odious in their brutal mirth or callousness'* but it was they who were no doubt slanging it, not

---

* C. Dickens, letter to the *Times* (14 November 1849).

her. Dickens might claim himself appalled, but as ever the attentive plot-maker, used her, at least in part, for the character of 'Madame Hortense' in *Bleak House*.

A decade later, and in America, appeared what might be termed a piece of anomalous lexicography, aimed it was said at women and offering them nothing but criminal slang. The idea that women might not be as knowledgeable of the more intellectually demanding end of the English language was a wearisome tradition. The first English dictionary, Cawdrey's *Table Alphabeticall of . . . hard usual English Wordes* was published in 1604. It professed itself 'gathered for the benefit & help of Ladies, gentlewomen, or any other unskilful persons'. What it offered the users an opportunity to 'more easilie and better vnderstand many hard English wordes, which they shall heare or read in the Scriptures, Sermons, or elsewhere, and also be made able to vse the same aptly themselues'. The aim was upwards, not at the linguistic gutter. This new lexicon went in quite another direction.

The Ladies' Repository, published by the Methodist church in Cincinnati and edited by a succession of preachers, had been launched in 1841. Its aim was to provide women with something other than the usual diet of romantic stories and fashion tips, and replace it with moral earnestness, a selection of poetry and useful information on history and science. Not that it was all morals and didactics: it wished, said its editor, to entertain as well as instruct. It was to that end, perhaps, that from 1853 it also carried a section headed 'Apothegm, Wit, Repartee, and Anecdote'. In 1859 there appeared an article on slang. It was headed 'The Flash Language' and appeared as part of a feature 'Pencilings from Pittsburgh', based on conversations between its compiler, the Rev. B.F. Tefft, and a convict he encountered in the Pennsylvania penitentiary. There are 190 terms, all of which are, as would be expected, cant. Although the terms are not new, there is no specific dictionary cited as a source. A number of terms are defined in a specifically American context (e.g. a mention of the usually un-English 'steamboats' at *sneak*) and the detail of certain terms regarding housebreaking implements suggests that Tefft's informant was a knowledgeable professional.

Quite what America's middle-class, God-fearing womanhood were meant to do with *chiv*, a knife, *croaksman*, a murderer, *blind charley*, a lamp, *thimble-crib*, a jeweller's shop or *sun*, 'a bit constructed so as to cut a large hole in a door . . . There is no preventative but sheet iron' is hard to know. Perhaps some were inspired to a new life of crime. On the other hand they might have known some of the terms that appeared in other issues: *bapsouse*, a jocular term for beat up, *beau-catcher*, a lovelock (and defined by Hotten as 'the mark at which all the Puritan and ranting preachers levelled their pulpit pop-guns, loaded with sharp and virulent abuse'), *Choctaw*, unintelligible language, *clay-eater*, a poor white Southerner and the dismissive exclamation, *your granny!*

No city, no slang. If the uninitiated, keen to disentangle life on the wild side, encountered the counter-language, they needed a translation. Aimed, as was so much else, at a male reader, there appeared in both the UK and US (i.e. London and New York) a variety of anonymous 'guides' to the local low life. These tended to give a rundown on notorious dives, brothels and their inmates, a flash vocabulary, and perhaps a contrived 'conversation' between a bunch of criminals. One such was the *Swell's Night Guide*, authored by one 'F.L.G.', published in London in 1846.

This offered the usual components ('*Apple dumplings*, a woman's bosom, dugs, cat's heads, milk shops' . . . '*Ars music*, [. . .] the creaking of a bedstead when natural operations are being performed thereon') with a 'conversation' that was especially revelatory of what a criminal woman should be assumed to know. The *Guide* offers us a chat between a Gonnif (a thief) and a Schikster (who seems to combine prostitution and petty theft). Both words come from Yiddish, both had been absorbed into London's underworld vocabulary.

The centrality of women to crime is obvious. Not only are we given such figures as 'Slippery Sall, the Oakley-street stunner' ('Sall was held in great tip [highly admired] among the kiddies and shakes [criminals of both genders], as well on account of her patter, as her pluck and beauty . . . An out-and-outer [exemplary figure] she is to go and no mistake, a rattling piece [very attractive woman] and a stunning charver [in more accessible slang, "a great fuck"] , s'elp my never' and Bet Flab 'the Yarmouth Bloater', but we have a French contingent 'These Femmes de Francois have given a foreign cast to the entertainments, customs and grubbery department; and Lady Bull has followed the example of John Bull by getting into the French style . . . The French shicksters fight *coakum* [use their heads, from Yiddish *kochum*, knowledge] better than our shakes [from *shakester*, a woman, itself like *schikster* from Yiddish *shiksa*]; they do not lush [drink] nor scrap, and can sweeten [con] a swell better; they are not so barefaced in their prossing [asking for money]; though they know how to nail a cully [pull in a client] and *ball off a flat* [despoil a sucker].' Or Dutch Frow Christine, who tells her hearers of one client 'He cannot stand it, and I cannot stand it [. . .] he shall churn all night, but the butter will not come, and he bends de churn-staff.' There are gorgeresses [landladies of underworld pubs] such as Mother Ruckers who 'is in no way less notorious than is the crib [brothel]. [. . .] shes fly [aware of] to every fakement and cross dodge [form of criminality] [. . .] She is a rank screw, a dead *grab* and a stinging *nark* [all mean miser], [. . .] vill have her tin [money], cos malling of it [giving credit], von't furnish *monjary broad* [put food on the table].'

The bulk of the talk is about a robbery. The Schikster asks, the Gonnif reports back. An excerpt runs:

Schikster: Did you fake the slum [do the job], cully [mate], last darky? [night]

Gonniff: Faked it rumbo [did it fine]: copped the lob [grabbed the cash register], darked the hommo of the cassey [knocked out the owner], and scarpered with the swag, bona.

Schikster: What's the slums of the swag? [what did you get?]

Gonniff: Oh, all sorts of slums; prickers and chives [knives and forks], suppers and spreaders [watches and chains], fawney and fogles [rings and silk handkerchiefs] . . .

Schikster: And how about the lushy cove? [the drunk]

Gonniff: Oh, Sall planted him in the dunniken [lavatory], pinched his kicksters [trousers] and his shaker [jacket].

This is deep slang, hard even for criminals to nail down. But in no way need we feel that it has the least gender restriction.

It may not have yielded full-scale memoirs, but petty crime is not without its rewards for the slang searcher. After all, such criminals were very likely to have used a variety of counter-language, including the obscene. Anthony Rhys of upsetvictorians.blogspot, who is compiling evidence from the police and newspaper reports of mid-nineteenth-century crime in a couple of especially squalid Cardiff streets, sums things up:

> Firstly the people in my book MUST have sworn. I know you should never assume things in history but come on, you've got the roughest streets in Cardiff full of the roughest career criminals mixed in with boat loads of sailors and copious amounts of alcohol and opium. The question is what language did they use?

The primary source seems to be police reports. These would be read out in court, although by then the choicest terminology would have been redacted or at least bowdlerised. By the time the regular court reports appeared in the press, the realities would have been reduced to the anodyne, with (at least in the less staid papers) sniggering facetiousness to taste.

This seems to have been the contemporary way. The court reports of the Cardiff press and of Australia's main 'sporting' paper *Bell's Life in Sydney* (a local version of the London original) have much in common. *Bell's* uses some twenty-one terms for a whore: *angel, blowen, buffalo gal, chicken, cruiser, Cyprian* and *Paphian, demi-rep, dress-lodger, duck, faggot, frail* (*sister*), *moontrotter, nymph of the pave, pigeon, quean, soiled dove, thing, trotter, unfortunate* and *vestal*. A number of these appear in Cardiff, e.g. *unfortunate*, the description 'interesting' appears in both cities with the implication of prostitute. On the whole these were not limited to a single place: these were the euphemisms that the mid-Victorians had chosen.

Bell's Life, for all the raciness of its coverage of sport (which demonstrated slang's definition of the term as much as it did that of standard English) opted to defuse any possibility of offence when it dealt with the police courts. It played up to what was probably a male readership, and thus as well as reporting on some 'unfortunate's' offence and on at least a version of the language she used, it also opined on her looks and by extension character. She might be 'a tidy little Emeralder', 'a natty little piece of property', 'a measley faced moontrotter' or a 'free-hearted damsel'. Her 'countenance' might bear 'ample testimony to its sufferance from the heat of the sun in the rocky regions, together with a penchant for an "odd nobler"' [i.e. glass of liquor]; she might be 'deeply pitted by the smallpox'. The Sydney courts witnessed a variety of slang, but kept it 'clean'. Racial stereotyping, on the other hand, was not a problem. If the same 'Emeralder' was facing charges of 'being drunk and using obscene language' the reader encountered none of it. On the other hand her reported speech would be awash with *begobs* and *begorrahs*, and other staples of the stage Oirishwoman. The same went for Blacks (invariably *cuffy*, *sambo*, *snowball*) and Chinese (a *John*, *pigtail* or *celestial* who always substituted swearing on the bible by the smashing of crockery), and the speech of both groups would be transliterated into some grotesque approximation of their supposed pidgin.*

Perhaps the coarsest example was a report of onlookers barracking a girl: 'They called her a b[loody] w[hore], the favourite waterside appellation for every trotter in petticoats.' Otherwise one finds girls talking about a *bunch of fives* (the fist), a *trap* (a policeman), *taking malt above the meal* (getting drunk), *kicking up a shindy*, *give it to* (attack physically), *down with the dumps* (pay over the money) and an insult: *snotty-nose*. In 1846 the paper reported that 'She heard the [female] defendant call her a

---

* There were as yet insufficient Jews: fifty years later the Australian press rejoiced in *ikey-mo*, *God-knows-who*, *sheeny*, *old clo* and *porker* with predictably accented reported speech.

d—d b—h and tell her [. . .] she would give her the d—st walloping she ever got in her life."* On the whole, however, it was pretty restrained and a typical report told how a young woman used 'a variety of expletives not to be met within Johnson or Walker's Dictionaries; but with which the lovers of cant and filthy garbage in Sydney are most familiarly conversant'.† Unfortunately the paper, however much it might boast of its 'sportiness', offered no further detail.

The Cardiff police reports are far more frank, although they took a while to reach that point. As Anthony Rhys explains,

> Unfortunately the police, who were the ones charging the prostitutes, pimps and thieves [. . .] often report using the 'she used disgusting language' format without repeating the words. [. . .] Luckily however this changed in the 1860's and the court transcriber Mr Rees was kind enough to write down a LOAD of the swear words that the police reported.

Thus such reports as that of 1849 in which P.C. Lewis Young 'very graphically described the lady's interesting conduct' but 'said that her language was so bad—so disgustingly vulgar that he was ashamed to repeat it'‡ were replaced by a selection of what, at least at the time, were considered real filth.

For examples of the kind of language that might have been used, usually by one woman to another woman or by a woman responding aggressively to a policeman who had in some way reprimanded her, there are these from Anthony Rhys' researches. All were used in 1850s to 1860s.

---

* *Bell's Life in Sydney* (13 February 1846), p.3/2.
† *Bell's Life in Sydney* (3 April 1847), p.3/2.
‡ *Cardiff Merthyr Guardian* (8 August 1849), p.1.

'You are the b[ugge]r that took the tobacco from me'

'There's the b[lood]y thief, kill the b[ugge]r'

'Bloody whore'

'She said to her sister to look at me standing in my door the stinking Bitch'

'Defendant called me a bloody shit'

'[I] did not strike her, I called her a nasty dirty slut'

'[She] called _____ a bloody fucking cow'

'She was telling women to go and fuck their mothers'

'Saw prisoner on Bute Road—some sailors passed. She used most disgusting language. She told sailors to kiss her cunt'

'When told to move on by the policeman she said she would when she pulled off her drawers—she pulled them off and told me to kiss her arse'

'She began abusing us and made use of the most indecent language. She rose up her clothes behind and said kiss my b[lood]y arse."

If such effings and blindings are truly verbatim, their creativity or rather absence thereof, is disappointing but very likely accurate. Half or wholly drunk, in the midst of a shouting match, lacking much in the way of articulacy or wit, it's the sort of thing that gives slang a bad name. The same thing – though never so explicit – is to be encountered in much 'proletarian' fiction, specifically the late nineteenth-century 'Cockney novels' that focused on the rougher areas of London's East End. Arthur Morrison's *Child of the Jago* (in real life a hyper-squalid area near Brick Lane known as the Old Nichol) or *Tales of Mean Streets* (with a similar backdrop) include a number of women, but these are not the feather-bedecked party animals of the music hall.

---

* For details, dates, sources and many more examples, see http://upsetvictorians.blogspot.com/2017/11/kiss-my-bloody-arse-swearing-in.html

Marie Lloyd at her most hard-done-to never sank to these depths. Nor are Morrison's women directly criminal, though their husbands often are, and their own activities often aid and abet what they consider no more than their partner's job: keeping the family afloat with ends definitely justifying means. If anything they are stern upholders of the law: the law of their local enclave. They persecute – with words and deeds – those of their society who cannot or will not fit in. If that includes accepting a regular nightly bashing from a drunken husband, so be it.

As for slang, at least one Morrison woman, mother to Dicky Perrott (the 'Child of the Jago'), is less than happy.

The boy returned to his box, and sat. Then he said, 'I do n't s'pose father's 'avin' a sleep outside, eh?' The woman sat up with some show of energy. [. . .] 'No, I ain't seen 'im; I jist looked in the court.' Then after a pause, 'I 'ope 'e's done a click,' the boy said. His mother winced. 'I dunno wot you mean, Dicky,' she said, but falteringly. 'You you're gittin' that low an' — '

'Wy, copped somethink, o' course. Nicked somethink. You know.' 'If you say sich things as that I'll tell 'im wot you say, an' 'e' pay you. We ain't that sort o' people, Dicky, you ought to know. I was alwis kep' respectable an' straight all my life, I 'm sure, an'— '

'I know. You said so before, to father — I 'card: wen 'e brought 'ome that there yuller prop the necktie pin. Wy, where did 'e git that? 'E ain't 'ad a job for munse an' munse; where's the yannups come from wot's bin for to pay the rent, an' git the toke, an' milk for Looey? Think I dunno? I ain't a kid; I know.'

'Dicky, Dicky! you must n't say sich things!' was all the

mother could find to say, with tears in her slack eyes. 'It's wicked an' an' low. An' you must alwis be respectable an' straight, Dicky, an' you'll get on then.'*

There are cheerier moments. For all that her home turf is The Cut, near Waterloo, no-one could epitomise the 'chirpy cockney sparrer' of popular myth more than the eponymous heroine of Pett Ridge's *Mord Em'ly* (1898). Mord is poor, her mother a nervous wreck and her father 'away' (i.e. in prison) but if she runs in the streets as the junior member of the all-girl Gilliken Gang, there is no malice let alone hard-core criminality in her. (Nor in the gang whose leader subsequently joins the Salvation Army.) Dicky Perrott of the Jago sees crime as an escape from wretchedness, 'Young Alf', the hooligan of Clarence Rook's take on the theme *The Hooligan Nights*, is a career villain (though he will die serving in the Boer War), but Mord Em'ly is above all a feisty young woman, enjoying life, and giving as good, if not better than she gets.

'Know this feller, don't you?' asked Miss Gilliken, jerking her head in the direction of the youth.

'Seen his mug before,' said Mord Em'ly, looking at him casually. 'Can't say I know his name.'

'Name of 'Enery Barden,' said the youth, in a deep, hoarse voice, stepping forward, and introducing himself awkwardly. 'Got a job at the Willer Walk Station; also to be met with, Saturday evenings, at the boxing-saloon of the Green Man.'

'Where did ye find it?' asked Mord Em'ly of Miss Gilliken, with a satirical accent.

* A. Morrison, *Child of the Jago* (1896), pp.13–14.

'Who are you calling "it"?' demanded Mr. Barden aggressively. 'P'r'aps you'll kindly call me "'im" and not "it"!'

'P'r'aps I shall do jest as I like,' replied Mord Em'ly. She
turned to Miss Gilliken. 'Did you win it in a raffle?'

'I'll tell you presently,' said Miss Gilliken.

'Sometimes they give 'em away,' said Mord Em'ly thought-
fully, 'with a packet of sweets. I 'ave seen 'em offered instead
of a coker-nut or a cigar at one of these Aunt Sally—'

'Look 'ere!' interrupted Mr. Barden crossly. 'You think
you're jolly clever, no doubt.'

'Think?' repeated Mord Em'ly. 'Don't I know it?'

Unsurprisingly she lacks the cant that informs the other two.
Her slang is gentler: *act the giddy goat, soft* (a weakling), *song and
dance, stony* (broke), *bounder*; it often appears as interjections:
cheese it!, give over!, I don't think, s'elp me greens!, language!, or in
imagery: someone has 'a face on 'im like half-past six'. It represents not her femininity – her verbal sophistication can outwit
virtually every male she meets – but her 'civilian' status. Mord's
slang would not have defeated the middle classes, and the book
was a best-seller.

But Mord is no bad 'un. South London she may have been
but the area's notorious Forty Elephants Gang, an all-girl mob
specialising in shoplifting and when necessary violence, wouldn't
have given her the time of day. For an uncompromising criminal
it is necessary to skip forward thirty years. To one who would
not only have been recognised by the Elephants, but whose lover
was best mates with the brother of one of their most ferocious
members.

Back with Mord, her language and what modernity terms
attitude are what make her indomitable. She is poor, working

class, she lives that life, but she gives no quarter. She is always, unconquerably, herself. Never more so than when, sent off by her mother on behalf of the family budget, she arrives in still bourgeois Peckham to become a maid.

'This, dears,' said the youngest sister, 'is the little girl who has come after the place. She looks willing, and my idea is that we might take her for a month, at any rate. Her mother is a good worker.'

'I expect Letty is right,' said one of the elder sisters. 'What is your name, my girl?'

'Mord Em'ly.'

Name interpreted by the youngest sister.

'Oh, you must really learn to pronounce distinctly. You should say Maud, and then wait for a moment, and then say Em-ily.'

'All very well,' said Mord Em'ly, 'if you've got plenty of time.'

'Are you a hard worker, my girl?'

'Fairish, miss. I ain't afraid of it, anyway.'

'I think we shall decide to call you Laura if you stop with us.'

'Whaffor?' demanded Mord Em'ly.

'We always call our maids Laura,' explained the eldest of the ladies complacently. 'It's a tradition in the family. And my youngest sister there, Miss Letitia, will look after you for the most part. My other sisters are engaged in—er— literature; I myself, if I may say so without too much confidence, am responsible for'—here the eldest sister looked in a self-deprecatory manner at the toe of her slippers—'art.'

'My sister Fairlie,' went on the eldest lady in a lecturing

style, and pointing with her forefinger, 'writes under the pen name of 'George Willoughby,' and has gained several prizes, some of them amounting to as much as one guinea. My sister Katherine pursues a different branch. Her speciality to use a foreign expression, is the subject of epitaphs—queer epitaphs, ancient epitaphs, pathetic epitaphs, singular epitaphs, amusing—'

'Talking about epitaphs,' interrupted Mord Em'ly, 'how much do I get a year for playing in this piece?'

Unsurprisingly Number 18 Lucella Road, SE does not hold her long. The bright lights of Walworth are far more alluring.

What matters is freedom and after a series of misadventures which include reform school (and she is, to an extent 'reformed', or certainly enough to allow her discharge), she sails off with the one boy who, still on her own terms, she has permitted to woo her. They are destined for a new life in that emblematic land of liberty: Australia. Walworth may have teemed with Mords but real-life London would have trampled their joyous self-sufficiency. Like his cockneys, Mord's merry life is Pett Ridge's fantasy: its only hope was to journey to what was still a fantasy land.

While still in the East End but no longer in fiction, we have *Seven Years' Hard*, the Reverend Richard Free's memoir of his days as a church 'missionary' in the Isle of Dogs, otherwise known as Millwall, 'the city of desolation' as the author terms it.

The supposed transcription of working-class speech is always problematic. The Reverend mocks 'soup-ticket philanthropists' but whether his docklands' women really spoke as he sets them down is unknown. On the other hand his contemporary Henry Nevinson, who combined war reporting with a little East End sociology, termed his excellent book . . . 'an intimate knowledge of working life.'* Let us agree.

Example 1: A neighbour informs Mrs Wilderish of a relative's imminent death. Mrs W. is not wholly convinced:

'Death-rattle!' echoed Mrs. Wilderish, with a sniff of contempt. 'The rattle needn't mean death, not if you've got your wits about you. Look at my Lizzie. She was a gorner [goner], if you like. There wasn't much left of 'er to pray about, I can tell you. Well, we was sitting waitin', wen sure enough comes 'er death-rattle. Up I jumps in a rare flurry, nea'ly knockin' the beer-can over it was a gallon, an' 'eavy, wen I'm blest if that there child di'n't open 'er eyes an' arst for a drink. You don't suppose we giv' it "er? Not 'arf! We tilted that gallon-can down her throat, an', Lord love you! she sucked at it an' sucked at it well, she might 'a drinked a pint. That child got better! Ah, nobody knows wot liquor can do 'cept them wot 'as put it to the test. Death-rattle, indeed! Give me beer!'[†]

Example 2:

East End women. Indeed, wife-beating is such a recognised institution, that a husband would lose caste should he so far forget his marital privileges as to be a total abstainer in this respect.

'Wot's up, Bella?' solicitously inquired a young woman, in my hearing, of a friend whose appearance indicated that she had been in the wars. 'Oh, nothink!

* H. W. Nevinson, *Essays in Rebellion* (1913), p.56.
† Rev. Richard Free, *Seven Years' Hard* (1904), p.65.

On'y my mate chastised me last night; so I've got to go about with a couple o' coloured eyes.' 'Does your father ever wallop you?' Lizzie Haggerston was asked by a small girl friend. 'Not 'arf! I might as well be his wife!' was Lizzie's answer.

Sometimes, however, the mare is the better horse, in which case I am uncertain whether the condition of the 'henpecked' husband is not more pitiable than that of the chastised 'wife'.

'Why has Mrs. Templar taken to drink?' I once inquired of that lady's friend.

'Well, she's got a lot to put up with; and when I tell you as 'ow 'er 'usband openly defies 'er, you'll understand."

Example 3:

As the local vicar, Free dispensed a good deal more than religion. Locals having problems with their landlord hoped to find him an ally. These, or so he assures the reader, are some of the letters he received. Writing to the clergy meant they abandoned slang, but that only achieved a degree of literacy:

Mr. Free Mr Blinker as start this morning thank god but i had a Letter from the Land Lord to say if not the Weeks rent when Collector Call to day between 3 and 4 to prevent further proceedings but i cant give him Eny think till Saturday as Mr. Blinker wont get it till then it will be 2 Week on Monday due but what make him so sharp i is as soon as he Can get you out he does the place up and put 1/6 moor on than are 4/6 down now.

* Free op. cit. p.130.

pleas Mr. Free are they to Come down for The Soup

pleas Mr Free i am sorry to have to ask you again Mr Gropp as not do a day work now 3 Weeks to morrow i did a little last week and hope to do a little this week i was going to ask you if you Could lend me 4/ till Saturday for the Landlord to night to save him sending the Brokers in i dont whant to go to the Workhouse if i can help it he will be heare about eaight to night.

The first of modern crime's female memoirists was published in 1928, though her career was over and she would die two years later. May Sharpe, self-christened 'the Queen of Crooks', was born either Beatrice Desmond in 1876 or May Duignan and five years earlier. In both cases she was the daughter of an Irish farmer. Constricted by her conservative upbringing – rigid schooling, claustrophobic home-life – she 'borrowed' £60 from her father's bankroll and skipped to America. She was just fourteen. Her first husband, Dal Churchill, was a classic Western 'baddie', robbing banks and holding up railroad trains. May 'liked what money could do' and he had plenty. But not for long: a heist failed, Churchill was wounded, captured and lynched.

According to her memoir this was her moment of truth. The goodtime cutie turned super-criminal avenger, pitting herself against a world that had stolen, then violently executed her man. 'When you want to go wrong,' she explained, 'it is very easy to accomplish your purpose.' Based in Chicago's red-light zone, the levee, she turned herself into a mistress of brothel-based fraud, specialising in the badger game and working in panel houses. From there she escalated things to blackmail, operating on much the same principle: the men she ensnared would rather pay than have their peccadilloes exposed to a censorious social world.

She fleeced everything that moved at the Chicago World Fair of 1893 and once that was exhausted, moved to New York. Here, like Marm Mandelbaum, she managed to mix lucrative criminality with infiltrating the social whirl. She met such as Mark Twain and the actor DeWitt Hopper and having got it, duly flaunted it as well. From New York, where she kept her savings fat with fake 'breach of promise' complaints, she sailed east to London. Here she met one Eddie Guerin, another Irish-American and another criminal.* Their biggest heist was the American Express office in Paris (Guerin hated France, having already spent a decade in the country's prisons). Just as they seemed to have got away with the job, it fell apart. The lovers were captured: Sharpe got five years and was out, pardoned, after less than three. Guerin was sent for life to the notorious penal encampment of Devil's Island (recently home to Alfred Dreyfus, railroaded as an alleged spy by the anti-semites of the French establishment). Remarkably he managed to escape after just three years.

Both returned to London. Here May had a new boyfriend, Charlie Smith, yet another villain. Guerin, convinced May had grassed him up, promised her a variety of punishments: lopping off her ears, tossing acid in her face. In the event he and Smith ran into each other and started shooting, Guerin's gun jammed, Smith shot off two of his toes. However Sharpe and Smith were tried and convicted for attempted murder. He got life, she fifteen years. Pardoned after a decade she was deported to America. The good days would not return: she was poor, presumably lacking the old skills, and could barely find a place to live.

---

* Guerin was best pals with the up-and-coming London villain Billy Hill, on his way to becoming what he, at any rate, termed the 'Boss of Britain's Underworld'; Hill's sister, Maggie, a terrifying sociopath who seemed to relish violence for its own sake, was second-in-command of the Forty Elephants.

There would be a final scam: in 1927 the reformed British con man turned journalist Netley Lucas published a history: *Ladies of the Underworld*. His publisher saw a marriage of financial convenience: Lucas and a genuine underworld lady, the Queen of Crime, May Sharpe. They duly played the game and reaped rewards in book sales and press coverage. The truth came out, but no matter: one best-seller sparks off another and after Lucas's effort, May's memoir appeared in 1928, even if she didn't seem to profit. She would die in poverty in 1930, bereft of money, health (she had cancer) and any vestige of a happy ending. According to Lucas (in his memoir *My Selves*) she'd lost her looks and lived in a cheap hotel room, awash with dirty magazines, fag packets and empty liquor bottles. Still, as her memoir concludes: her only regret was being caught.

May's autobiography is as slangy as one might expect from a professional criminal. In all she offers some three hundred examples. It is a predictable list, and very much of its time. Though she is relatively prudish when it comes to sex. There are many more terms from confidence trickery. Perhaps this reflected her self-description, her days with the badger game and in the panel houses notwithstanding, as 'artist'. If there are few 'female-specific' terms other than those dealing with prostitution why should there be? Perhaps the oddest entries, given that she was ultimately an American, were sixty-odd terms of rhyming slang, which she presumably picked up from her days in London. She headed her list 'the language of the underworld', but of course it wasn't: more the language of the London Cockney.

She also stands as the first recorded user, at least in print, of seventy words and phrases. Setting aside the rhymes, they include:

Aunt Jane (the border town of Tijuana, Mexico), *bend* (to allow oneself to be corrupted), *bum soup* (diarrhoea), *call out* (to use a stolen cheque to pay one's bills), *cokey* (a drug addict, but not a cocaine user), *connector* (a beggar), *creep* (a sneak thief), *drizzle* (nonsense), gopher (a robber who tunnels under and thus into his target, e.g. a jewellery store), *hop on* (to beat up), *john elbow* (a police officer), *lay up* (to hide), *lean on* (to trust, to depend on), *locate* (to target a victim for a con trick), *lose out* (to be swindled), *Mrs White* (a narcotics dealer, presumably female), *pay-off* (*man*) (a confidence trickster of either gender), *black pill* (a measure of opium), *piperheidsick* (to look; a play on slang *pipe*, to look and the brandname of a popular champagne), *take the rap* (to go to prison), *rapper* (an informer), *sad* (a sadist; she also notes *masoch*), *scream* (a good time), *take a sleigh-ride* (to use morphine), *sneak job* (house-breaking), *steerer* (a crooked lawyer or an agent who supplies such a lawyer with clients), *straighten out* (to act in an acceptable manner; to abandon one's bad habits), *tie up* (to link) and *wires* (the electric chair).

Around a decade later, in 1937, came *Sister of the Road* by 'Boxcar Bertha', properly Bertha Thompson. Despite still being advertised as a 'raging slab of real American history you're not likely to find in the textbooks' and publicised as the real-life Thompson's genuine autobiography – 'one hell of a rugged woman's hard-living depression-era saga of misadventures with pimps, hopheads, murderers, yeggs, wobblies, and anarchists'* – the book is acknowledged as fiction and it seems that Ms Thompson was made neither of flesh nor blood but only of type-writer ribbon. 'Her' story was written by the American anarchist (and onetime lover of the radical campaigner Emma Goldman) Ben Reitman. Reitman coupled his own left-wing politics with

---

* Blurb by www.akpress.org/sisteroftheroad.html (2002).

working as a doctor-cum-educator in the hobo community; in a world of exaggerated nicknames his – perhaps self-proclaimed – was 'King of the Hobos' though he seems to have abandoned the rods as a teenager.

It remains a slang-heavy work and there was no reason why 'Bertha's' voice didn't represent the kind of people who *rode the rails*, cooked in *jungles* and suffered the attentions of *shacks* and *horstiles*. Reitman claimed her to be a composite of several radical women he knew and it is their voices that he is channelling.

Setting aside more general terms, 'Bertha' deals with what 'she' (or those on whose knowledge Reitman drew) might have used on a regular basis. She lists a detailed taxonomy of hobos: a. *Blinkey* (blind) b. *Deafey* (deaf) c. *Dummy* (dumb) d. *D & D* (deaf and dumb) e. *Army* or *wingey* (armless) f. *Peggy* (legless) g. *Crippy* (paralysed) h. *Fritzy* (epileptic) i. *Nuts* (feeble-minded or insane) j. *Shaky* (with pronounced tremors). And added *blisters* (those who use fake sores to elicit extra sympathy), *ghosts* (those who simulate pallor, haggardness, or coughing to imitate a tubercular patient) and *floppers* (those who sit or flop down in front of a church or building and give the impression of being cripples). Non-specific hobos were *bindle stiffs* (from their *bindle* or bundle), *gandy dancers* (originally used of railroad maintenance crews) and, if women, *battleaxes*. To ride (a freight train) was to *flip* (a freight). The enemy was a *shack* or *railroad dick* and a warning of his approach an *air loft* or a *buzz*.

There were, inevitably, drugs, with opium as the intoxicant of choice. The jargon was explained: 'This particular outfit, or "layout," consisted of six bowls and four stems, three small traveling lamps that burned peanut oil, a dozen yen hoks, (like a crochet hook, but finer and more flexible, used for preparing the opium pill) and three yen shee gows, steel instruments for removing the yen shee or ash from the inside of the bowl.' There were also references to the *chef* (who cooks the pill of opium), to a *connection* (a dealer) and *dog* (the residue of second-rate opium). Drink came in the form of *dago red* (cheap, possibly home-made wine) while a *muggle* was a marijuana-filled cigarette.

Prostitution offered a mini-lexis of *the game*: the *working girl*, *hustling girl* and call-girl (who was summoned by 'phone); the *gold-digger*, the *broad* and the *baboon* (an especially hard worker); pimps were a *daddy* or a *coffee-and pimp* (a second-rater with perhaps one girl in his *stable*). Prostitutes offered *Greek* (anal sex) and *half-and-half* (fellatio plus full intercourse).

Perhaps the largest vocabulary was that of criminality. The pickpocket was the primary villain: a *cannon*, *clout*, *gun* or *whizz*; a *derrick* or *booster* was a shoplifter; a *heavy man* a burglar, a *duke player* (from *duke*, a hand) a cheating gambler, a *beater* a swindler and a *heel* a sneak thief. To arrest was to *guzzle*, *glom* or *grab off*. A *hotel* or *bughouse* was a prison, while *Bughouse Square* was generic for any centre of urban life, typically Union Square, New York City, or Washington Square, Chicago, where tramps, vagrants, the more or less deranged and any other eccentrics gather. To be *down* was to be in jail where a *fresh fish* was a new inmate.

Bertha wasn't alone, nor even first in her field. In 1917 there had been Ethel Lynn's *The Adventures of a Woman Hobo*. She offered a small vocabulary, among its terms: *bindle stiff*, a hobo (who carried a *bindle*, i.e. bundle), *flophouse*, a cheap lodging house, *plute*, a rich person, i.e. a plutocrat, *brakie*, the brakeman on a train, *honey-dripper*, a term of affection, *copperhead*, a Northerner who had fought for the Confederacy, *skate*, to rush away, *tuckered out*, exhausted and *gritty*, tough.

In her 1968 memoir *The True Story of Bonnie and Clyde*, Emma Parker, the mother of Bonnie, she of the much-fêted Depression-era his-and-hers bank-robbers and that year's hit movie, claimed that when she heard her daughter starting to use what she termed bandit slang, she witnessed 'a strange and terrifying change taking place in the mind of my child'. There can be no doubt that the gun moll of the 1930s would have used the same kind of language that typified her boyfriend. If it wasn't much recorded then nor is the day-to-day talk, via pillow or elsewhere, of any pair of young criminals. In Bonnie Parker, however, we do have a tangible exception: the poems she wrote down either while on the run or while in jail. One, the mawkish 'The Ballad of Bonnie and Clyde' (otherwise 'The Trail's End') was excerpted in the movie of their life; it was mainly in standard English though we do find the odd incursion of slang, for instance a newsboy's comment:

'I wish old Clyde would get jumped.
In these awfull hard times;
we'd make a few dimes,
if five or six cops would get bumped'

There was also 'The Street Girl'. It starts with a common Parker theme: the farm girl running after the bright lights, and, for a while, things look good:

I soon got a job in the chorus,
With nothing but looks and a form.
I had a new man every evening,
And my kisses were thrilling and warm.

Despite the offers, she resisted 'some old Sugar daddy with dough' but young suitors were a different matter.

> Then I fell for the 'line' of a 'junker',
> A slim devotee of hop,
> And those dreams in the juice of a poppy,
> Had got me before I could stop.

Once her lover leaves her 'in a hop joint one nite', it's downhill all the way.

> Well, I didn't care then what happened,
> A Chink took me under his wing,
> And down in the hovel of hell,
> I labored for Hop and Ah-Sing.

She gets busted, takes the cure on 'the Island' (Blackwell's Island, NYC), but has no illusions of reform. For,

> A man can break every commandment,
> And the world still will lend him a hand.
> Yet a girl that has loved, but unwisely,
> Is an outcast all over the land.

Of all her doggerel the hundred lines of 'The Story of Suicide Sal' was best known. It was found during a raid on their hideout in Joplin Missouri in April, 1933. Jotted down in a notebook she had picked up during a bank raid in Burkburnett, Texas, it conveniently marked nearly all instances of what she considered to be slang with quote marks. The poem was published across the country; the pair had less than a year to live.

We each of us have a good 'alibi'
For being down here in the 'joint;'
But few of them really are justified
If you get right down to the point.
You've heard of a woman's glory
Being spent on a 'downright cur,'
Still you can't always judge the story
As true, being told by her.
As long as I've stayed on this 'island,'
And heard 'confidence tales' from each 'gal,'
Only one seemed interesting and truthful—
The story of 'Suicide Sal.'
Now 'Sal' was a gal of rare beauty,
Though her features were coarse and tough;
She never once faltered from duty
To play on the 'up and up.'
'Sal' told me this take on the evening
Before she was turned out 'free,'
And I'll do my best to relate it
Just as she told it to me:
I was born on a ranch in Wyoming;
Not treated like Helen of Troy;
I was taught that 'rods are rulers'
And 'ranked' as a greasy cowboy.
Then I left my old home for the city
To play in its mad dizzy whirl,
Not knowing how little pity
It holds for a country girl.
There I fell for 'the line' of a 'henchman,'
A 'professional killer' from 'Chi;'
I couldn't help loving him madly;

For him even now I would die.
One year we were desperately happy;
Our 'ill gotten gains' we spent free;
I was taught the ways of the 'underworld;'
Jack was just like a 'god' to me.
I got on the 'F.B.A.' payroll
To get the 'inside lay' of the 'job;'
The bank was 'turning big money!'
It looked like a 'cinch' for the 'mob.'
Eighty grand without even a 'rumble'——
Jack was the last with the 'loot' in the door,
When the 'teller' dead-aimed a revolver
From where they forced him to the floor.
I knew I had only a moment—
He would surely get Jack as he ran;
So I 'staged a "big fade out"' beside him
And knocked the forty-five out of his hand.
They 'rapped me down big' at the station,
And informed me that I'd get the blame
For the 'dramatic stunt' pulled on the 'teller'
Looked to them too much like a 'game.'
The 'police' called it a 'frame-up,'
Said it was an 'inside job,'
But I steadily denied any knowledge
Or dealings with 'underworld mobs,'
The 'gang' hired a couple of lawyers,
The best 'fixers' in any man's town,
But it takes more than lawyers and money
When Uncle Sam starts 'shaking you down.'
I was charged as a 'scion of gangland'
And tried for my wages of sin;

The 'dirty dozen' found me guilty—
From five to fifty years in the pen.
Tomorrow I'll be on the 'outside'
And I'll 'drop myself' on it today:
I'll 'bump 'em' if they give me the 'hotsquat'
On this island out here in the bay . . .
The iron doors swung wide next morning
For a gruesome woman of waste,
Who at last had a chance to 'fix it.'
Murder showed in her cynical face.
Not long ago I read in the paper
That a gal on the East Side got 'hot,'
And when the smoke finally retreated,
Two of gangdom were found 'on the spot.'
It related the colorful story
Of a 'jilted gangster gal.'
Two days later, a 'sub-gun' ended
The story of 'Suicide Sal.'

Bonnie Parker's poems, probably unconsciously (though they seem to have been permeated by every cliché the fictional versions of the criminal world could offer), are deeply informed by what one might see as a pulp ethos, i.e. the same kind of sensibility not to mention vocabulary, as that of the then popular pulp magazines, specifically those of the noir-infused detective pulps such as *Black Mask*, *Detective Fiction Weekly*, and further down the market, *Gun Molls* and *Spicy Detective*.* As to

* It was the publisher of this latter, Frank Armer, who in 1935 published *Sex in Detective Fiction – Do's and Don'ts*:
1. In describing breasts of a female character, avoid anatomical descriptions.
2. If it is necessary for the story to have the girl give herself to a man, do not go too carefully into the details. You can lead up to the actual consummation, but leave the rest

the authors, it is hard to know who exactly was who: a series character would have many writers taking turns to sign as a single totemic by-line; women, just as they continue to do in other creative environments, often signed themselves as men. For instance C.B. Yorke created such female stars as gang boss Queen Sue and private eye Yola Yates: '[She] twisted forward, freeing the gun in her pocket. "Mobsters with a Tommy!" she shouted. "Gun 'em, guys!"'. On another occasion a man asks, 'Why the gun play, Sister? . . . Who are you?' 'Just a woman — ' she said evenly, and after a brief pause, ' — detective.' Like Yates, Yorke's Queen Sue was a staple of *Gangster Stories* (1930–32). Titles included 'Arms and the Moll', 'Mother of Guns' and 'Snowbound'('My right hand shot under the hem of my dress and came out with my gun in my fingers'). Yorke was also responsible for gun moll Velma Dare. To quote Jesse Nevins' blog *The Best of the Encyclopedia of Pulp Heroes*:

> Velma Dare is a stick-up woman fresh from a two-year stint in the joint. She was framed for a crime she didn't commit: "Buck and I had pulled some jobs the cops never got wise to, but we hadn't been near the Gladstone Theatre." A "yellow-bellied stoolie and a crooked dick" sent Dare and her partner Buck Evans away, but before she'd gone she had uttered a threat to get even with the stoolie and the dick. She changed

up to the reader's imagination. This subject should be handled delicately and a great deal can be done by implication and suggestion.
3. Whenever possible, avoid complete nudity of the female characters. You can have a girl strip to her underwear, or transparent negligee, or nightgown, or the thin torn shred of her garments, but while the girl is alive and in contact with a man, we do not want complete nudity.
4. A nude female corpse is allowable, of course.
5. Also, a girl undressing in the privacy of her own room, but when men are in the action try to keep at least a shred of something on the girls.
6. Do not have men in underwear in scenes with women, and no nude men at all.

her mind about the threat ("women do that – often") and
when she is released from prison she is "determined to mind
my own business and keep out of any jams with the cops."
But people begin dying, and the police blame Dare, and she
finds it more difficult than she'd intended to break free of the
underworld. Fortunately, she has her skills as a criminal,
including marksmanship, and the friendship of "hard boiled
flattie" Detective Captain Lon Colby to help her remain free
and unkilled.*

Velma is properly tooled up for a slang-ful narration:

A *frame's* a frame, no matter how you look at it. But some-
     times you can't prove it, and this was one of those times
Our *mouthpiece* had tried to carry the case to a higher court,
     but failed
Bert Frome had gone to a lot of trouble to *frame* that evidence
Buck and I *took the rap*. There was nothing else to do about
     it
The defense was trying to *pull a* legal *fast one* by claiming
     that we were framed
But that didn't alter the fact that the evidence was *phoney*
And now I wondered who was making me a *goat*
Clam Seibert was *in the spot*, but I hadn't put him there
Velma Dare was going to *knock over* the man who had *stooled*
     on me and Buck
A friendly barman in a *speak* had *tipped* me the news
I hadn't broken away completely from the underworld even
     though I was *going straight*

* http://jessnevins.com/blog/?p=594

Buck and I had never *tied up* with any of the gangs or the
  rackets that *worked* the city

[L]ucky enough not to get picked up too often by the *bulls*

Death and the cops had caused quite a change during the
  two years I'd been in *stir*

[T]here were a lot of new faces everywhere I went. I knew
  they all weren't just *floaters*

There was nobody I could go to in the underworld for the
  lowdown on it all

Clam Seibert had become prosperous in the *booze racket*
  while I had been serving *time*

I knew what would happen as soon as Clam *stopped a slug*

He'd know a lot of things about the new *line-up* in crime

He'd been the first *dick* to *run me in*

[H]e had paid his debt to society by serving a *stretch in the
  pen*

My nerves were *shot* from worry

[I] was *on the prod* twenty hours yesterday, trying to run that
  down

I *sent* you *up* once, and I'll do it again

Think I'm *sap* enough to tell the world—if I was *giving* a guy
  the works?

Lamming won't help me. I can't fight a murder charge by
  long distance

'He's crooked—or was,' I said as a feeler. Nodding, Colby
  said: 'Yeah, liquor's made *bums* out of lots of cops.'

[H]e was taking *graft* from three or four *fences*

'I won't be a *fall guy!*' I blazed

Dizzy Malone was another first-person femme. 'A real gun
moll—a jane with a purple paradise and a red past—but a sport.'

As her creator Perry Paul explained in 'The Jane from Hell's Kitchen', in the October 1930 edition of *Gun Molls*, 'Her *moniker* was a *stall*. They called her *Dizzy* because she most decidedly wasn't.' Dizzy's been bad, still is, but she's fighting on the side of goodness. She's hot stuff, in every sense. 'A flash of chiffon and silk—the door opened and a girl backed her quivering body against it, her mouth open, panting . . . "Dizzy Malone," he gasped. "The same gorgeous body and all!" ' Dizzy – pictured in cloche hat, full-length fur, seamed stockings (silk presumably) and a cigarette holder – takes no nonsense. The story ends when her treacherous lover takes to the air and she downs his plane with the machine-gun mounted in her own.

Like Queen Sue she's got pulp lingo to spare.

Now collapse, *stuffed shirt*, while I put on the loud speaker
That guy [. . .] that's disappeared. I gotta *hunch* who *lifted*
    him
No more *cracks* like that then, *big boy*
I came here to make you a proposition, not to *turn anyone*
    up
He gets a *phoney wire* to come see you
Your job is to get Burke back and turn up the guy that *pulled*
    the job
A guy [. . .] put the *double-X* on me
I was his *moll*. We *worked* a good *racket*. We piled up a stake,
    a big one
We were all set to *beat it for the sticks*
Then some *fly dick framed a rap* on him
My man went *stir-bugs* up there
Baldy Ross [. . .] a *straight-shooting* guy, gets *lit* out in *Chi*
    with a *cokie* that's a *rat*

A copper gets *bumped off*
They *put him on the spot* for the rat he was
While the Ghost's in the *'Can'* some *wise yegg* gets the Kid
    coked up
A watchman gets *knocked off*
You *send* him *up the river* and he *fries*
He comes outa the *Big House* completely *bugs*
That black-haired *flossie*, Spanish Lil *gets her hooks into* him
She *takes* him for his *wad* and the Ghost is *flat*
He taught me [. . .] how to work rackets the *flatties* never
    heard of
I can spring this *bozo* Burke
Somebody'll get it in the neck all right
Throwin' *coin* around like a *coked-up* bootlegger
There's only person that can *put the skids under* him [. . .]
    and I'm that baby!
I'm no *squealer* [she gets third degree]

Pulps were of course the antitheses of what is known as the Golden Age of crime fiction, headed by the vastly popular Agatha Christie and sustained by her many imitators on both sides of the Atlantic. The modern equivalent is probably the 'cosy': the heroine (for it is invariably she) lives far from the big cities and while she has some kind of career – bookseller, restaurateur, clothes shop owner, dog trainer – is as far as possible from anything resembling a private eye. Her one source of professional input will be a friend, conveniently a local cop. Cosies resemble Christie's Miss Marple books and latterly the TV series *Murder She Wrote* featuring the 'mystery writer and amateur detective Jessica Fletcher' (Angela Lansbury). Sex and violence are strictly off-stage, if anywhere; forensics are irrelevant; all that matters is the sleuth's feel and instinct (those stereotypically 'womanly' attributes) and as ever in an era which rejoices in disdaining any form of 'expert' or 'intellectual', common sense. Other perhaps than in some walk-on playing strictly for laughs, there is no slang.

There was, starting around 1950, a fashion for lesbian pulp. Or rather lesbian dime novels since overtly at least, the pulp magazine publishers stayed very straight. The first appears to have been Tereska Torrès' *Women's Barracks* (1950).* It was billed as 'the frank autobiography of a French girl soldier' and set in the London barracks of the women members of the Free French forces during World War II. The book sold over two million copies, though what proportion of readers actually shared the heroines' tastes and how many were men looking for cheap thrills is unknown. No matter, the book proved the market and publishers such as Newstand Books (*Lavender Love Rumble, Bitter Love, Lesbo Lodge* etc.) and Fawcett's Gold Medal Publications quickly capitalised on it. The authors were invariably pseudonymous, but among the best known were 'Sloane Britain' (real name Elaine Williams) who wrote the popular *First Person Third Sex* (1959); the intensifying assault on such novels by the censors, and a growing personal unhappiness culminated in her suicide in 1964. Other authors included 'March Hastings' (Sally Singer) whose titles included *Veil of Torment* (1959) and *Fear of Incest* (1959) and perhaps most important of all, Maryjane Meaker (1927–), writing as Vin Packer (whose plots might offer lesbian pulp such as *Spring Fire* (1952), or tales of heterosexual urban teen gangsters in books such as *The Young and Violent*, 1956). She also wrote as Ann Aldritch for a series of five books,

---

* This seems to have predated the first example of gay pulp: George Viereck's prison-set *Men into Beasts* (1952).

all non-fiction and including *We Too Must Love* (1958) and *Take a Lesbian to Lunch* (1972). The list served, as she put it, to provide 'resource books' for girls, often trapped in small towns, who had no other way of finding out about the lesbian world. Frustratingly, while Meaker embellished her mean streets with the necessary 'JD' (i.e. juvenile delinquent) slang, she didn't feel the need, or perhaps know anything equivalent for her lesbian work. Since then she has specialised in young adult fiction (as M.E. Kerr) and children's books (as Mary James).

Given its contemporary notoriety, Britain's Profumo Affair of 1963 (a wondrous gallimaufry of sex and drugs though perhaps no rock 'n' roll, which offered an irresistible dish of government ministers, pricey call-girls, possible Russian infiltration, slum landlords and their minders, Notting Hill's West Indian community, an upmarket osteopath-cum-pimp and all bathed in a sauce of cross-class high jinks) ought to be filed as crime. One of its lesser stars was Mariella Novotny, probably born Stella Capes and who as the London writer Peter Watts has put it 'almost certainly wasn't the niece of former Czech President Antonin Novotny as she claimed, nor had she spent four years in a Soviet camp'. She probably did host the notorious Man in the Mask orgy (who he? a government minister was the best bet) and allegedly garnished the evening with a dinner featuring peacock and badger before retiring to bed, corseted and whip-wielding, with six 'naughty boys'. She also, ten years later, wrote 'a fictionalised account of her adventures called *King's Road* and one of the worst books I've ever read.'* True, perhaps, but very slangy. Indeed one of the few contemporary women-authored books to offer, in 1971, the slang of swinging London, its emphasis more on drugs

* https://greatwen.com/tag/mariella/ (3 June 2011 accessed 17 December 2018).

than crime and offering such as: *mind-bending, freaky* and *freak-out, hung up, have a loon, turned on, bring down*. In 1969, Jenny Fabian, plus co-author Johnny Byrne, brought out her lightly fictionalised autobiography *Groupie*. The best-recalled term was probably *plate*, as in the rhyming slang *plate of meat*: to eat, i.e. fellate (seemingly the rockstar's service of choice) while the pair also came up (used presumably at a fearful publisher's behest) with *manny*, a bowdlerised rendition of the hippie slang *mandy*, i.e. the drug mandrax (methaqualone).

Slang-speaking women abound in more recent crime writing, typically the work of UK crime writer Dreda Say Mitchell (writing from a British black perspective), Sara Paretsky's hard-boiled Chicago private eye, V. I. Warshawski, or Leigh Redhead's Australian stripper-sleuth Simone Kirsch. The lexis still confers authority, but the need is not so pronounced: slang is used, as far as possible, seamlessly. The quote-marks that bespattered Bonnie Parker's 'Suicide Sal' are no longer necessary. And slang is no longer a membership card for criminality. If Velma Dare, Dizzy Malone or Queen Sue emerged from their graves into modernity, they would not need to display their laddish lexis in every syllable. They would demonstrate other proofs of their eminent qualifications for trouncing the patriarchy.

It is not so much the patriarchy but the entire world that threatens Anais, the heroine of *The Panopticon* by Jenny Fagan (2012). The title acknowledges the omni-present surveillance of the original panopticon, a privacy free prison invented by the social theorist Jeremy Bentham. The theory was that all inmates could be observed, but had no idea when it was actually happening. The aim was to force self-regulation; the actual effect was paranoia. Anais' mother, giving birth in a psychiatric hospital, immediately vanished, leaving the infant to a succession of substitute carers. She was adopted and brought up by a prostitute who is knifed to death by a client. She plays her 'birthday game', dreaming of other might-have-been lives, with a sophisticated if stereotyped Parisienne existence at the top of her lists, but in fact seems condemned to an infinite round of foster-parents, careless (but not carefree) care-homes and every other dumping ground wherein such unfortunate children are placed. The reader meets her at fifteen, tough, mouthy, veteran of a pile of files and charge-sheets. Next stop, she is assured, will be a secure unit and thereafter, inevitably, adult prison.

Irvine Welsh blurbed the book: logically so, since Anais' first-person monologue surely owed much to the master of Leith-speak. (Welsh and Fagan use sixty-six terms in common.) Not as pervasive as in a Welsh novel, one can occasionally put down the slang dictionary, but such is the core of her speech – which drifts in and out of Welsh's phonetic spelling (usually in elisions of verbs: 'umnay': am not, 'isnae', is not, 'didnae', didn't) – and the book offers nearly two hundred examples of the counter-language. Written by a young woman, voiced by a teenage girl, there is definitely no ventriloquy here. Yet the slang offers little or no gendering. Masturbation for girls is still *wanking*, there is no variation to reference the clitoris; there are various combinations with *arse* (*arsepiece, arsehole, up the arse*), *fuck* (*fuck around, fucked, shut the fuck up, flying fuck, away to fuck!*), *shit* (*shit-pit, shit oneself, shitness*) and *piss* (*pisshole, piss on*) all equally available in masculine speech, as are those with which Anais embellishes *cunt* (*take the cunt, cuntface*); only, as ever, is menstruation strictly dressed in pink: *fanny pad* for a sanitary pad is girls only. The only other contender might be *knick-knacks*, knickers; but such 'female' terms as *lesbo* (lesbian) and *paps* (breasts) gain a gender only by association, not by use. There are a few Scotticisms, such as *spraff*, to chatter, and *pish* rather than *piss*, but the slang is usually quotidian. Only *on chucky* for on credit seems arcane, as might *chore*, to steal (usually to shoplift) which comes straight from Romani and before that Hindi.

Finally, the modern girl gang American-style. These gangs, generally 'auxiliaries' of their male equivalents, but occasionally autonomous and girls-only, have elicited much sociological study. Two books – *8-Ball Chicks* (1997) by Gini Sikes and *One of the Guys* (2001) by Jody Miller – also feature a range of relevant slang. Both focus on American gangs, with *8-Ball Chicks* covering Los Angeles, San Antonio and Milwaukee, whereas *One of the Guys* looks at membership in St Louis, Missouri and Columbus, Ohio. The girls are all African-American or Hispanic.

As its title suggests, *One of the Guys* depicts a world, and a vocabulary, that is very much drawn on male example. Much of the slang reflects the jargon of gang membership. The interviewees are all part of a *click, clique* or *set*, a small local gang, part of the larger gang but working autonomously in its own neighbourhood or area of influence. To attack that set is to *set-trip*.

In the gang's hierarchy are *Gs* (gangsters, sometimes *soldiers*) and *OGs* (original or senior gangsters). Junior members are *BGs* (baby gangsters) or *little locs* and to be initiated is the transitive verb *jump in* or *jump in the hood* (where 'hood' means not just the larger neighbourhood but also the highly localised area – a street, even a section of a street – dominated by a single gang). Jumping in, also *beating in*, the process – the *beat-down* – requires established members beating the initiate; girls may also experience *sexing in*, in other words the original meaning of *gang-banging*, before the term took on that of joining and operating within a gang. Voluntarily or otherwise, some girls may be subjected to a *train*, multiple heterosexual sex, which the male members *run* on them. One wears *colors*, typically a red or blue *rag*, a bandana (but the term includes any gang-coloured accessory), denoting one's membership of the Bloods or Crips, the primary branches (there are many sub-sets) of the US gang world. The Crips' blue is also known as *flu*, the Bloods' red as *dred*. *B-town* is a figurative 'home' for all Bloods; *C-town* for Crips. To the Crips Bloods are *Slobs*, the reverse insult is *Crabs*.

To join and then espouse a gang is to *claim* or to *true*, and the latter also covers one's subsequent adherence to gang rules. To state one's loyalty is to *pump up* while making a physical identification by openly displaying one's gang sign is *throwing up* or *stacking*. *To have someone's back* is to take care of a fellow member. Those who break them are given a *V*, a violation, which may well incur some form of violence, meted out by the *big dog*, the (male) gang boss. Girls fight as well as boys; those who do not stay *on the porch*, one step nearer activity than the old African-American *in the house*: those who completely eschew street life.

Sikes's interviewees use some of these – *jump in* (as well as *jump out*, to ritually beat up a member prior to their leaving the gang), *Slob*, *claim*, *click* as in *click into*, to join a gang – but add others, often emphasising the carry-over of an older Hispanic gang tradition. Thus *cholo* (and *chola*) and *vato*, Mexican gang members; *la vida loca*, literally 'the crazy life' and thus the gangster lifestyle. The book also lists *banger*, i.e. gangbanger or gang member; *new booty*, an initiate, *peewee*, a junior member, *shot caller*, an authority figure; *dickies*, baggy trousers; *earn one's stripes*, to commit crime to advance status; *walk-by*, the equivalent of the *drive-by*, with the shooter(s) walking rather than driving past in a car; *wife*, a gangster's permanent girlfriend; *scandalous*, an all-purpose negative and *roll in*, used in the context of *sexing in*, and referring to the rolling of a dice by a female recruit to a gang to ascertain how many members will have sex with her. Whether such terms are so obvious as to have been deemed unworthy of comment, there are no terms that mean specifically 'female gang members'. The girls of the Fifties' gangs were *debs*, but that word vanished as surely as the *debutantes* on which it was based.

Of the remaining slang both books feature sex, violence, drugs, crime and a selection of non-specific terms.

From sex, the penis is variously a *thing, stuff* and a *cock*, which can also be a vagina (the southern and African-American use), *pull* (or *run*) *a train, sloppy seconds, pity fuck, put the make on, give it up, get off on, get one's nut off, go with* and *hook up*. Sexually available girls (disdained even as they fulfil male desire) are *skanks, sleazes, bitches* and *hos*. Violence gives *gaffle*, to ambush, *jack*, to rob with violence; *scrap and squat*, a fight; a *cat fight* is between two women; *buck, get into, go off on, hit someone up* and *take care of* all mean to attack or fight with. To beat up is *catch, whip* or *whup, stomp* and *bounce*; a *shot* is a blow. To kill, usually by shooting, is to *smoke*, to *light someone up* or to *put in work*; the shooter is a *triggerman* who uses a *gat* or *gauge*. Drugs focus on marijuana and (crack) cocaine (the *eight-ball* of Sikes' title refers to a measure of 3.5 gms/one-eighth ounce of cocaine, though it can also be a bottle of Old English 800 beer). There are only two terms for alcohol: *forty*, a 40-oz bottle of beer and *rotgut*, cheap wine. Otherwise marijuana is *bud* or *weed*; a *herbal* is a simple marijuana *joint* while a *primo* is a joint laced with cocaine and/ or heroin; *sherm* is PCP and a *shermhead* smokes a mix of marijuana and PCP (a *sprayhead* sniffs paint sprays). One can be *coked up* (after *hitting the pipe*), *turned-on, high* or *flying high* and *buzzed*. *Dope fiends* and *geekers* are addicts and one *connects*, buys drugs, in a *dope house* (where they can also be consumed).

Like the 'general' terms, among them *ball* and *roll*, to live in a given way, *chill*, to relax, *cool with*, friendly, *crap*, nonsense, *in the wind*, on the run, *knucklehead*, a fool, *shorty*, a youngster, *ride*, automobile, *punk*, a coward, *props*, respect, *motormouth*, a verbose talker and *jaw* to talk, *talk shit*, to insult, *wannabe*, an aspirant , or exclamations such as *dag!* or *blow me!* there is nothing exceptional about any of this. The slang of sex, violence and drugs reflects the larger worlds of such phenomena; they are not especially new, though some will be, and beyond the purpose-built gang jargon, the terms used have a variety of origins. Nor, even if some describe given perceptions of women, are any 'female'. If, on the whole, female gangbangers are seen, as suggested, as part of male gangs, and as such – for all their skills at fighting and robbery – remain dependent on the word, and the words, of big dogs and the shot-callers.

7. Working Girls

WHETHER OR NOT the 'oldest profession' can justify that name is irrelevant here. (As a construction it was claimed for cattle-rustling in 1848, and agriculture in 1860. The link to commercial sex is far from old: the *OED*'s first recorded use is 1922, although the *New York Times*, on 26 February 1893, made the connection when it absolved a young woman of membership in 'what has been called the oldest profession in the world'. Whatever its antiquity, one senses that no professional has ever wished to use it.) No matter the euphemism, the selling of sexual services scores high in any taxonomy of slang terminology: the working girl has long been beloved by slang users. Half a millennium's development of the counter-language offers just over one thousand terms for prostitute.* Her profession adds sixty-eight more; the brothel a further 312 and its keeper, the bawd or madam, twenty-six. From males, the pimp is good for a further three hundred; the client for thirty-nine.

How then, do things work from the opposite direction: the use and creation of slang by prostitutes. By such logic as

---

* I have used both *whore* and *prostitute* in the text; the current *OED* revision records the former from a.1100 and the latter from 1607 and my aim, doubtless imperfectly achieved, has been to match the term to the background chronology. That said, *whore* tends to be the preferred term in most source material prior to the 19th century.

underpins this investigation, she should be a repository of woman-created, woman-specific language. Her job, while it is based on interactions with the opposite sex, is at the same time defined by the line that is drawn between those who supply a service and those who pay for it. That the service happens to be sex is ultimately irrelevant, even if moralising has always ensured that it is anything but. Yet for the dividing line, and the inference that on the professional side of the line there should evolve a specific jargon, it is hard to find.

In 1862, Henry Mayhew, Britain's pioneer sociologist, devoted a whole volume of his *London Labour and the London Poor* (Vol. IV: 'Those Who Will Not Work, Prostitutes, Thieves . . .') to commercial sex. As ever there were a number of interviews (these, it seems, were carried out at least in part by his brother Augustus, who tended to be deputed to what his elder sibling adjudged the less appetising tasks: he had already dealt with the grim cruelties of the rat pit). For the most part the girls seem paradoxically well-spoken: they may have presented themselves to clients as the fallen daughters of country vicarages, but surely there were a few working-class women among them. It is possible that Mayhew, like Dickens, was prey to his era's fantasies of female purity. His real-life whores were therefore mainly well-spoken, just as the fictional Nancy, in *Oliver Twist*, manages to speak standard English when all around her – Sykes, Fagin, the Artful Dodger and company – were imbued with proper cant. (Oliver too, though fresh from the 'work'us', has magically gained his aspirates.) No 'grande horizontale' (the French euphemism for the cream of courtesans) her peers would have called this lowly whore a 'twopenny uprighter' – Dickens was far too kind for that.

Writing on prostitution in Paris in 1836, Alexandre

Parent-Duchatelet (a hygiene specialist who had already written on the city sewers) kept to the script: In a chapter headed 'Do prostitutes have a special slang?' and claiming to have done the necessary fieldwork, notably in the city's major clap clinic, he answers disappointingly, no. There were a few expressions: terms for the Morality Office (*rails*), the police (*fliques* and forerunners of the modern *flics*), plain girls (*roubiou*) and pretty ones (*Gironde*, 'a pretty one', itself from Latin *gyrus*, a circle and thus denoting a 'curvy cutie') or *chouette* (literally an owl but note that cliché of French affection '*mon petit chou*': 'my little cabbage'), for a girl who had a boyfriend (*largue*, otherwise used of ropes which are 'loose' or 'slack') and for that lover (*paillasson*, either a doormat or a 'braided straw mat that is used on construction sites to cover cut stones and building materials to protect them from impact, weather and the sun'; the implication being that the lover protects the girl who is, after all, 'on the stones'), but that was it. He adds that such terms changed over the years (over the last fifty-odd years *paillasson* for instance had been *greluchon* from a fantasy Saint Greluchon, supposedly capable of curing sterility, *homme à qualité* – a 'fancy man' – and most recently *mangeur a blanc*, from *blanc de poulet*, 'white meat' and slang for the girl herself, though devoid of the racist overtone that the English slang carries), but the lexis went no further. Essentially, since whores tended to hang out with thieves, they also borrowed their slang.

This was a common theory. Whores lacked the wherewithal – intellectual, professional – to come up with proper slang. It was all superficial stuff. Not only that, but it wasn't true slang, or not in the way of criminal slang which sprang, it was claimed, from the very essence of those who spoke it. It was simply a pose, an adopted, superficial jargon, taken up and dropped with as little relation to the girl herself as the clothes that a 'dress lodger' might hire out from her profiteering landlady. As a commentator put it, perhaps disappointed to find insufficient depravity, 'The filthy talk of so many of our streetwalkers is only professional slang, implying no proportionate depravity of heart – learnt in a few weeks, and to be unlearnt, perhaps as quickly.'*

A century later, the American David Maurer, whose work devoted itself to listing the lexes of a variety of criminal specialities, was another to dismiss the idea of such a language: the girls, by every aspect of their nature, lacked the necessary creativity. One wonders how hard and indeed if he bothered to look. But perhaps the girls, unlike the hapless denizens of death row, who were apparently pestered by the eminent lexicographer, decided not to talk. Hollywood's Sugarpuss O'Shea may have been happy to teach jazz slang to Professor Potts in *Ball of Fire* (1941) but this was a very different ball game, and if the word *jazz* entered the picture, it had a very different sense.

Whatever Maurer's private attitude to women in general, let alone sex-workers, this is an essay that seems shot through with misogyny. In virtually every line he compares her with the macho sodality of male criminals, 'real' men who create the red meat of 'real' slang, and finds her in every way wanting. Were this a noir fiction, one might wonder as to the writer having had, at some undisclosed time, an unfortunate experience – impotence, the clap – when visiting his local good-time girl and remaining vengeful as regarded all her sisterhood. As regards her slang, or lack of it, Maurer has not a word to say in the whore's favour. And to justify what he undoubtedly sees as a failure on her behalf, he eviscerates her intelligence, her upbringing, her social

* *Tait's Edinburgh Magazine* (August 1858).

class, her psychological inadequacies, her lifestyle and much besides. All fail and it is because they do that she, alone of any criminal grouping, cannot come up with slang.

According to Maurer, on the one hand in thrall to the 'real men' of professional crime, and on the other taking almost personal pains to render the whore wordless, 'one might classify their speech as colloquial American' . . . they are 'unconscious entrepreneurs of second-hand argot' (leaned from their male criminal associates) and 'lack the sophistication to make and acquire an artificial language for themselves'. Her linguistic skills are those of a 'semi-literate farm wife': the background from which he suggests many whores emerge. He grants them a scant fifty words and cites only five: *on the line*, in a brothel or *house*; *work the streets*, *crib* (a room), and *call-house*, whence she is summoned by phone by her pimp or madam. Prostitution, he claims, holds a 'very low position in the hierarchy of the crime-world' which in turn 'denies the prostitute all claim to true professional status'. No wonder, he adds, that she lacks professional pride, allegedly the primary motive for slang creation. In such a situation she feels inferior, 'there is no incentive, no advancement', and her speech never attains the argot-y colour of her properly criminal 'cousins'. Then again, says Maurer, she has no need for slang: her work – failing to pull down major scores, and merely selling a 'biological' service – has no need for secrecy. In addition she is socially inadequate and turns for help to drink and drugs and 'a thousand pitiful compensatory artifices' (make-up, dyed hair, framed photographs of celebrities she could never meet, self-dramatisation in 'synthetic autobiographies which they come to believe'). In the end: compared with 'other professional criminals' she is stupid.

The contradictions are obvious. Does every male criminal

lead an ascetic existence, never sampling stimulants? Are none of them born other than the renegade alumni of Ivy league aristocracy? Is each criminal, as he seems to believe, a buccaneering self-promoter, taking what he wants when he wants it and boasting of it in self-created slang? Is every robbery productive of millions? Simplest of all: were women excluded from big-time crime? Nonetheless, Maurer had clout, at least linguistically. It is an image that has persisted. Pimps, celebrated in a number of books, and with the added linguistic garnish of usually being (in memoirs and fictions) black and thus argotically extra-articulate, are granted a large vocabulary. Their *flatbackers*, *mud-kickers*, *bottom women* and the rest, are not.

The silent whore is an image embraced even by her sisters. Though the causes may not be those proposed by the professor. Talking online, in 2018, to a modern sex worker who has taken the Twitter handle @dollymopp*, it was suggested that sex-workers still resist slang. Why? Because slang is so consistently antagonistic to the profession and to those who work within it. This is undoubtedly true: whatever the context slang has a problem with congratulation. But prostitution and its ancillary world have created a substantial lexis, and its use surely cannot be restricted to those who are not part of that world.

So the whore does have slang. Perhaps the girls and madam weren't sitting around in the seventeenth-century London's Hollands Leaguer, nineteenth-century Chicago's Everleigh Club, or mid-twentieth-century Paris' Le Chabanais, working

---

* In nineteenth-century slang *dollymop* is defined variously as a prostitute specialising in sailors, a slovenly servant-girl, and a part-time prostitute, often a servant or shopgirl, especially a milliner, who occasionally sells her body to supplement her otherwise meagre income (the equivalent of the Parisian *grisette* or *midinette*); *dolly* is self-evident while *mop*, in standard English a young whiting or gurnard, is yet another of slang's equations of women and fish and here reminiscent of the old German slang *Backfisch*, a teenage girl, literally a 'fish for baking' and used today, asexually, for 'fried fish'.

team-handed on yet another synonym for an impotent, but usefully wealthy old man, nor the street-walkers clustering under a convenient lamp-post to develop new variations on 'kerb-crawler', but the words are to be found.

And if one French expert decried the whole idea, there were others who applauded it.

Brigitte Rochelandet, in the introduction to her book *Les maisons brothels autrefois* (1999, 'the brothels of yesteryear'), explains the place of slang in the world of prostitution and brothels: 'This world has its own language, unromantic, marked by raw and provocative vulgarity. This picturesque talk, slang for the sidewalk, shocked the self-righteous, stirred up customers and was not appreciated by the police, who saw in it a secret code!' and Jean Alexandre, prefacing his mini-dictionary *L'argot de la prostitution du XIX a nos jours* (1987) stressed the extent to which 'The whore has played a primordial role in the propagation of slang . . .' They, of course, were looking to France, where prostitution (and for many years brothels) has always been considered in a less viciously condemnatory manner than it has in the Anglo-Saxon world. Still, English speakers can make their contribution too.

As with scolds, the seventeenth century offered a number of dialogues, supposedly conducted between whores or whores and pimps. As in pornography, where such conversations, typically case between an older, experienced woman and a younger, perhaps virginal one, these were a useful convention. The form still existed in de Sade's *120 Days of Sodom* (1789) where the long, egregiously bizarre orgy that forms the 'plot' is 'narrated' (or even curated) by four specifically imported whores. As Maya Guarantz has noted, such women are 'taxonomists of the perverse'.

In 1641 there appeared *The sisters of the scabards holiday: or, a dialogue between two reverent and very vertuous matrons, Mrs. Bloomesbury, and Mrs. Long-Acre her neare neighbour. Wherein is discoursed how terrible, and costly the civill law was to their profession; and how they congatulate* [sic] *the welcome alteration* – the scab[b]*ard* being both a literal translation from Latin and euphemistic slang for the vagina. The sisters throw in a little slang: *commodity,* for the female genitals, *mackeral-tail'd gentleman* for pimps and the *smell-smock crew* for their clientele. They also name check such well-established centres of commercial sex as 'Turnmill-street, Goulding- [i.e. Golden] lane, Beech-lane, Pick-hatch and in all other places where any of our societie remains'. The names of Mesdames Bloomesbury and Long-Acre add the north side of Oxford Street and Covent Garden to the list.

A dialogue between Mistris Macquerella, a suburb bawd, Ms Scolopendra, a noted curtezan, and Mr Pimpinello an usher, &c. Pittifully bemoaning the tenour of the Act (now in force) against adultery and fornication followed in 1650. The bawd's name, Macquerella, was a feminised ancestor of modernity's *mack,* a pimp; *Scolopendra,* slang for prostitute, borrowed a standard English word meaning centipede or millipede, and which Bullokar in his *English Expositour* (1616) described as 'a fabulous sea-fish which feeling himselfe taken with a hooke casteth out his bowels vntill hee hath vnloosed the hooke and then swalloweth them vpagaine'. Their conversation includes *cully* and *smock-coat swain,* clients, *do penance in a halter,* to be hanged, *upper weed,* a garment, *pensioner of the placket,* a pimp, *placket* being the slit at the top of an apron or petticoat, facilitating dressing and undressing and by metonymy both the whore and her vagina, *doxy* and *tib* ('a typical name for a woman of the lower classes' *OED*), both whores, the *French disease,* syphilis and *roasted*, diseased, *tails* and *toys*, the female genitals, *Master Mentula*, the penis (*mentula* was the primary Latin slang term), and another Latinism *rem in re*, intercourse or literally 'thing in thing'. They bemoan the effect of new laws on past pleasures: 'all's lost,' says Scolopendra. The only solution: curtained windows and well-locked doors; 'trading' will continue, but 'cunningly, clandestinely and obscurely'.

There was little slang in the lengthily titled *The crafty whore or, the mistery and iniquity of bawdy houses laid open, in a dialogue between two subtle bawds, wherein, as in a mirrour, our city-curtesans may see their soul-destroying art, and crafty devices, whereby they insnare and beguile youth, pourtraied to the life, by the pensell of one of their late, (but now penitent) captives, for the benefit of all, but especially the younger sort. Whereunto is added dehortations from lust drawn from the sad and lamentable consequences it produceth* (1658)— *needle* for penis, *cully* again and *opticks* for eyes – but *The Whores Dialogue* (1668) was more productive. Its conversation offers a *house* (*of delight*) a brothel with its owner an *abbess* or *Mrs*, a bawd, her employees the *lady of pleasure*, the *fish* and the *bona roba, blade*, a rake, *clap, pox* and a *blow with a French faggot stick*, all syphilis, *pocky*, diseased, *buzzard*, an old unattractive person, *cully, fireship*, a diseased girl, 'hot' in a far from good way, *hector*, a minder or thug, *meat*, the female body, *trapan*, to trick, *pump* to punish with a soaking and *sir-reverence*, a piece of excrement.

In 1676 comes *The Night-walkers declaration, or, The Distressed whores advice to all their sisters in city and country set forth (by way of confession) out of a deep sense of the tribulations they have lately suffered*. The distressed whores – known as *misses* and pursuing what had once been 'a pleasant and thriving undertaking' – talked of *cully-catching*, picking up men and *trepanning*. One might also *smuckle a cully*, unrecorded elsewhere, which suggests some element of violence, what would later be termed the *Murphy game*. They were paid in *georges*, sovereigns, but lived in fear of being sent to the *hemp office*, a prison, where girls would supposedly learn respectability by beating hemp. They mention the *bullies* and *hectors* who work as pimps or brothel heavies, call their profession *traffique* (as in modernity's *trafficking*) and warn against wearing 'the white colours', the white apron which was their well-known badge of office.

There is also a general complaint regarding this 'unfortunate sex of ours! whose lot it is, if *young* and *handsome*, to be punished as *Whores*, if *old* and *ugly*, to be Carted [whipped at the cart's tail] for *Bawds*, or burn'd for *Witches*; if honest to *starve*; if free and complaisant, to be rail'd on, *Pox'd*, *Trepan'd*, and *Bridewell'd* [imprisoned]; and all this by an *ungrateful* Generation. whom we endeavour, through so many dangers, to *oblige*.'

Around 1650 there appeared in Italy *La Puttana Errante* ('The Wandering Whore'), a dialogue between Magdalena, an experienced old bawd, and Julietta, a relatively innocent whore. It declared no author but its format – a dialogue – and its inclusion of thirty-five plates illustrating the positions of intercourse, echoed the earlier *Ragionamenti*, created around 1525 by Pietro Aretino, a wit whose scathing satires had earned him the title 'the Scourge of Princes'. The text itself would not be translated until 1827, but between 1660 and 1663 there appeared a succession of pamphlets using the title 'The Wandering Whore'. Their format, a dialogue between the old whore and the novice, aped that of the recently published *Puttana Errante* and indeed simply English-ed its title.

In all there were five pamphlets, each of sixteen pages and cheap enough to satisfy the purses of any reader in search of accessible titillation. The first was *The Wandring Whore*, sub-titled: 'A Dialogue between *Magdalena* a Crafty Bawd, *Julietta* an Exquisite Whore, *Francion* a lascivious gallant And *Gusman* a Pimping hector. Discovering their Diabolical Practises at the Chuck-Office. *With a List of all the Crafty Bawds, Common Whores, Decoys, hectors, and Trappaners and their usual Meetings.*' Its publisher, and very likely author John Garfield (of whom we have no further information), claimed that it had been 'Published to destroy those poisonous Vermine which live upon the ruin and destruction of many Families.' The reality was that like many pornographers before and since, Garfield used his proclaimed disgust to offer as much smut as he could get away with. Like the later *Catalogue of jilts, cracks, prostitutes, night-walkers, whores, she-friends, kind women, and others of the linnen-lifting tribe* (1691) and the multiple editions of the eighteenth-century's *Harris' List*, it promoted a list of currently working girls.

Follow-up titles included: *The wandering whore continued* (1660) which featured the same discussion group; *Strange nevves from Bartholomew-Fair, or, the wandring-whore discovered her cabinet unlockt, her secrets laid open, vnvailed, and spread abroad* (1661); *Strange & true nevves from Jack-a-Newberries six wind-mills, or, The crafty, impudent, common-whore (turned bawd) anatomised and discovered in the unparralleld practises of Mris Fotheringham . . . with five and twenty orders agreed upon by consent of Mris Creswell, Betty Lawrence* (1661) and *The Wandring-Whores complaint* (1663).

The Wandring Whore offers a mix of stories, focusing either on criminal trickery or on sexual pleasures, invariably ascribed, however, only to degenerate foreigners. It is full of bawdy humour and uses a number of military and naval images. And like later guides to London prostitutes it names streets and real-life whores such as the sailors' helpmeet Damaris Page (mentioned by Pepys) and Madame Cresswell (a successful madame for thirty years until her arrest in 1681).

Cresswell can also be found in *The whore's rhetorick calculated to the meridian of London, and conformed to the rules of art* (1683) by 'Philo-puttanus', i.e. 'whore lover'. It offers some 130 examples of contemporary slang. There are the first uses, which include *as long as one's arm, tearing,* for impressive, *cock-broth,* a strong soup, presumably seen as a sort of culinary viagra, and *hit,* to take effect. There were the predictable range of sex-related terms which offer both the obvious: *cunny, cunt, fuck, ride, stallion* and *tail,* and the more imagistic: *the best in Christendom* (the missing word being 'cunt'; the phrase was usually found as a toast), the *touchhole,* the *fancy bit* and the punning *low countries* for vagina. The penis was often a *trapstick* and another bawdy pamphlet, 'Mercurius Fumigosus' noted how a milk-woman 'bitt off her Husband's *Trap-stick* because she found him at *Trap-ball* in her Neighbour's ground'.[*]

There were a variety of xenophobic terms for venereal disease: the *French pox* and the *Neapolitan disease,* both of which *burned* the victim, plus the *Italian padlock,* a chastity belt. As well as to be *clapped, peppered* and *pocky.* The *Whore* also offered what may be the earliest take on 'as the actress said to the bishop', in this case 'Every man to his trade, as the Rat-trap-maker said to the Parson'. Intercourse was *business, fancy work, knocking* or *dancing* and a prostitute was a *buttock,* a *hackney* or a *trader;* her pimp a *smock merchant* and her client a *rumper.* She worked in a *dancing school,* or brothel. Of particular note was the title's

---

[*] *Mercurius Fumigosus* 17 (September 1654), p.152.

reference to the *chuck office*. This was a 'game' whereby a whore would stand on her head, exhibiting her spread vulva and clients would throw coins into her exposed vagina. As the first edition of *The Wandring Whore* reported in 1660: 'Witness Priss Fotheringham's Chuck-office, where upon sight thereof, French Dollars, Spanish pistols, English Half-crowns are as plentifully pour'd in, as the Rhenish wine was into the Dutch wenches two holes till she roar'd again, as she was showing tricks upon her head with naked buttocks and spread legges in a round ring, like those at wrestling neer the Half-crown-chuck-office, call'd Jack-a-newberries-six windmills.'* Ms Fotheringham's own name for her vagina was the *rima magna*, the great cleft, the cash-tossing punters were *cully-rumpers*.[†]

The language of seventeenth-century sex, as seen in *The Wandring Whore* and its various clones, was nothing if not inventive. As well as the terms noted above, a selection of those referring to intercourse included *basket-making, bestial back-slidings* (either rear-entry position intercourse or sodomy), *the blow that never smarteth, latitudinarian principles* (Latitudinarians were opposed to Puritan self-denial, which they considered harmful), *the monster with two bellies* (playing on Shakespeare's *beast with two backs*, coined for *Othello* in 1604), *the path that is first trod, violin-playing* (a play on *instrument*, both vagina and penis) and *letting blood near the leg and loin*. As well as the established attributions to France and Italy, venereal disease could be the *Covent*

---

* A blue sign, mimicking the official memorials, has been mounted in honour of Ms Fotheringham in Whitecross Street, EC1, known as one of her era's great centres of vice and still cited among London's most wicked and dangerous streets by nineteenth-century sociologists. For further detail see G. Williams, *A Dict. of Sexual Lang. and Imagery in Shakespearian and Stuart Literature* (3 vols 1994) I 242.
† There was a male equivalent: the *Prick-Office* whereby a man stood on his hands naked and with 'T[arse] upwards' and had the tip of his 'Trapstick' kissed by a succession of women who paid for the privilege.

Garden gout and the *Piccadilly cramp*, and to suffer it was to be *clapt under the hatches*, to *learn French*, and to be *shot between wind and water*. As is obvious, many of these terms were puns.

After the seventeenth century's dialogues, the eighteenth and early nineteenth turned to memoirs. Fanny Hill may have been a fictional figure but the subjects of these supposed 'autobiographies' were not. The best-known madams of an earlier age, such as Damaris Page 'the great bawd of the seamen' who had flourished c.1650 in London's dockland red-light district Ratcliff Highway, achieved no more than an occasional walk-on as regarded print (for instance Page and Fotheringham's joint appearance in a pamphlet of 1660: *Strange and true Conference between Two Notorious Bawds, During their Imprisonment and lying together in Newgate . . .*' supposedly authored by 'Megg. Spencer', a well-known bawd herself and self-appointed 'Overseer of the Whores and Hectors on the Bank-Side.'). Her successors are recorded, quite literally, in chapter and verse.

Among those name-checked were 'Mrs Elizabeth Wisebourn' (1721), 'The effigies, parentage, education, life, merry-pranks and conversation of the celebrated Mrs. Sally Salisbury' (1722–3, and accompanied by a number of similar works), 'the celebrated Miss Fanny M' (1759) which included the rules of the Whores Club ('1. Every member of this society must have been debauched before she was fifteen') and 'Miss Kitty F[ishe]r (1759), whose 'uncommon adventures' were also recorded as 'Horse and away to St James' Park' (1760).

The list also includes 'Genuine memoirs of the celebrated Miss Nancy D[awso]n' (1760) whose book of 'jests' (Nancy was perhaps paid to lend her celebrated name) was a popular bestseller. Nancy was as much dancer as whore, taking a role in the

1759 revival of Gay's 1728 hit *The Beggar's Opera*. Here she performed her speciality: the hornpipe (the punning potential of which may possibly have been observed). She died in 1756, leaving a variety of dances, sailor songs and this nursery rhyme as her memorial:

> Nancy Dawson was so fine
> She wouldn't get up to serve the swine;
> She lies in bed till eight or nine,
> So it's Oh, poor Nancy Dawson.

As well as non-specific round-ups of the foremost ladies of the town, such as *Characters of the present most celebrated courtezans* (1780) there were also such leering collections as *The prostitutes of quality; or adultery à-la-mode. Being authentic and genuine memoirs of several persons of the highest quality* (1757). The lip-smacking allure of posh totty is nothing new.

Other memoirs included *The women of the town, or Authentick memoirs of Phoebe Philips* (1801), *The Secret memoirs of Miss Sally Dawson* (1805), *A curious and interesting narrative of Poll House and the Marquis of C****** (1820), *Memoirs of the celebrated Lady C*****m* (1820), *Memoirs of the life of the celebrated Mrs Q------* (1822). A trio of early nineteenth-century ladies – Margaret Leeson (1797), Harriette Wilson (1825) and Julia Johnstone (1825) – were keen to add in all their titles that the work had been 'written by herself'. Unfortunately, even were this truly the case (and it would appear to have been so in that of Margaret Leeson) the ladies were at pains to present a respectable image, at least in their vocabulary. No slang here.

Perhaps the best equipped for our purposes was Jane Davies, the 'genuine memoirs' of whom, now fêted as 'the late celebrated', appeared in 1761. Jane came from Edinburgh, where she had joined the game as a teenager. There she had been clapped, then cured and was 'allow'd [i.e. acknowledged] to be the heartiest girl in town'. This seems to have arisen from the fact that she 'surpassed all her sister whores in swearing and obscene talk'. As a later comment puts it, she possessed 'a peculiar turn to that species of eloquence, which though not treated ... by Quintilian or Longinus [both Roman rhetoricians], is generally understood in the metropolis, and goes by the name of Billings-gate'.

She could also drink any man beneath the table, pausing only to empty his pockets of such money as remained before marching off. A later trip to Ireland, to recruit new girls, after she had become a Covent Garden madam, showcased both her talents. The ship ran into a storm and while weaker folk might wail and/ or vomit, not Jane: 'She drank flip [beer, spirits and sugar mixed and heated], and cursed as loudly as any sailor of them all.'

Ms Davies made no pretence to sisterhood. While she had to acknowledge the need to regard men – her paying customers – as deserving of at least counterfeit politeness, her dealings with women, be they the brothel's inmates or the maids who cleaned after them, were antagonistic and her term of choice was *bitch*. 'She scarce ever spoke to [maids] without using the appellation of ragg-doll b—h, or some other epithet equally indelicate.' Unsurprisingly few maids stayed much beyond a week. Her house was known for its foreign girls – she made regular recruiting trips to France and established a pan-European network of bawds, trading girls between them (such travellers often miraculously regaining their maidenhead as they stepped off the boat). This did not spare a particular girl's French maid who, perhaps somewhat homesick, entered the brothel kitchen and started preparing *potage*, no doubt to some rich old provincial recipe learned at the maternal knee.

> Old Jenny [Davies] who had a good nose soon smelt the stink of leeks, and called out, G—d d—n me, who is that poisoning my house below. Answer being given her That it was only M—le's maid making a little soupe. D—n the French b—h cried Jane, I'll give her a bellyful of soupe by and by. So Jane having provided herself with a close stool pan [a chamberpot] which was full, ran to her, and throwing it full in her face, cried, Here you French b—h, here's soupe enough for you, you shall never wanted for soupe . . . I'll season it for you you b—h, G—d d—n ye.

The memoir runs from one lurid anecdote to another. Another tale concerns a brother and sister (again French) who, wholly ignorant of their true relationship, she had as she believed introduced to each other (pimping out the girl to her brother). Despite a plot which might seem to be leading to farce if not actual incest, Ms Davies would be for once the victim. The pair robbed her, and left, after poisoning her supper. Her response was predictable:

> G—d eternally d—n all the French b — ches! may their own country disease, the p—x, rot them to the bone! May they be all covered over with ulcers, their noses drop off, and may they all die upon a dunghill and the devil run away with their souls! Amen.

There followed 'a good deal more, in the same stile and tone'. At which she fainted and was 'quite unfit for business that day'.

She was seventy-four at her death, a respectable sum of years. The compiler of her memoirs concluded thus: 'Old Jane had a particular talent for smart sayings, though there generall enter'd a good deal of that sort of humour into them, which is common among fish-women and upon the Thames. A Person who was intimately acquainted with her made a collection of her bons mots and [. . .] we shall publish it entire.'

Sadly, this embryonic clickbait was unfulfilled. The small print, as it were, made it clear that such a 'best of . . .' compilation would only appear were the memoirs a hit. We must assume, in the compilation's absence, that this was not the case.

Bawds

If street girls, as various male experts claimed, lacked a rich slang vocabulary, this could not be said of those who worked in brothels. There are well over three hundred terms for the *buttonhole factory*, the *cavaulting school*, the *fuckery* or the *meat works*. The bulk compound a term for a girl – *doll, moll, nanny, bat, chicken, badger, heifer* – with that of a place – *crib, shop, ken, joint* and notably *house*, which provides twenty-five, including *house of sale, of state, of civil reception, of convenience* and *of delight*.

France, with its blank-windowed *maisons closes*, their doors often adorned with an extra-large street number (thus the name *maison à gros numéro*; it was also used as *big number*, by US soldiers in World War I) so as to ensure that no potential client wandered by unknowing, had many more: among them the *magasin des fesses* (the buttock-shop), *poufiassebourg* (whore-town), *pince-cul* (arse-pincher) and *poulailler* (the chicken-house) as well as such basics as *maison des putes* (whore-house) and the euphemistic *mauvais lieu* (bad place). Isolated, enclosed, a claustrophobic home to a regular (if rotating) population, they, like the larger city around them, provided the perfect basis for slang generation.

To what extent those who worked within a brothel coined their slang names is impossible to discern. In many cases such terms were coyly euphemistic or broadly humorous (plays on 'school', 'academy' or 'convent'); there was nothing as harsh as France's *maison d'abattage*, literally 'slaughterhouse', the lowest level of establishment, where a girl might be sent as a punishment and there forced to suffer scores of clients, usually poor workers queuing down the street, every day, and especially at weekends. (Paris had thirty-eight such brothels in 1938, some were situated near the city's actual abattoirs to provide for the butchers.) Given the evidence of such terms, many seem to have been conjured up for print, used by journalists or writers of varying levels of sociology to shield their readers from anything simpler. It is unlikely that many of those who were employed within had any time for such linguistic playing around. (The unveiled cruelty underpinning the French 'slaughterhouse' does suggest that this might well have been coined by those who were sent to work there.)

Brothels were women-only establishments. There were the male clients, of course, and since they occasionally got out of order to an extent that could not be tolerated even from paying customers (as did the girls, who had no such economic protection) they employed a variety of 'minders' and 'heavies': the *bone-setter*, the *bully-rock* or *bully-back*, the *hector* and the *twang*. The nineteenth century used the unadorned *bludgeoner*; Australian brothel girls called him a *bumper-upper*, and teased those blokes who 'couldn't get a job as a bumper-upper in a brothel'.

At the top was the bawd, which seems to be an abbreviation of Old French *baudetrot* and English *bawdstrot*, a procuress (a seventeenth-century version is *bronstrops*). The *OED* notes this but rejects a link to *baude*, joyous (though this may have been a nod to contemporary – the entry was written in 1887 – moralising). *Madam*, the modern version, was an eighteenth-century invention, essentially a euphemism. Her fifteenth-century employees called her a *mackeral* or *macquerella*, which was not, subsequent theories notwithstanding, yet another equation of women and fish, but linked to the Dutch *makelaar*, a merchant, in this case of flesh (thus the use of *mackeral-tail'd gentleman* and *Madame Macquerella* above). That said, another synonym was *fishmonger*. The brothel was, mockingly, an abbey (*l'abbaye de s'offre-tous*, the abbey of available to all, in France) which made the bawd an *abbess* and the girls *nuns*. She was also a *provincial*, properly the local head of a religious order.

As time passed, the girls came up with new suggestions: she could be an *aunt*, a *three-chinned dame*, a *buttock-broker, flesh-broker* or *flesh-fly*, a *wafer-woman* (posing as a legitimate maker of wafers, i.e. filigree), a *landlady*, a *covess of the ken*, a *crib-* or *house-* or *kip-keeper*, and a *house-mother*.

Indeed and above all she was a *mother: Mother Cunny,** *Mother Midnight, Mother Nabem* ('grab them', presumably the clientele) and even blunter *Mother Knab-Coney* ('snatch-sucker') and *Mother Damnable* who like her 'sisters' was usually generic but in Caulfield's canting dictionary *Blackguardiana* (1793) is printed a

---

* A real life, if nick-named bawd; she appears as co-sponsor of *The Ladies Champion, Confounding the Author of the Wandring Whore* (1660) alongside other madams such as Megg. Spencer, Priss Fotheringham, Damaris Page, Su. Leming and Betty Laurence. Her wholly fantasised 'Life' is also conjured up in *The Practical Part of Love* (1660) wherein the author creates a catalogue of imaginary volumes worthy of belonging to 'Love's Academy'. A real-life Joan Cunny (or Cony) also known as 'Mother Cunny' was hanged for witchcraft in Chelmsford, Essex in 1589.

picture of a bawd entitled 'Mother Damnable of Kentish Town Anno 1676' with an accompanying verse which notes that 'So fam'd, both far and near, is the renown, / Of Mother Damnable, of Kentish Town'. She could be, tongue well in cheek, the *mother of the maids* who in respectable life was governess to the Queen's maids of honour. France offered *Mère Caca*: Mother Shit.

The mid-nineteenth century's celebrated Mother Willitt of Gerrard Street (London's modern Chinatown) was proud of her work: 'So help her kidnies, she al'*us* turned her gals out with a clean arse and a good tog, and as she turned 'em out, she didn't care who turned 'em up, cause 'em vos as clean as a smelt* and as fresh as a daisy — she vouldn't have a speck'd un† if she'd know'd it.' This was presumably during the madam's gentler period. Hitherto a terrifying figure, she seemed to have turned soft: a commentator noted that she 'has now turned to the pious dodge, and calls them her *darters* [daughters], her *chickens*, and *kids*.'

Relative modernity was less inventive. She became the *she-boss*, a *strong-arm woman* and a *nookie bookie*. There was also the mysterious *Mrs Lukey Props* of whom, sadly, we know nothing.

Various 'mothers' crop up in whore literature. Among them Mother Cresswell or Criswell, whose authority supposedly lay behind the pamphlet *Strange & true nevves from Jack-a-Newberries six windmills* (1661) and who is exhumed by the satirist Thomas Brown in his *Letters from the Dead to the Living* (1702) as '*Madam* CRESSWELL of pious Memory'. Writing to her 'sister in iniquity' she explains that 'My home was always a sanctuary for distressed ladies' and 'The clergy, I think, were beholden to me, for many a

---

* Slang uses *smelt*, but only to mean a half-guinea or $5.00 coin; it is thus one of the few fish that have escaped being co-opted as a woman or her genitals.
† Usually used by costermongers in the context of spoiled fruit; *fruit* itself can mean a sexually generous girl, but not before 1900 though such fruits as the *cherry* were long since adopted by slang.

poor parson's daughter have I taken care on [and] taught her a pleasant livelihood.' The letter, written deadpan but awash with doubles entendres, refers to a *nunnery* and a *boarding-school,* both brothels, to noblemen 'notwithstanding they had *deer* [i.e. mistresses; the era also has the *Whetstone Park deer*, a whore and named for a brothel street to the north of Lincoln's Inn Fields] of their own, us'd to come to my park a *bit of choice venison'* since 'within my pale it was all-year rutting time', and to the *scuts* of *bucks* and *does'.*

Hogarth includes 'Mother' Elizabeth Needham in plate 1 of *The Harlot's Progress* (1731), as she welcomes the country-girl Moll Hackabout* off the London stage with the notorious debauchee, 'rapemaster-general' Colonel Francis Charteris, accompanied by his 'Lieutenant' and pimp John Gourlay, leering from a doorway. Mayhew notes the profession but his own interviewee speaks 'standard' though there is a report of the use of *ax*, and its prompt explanation as 'ask'.

For a substantial picture of a madam and her vocabulary, offered in her own words, one needs fast forward some three hundred years: *Nell Kimball, Her Life as an American Madam* was published in 1970 (edited by the writer Stephen Longstreet), and written apparently in 1930. Its story went back further, covering Ms Kimball's professional life from the end of the US Civil War to 1917.

Nell Kimball, or such was the name she adopted, was born into rural poverty in South Illinois in 1854. She was the youngest of twelve siblings, four still born, two more dead as infants

---

* *Hack about* suggests violence and Moll will suffer (and die), but the verb also plays on the usual equation of whores as women one can *ride*: *OED*'s definition 2b has to use a horse for general riding . . . 'to ride a horse, typically in the countryside, for pleasure or exercise.

and the remaining five dying in various circumstances: alcoholism, childbirth, outlawry and illness. Aged fifteen she quit the hardscrabble life when she absconded with a farmhand, Charles Owens, who had come back from the war minus a hand. When he walked out on her in St Louis, she volunteered her charms to Fliegel's, one of the city's top 'sporting houses'. Here she was known as 'Goldie' and, unlike her spendthrift companions, she banked her takings (one third of her price – the rest went to the boss) and in 1872 quit the brothel to become the kept mistress of a local bigwig. Two years later he paid her off with $1000 cash and $10,000 in railroad shares. Next keeper: Monte (no recorded surname) who had his own career, safecracking. Unfortunately this came with a downside, notably three bullets in the chest, leaving Nell a widow, and briefly (her baby Sonny died of diphtheria) a single mother. By the early 1880s she moved to New Orleans and, after cashing in her shares, established one of the town's best whorehouses in Storyville, its red-light zone (also known as the *Swamp*). It lasted until a sadistic customer killed one of her girls (he was trying to set her on fire). Nell moved again: to San Francisco and operated another house there, staying three years before returning to New Orleans. In 1917, as the boys marched off to war in Europe and those she termed *bluenoses* and *holy Joes* finally managed to shut Storyville down, she finally quit – she was sixty and 'feeling stiff in the joints'. She threw a final party then cashed up once and for all.

Around 1930 she wrote it all down; she lacked much schooling but proved herself a natural raconteur: In 1932, needing money, she showed the manuscript – a near-illegible mess of crossings-out, rewrites and additions in both ink and pencil – to Longstreet. At the time it was impossible to publish. The language was simply too raw for print. So perhaps was its unvarnished honesty: as her unabashed summation put it, 'I served a vital need . . . I offered a good product, kept everybody's secrets, and saw to the health and wellbeing of everyone concerned.' Not until 1967 did Longstreet find a taker and the book appeared in 1970.

Kimball's *Life* offers around 260 slang terms. Of these around 40 per cent refer to sex.

Unsurprisingly she offers a number of synonyms for her 'office': the *banging shop, cowyard, cathouse, kip, knocking shop* and *crib*. She also has the *fairy house*, for gay clients and the *hot-sheet hotel*, the high turnover house of assignation. A *fancy man* works as a minder, and she mentions, but does not practise, the *badger game*. Intercourse is as productive as would be expected: *fuck* (*like a mink*), and *futz* plus the *fucker*, he who has sex; *bang, dip one's wick, get one's ashes hauled* or *haul someone's ashes, hump* and *schtup*. The act itself is a *lay, nookie*, a *piece of ass* (also a woman), *it* (thus *get it*, to have sex). *Screw* multitasks as a verb, a noun and as a job description: the *screwing trade*, otherwise known as *peddling gash*. A single act of paid sex is a *trick*, which one *turns*. To *shoot one's wad* or the Biblical *spend* mean ejaculate and what a man delivers – *spunk* or *stuff* – is a *load*. Virginities – genuine or more likely otherwise – are taken (*cop a cherry*) and women impregnated (*knocked up*); there are gang-rapes (*gang fucks*). To *horse around* is merely sexual play. The working girls are variously *bints, dollies, flappers* (a sense of the word that precedes the gentler evocations of the Twenties), *kates, kittens, ladies, stunners* and *hookers*; a *goldskin* is a light-skinned black girl and a *cadet* one who travels the small towns recruiting new whores.

The giblets with which clients and girls perform are displayed. The vagina is a *quiff, muff, snatch, split, crack* and a *cunt*, which is also used to equate the girls with their profession ('Free cunt is not good cunt, we agreed') and as such alternates with *meat*. The penis is a *joint*, *wang* or *dick* and a large one renders its possessor *well-hung*. Breasts are *tits*, *knockers* and *boobies* and *duff* the buttocks. The pubic hair is *fuzz*. If terminology is a guide, a brothel speciality is oral sex. Fellatio appears as *blowing*, *copping a joint*, *face* and *face job* and *Frenching*, plus the imagistic *getting one's hat nailed to the ceiling*. Cunnilingus is *eating pussy*, *muff-diving* and enjoying a *seafood mama*. The cunnilinguist, straight from Victorian porn, is a *gamahucker* [*sic*]. There are a variety of 'non-standard' *freakish* terms: *AC/DC* and *bi*, for bisexual; *daisy chain*, a spintry; *dry fuck*, frottage; *cornhole* and *Italian game*, anal sex; *ream out*, to penetrate the anus with penis or tongue and *sixty nine* or *fork and spoon*, soixante-neuf. She has a few homosexuals, whether male: *sissy*, *queen* (sometimes *screaming*), *Greek* and *lavender*; or female: *dykes*; a *drag joint* is a transvestite club. Men include a *boyo*, a *chicken*, an underage boy, the (self-proclaimedly) ultra-virile *stud* or *cocksman* and the sexualised *tomcat* who goes *vetting*, seeking sexual adventures. His antithesis is the *duff flogger*, the masturbator, reduced to *jerking off*, *diddling* and *pulling his pud*. The client ideally uses a *thing*, a condom; if he gets *clapped* it is known as a *dose* or *old rale* (perhaps from dialect *rail*, to stagger), or *big* (syphilis) *casino* or *little* (gonorrhea) *casino* (which are both, fittingly, games of chance).

If David Maurer can be dismissed as biased, even ignorant when it comes to whore speech, then he seems right enough in linking some prostitute slang to that of those with whom they associated: clients – louche or otherwise – and the underworld. When she is not talking sex, what we find in the *Life* is very much of her era and embraces the vocabulary's primary interests.

Her smarter clients might not have understood, but the villains undoubtedly would have had no problems.

There is, for instance, crime: A *brain* is a clever criminal and a *mobsman* a gangster. *Bushwhackers* and *highbinders* deal out violence, *sandbagging* or *whomping* or using *mickey finns* (knock-out drops), *chivs* (knives) or *hoglegs* (pistols) all of which leave victims *mangled.* Safebreakers are *jug-heavies* and *cribmen,* using *dinah* (dynamite). The forger can be a *penman* or *paper-hanger* (bad cheques), the con-man a *grifter* or *flimflammer;* the *shill* lures the gullible to *buck the tiger* (play faro) or play the *shell game* (three-card monte) in the hope of *cartwheels* (silver dollars) or *frogskins* (notes). Chased by those *goons* or *dicks* who are not to be *sweet-talked* with *pay-offs,* you *do a skip* to the *coop* (a hide-out). Your last words are *Goodbye, Charlie it's all over,* and you *take the deep six* (suicide).

There are drink and drugs. The *hard stuff* (spirits), *corn, rotgut* and *skull-cracker* (strong, if usually illicit whiskey); it's a *hog-wallow* (boisterous party) and as *snort* (shot of liquor) follows snort you get *bottled* (drunk) and sometimes *cat up* (vomit). *Gow* is opium and *snowbird* a cocaine user, who *sniffs* their drug of choice.

Important individuals are *muck-a-mucks, nabobs* and *sockdolagers;* they are *high-ass* (haughty), *it* (the fashion), *gussied up clothes horses* (well-dressed) and *flannel-mouthed* (well-spoken); the *double-dome* is an intellectual who *has a head on.* The out-of-towner is a *jake, peckerwood* or *redneck* from a small town or *one-night stand;* in town he *rubbernecks* at the sights. The fool is a *burrhead, chowderhead* or *knothead* and his madder peers are *whacky, cuckoo, off their trolley* or *soft in the head.*

Kimball uses a good deal more and if there is any lesson, it is lexicography's eternal stricture: everything is much older than you might expect. Linguistically there is nothing exceptional here, other than to note that a woman, albeit a brothel-keeper, could employ as much (maybe more) slang than any of her contemporaries. If you moved in a given world you used the pertinent language. Gender simply didn't come into it.

The Girls

How did the girls talk? Much early material, e.g. the Whore Dialogues, was most likely ventriloquised, though its anonymous authors were not automatically men. In a more useful world it would have been the women in question, an enthusiastic gaggle of court ladies, rather than their creator Thomas Urquhart, who came up with so splendid a taxonomy of terms for the giant Gargantua's penis in Urquhart's mid-seventeenth-century translation of Rabelais. So gross a member – and its owner was still in the cradle – doubtless merited so extensive a list:

> One of them would call it her *pillicock*, her *fiddle-diddle*, her *staff of love*, her *tickle-gizzard*, her *gentle-titler*. Another, her *sugar-plum*, her *kingo*, her *old rowley*. her *touch-trap*, her *flap dowdle*. Another again, her *brand of coral*, her *placket-racket*, her *Cyprian sceptre*, her *tit-bit*, her *bob-lady*. And some of the other women would give these names, my *Roger*, my *cocka-too*, my *nimble-wimble, bush-beater, claw-buttock, evesdrop-per, pick-lock, pioneer, bully-ruffin, smell-smock, trouble-gusset*, my lusty *live sausage*, my *crimson chitterlin, rump-splitter, shove-devil, down right to it, stiff and stout, in and to, at her again*, my *coney-borrow-ferret, wily-beguiley*, my *pretty rogue*.

Whoring literature's supreme narrator, Fanny Hill, the 'Woman of Pleasure' whose novelised 'memoirs' were created by John Cleland and published in 1748–9, was certainly a male creator's mouthpiece. The entire book is in addition an experiment; the creation of porn without the usual obligatory 'dirty words'. Fanny (whose own full name is a far from elaborate play on 'mount of Venus') is lavishly inventive:

> When our mutual trance was a little over, and the young fellow had withdrawn that delicious stretcher, with which he had most plentifully drowned all thoughts of revenge, in the sense of actual pleasure, the widened wounded passage refunded a stream of pearly liquids, which flowed down my thighs, mixed with streaks of blood, the marks of the ravage of that monstrous machine of his, which had now triumphed over a kind of second maidenhead [. . .] Coming out with that formidable machine of his, he lets the fury loose, and pointing it directly to the pouting-lip mouth, that bid him sweet defiance in dumb shew, squeezes in his head, and, driving with refreshed rage, breaks in, and plugs up the whole passage of that soft pleasure-conduit pipe, where he makes all shake again, and put, once more, all within me into such an uproar, as nothing could still, but a fresh inundation from the very engine of those flames, as well as from all the springs with which nature floats that reservoir of joy, when risen to its floodmark.

Setting aside the dubious masturbatory potential of such passages (and thus runs the whole book) we may have to accept that this was probably not the meat-and-potatoes monologue of the average *sporting lady*, *daggle-tail* or *nymph of darkness*. Even in the

eighteenth century. Only in talking of her brothel does our heroine seem to approach reality. The place is a *house of conveniency*
(a *house of convenience* was merely a privy); its bawd an *abbess* or
mother, her fellow whores *hackneys* (like the hackney horse they
are 'for hire' and can be 'ridden') and *misses of the town* and their
clients *cullies*. These were terms a real-life 'Fanny' might not have
coined, but would surely have known and used.

A century on and we encounter the interviewees who appear
in Henry Mayhew's 1862 volume. While the bulk of Mayhew's
published interviews with full-time working prostitutes (almost
certainly the first material of their kind), are frustratingly slang-
free (either as transcribed or bending like Dickens and many
others to Victorian conventions as regarded women, of no matter
what type), for instance the very standard English delivery of 'a
gay woman at the West End of the metropolis', there were others.
The 'Sensitive, Sentimental, Weak-Minded, Impulsive,
Affectionate Girl,' declares Mayhew,' will go from bad to worse,
and die on a dunghill or in a workhouse.' One woman, most of
whose customers were sailors, had what Mayhew termed a 'good-
natured expression' but was 'pointed out to me as the most
violent woman in the neighbourhood'. That established,
Mayhew's transcription allowed her to speak relatively roughly,
and he leads her by commenting that he had heard that she
could be 'very passionate and violent':

> I believe yer. I knocked my father down and wellnigh killed
> him with a flat-iron before I wor twelve year old. I was a
> beauty then, an I aint improved much since I've been on my
> own hook. I've had lots of rows with these 'ere sodgers, and
> they'd have slaughter'd me long afore now if I had not pretty
> near cooked their goose. It's a good bit of it self-defence with

me now-a-days, I can tell yer. Why, look here; look at my arm where I was run through with a bayonet once three or four years ago.

[. . .]

You wants to know if them rowses is common. Well, they is, and it's no good one saying they aint, and the sodgers is such ——cowards they think nothing of sticking a woman when they'se riled and drunk, or they'll wop us with their belts. I was hurt awful onst by a blow from a belt; it hit me on the back part of the head, and I was laid up weeks in St. George's Hospital with a bad fever. The sodger who done it was quodded, but only for a drag [imprisoned for three months], and he swore to God as how he'd do for me the next time as he comed across me. We had words sure enough, but I split his skull with a pewter, and that shut him up for a time. You see this public [house]; well, I've smashed up this place before now; I've jumped over the bar, because they wouldn't serve me without paying for it when I was hard up, and I've smashed all the tumblers and glass, and set the cocks agoing, and fought like a brick when they tried to turn me out, and it took two peelers to do it; and then I lamed one of the bobbies for life by hitting him on the shin with a bit of iron – a crow [bar] or summet, I forget what it was. How did I come to live this sort of life? Get along with your questions. If you give me any of your cheek, I'll —— soon serve you the same.

Among those who are willing to talk is 'another woman, commonly dressed in old and worn-out clothes; her face was ugly and mature; she was perhaps on the shady side of forty. She was also perambulating the Mall. I know she could only be there for one purpose, and I interrogated her, and I believe she answered my queries faithfully.' As she explains, while she does speak in slang, it is for 'professional purposes', i.e. eliciting some extra cash, and the interview suggests a very well-worn bit of patter.

'I have a husband, and seven small children, the eldest not yet able to do much more than cadge a penny or so by cater-wheeling and tumbling in the street for the amusement of gents as rides outside 'busses. My husband's bedridden, and can't do nothink but give the babies a dose of '*Mother's Blessing*' (that's laudanum, sir, or some sich stuff) to sleep 'em when they's squally. So I goes out begging all day, and I takes in general one of the kids in my arms and one as runs by me, and we sell hartifishal flowers, leastways 'olds 'em in our 'ands, and makes believe cos of the police, as is nasty so be as you 'as nothink soever, and I comes hout in the Parks, sir, at night sometimes when I've 'ad a bad day, and ain't made above a few pence, which ain't enough to keep us as we should be kep. I mean, sir, the children should have a bit of meat, and my ole man and me wants some *blue ruin* to keep our spirits up; so I'se druv to it, sir, by poverty, and nothink on the face of God's blessed earth, sir, shou'dn't have druv me but that for the poor babes must live, and who 'as they to look to but their 'ard-working but misfortunate mother, which she is now talking to your honour, and won't yer give a poor woman a hap'ny, sir? I've seven small children at home, and my 'usban's laid with the fever. You won't miss it, yer honour, only a 'apny for a poor woman as ain't 'ad a bit of bread between her teeth since yesty morning. I ax yer parding,' she exclaimed, interrupting herself –'I forgot I was talking to yourself. *I's so used though to this way of speaking when I meant to ax you for summut I broke off into the old slang*, but yer honour knows what I mean: ain't yer got even a little sixpence to rejoice the heart of the widow?'

Mayhew persists: 'You call yourself a widow now,' I said, 'while before you said you were married and had seven children. Which are you?'

'Which am I? The first I toll you's the true. But Lor', I's up to so many *dodges* I gets what you may call confounded; sometimes I's a widder, and wants me 'art rejoiced with a copper, and then I's a hindustrious needle-woman thrown out of work and going to be druv into the streets if I don't get summut to do. Sometimes I makes a lot of money by being a poor old cripple as broke her arm in a factory, by being blowed hup when a steam-engine blowed herself hup, and I bandage my arm and swell it out hawful big, and when I gets home, we gets in some *lush* and 'as some frens, and goes in for a regular *blow-hout*, and now as I have told yer honour hall about it, won't yer give us an 'apny as I observe before?'

Finally we meet a sixteen-year-old, veteran of 'low-lodging houses, where boys and girls are all huddled promiscuously together' her story 'discloses a system of depravity, atrocity, and enormity, which certainly cannot be paralleled in any nation, however barbarous, nor in any age, however "dark." The facts detailed, it will be seen, are gross enough to make us all blush for the land in which such scenes can be daily perpetrated. The circumstances, which it is impossible to publish, are of the most loathsome and revolting nature.' There is, of course, little detail of these 'wicked goings-on'. And the voice that tells them, perhaps coached by some missionary, uses the simplest of standard English.

In the end we must take what we are given. In 1858, in his *History of Prostitution*, William Sanger was, like all reformers, wholly without doubt. His job was as the resident physician at New York's Blackwell's island prison but he had no qualms when it came to international pontification. Talking of these same cheap lodging houses,* he declared that:

Obscenity and blasphemy are the staple conversation of the inmates; every indecency is openly performed; the girls recite aloud their experiences of life; ten or a dozen sleep in one bed, many in a state of nudity. [. . .] Unmitigated vice and lustful orgies reign, unchecked by precept or example, and the point of rivalry is as to who shall excel in filth and abomination.

A pity that he recorded not a word. Doubtless it was all too far away and recycling Mayhew was much less demanding.

Although one can come upon the occasional glimpse of language 'live': for instance the street-walking centre of London's Haymarket was known as 'Hell Corner' with its ads, presaging the tarts' cards of modernity, of 'Beds to Let' and 'For private apartments, ladies'. Again, just as has followed, brothels might masquerade as a 'massage rooms, baths, foreign language schools, and rheumatism cures'.† Some girls, says Ronald Pearsall, went so far as to hire sandwich men who, with suitably disguised

* W. Sanger, *History of Prostitution* (1858), pp.324–325.
† R. Pearsall, *Worm in the Bud* (1969), p.265.

wording on their boards, advertised their wares around the local streets. Meanwhile the authorities, backed by handwringing politicians and others keen to parade if not actually back up their preaching, talked in another form of slang of 'unfortunates' who were lost amidst 'the Great Social Evil' (labelled by the French visitor Hippolyte Taine 'the fouled hindquarters of English life'). The girls in turn called them, at least the clergymen, *dodgers*, as in *devil-dodger* and asked them, as they did every interested party, 'Are you good-natured, dear?' (very euphemistic compared with today's 'Do you want business?').

Modern street-walking has gained a number of practical terms: *git-down time*, to start a day's (or night's) 'shift'; to *break luck*, to find one's first client; to *catch* or *clock*, to find subsequent men; *trap*, the number of customers a prostitute is assigned as a daily tally by her pimp to reach a financial target (*trap money*); thus the money she earns each night. The prices vary but the service is divided in X for the girl and Y for the room, thus the *ten and two* of the 1980s. The potential vocabulary of the *pussy game* is far greater if one factors in pimp-talk, a storied lexicon and as such much listed in fiction, typically the work of Iceberg Slim (Robert Beck) or such quasi-scholarly studies as Christine and Richard Milner's *Black Players* (1972). The former includes nearly a thousand terms (though not all pimp jargon), the latter over 170. Their girls would have known and used some of them, e.g. *stable*, a single pimp's string of girls, *bottom woman*, the most important woman therein, *sweet mack*, one who was kind to his employees and *gorilla pimp*, one who rules through violence, *star* or *stallion*, a top money-maker, *cop and blow*, to exploit a girl for as much as possible before, inevitably, she moves on, to *choose*, for a pimp to select a new whore (and receive the voluntary donation of her prior earnings known as *choosing money*), *turn out*, to start an uninitiated girl (a *square broad*) in her job as a *lady*, a *bitch* and of course a *ho*.

Clients

If one area can be firmly ascribed to the working girl's vocabulary – whether on the street or behind the brothel's door – then surely that is the client. The first of these, *rifler* (1560) develops the verb to *rifle*, to have intercourse and uses, as does much sex slang, an animal-related image: *rifle*, of a hawk, to tread the hen; in terms of the client there may be backup from *rifle*, to despoil, to plunder, although it is more likely the girl who takes on that particular role. The seventeenth century offers *cunni-catcher*, punning on *cunny*, i.e. *cunt* and on cant's *coneycatcher*, a confidence trickster. There are *cull* and *cully* (which otherwise mean 'fool'), *rumper*, *trooper* and *suburbian trader*. This last, notwithstanding its extra 'i' (and the fact that the *trader* was more usually and logically the working girl herself) comes from London's original suburbs, areas immediately outside the city walls. For instance Clerkenwell to the north or Southwark to the south, doubly distanced by being across the river. Such areas, where a variety of 'stink industries', e.g. tanning or butchery, were allowed, were also known for whores and brothels.

The eighteenth century added *bully* (usually a brothel 'minder'), the jokey *husband*, a *flat* (again equating with 'fool') and paradoxically *pimp*. Thus the courtesan Sally Salisbury's *Authentick Memoirs* (1723): 'If the Pimp bleeds well, I'll glut you' (*bleed*, as in yield a good profit, *glut* as in give a substantial share). Finally the century seems to have originated *pick up*, as in attract a client, and the phrase 'Is he foolish or flash?' used among professionals to distinguish a casual, wham-bam customer from a more sophisticated (and regular) client.

Much is down to records but it seems hard to believe that such records yield a mere trio of nineteenth-century terms: *pross* (nothing to do with *pro*stitute, but extending a slang term meaning one who is easy to sponge on; the origin may be *prose*, to talk at length), *daddy* and *live one*, a more general term which suggests a sucker. The West End girls apparently, called the self-professedly do-gooding prime minister Gladstone 'Old Glad-eye'.* The twentieth, on the other hand, proves itself fecund.

Terms include *jockey* (i.e. a rider), a *date* (playing on a more innocent version, just as does *party*, for a paid encounter), *action*, *trade* and *fare* hint at economics; *mark* (more usually found among con-men) and *vic* (i.e. victim) suggest exploitation, and *meatball* and the Sixties' *gonk* (from a large squashy toy, much loved by British teenagers) are hardly flattering. A final trio are perhaps most important. The *punter*, which started life around 1700 as a gambler, and by the 1930s had expanded to mean any member of the general public, rather than an initiate into matters sometimes licit but more usually not. This equated with a customer, and thus a prostitute's client. *John*, generic for any man, has meant variously his penis (from 1838) a lover (from 1884), a free-spending sucker (1908) and thence, and combining all three, a prostitute's client, with somewhat contemptuous overtones (perhaps from the common-ness of the given name).

The third term, *trick*, is perhaps the most pervasive, at least in America. Trick is first recorded in any sexual context around 1550: it means any form of sexual intercourse but gradually focuses on the paid variety. By 1925 trick had moved from act to

* R. Pearsall op. cit. p.251.

individual: the prostitute's client, with the underlying suggestion of trickery, i.e. failing to give that client his money's worth.
The term has also meant a casual (free) sex partner, a prostitute
and anyone who is easily manipulated, typically a long-term
admirer who is never allowed sex, but merely kept in tow for the
material pleasures they offer. The etymology is debatable. As
noted, there is standard *trick*: a deception but one may note J.L.
Dillard in the *Lexicon of Black English* (1977): 'The term *trick* for
the sexual performance of a prostitute probably comes, ultimately, from the voodoo term for achieving control (often sexual
control), possibly reinforced by the nautical term meaning "a
task".'

Trick, even limited to the world of prostitution, is remarkably
flexible. It offers *trick-ass*, a general derogatory term, the implication is of sexual inadequacy (for a man) or promiscuity (for a
woman); *trick baby*, an illegitimate child born to a prostitute
(given no positive evidence to the contrary, the prostitute-
mother assumes the father to have been one of the paying
customers, known as a *trick-daddy*); *trick-bag*, of individuals a
fool, one who thinks they are better than they are and of circumstances a no-win situation (the term mimics *scumbag* and the
underlying assumption is that no-one but victims pay for sex
and that such a victim deserves whatever happens to him); *trick
broad*, a prostitute; *trick dough* or *trick money*, the money earned
by a prostitute; *trick house*, a brothel and *trick pad* or *trick room*,
an apartment, room or hotel room used by prostitutes to entertain their clients; *trick suit*, a prostitute's dress that can be
removed easily and is thus suitable for business. To *beat a trick* is
to rob a client and a *boss trick* or *champagne trick* pay well.

Whatever Maurer may have believed, the prostitute has
created work-specific jargon. There are times, based on the

length of the encounter: a *short-timer*, a client who pays for a *short time* — around fifteen minutes; the provider is a *short-time girl*. A *long shot* who spends longer than the usual time. An *all-nighter* or *all-night-man* who pays for a whole night's sex, itself known as an *all-nighter*. The *matinee*, who makes his appointments for the afternoon (*matinee* in wider use refers to afternoon, and often adulterous sex) and the *sleeper*, the last client of a night. Looked at for the long term there is the *steady*, another word borrowed from dating: a regular.

Special Services

Prostitutes, unless called upon to be otherwise, are remarkably forgiving. Once the client moves beyond *vanilla* sex (the most basic and unimaginative of flavours – both of ice-cream and of sex), and assuming the girl agrees with what is requested, there seem to be few if any limits. You pays your money and . . .

The variations on the theme may have existed earlier, but they were rarely recorded. Flagellation was variously *barking* (from *bark*, the skin), *bum-tickling*, the *English disease* and most recently *fladge*. A *flogging cully* or a *flogster* was a fan thereof and the sexual beatings are recorded from the seventeenth century on. There was also the *posture moll* (plus a whore who named herself Posture Moll to underline her speciality): such women specialised in stripping and adopting sexually arousing positions before their customer; sometimes paired up with a man to demonstrate what might be on offer.

But the idea of a prostitute's menu of services (known in its entirety as *the works*), and the details it held is very much a twentieth-century phenomenon. Those who chose from such menus could be *queer johns*, *freaks* or *freak fucks* or *twists*. The earliest term seems to have been a *French date* (oral sex). National stereotypes played a major role, including *Roman culture*: orgies, *English*: B&D, *French*: fellatio, *Greek*: anal, *American*: missionary position and *Swedish*: dressing in rubber, PVC, etc. In addition one encounters *Italian* or *Russian*, both involving rubbing the penis between the buttocks; a *Roman shower*, vomit play; and *Spanish*, i.e. *ATM* (ass to mouth) in which the penis, a sex toy or a finger, having first penetrated the anus, moves on to the mouth.

Very popular was *around the world* or *roundhouse*, licking and sucking the partner's erogenous zones, including the genitals and sometimes the anus; thus *halfway around the world*, fellatio and anilingus only. The *freak fuck* requested any unusual or possibly physically dangerous service; the term was also a prostitute's name for taking on three men – in her anus, vagina, mouth – simultaneously. Freaks could be choosy: the *mammy freak* demanded only large, motherly black women; the *needle freak*, a prostitute's sadistic client who derives pleasure from hiring a woman with large breasts and paying her for every needle she permits him to stick into her flesh; the *no freak* wanted the girl to simulate the role of a rape victim, screaming 'No!' and 'struggling' before he overpowers her. A *cum freak*, however, is a prostitute deemed to enjoy the sex even more than its earning potential.

Women could also entertain a *bennie*, a client who prefers to give oral sex rather than have sexual intercourse (perhaps from *bend down* or *bend over*); a *beat*, a masochist; a *looker*, who wishes only to look at a prostitute, who is usually naked, though he may occasionally fondle her breasts or a *tin soldier*, usually a middle- or upper-class client, who doesn't want sex but only to act as a servant or 'slave' to the prostitute. A *sniffer* sniffed used underwear and in sadomasochistic scenarios, there was a *mole* (with a possible link to the Hebrew *mohel*, one who performs ritual circumcision) a dominatrix who slits or pierces her masochistic client's penis; the term extended to the penis thus pierced or slit and the man who has such a penis. Then there was the *happy ending*, masturbation to orgasm offered in a massage parlour. Meanwhile the prostitute could augment her daily turnover by judicious use of the *middle finger*, when applied properly to the anus this would speed up orgasm and make way for the next client.

None of these have vanished. For the last few years a number of online websites, usually offering escort services and highlighting the services their girls may offer, have been offering a lengthy glossary of common adult industry sex terms, abbreviations, codes, codewords, terminology, acronyms and allied lingo. These are some of them:

Asian = anilingus
Asian Cowgirl = girl on top, squatting
Babyback = petite, young, attractive Asian
Balloons = breast implants
BJ = blowjob = oral sex = fellatio
BB = bareback = without condom
BBBJ = bare back blow job = BJ without condom
BBBJTC = bare back blow job to completion
BBBJTCIM = bare back blow job to completion in mouth
BBBJTCNQNS = bare back blow job to completion, no quit, no spit
BBBJTCWS = bare back blow job to completion with swallow
BBBJWF = bare back blow job with facial

BBFS = bare back sex

BCT = ball & cock torture

BFE = boyfriend experience

Blue Jay = blow job

Blue Pill = Viagra

Butter Face = everything looks good, but her face

Cash and Dash = ROB (i.e. a Rip Off Bitch) who takes your money and runs

CDS = covered doggy style = doggy style sex with condom

CFS = covered full service = Sex with condom

CG = cowgirl = girl on top facing you

CIM = cum in mouth

CMD = carpet matches drapes, typically a natural blonde

COB = cum on breasts / COF = cum on face

Cowgirl = CG = girl on top facing you

Cover = condom

DATO = dining at the o = anilingus

DATY = dining at the y = cunnilingus

DDP = double digit penetration, vagina and anus

DDE = doesn't do extras (PS only)

DTTC = deep throat to completion

Fire and Ice = a blowjob switching between hot drink and ice

Get Brain = blow job

GFE = girlfriend experience

GND = girl next door

Hardwood Floors = clean shaven pussy

HDH = high dollar hottie / LDL = low dollar looker (opposite of HDH)

Half & Half = oral sex & intercourse

LE = ellie = law enforcement

Mohawk = thin rectangular strip of pubic hair

MSOG = multiple shots on goal = multiple orgasms allowed

OWO = oral without condom

OWOTC = oral without condom to completion

Party Hat = condom

Pearl Necklace = cumming on breasts

Rimming = anilingus

Reverse cowgirl = RCG = girl on top facing away

Reverse Massage = you massage her

SOG = shot on goal = one orgasm

Southern France = BBBJ

Spinner = very petite, small girl

Stroll = path frequented by street walkers

Teabag = man squats and dips balls in partner's mouth

Tossing Salad = anilingus

TUMA = tongue up my ass

UTF = untranslated french = BBBJ

Trickery/Fraud

Those who are determined to dismiss her as no more than the passive provider of a biological function, deprive the working girl of agency. Again, one wonders just how much such commentators know of those they disdain. The canonical trio, the alluring whore, her violent pimp or some kind of thug-cum-thief and the hapless, *cunt-struck* (sex-blinded) and thus vulnerable client, play out one of slang's long-established cameos. It may safely be assumed that of those involved, two at least would have used the terminology.

When this fraudulent 'game' was instituted is unknown – probably around the time that prostitution joined the professions – but slang picks up on it in 1591 in Robert Greene's *Notable Discouery of Coosnage* [cozenage, or trickery]. 'Now daily practised by sundry lewd persons called Connie-Catchers [confidence tricksters] and Cross-biters [swindlers] . . .' He cites the 'Cross-biting Law' and subtitles it, 'cosenage by whores'. He lists the players: the whore herself, here known as the *traffique*, the sucker or 'coney', this time termed the *simpler* [he, like the celebrated Simon of nursery notoriety, is *simple* or foolish], and the *cross-biter*, who beat and robbed the unfortunate punter. The plot was simple: the girl was picked up, took the client back to her room, and before he had finished what he had paid for, the thief either quietly rifled his clothes – he was too preoccupied to notice – or noisily announced himself as the outraged husband of this poor, debauched young woman. Sometimes he was a lover, sometimes a brother or even father. No matter, what followed was invariably the same: only a substantial payoff would avoid either a beating or exposure.

We find it again in 1845, now renamed the *badger game* or *badger lay* (*lay* or *law* covered a variety of criminal schemes). Why *badger*? Because in nature the creature is nocturnal and carnivorous; the prostitute and thief also 'devour' their victims after dark. It was played in a *badger crib* or *badger house* (a whole brothel devoted to the con) by a *badger moll* or *badger worker*.

Alternatively, and a century later, it was the *Murphy game*. Again, the etymology remains debatable, with current theory suggesting that the strolling client encountered a pimp who asked him if he would like to meet 'a lovely woman called Mrs Murphy'. Once aboard the train, all moved on well-worn rails.

There was a marginal variation, known as the *panel game*. It was explained in 1868 by the reporter James D. McCabe in his exposé of New York vice, *Secrets of a Great City*.

This method of robbery is closely connected with street walking. The girl in this case acts in concert with a confederate, who is generally a man. She takes her victim to her room, and directs him to deposit his clothing on a chair, which is placed but a few inches from the wall at the end of the room. This wall is false, and generally of wood. It is built some three or four feet from the real wall of the room, thus forming a closet. As the whole room is papered and but dimly lighted, a visitor cannot detect the fact that it is a sham. A panel, which slides noiselessly and rapidly, is arranged in the false wall, and the chair with the visitor's clothing upon it is placed just in front of it. While the visitor's attention is engaged in another quarter, the girl's confederate, who is concealed in the closet, slides back the panel, and rifles the pockets of the clothes on the chair. The panel is then noiselessly closed. When the visitor is about to depart, or sometimes not until long after his departure, he discovers his loss.

The site of the robbery was the *panel crib, den, house, joint* or *store*, all of which were a purpose-built brothel (Chicago May Sharpe mentions a *dipping house*, 'They were like booths, into which you took your man. If you succeeded in getting him in, the landlady soon helped you trim him'); the game could again be a *lay* (although the *panel dodge* was about passing counterfeit money). The male performer was the *panel thief, panel, paneller* or *panel worker*; his female accomplice the *panel woman*.

Another variation was the early eighteenth-century *buttock and twang*: in this case the prostitute worked as both lure and robber and her accomplice merely as a thug. Captain Alexander Smith, in his *Lives of Most Noted Highway-men* (1714) laid it all out:

She [went] upon the Buttock and Twang by Night; which is picking up a Cull, Cully, or Spark, and pretending not to expose her Face in a Public House, she takes him into some dark Alley, so whilst the decoy'd Fool is groping her with his Breeches down, she picks his Fob or Pocket, of his Watch or Money, and a giving a sort of a Hem as a signal she has succeeded in her Design, then the fellow with whom she keeps Company, he knocks down the gallant, and carries off the Prize.

There were other names for the basic game. The *touch game* (mid-nineteenth century); the *dark lurk* (late nineteenth century); the *creep* (1920s); *bilking* (which took place in a *bilking house*); Australia's *ginger* (1940s) and its necessary *gingering joint*. Finally the *crocodile scam* (1980s), named for the amphibian which opens its jaws to embrace, then kill its victims and the *bawdy-ken dodge*, literally 'the brothel trick'. Girls who lured in such victims have been *skinners* and *clippers* (from *skin* and *clip*, to steal or defraud) or *flashtails*. A *shoful-pullet* (a 'second-rate chicken', shoful began life as counterfeit money or a cab, especially when unlicensed, and seems to come from Yiddish *schofel*, rubbish) was that ever-popular illusion the 'virgin', offered at a high price, thus usually to the jaded and wealthy, whose maidenhead is wondrously renewed for each successive defloration. A *bawdy-house bottle or bawdy-house glass* were used for nothing more sinister than serving short measure; the visible liquor might reach the top of each, but the bottom, of glass or bottle, was far thicker than was usual. The *b-drink* (consumed by a *b-girl*) was a drink that resembles whisky (and charged as such) but is in fact cold tea; served to the female companion of a man, or homosexual customer, who has entered a club in the hope of sex. A *down*, from down, short weight, was synonymous. The client rarely fought back: the sole term, available in more general use, was *georgia*, to enjoy the girl's services but to renege on her fee. The term was originally used by African-Americans who had long since moved north and meant to play a confidence trick on a person only recently arrived from the south (whether from Georgia or another deep south state) and is thus naïve as regards the northern, urban world.

8. Women of the Town:
G'hals, Donahs and Larrikinesses

THE MOB, AS in the full-scale burning, looting and murdering seen in London's late-eighteenth-century Gordon Riots, had effectively disappeared by the mid-nineteenth century. There were occasional one-offs, such as the racially-based Draft Riots that hit New York at the outbreak of the US Civil War, and there were continual skirmishes between the many 'gangs of New York', but while middle-class Londoners or New Yorkers, among others, might see such working-class areas as the East End or the Lower East Side, both confluences of slum housing and an influx of immigrants, as potential – and on occasion quite literal – plague spots, only the obdurately stupid (or those with a political career to promote) truly believed that the masses were about to take over in Mayfair or Murray Hill.

What had taken its place was more fragmented, though equally indisciplined, other than internally: the gang or what Australia termed the *push*. New York hosted, as Herbert Asbury has memorialised, a number of criminal gangs, often the fighting arms of more ostensibly respectable political parties and in turn drawing on the prejudices of one or another of New York's immigrant communities. As Asbury noted, women were wholly welcome. The front lines of gangsters 'blazed away at each other with musket and pistol, or engaged in close work with knives, brickbats, bludgeons and teeth'. Meanwhile, hovering round the edges and picking off the weaklings were a gang's womenfolk, 'always ready to lend a hand or tooth in the fray'. Not for the first time were the female fighters ranked as the most ruthless. In the Draft Riots of 1863, which pitched white nativists against African Americans, 'it was the women who inflicted the most fiendish tortures upon Negroes, soldiers and policemen captured by the mob, slicing their flesh with butcher knives, ripping out eyes and tongues, and applying the torch' to those who, first drenched in oil, were hanged from trees. We may hope that Asbury, something of a cut and paste artist, was exaggerating.

Some of the ladies' auxiliary were exceptional even by these standards. Hell-Cat Maggie (real name unknown) fought alongside the Dead Rabbits, one of the top gangs of the downtown Five Points district, the ultimate in mid-century slum badlands. Maggie, it was believed, filed her teeth to points and lengthened her fingers with sharpened brass nail extensions. Later in the century the Gophers, from Hell's Kitchen (on the West side), could call upon Annie Walsh, better known as Battle Annie, who ran their women's section, the Lady Gophers, officially known as the Battle Row Ladies' Social and Athletic Club; mobbed up, they ran from between fifty to a hundred deep, carried clubs and were regularly hired as muscle in labour disputes; they were indifferent as to the side that paid their fees.

The Whyos or Why-O's were another of the Bowery gangs, Asbury terms them the 'greatest' of those that emerged immediately after the Civil War. Prefiguring the modern rite of *blood in blood out* (i.e. kill to gain membership, be beaten up to leave) it was said that no-one joined without proving their ability to murder. Among the thugs, brawlers, sneak thieves, burglars and pickpockets drawn to the gang was one Danny Lyons, exceptional in such a macho cast (fellow members included Hoggy Walsh, Fig McGerald, Googy Corcoran and Baboon Connolly) for his using girls, albeit those for whom he was their pimp, as consigliere. Lizzie the Dove, Gentle Maggie and Bunty Kate were among those who gave him strategic advice. They were less tolerant of each other. When in 1888 Lyons was hanged for murder Maggie and the Dove argued over who had been his real favourite and who had in turn loved and now mourned him more. They met to discuss the matter but drink got the better of their conversation and Gentle Maggie saw off Lizzie the Dove with a cheese-knife in the throat. Lizzie lived long enough to assure Maggie that they would meet again in hell, and promised there to scratch her eyes from her head.

Another of the Whyos' heavy hitters was Beezy or Bezie (presumably from Elizabeth) Garrity, killed by accident in 1887 when she was hit by a stray bullet during a gangland set-to. Beezy, according to her 'obituary' in the *Oakland Tribune,* was 'a typical Whyo girl'. 'Almost worshiped' by the gang – both men and women – she was 'so strong and coarse and violent and depraved.'

'She was fairly good-looking with shoulders proportioned like the fore-quarters of an ox and yet with a waist that tapered till the belt of a Murray Hill belle would hang loose on it. She could drink like a brewer, could not speak a sentence or a phrase without an oath in it, could throw any man in the gang with a simple side hold and always stood ready to go to jail rather than tell a policeman anything.' Sadly, yet again, no-one thought to take notes of her delivery.

Beezy's *pièce de resistance* was an exhibition of what she called 'nerve'. This entailed challenging any of her male companions to hit her, as hard as they could, square in the face. Given that a Whyo liked nothing better – 'hitting women and robbing drunkards are the joys [he] prefers to anything, even . . . robbing his parents of whatever they have that can be pawned' – she didn't lack for challengers. Beezy set herself, up strode a thug, drew back a fist and lashed out as hard as he knew. She might stumble backwards, but never, ever admit to pain. They loved her for it.

'Sadie the Goat', properly Sadie Farrell, was quite literally a legend. There exists, in other words, no proof that she actually existed. Only a garland of anecdotes. Fact or fiction, she had won her name by her personal style of mugging: a goat-like head-butt to the stomach that left her victims winded and vulnerable. Around 1869 Sadie was wandering the West side waterfront; here she allegedly witnessed a bungled attempt to strip a moored sloop of its cargo. She volunteered her skills to the incompetent *ark ruffs* (river pirates) known as the Charlton Street Gang and was soon elevated to running the show. She turned them into real pirates, stealing a boat and marauding up and down the East coast along New York State. The ship flew the Jolly Roger and victims, it was said, actually did walk a plank. It did not last. Local vigilantes fought back, killing a number of members. Sadie, now 'Queen of the Waterfront' returned to dry land, and – other than her celebration in various posthumously penned ballads – to invisibility.

Sadie, while 'alive' had also fallen foul of possibly the most notorious of her sisters: Gallus Mag, bouncer and general facto-tum of the Hole in the Wall, a brutally criminal tavern on Water Street, a thoroughfare then basking in one of the city's bloodiest of red lights. A six-foot-plus immigrant Brit she dominated the tavern, a pistol in her belt and a bludgeon strapped to her wrist.

Her trousers – she scorned skirts – were held up by braces, or in American *galluses*. Her speciality was to club a victim to the floor, then use her teeth to drag him by an ear to the front door, where she kicked him on his way. If he protested the treatment, she simply closed her teeth harder, and off came the ear. It was then added to a number of predecessors in a large jar of pickle. Not for nothing did those few police who dared enter the bar brand her the most savage female they had ever met.

It was Sadie's error, perhaps inescapable, to engage in a vendetta with Mag. They fought, she lost and off came her ear. However on her return from the sea the women made peace. Mag returned the ear which Sadie encased in a locket, wearing it round her neck for what remained of her life. Thus, at least, runs the story.

These were the tough cookies, egregiously savage even for nineteenth-century New York's violent and blood-soaked streets. It is unfortunate that they remain voiceless; they are, after all, the very exemplars of that much-sought-after figure, the strong working-class woman. Nor can one even claim deliberate suppression: we do not have much from their male companions. The reality is that slang depends on cities, and America's cities, whatever they may have become, were mainly in the process of becoming. The language they generate, which now dominates the slang lexis across the world, had yet properly to arrive.

A gang did not, however, have invariably to be criminal, they were, at least in the US, as likely to be allied to a political boss as to a *Brain* or *Mr Big*. Sometimes they were not even a gang in the traditional sense – no organised violence, no overt criminality – but more a social phenomenon, defined by clothes and speech and perhaps occupation, such as London's rumbustious costermongers or the rough-housing butchers and volunteer fire-fighters who made up New York's *Bowery b'hoys* (a spelling and pronunciation that referenced the Irish origins of many members). Predecessors, one might suggest, of the succession of youth cults that emerged post-World War II. As much as anything they represent unfettered working-class hedonism and their simple refusal to accept the mores of bourgeois society; their overtly displayed preference for less genteel pursuits could be enough to have them pilloried, as were Australia's *larrikins* or, again in the States, and strictly in New York City, the *b'hoys*.

As far as women and girls were concerned, their role remained subordinate. There are no 'girl gangs'. Instead there were versions of what later generations might term 'debs', the female sidekicks and/or girlfriends of the gang's male members. Thus the Bowery b'hoy came with his *g'hal*, the larrikin with his *larrikiness* and the coster with his *donah*. The first two, at least as recorded, seem less vocal than their partners; the donah, verbal or otherwise in life, created the template for a whole subset of highly popular entertainment, as paraded on the stages of Britain's music halls.

The b'hoy himself might be a butcher, a manual labourer or a club bouncer; most often he was also a 'fire laddie', running to put out blazes with one of city's fire companies, fiercely antagonistic groups whose scuffles over access to the nearest fire hydrant might well persist longer than the fire itself. Naturally, he had a uniform:

> The Bowery Boy promenaded his favorite thoroughfare with his head crowned by a high beaver hat with the nap divided and brushed different ways, while his stalwart figure was encased in an elegant frock coat, and about his throat was knotted a gaudy kerchief. His pantaloons, out almost as full

as the modern Oxford bags, were turned up over his heavy boots. The hair on the back of his head was clipped close and his neck and chin were shaven, while his temple locks were daintily curled and heavily anointed with bear's grease or some other powerful, evil-smelling unguent.[*]

He often sported a bright red shirt, indicating his connection with the fire companies who were similarly attired. He had a rolling walk, a surly manner, puffed regularly on a 'long nine' cigar tipped up at forty-five degrees into the air and, of course, came out with a good line in slang.

The B'hoy was easily recognisable, and his gang was one of those who were exploited in the sectarian rivalries of contemporary politics. But if he was fact, it would take fiction to render him omnipresent. The first night of Benjamin's A. Baker's play *A Glance at New York in 1848* opened at the Olympic Theatre on 15 February 1848. It starred the actor Frank S. Chanfrau as 'Mose', the Bowery B'hoy and member of the city fire department. Chanfrau was Bowery-born and had been a member of a fire company; and Mose had a real-life origin, one Moses Humphreys, who was a printer on the New York *Sun* and a runner with the fire brigade's Lady Washington engine company No. 40; he was also well-known as a tough fighter. Like Pierce Egan's *Life in London*, and the play based on his book, it was more *tour d'horizon* than sequential, plotted narrative, but unlike Corinthian Tom and his country cousin Jerry, the cast experienced only those scenes already well-known to working class New Yorkers. Though such plot as it did have – streetwise New Yorker Mose shepherding the naïve yankee George through the

---

[*] H. Asbury, *The Gangs of New York* (New York 1928), p. 32.

snares and delusions of the metropolis – was slightly reminiscent of Tom's education of Jerry.

In the end there would be a procession of sequels. Among them were *The Mysteries and Miseries of New York* (1848 and based on Judson's 'exposés'), *Mose in California* (1849), *Three Years After; or, A Sequel to the Mysteries and Miseries of New York* (1849), *Mose, Joe and Jack* (1849), *Mose in France* (1851) and *The Newsboy of New York; or, Mose in Town* (1852); the last, and somewhat belated, was *New York As It Is and Was* (1871). They were each toured across the States, opening in every major city. Plots were rudimentary but all capitalised on Mose and his associates: Sykesy, his second in command, his friends Joe and Jack and perhaps anomalously for so determinedly macho a world, his girlfriend, Lize.

Lize, again like Mose a template drawn from thousands, was also deemed worth of description and analysis. For the first time young women had joined the workforce – other than as servants – and the writer G.G. Foster dealt with her at length in *New York by Gas-Light* (1856):

> The g'hal is as independent in her tastes and habits as Mose himself. Her very walk has a swing of mischief and defiance in it, and the tones of her voice are loud, hearty and free. Her dress is 'high,' and its various ingredients are gotten together in utter defiance of those conventional laws of harmony and taste imposed by . . . the French mantua-makers of Broadway. The dress and the shawl are not called upon by any rule recognized in these 'diggins' to have any particular degree of correspondence or relationship in color—indeed, a light pink contrasting with a deep blue, a bright yellow with a brighter red, and a green with a dashing purple or maroon, are among

the startling contrasts which Lize considers 'some pumpkins' and Mose swears is 'gallus!'* But the bonnet!—that is the crowning achievement of the out-door adornment of the full-rigged g'hal. It is of various materials at different times—though without any special regard to the season—but we believe that white chip and fancy straws are the favorite patterns. The outside is trimmed with a perfect exuberance of flowers and feathers, and gigantic bows and long streamers of tri-colored ribbons give the finishing touch to a hat which, resting on the back of the head, extends its front circumference just round from ear to ear across the top of the forehead, leaving the face entirely exposed, and the eyes at full liberty to see what is going on in every direction.

The newest invention in the costume of the g'hal is a fascinating article of outside gear, termed by some a 'polka,' but generally known as a 'monkey-jacket.' It is cut like a gentleman's tight sack to fit the back and shoulders smoothly, and reaches halfway down the thigh. When neatly cut and fitting to the figure of a plump, healthy and elastic-limbed g'hal, with the full-skirted dress swelling out voluptuously from beneath it and undulating like a balloon, it certainly has a very exhilarating appearance.

Both parties were keen on hairstyles, notably what he termed a *soap-lock* and she a *spit-curl*. Both involved the curling of one's side hairs and the gluing of the resulting creation to the skull beneath.

---

* This is not the *gallus* that holds up Meg's *inexpressibles* but a variation on slang's *gallows*, lively and spirited; first-rate and satisfactory. The origin either takes slang's established bad=good trope to equate death on the hangman's gallows as something admirable, or a link to Scottish *gallows*, rascally, dissolute.

The generic Lize came in two varieties. One was the relatively subordinate Lize of *Glances at New York*. (The character was only added after a couple of months' performances; 'Lize' gave a part to a local favourite, the actress Mary Taylor, whose 'luscious' voice' was much beloved of her fans.) She has a couple of scenes and performs a song she's picked up from the Christy Minstrels. We see her in a tea shop where she orders 'A cup of coffee and nine doughnuts' (Mose goes for pork and beans, adding 'don't stop to count de beans'). Mainly she acts as Mose's adoring sidekick, telling her friend Jenny 'that Mose of mine is such a dear fellow— he don't care for expense—not he —he thinks there's no gal like me in this village. You ought to see him in de market once, I tell you— how killin' he looks. De way he takes hold of de cleaver and fetches it down is sinful! Dere's no mistake but he's one of de b'hoys!' When Jenny suggests that Bill Sykes (Mose's best pal Syksey) has been 'cuttin' round you', Lize laughs her off: 'Syksey tried, but I bluffed him off—he's got to look a little more gallus, like my Mose, afore he can commence to shine.'

As a later commentator added, 'Lize . . . shares with Mose his most endearing trait—a hearty, matter-of-face self-esteem. When Mose compliments her with "You're a gallus gal" she readily responds "I ain't nothin' else."'* Mose is also worried about Sykesy's advances.

Mose. Now, look a-here, Lize, I go in fur Bill Sykesy 'cos he runs wid our merchine—but he musn't come foolin' round my gal, or I'll give him fits!
Lize. La! Mose, don't get huffy 'cause I mentioned him; but

* F. E. Dudden, *Women in the American Theatre: Actresses & Audiences, 1790–1870* (1997), pp.104ff.

I'd rather go to Christy's. Did you ever see George Christy play de bones? ain't he one of 'em?

Mose. Well, he ain't nothin else.

Lize. And that feller with the tambourine musn't be sneezed at neither.

Mose. Yes, he's some.

Lize. Do you know I've been learnin' one of their songs— and if it wasn't for bein' in the street, I'd sing it for you.

Mose. It's too early in de mornin' for many folks to be out— so you're safe. Blow your horn.

Lize offers 'Lovely Mae', a popular song of the time, and it has the right effect:

Mose. [*Affected.*] Well, I'm blowed if that ain't slap up. Lize, you can sing a few.

Lize. You ought to hear Jenny Boget and I sing at the shop. We can come it a few, I can tell you. But I can't stand talking here—I must go to the shop. Drive on with your meat, Mose.

Mose. What time will I come up to your shanty?

Lize. Any time after tea. [*Going*].

Mose, in his rough-and-ready way, was smitten. Even if business has to come first:

She's a gallus gal — she is; I've strong suspicions I'll have to get slung to her one of these days. But I musn't forget my butcher-cart. [*Goes up.*] I say, boy, yer better drive the cart right up to de slaughter-house. The customers are all sarved. What! yer don't know where de slaughterhouse is yet? Well, drive up Chrystie Street till you smell blood, and dere stop.

Foster also notes her language, offering a contrast in class conversations in *New York by Gas-Light*. If slang made the streetwise man, then it also made the woman:

'Do tell me all about your fine parade with the Hoosah troop yethterday, Mither Thmith,' lisped a young lady of the Upper Ten to a dandy Hussar, the other evening at a party in the Fifth avenue.
'Oh I assure you, we had a most chawming time, my deah madam—perfectly chawming.'

On the same evening Mose returned from a grand fireman's parade and target-excursion, and was met by Liz at the door.

'Well hoss, what kind of a time'd ye hev—say?'
'Well now yer'd better *bleeve* we hed a gallus time! Give us a buss, old gal! Guess I seen ye lookin' out erther winder this morning—*I* did.'
'Oh git out—*you Mose!*'*

A second Lize, playing a substantial, even starring role in *The Mysteries and Miseries of New York* (1847) by 'Ned Buntline' (proper name Edward Judson) is a very different figure. Given the dates it is hard to work out the crossover, and the *Mysteries* was made subsequently into a Mose play. Copyright was hard to sustain on so hugely popular a set of characters.

* G. G. Foster, *New York by Gas-Light* (1856), p.174.

Buntline offers readers a portrait of this Lize that, without going into her dress, suggests a very different figure to the happy-go-lucky g'hal of *Glances*.

Very tall, nearly or quite six feet in height; a form well-proportioned; a carriage rather graceful; features that once must have been remarkably handsome, and even yet are fine and regular, though the hollow cheek, and high cheek-bones, and narrowing chin, denote the havoc of time and dissipation; a large, piercing eye of hazel; lips which now are thin and close, set over white and regular teeth — lips which have firmness written in their expression; a high brow, upon which crescent shaped and delicately pencilled eyebrows are seen; dark hair, even yet soft and glossy, though thinned and shortened. See this — and fancy a touch of paint on either cheek, and a coat of powder on a rather slim neck and broad uncovered shoulders, and 'Big Lize, of Thomas Street,' is before you.

Her first appearance, rescuing a younger woman from rapists, is also some way from her doughnut-guzzling, up-for-fun namesake. If there is one thing that unites them, it is their use of slang.

'God protect me !' murmured the girl, then with a kind of desperate firmness in her manner, she pressed forward to try to force her way from amongst the crowd of drunken libertines. But he who had won in the toss-up, clasped her firmly in his arms; in vain she tried to spring from his grasp. Then she uttered a wild, piercing cry — a shriek of terror and agony. And it was not in vain, for the next moment a tall form stood among the laughing young men; two or three heavy blows were heard and felt rather than seen, and with each blow one of the party laid down. Before Harry could turn to see who it was that interfered, a large bony hand reached his cheek, and though struck by its open palm, he let go of the poor girl and staggered up against the lamp post.

'Big Lize, of Thomas Street !' he muttered, as he saw the tall form of the one who had struck him and his companions.

'Yes, I am Big Lize, you lushy Swell!' cried the woman, 'and I can maul every sneaking mother's son of ye! What d'ye mean by stoppin' this ere gal against her will?'

'It's none of your business; go look out for yourself, you thieving catamaran!' cried the young man . . . again springing toward the poor sewing girl, who shrank behind the huge form of her protectress.

'You will have it then, my covey; you're mighty fond of my mawley!' cried Big Lize, as with another blow, she landed him clear down the stairs of the oyster saloon, which was behind him; and then turning to the girl, she cried, 'Cut and run, my darling! Hays is the word, and off you go! I'll see that they don't follow you.'*

If Lize's slang – *lushy* for drunkard, *covey* as a term of address to a man, *mawley* for hand – seems reminiscent of what was used in London at the time, then so it was. As George Washington Matsell's American (and thus essentially New York City) slang lexicon *Vocabulum* made clear a few years later, slang was one more of the emigrants who had brought the habits of the old world with them to the new.

* 'Ned Buntline', *Mysteries and Miseries of New York* (1848), pp.11–12.

But if there is misery in Lize's world of crime there is also mystery: her own antecedents. Buntline's plot is straight out of the penny-dreadful playbook. Angelina, the rescued victim, flees, the attackers slink off, and:

> Lize stood and gazed at them a moment, while upon her dissipation marked, but yet firm features, a freezing expression of scorn and contempt settled; then as she turned away and walked up the street, that expression gave way to one of deep sadness, mingled apparently with satisfaction at the act which she had just performed.
>
> 'God bless me!' she murmured, repeating the last, grateful words of the poor girl whom she had protected. 'Yes, I have need of such prayers; for God, or man, or the devil, or all together, seem to have cursed me! Oh God! I once wore the stamp of innocence on my brow — once I rode along these very streets in my father's carriage, and now.'

The soliloquy – no slang here, of course – is soon cut short as a voice breaks in:

> 'Hallo, old gal, where are you stavin' to? Have you lifted anything to-night?'
> [. . .]
> 'How d'ye, Charley, my chum! I haven't lifted nuthin' as yet; but I mauled some o' the bigbug swells a bit ago. If you'd been there you might have larnt 'em some lessons in the knucking line?'
> 'What, warn't none of the files on the tramp?'
> 'Not a mammy's son of 'em!'
> 'What did you maul the swells for?'

''Cause they were abusin' a gal — a poor bit of a thing that hasn't got hell's mark on her yet — that's as innocent as I was ten years ago!'

'You might have been in better business, Lize. You're too blasted good-hearted to be on the tramp: but stir your pegs, old gal. I'm agoin' to the crib; see if you can't pick up some cove as wants to see the elephant.'

'Well, tramp along, chummy,' replied the girl; 'I'll see what's what, my chuck!'

And Big Lize leaves, off to seek a new victim for her panel-crib, 'for she has long been an active panel-thief'. She has indeed fallen very far. No matter: she has the obligatory 'heart of gold'. Lize dodges in and out of the plot, sometimes speaking standard English, especially to the unfortunate Angelina who seems destined to fall foul of brutes, and sometimes 'pattering flash'. Angelina will die as will Lize and they are buried side-by-side. It is all as mawkish as the most sentimental reader could desire.

The Mose and Lize boom wore itself out quickly; the papers were already saying their farewells to the Bowery's finest by 1850. The last we hear from our happy couple are in a couple of letters published in the small-town press, suggesting that as they did on stage, the pair had set off to make their fortunes in the Far West.

Syksey may be 'Bill Sykes' but Dickens' character has been dead a decade even if one critic liked the idea of the fictional 'brothers in arms, the cockney bully and the Bowery b'hoy'.* In any case, Mose and Lize already had their own equivalents, three thousand miles to the East.

Slang in fiction, consciously or otherwise, plays the role of a

---

* D. Symonds, *Broadway Rhythm: Imagining the City in Song* (2017), p.36.

guarantor of authenticity. It does this in *A Glance at New York*, where it helps underpin the validity of the characters' dips into the working-class city. It does the same in what may have been an influence on the *Glance*, Pierce Egan's slang-dense, semi-sociological guided tour of *Life in London* (aka *Tom and Jerry*) which in 1821 had appeared in print and very soon after on stage in London. The play arrived in New York in 1823 (and toured major cities). American-written sequels such as *Life in New York* (1844) and *Life in Boston* (1847) followed.*

It is possible that the print version of *Life in London*, specifically the scene in the East End gin shop 'All-Max' (*max* being slang for gin) is the first fictional portrayal of working-class Londoners 'at play' other than the various portraits of criminals, beggars or gypsies that had been seen in print or on stage.

Lascars, blacks, jack tars, coalheavers, dustmen, women of colour, old and young, and a sprinkling of the remnants of once fine girls, &c. were all *jigging* together, provided the *teazer of the catgut* [fiddler] was not *bilked* of his *duce*. Gloves might have been laughed at, as dirty hands produced no *squeamishness* on the heroines in the dance, and the scene changed as often as a pantomime, from the continual introduction of new characters. *Heavy wet* [strong beer] was the cooling beverage, but frequently overtaken by *flashes of lightning*. [gin] On the sudden appearance of our "*swell* TRIO," and the CORINTHIAN's friend, among these unsophisticated sons and daughters of NATURE, their *ogles* were on the roll,

---

* 'Tom and Jerry' had girlfriends too: Corinthian Kate and her friend Sue. Egan is too discreet to name their profession but they were supposedly based on Mrs. Maples and Harriette Wilson, both celebrated courtesans. They say little and when they do, it is in standard English. One illustration, later censored, has the girls *sporting the dairy*, i.e. revealing their naked breasts.

under an apprehension that the *beaks* were out on the *nose*; but it was soon made "all right," by one of the *mollishers* [girls] whispering, loud enough to be heard by most of the party, "that she understood *as how* the *gemmen* had only dropped in for to have a *bit of a spree*, and there was no doubt they *voud* stand a *drap of summut* to make them all *cumfurable*, and likewise prove good customers to the *crib*." On the *office* being given, the *stand-still* was instantly removed; and the *kidwys* and *kiddiesses* were footing the *double shuffle* against each other.[*]

Cruikshank's illustration shows a remarkably heterogenous group. Of the seventeen individuals pictured six are women (four 'of colour', which must be an early use of the phrase, plus a black babe-in-arms, and two, including the landlady or *covess of the ken*, white). Front and centre are Dusty Bob, a coal-heaver (and soon generic for a chimney sweep) still blackened from the day's work, who dances with Black Sal (seemingly a generic name for a black woman, as well as a possible link to the character and phrase *Aunt Sally*), resplendent in a pink bodice over a yellow dress with embroidered red flowers. Black Sal may have had other celebrity: London historian Lee Jackson[†] mentions 'the far-famed *mollisher*' Black Sarah who was fêted a few years later in the down-market *Town* magazine (a prototype lads' mag) as being pre-eminent among the docklands bachannale of the Ratcliff Highway. The 'sable' Sarah, also abbreviated to Sall, 'is not one of the insipid things they call genteel; she may be compared in maritime analogy, to a Dutch-built piratical schooner, carrying on a free trade under the black flag'. Jack (i.e.

[*] Ibid. pp.286–287.
[†] http://catsmeatshop.blogspot.com/2015/12/black-sall.html

Jack Tar, the sailor), adds the writer, is no racist, and 'not one of those "d-----d nasty particular sorts of fellow as stands nice about the colour of the craft, so long as she's a fast sailer." Such is black Sarah, and therefore a favourite with black and white; she is the very life and soul of the neighbouring *lush cribs* [pubs], and sticks to her locality as if she know no other.'

In 1844, in a short guide to the *New Sprees of London*, the anonymous author promised to 'introduce you to the [. . .] flash and slang Mots, Donners, and Cullies that's faking the slums on the cross'. That is, criminal men and women who specialise in break-ins and burglaries. *Donner*, which can also be found as *donah, done, doner, doney, donie, donna, donnah, donnie, donny, donor* and *dony* – a wealth of alternatives that attest to its wide-spread use – came from the stage (and later gay) jargon Polari, and ultimately the Italian *donna*, a woman. While the era (and slang as a whole) was spoilt for choice for terms for 'woman', it would become the term of choice for a Cockney *bloke's* equally Cockney girlfriend or partner. The 'old woman', in other words. It still appeared in twentieth-century crime fiction (often in America), but is essentially a London word, and faded with the previous century.

One of those synonyms was, in mid-century, *tart*, a word that has long-since turned pejorative (though not in Liverpool nor Australia where it remains neutral). In 1864, as defined by the latest edition of Hotten's dictionary, it played on the 'good enough to eat' trope of desirable womanhood and was far from derogatory; it also gives us some idea of how the average donah dressed:

Tart, a term of approval applied by the London lower orders to a young woman for whom some affection is felt. The expression is not generally employed by the young men, unless the female is in 'her best,' with a coloured gown, red or blue shawl, and plenty of ribbons in her bonnet — in fact, made pretty all over, like the jam tarts in the swell bakers' shops.

A colourful costume, and Lize, at least in her frivolous mode, would have admired it. It wasn't just ribbons; a donah could never have too many ostrich feathers; in 1894 Sydney's *Truth* warned against 'despoiling an ostrich to adorn a donah' and in 1897, pondering what would become his play *Pygmalion* (later the musical *My Fair Lady*) Bernard Shaw saw his mismatched duo Professor Higgins and Eliza Dolittle as: 'he . . . a west end gentleman and she an east end dona in an apron and three orange and red ostrich feathers.'

Beyond the penny-dreadful or shilling shocker, and the all-conquering minstrel show, imported from America in the 1830s, London's primary form of popular entertainment was the music hall. This in turn had descended from the 'free-and-easy' and the 'cock-and-hen-club', both held in pubs or taverns and both featuring male singers. The bawdiness, even downright obscenity of some of the songs, heavily larded with smutty doubles entendres, guaranteed that. The songs may have found their ancestry in the ballads collected by Pepys and Thomas Durfey a century and more before, but that didn't offer respectability. A woman (though certainly not what Victorians termed a 'lady') might just sing along with such ditties as 'He'll No More Grind Again', 'Mother H's Knocking Shop; or, A Bit Of Old Hat!' (*old hat* meaning the vagina) or 'I Am a Smutty Chimney Sweep'('When up the ladies' flues I creep, / The pleasure it is all my own') but she wouldn't stand up and lead the choruses. It was the same in the even less savoury *penny gaffs* (cheap, temporary theatres featuring obscene songs and suggestive dancing) even if, as moralising observers announced in shocked tones, 75 per cent of the audience were girls, some as young as eight. Mayhew visited one and was duly appalled.

The 'free-and-easy' proved too much so for Victorian propriety. In its place came the music hall, a far larger enterprise, both in their numbers around the country and in the halls themselves, capable of holding a substantial audience. There was also a great difference in style. Where the free-and-easy expected the audience to help make the entertainment and singers lead as much as performed the songs, the music hall began to make the singer the star, delivering the song to an audience, though they too might well sing along, at least for the chorus.

The free-and-easy, which also peddled food and drink and might well have hosted a number of working girls, had necessitated a loud and physically demonstrative delivery. The music hall had no need for this, but what made a star was not just a performance, but the identification of given performers with a specific character, with dress and diction to match.

There were a variety of 'characters' – the style began with the *lions comiques*, singing to the working classes in the *soup-and-fish toggery* of their alleged upper-class 'betters' – but among the most popular was the Cockney coster. Like the b'hoy and the larrikin he had a uniform,

> Now kool my downy kicksies—the style for me
> Built on a plan werry naughty,
> The stock around my squeeze a guiver colour see
> And the vestat with the bins so rorty
> [*chorus*]

I'm a Chickaleary bloke with my one, two, three,
Whitechapel was the village I was born in,
For to get me on the hop, or on my tibby drop,
You must wake up very early in the morning.
A. Stephens 'The Chickaleary Cove' c.1864

Like Mose, who was dressed for the part in the fire laddie's signature red shirt, the on-stage coster mimicked his real-life inspiration. Henry Mayhew listed the basics:

The costermonger's ordinary costume partakes of the durability of the warehouseman's, with the quaintness of that of the stable-boy. A well-to-do 'coster,' when dressed for the day's work, usually wears a small cloth cap, a little on one side. A close-fitting worsted tie-up skull-cap, is very fashionable, just now, among the class, and ringlets at the temples are looked up to as the height of elegance. Hats they never wear—excepting on Sunday—on account of their baskets being frequently carried on their heads . . . Their waistcoats, which are of a broad-ribbed corduroy, with fustian back and sleeves, being made as long as a groom's, and buttoned up nearly to the throat. If the corduroy be of a light sandy colour, then plain brass, or sporting buttons, with raised fox's or stag's heads upon them—or else black bone-buttons, with a lower-pattern—ornament the front; but if the cord be of a dark rat-skin hue, then mother-of-pearl buttons are preferred. Two large pockets—sometimes four—with huge flaps or lappels, like those in a shooting-coat, are commonly worn . . . The costermonger, however, prides himself most of all upon his neckerchief and boots. The costermonger's love of a good strong boot is a singular prejudice that runs throughout the whole class.

As for the donah, the coster girl:

> The general costume of the women or girls is a black velveteen or straw bonnet, with a few ribbons or flowers, and almost always a net cap fitting closely to the cheek. The silk 'King's-man' covering their shoulders, is sometimes tucked into the neck of the printed cotton-gown, and sometimes the ends are brought down outside to the apron-strings. Silk dresses are never worn by them—they rather despise such articles. The petticoats are worn short, ending at the ankles, just high enough to show the whole of the much-admired boots. Coloured, or 'illustrated shirts,' as they are called, are especially objected to by the men.

The silk neckerchief – the *billy* or *kingsman* and occasionally *solicitor* – was especially beloved. Coming in different patterns and colours, each style was accorded its own slang name. The *bird's eye fogle* or *bird's eye wipe* had a bird's eye pattern; the *canary* and *Spittleonian* (of Spitalfields-manufactured silk) were yellow; the *randalsman* (favoured by the prize-fighter Jack *Randall* 'The Nonpareil') had a green base and white spots; the *blood-red fancy* was red; the *blue billy* blue and the *cream fancy* had a white or cream background with a variety of patterns.

The main music hall costers were Albert Chevalier, Harry Champion and Gus Elen. Chevalier was sentimental, Champion played for laughs and Elen was grittiest. They dressed as costers and spoke, or rather sang, in their manner. Slang was a given. They all had their signature songs; among Elen's was the minatory 'Never introduce your donah to a pal.'

Elen sang no duets, but he would have had plenty of potential partners (and his main songwriter George LeBrunn, also wrote for the best of them, Marie Lloyd). If men portrayed costers then some of the female stars logically went for the donah. Again the costume, again the slang, again the opportunity for the audience to see an idealised, heightened version of themselves on stage. Academics have suggested that the music-hall costers and donahs had little to do with the real thing[*] – Marie Lloyd and others were consciously acting a part that could be adopted and discarded at will – but like modern villains who take on the attributes (clothes, speech) of Hollywood 'mobster' movies, the representation offered an aspirational model for many in the audience.

Not every female singer opted for the pose – Vesta Tilley (Matilda Alice Powles), male impersonator and creator of 'Burlington Bertie'[†] and 'Algy, the Piccadilly Johnny with the Little Glass Eye', chose to mimic the nobs, and indeed married one in real life and died as Lady de Frece – but some of those who did were ranked among the greatest ladies of the halls: among them Marie Lloyd, Lottie Collins, Jenny Hill and Bessie Bellwood.

The other thing that differentiated Tilley from the donahs was, as the *Daily Telegraph* put it following her final show (her last song earned an unprecedented forty-minute standing ovation) 'she has stood with the clean and wholesome song . . . when her rivals have gained applause and kudos by the suggestive and vulgar.'[‡] Victorian concepts of both 'wholesome' and 'vulgar' may have been somewhat extreme in their moralising, but the donahs, true to type, were not averse to a little

---

[*] D. B. Scott, 'The Music-Hall Cockney: Flesh and Blood, or Replicant?', *Music & Letters* (83:2, May 2002).
[†] The parody 'Burlington Bertie from Bow', a vast hit in 1915 and thereafter, was always associated with the male impersonator Ella Shields, its first performer.
[‡] *Daily Telegraph*, 7 June 1920.

nudge-nudgery. Like Max Miller, a generation or two in the future, they knew not to go 'too far' but the audience was generally complicit and no-one was complaining.

——————

Then a swell from the West winked his blinkers once at me,
And in course I tips 'im back a civil wink.
I was eating of some winkles from a paper in my 'and,
Which I offers 'im and then he stands a drink.

Then 'e says, 'If you will fly with me I'll put yer on the stage,
Where yer know the corster business now, is getting quite
    the rage!'
'What!' says I, 'You teach yer grandmother, my covey, to
    suck eggs,
D'yer think I'd ever go upon the stage and show my legs?'

Marie Lloyd 'G'Arn Away' (1892)

Marie Lloyd (Matilda Alice Victoria Wood) was undoubtedly the queen of the halls, one of the limited number of 'stars proper' of the variety stage who according to the *London Society* magazine, could 'almost be counted on one's fingers'.[*] Born in 1870 she launched her career in 1884, appearing, as 'Bella Delamere', at the Grecian Music Hall, attached to the Eagle (the City Road pub that gained immortality in the nursery rhyme 'Pop Goes the Weasel'). Thereafter she came on as herself and moved swiftly up the bill. By 1886 she was earning £100 a week (in 2019 purchasing terms around £12,500). At her pre-World War I peak she was a worldwide star. She toured Australia and the States. The *Los Angeles Times* termed her 'The Queen of Comedy Song' and

---

[*] *London Society* LXX (Jul–Dec 1896), p.31.

'a cartoonist of London types'.[*] Only in her unfortunate choice of husbands, there were three and each was to some extent abusive, did what seemed like infinite success elude her.

As noted in the *Oxford Dictionary of National Biography* 'Lloyd articulated the disappointments of working-class life, especially those of women.'[†] Less sentimental, à la Chevalier, than grimly realistic, she made it clear that a donah's lot could be a far from happy one: faced by domestic violence and financial worries her escape was drink or perhaps a lover. After all, as one of her most celebrated songs proclaimed, 'A Little of What You Fancy Does You Good'. But as that title and many others make clear, the great overriding theme was naughtiness, even smut, though the latter was never directly spoken. 'I always hold in having it if you fancy it / If you fancy it, that's understood' ran the chorus of 'A Little of What You Fancy' and for slang fans, both 'have it', and 'it' could easily run to alternative interpretations.

> She could play out the contrast between the persona of a song and her own stage presence: as a cockney child in the country, giggling as a bull 'wagged 'is apparatus', she wiped her nose on her sleeve and kicked aimlessly, dressed in one of the elaborate gowns she loved; she could add a top-spin of lewdness to the most innocent lyric and slip into amused contemplation of her own naughtiness; the title of one of her first commissioned songs, 'When you wink the other eye', symbolized her stage presence—the sense of sharing a secret with her audience rather than simply a smutty joke.[‡]

[*] *L.A. Times*, 29 March 1914, pt 3 p.1.
[†] *ODNB* 'Marie Lloyd'.
[‡] *ODNB* 'Marie Lloyd'.

T. S. Eliot, in the *Era* (1922), turned a blind eye to smut, claiming that 'There was nothing about her of the grotesque; none of her comic appeal was due to exaggeration';* *The Waste Land* owes much to the music hall. Others saw otherwise: for many, her whole shtick was exaggeration: sidelong glances, winks, grimaces . . . the popular gamut of the nudge-nudge, wink-wink style that underpins so much British humour. During her Australian tour of 1901 Melbourne's *Table Talk* noted her 'blue' songs, but added that while her lyrics 'get pretty close to the knuckle [they] never jump over the fence'.†

Her songs, unsurprisingly, are filled with slang. Well over 250 words or phrases. They are, by slang standards, almost wholly bland. Just as in her songs as a whole she might dance along the edge of obscenity, but it was all in the audience's mind. But if this was run-of-the-mill slang, it was exactly what her audience knew and what they used at home and work. It helped make her one of them and it shouldn't be surprising that a good 30 per cent of the slang she used overlapped with her fictional contemporary, E.J. Milliken's Cockney 'chap' par excellence, ''Arry', whose slangy 'ballads' appeared in *Punch* from 1878 to 1892 and whose given name became shorthand for any of his type.

As befitted any Cockney worthy of the name, there was rhyming slang: *almond rock* [frock], *darby kelly* [belly], *dicky dirt* [shirt], *God forbid* [kid/child], *heart of oak* [broke/poor], *how-do-you-do* [a to-do, a problem], *tealeaf* [thief] and *threepenny hop* [shop]. It is just possible that the first of these was used for its alternate, and far better known meaning, 'cock'. There was, as one might expect, *donah*: but the speaker, even through her lips, was male, telling her admiringly, 'Straight, you are a blooming "slap-up" little donah'.‡

* 'Marie Lloyd' in T. S. Eliot, *Selected Essays* (1951), p.452.
† *Table Talk* (Melbourne) 23 May 1901.
‡ T. & G. LeBrunn [perf. Marie Lloyd] 'Come Along, Let's Make Up' (1901).

As for *blue*, that was there, but only in the most patriotic of disa-vowals: 'Let them keep the blue, they're blue enough, French papers so obscene, / But let them keep their hands off English women's lives so clean.'* A little bit of Little Englander jingoism from the girl who brought fans 'The Coster Girl in Paris' and there confessed that 'if they'd only shift the 'Ackney Road and plant it over there, / I'd like to live in Paris all the time!'†

Obscenity – 'whatever gives an aged and impotent judge an erection' – like beauty, allows for a very subjective assessment. In the music hall context it was hard to miss the nods and winks, of course, but one had to be a dedicated bluenose to see actionable 'filth' in the words she used. By slang's standards her vocabulary was anodyne. She mentions *hot stuff* and a *bit of crackling* (as well *bit of goods* and *bit of stuff*) which meant a young woman and claims herself as *warm* and 'a little bit *fruity*'; a saucy joke was *spicy*; there are *spooning* and *yummy-yum*, two of the era's terms for love-making. Perhaps the nearest she gets to out-and-out smut is *agility* as in *The Wrong Girl* (1895): 'The day your gee-gee stumbled there / And threw you off, you know. / But you were up and on again / As agile as can be' / I said, 'Excuse me, sir, you've not / Seen my agility'. The 'riding' backdrop aside, even this required a bit of foreknowledge. It mimicked a joke that was published in 1888, but was probably a good deal older: 'A young lady was out riding, accompanied by her groom. She fell off her horse and in so doing displayed some of her charms; but jumped up very quickly and said to the groom: "Did you see my agility, John?" "Yes, miss," said he, "but we calls it cunt in the kitchen!"'‡

Drinks included *fizz* and *cham* (champagne), *b. and s.* (brandy

---

* E.W. Rogers [perf. Marie Lloyd] 'The Red and The White and The Blue' (1900).
† O. Powell & F. Leigh [perf. Marie Lloyd] 'The Coster Girl in Paris' (1912).
‡ 'An English Popular Story' in *Kruptadia* (1888–1911) vol. IV 394–395.

and soda, and *pongelo* (beer). *Half seas over* was drunk and a drink was a *drain* or a *sherbet*. There was also what might be termed swearing, but of the mildest sort: *bally, blessed, blooming, blow!, Jerusalem!, lumme!, no fear!, not much!, rather!* and *s'elp me bob!* Nothing, surely, to trouble the local watch committee. But the professionally offended live for offence, however thin the evidence, and Lloyd was not immune from attack. In 1894, when the license of one of her favourite venues, the Oxford Music Hall, came up for its annual renewal, it was strongly opposed.

The self-appointed censors specified two songs as 'objectionable'. Both seemed to depend upon knowledge of the forbidden. One, sung by Lady Mansel (Lillie Ernest before her marriage into the aristocracy) had the chorus 'What I saw I must not tell you now'; and referred to the 'saucy' results of various clothing malfunctions, high winds and mistaken entries into the men's dressing room. The other was Lloyd's 'What's That For?' otherwise known as 'Johnny Jones'. In this case Lloyd, dressed as a schoolgirl, offered such faux-naive verses as:

> Pa took me up to town one day
> To see the shops and sights so gay
> Oh how the ladies made me stare
> They nearly all had yellow hair
> And one of them – Oh what a shame
> She called Pa 'Bertie' it's not his name
> Then went like this (*kissing sound*) and winked her eye
> And so I said to Pa, 'Oh my'

and a chorus that had the 'schoolgirl' asking:

'What's that for, eh? Tell me Ma
If you don't tell me I'll ask Pa'
But Ma said, 'Oh it's nothing, shut your row'
Well, I've asked Johnny Jones, see
So I know now.

There were also problems with another verse, in which 'Ma' seemed to be making baby clothes. There were further objections to the flouncing of skirts by one singer, and the lifting of a female performer so that 'she was entirely exposed'. As the assiduous censor invariably demands, multiple visits were necessary to ascertain all this 'obscenity'. On one of these Madge Ellis, again as a schoolgirl, used the lines 'You show me yours fust, and I'll show you mine'. The offending item was a bruise, but it was too far up the thigh for propriety to remain silent. A gentleman witness complained that a young woman 'ogled' him. This time Marie Lloyd's 'He knows a good thing when he sees it' came under the disapproving glare.

My dear Uncle Sam is a jolly old cock
Who knows a good thing when he sees it
He's right up to snuff, he can tell you what's o' clock
And he knows a good thing when he sees it.
He once saw an up-to-date play in the West
And sweet Chorus ladies scantily dressed
Round to the stage door later on did he roam
And found 'something choice' coming out, going home

Chorus: *Then he stood it a supper at Scotts*
And bought it a bottle to please it
For its dear little waist

325

Seemed to tickle his taste
And he knows a good thing when he sees it

There was more of the same and one cannot deny that such lyrics were nothing if not suggestive. ('It' was long established in the sphere of sex; this was seemingly the first occasion on which the word was used to mean a young woman.) Perhaps the most interesting line referred to Lloyd's view of a gentleman's 'first class' *ticket*, perhaps cognate with her song title 'She'd Never Had Her Ticket Punched Before'.

Another lyric, that of 'Salute My Bicycle', in which the singer wore the new 'rational dress' (notably the 'bloomer suit') was deemed 'difficult'.

You see I wear The Rat'nal Dress,
Well how do you like me? eh, boys?
It fits me nicely, more or less,
A little tasty! eh, boys?
When on my 'bike' I make a stir,
Girls cry, 'My word!'
Men cry, 'Oo-er!'
And in this garb they scarce can tell,
Whether I'm a boy or 'gell'.

Chorus: *The fellows all 'chike',*
When they see me on my 'bike',
But I'm as cool as any icicle;
They can chaff me all they like,
But I never get the 'spike',
I only say, 'Salute my bicycle!'

Whether this was Lloyd's self-promotion as 'tasty' and in later verses 'sultry', 'saucy' and 'tricky' that worried the censors is unstated. Perhaps it was the implied transvestism of garments that defeated gender specificity, or the dismissive slogan that was in effect a euphemism for 'kiss my arse'.

Lloyd had no direct input to the hearing (the Oxford survived for a further year) but soon afterwards she was summoned before a London County Council committee and asked to sing some songs. As the *Sporting Times*' historian J.B. Booth put it in his memoir *Pink Parade*:[*]

Marie sang them, as a Sunday School child would 'speak its piece'—without wink, laugh, or glance—and they were supremely and utterly proper—and dull. The deputation rose to leave, but she stopped them. 'Now,' she said, 'you've had your show. I'll have mine. I'm going to sing you a couple of the songs your wives sing.' And she sang them, 'Queen of my Heart,' and 'Come into the Garden, Maud,' which quite suddenly acquired incredible improprieties.

'There!' she said triumphantly, 'if you can stand that sort of stuff in your homes I don't think there's anything much wrong with my little parcel!'

She would never convince those whose whole satisfaction depended on interfering in the pleasures of others. In 1912 she was banned from the Royal Variety Performance (had Edward VII still been on the throne things might have been different). The solution was simple: she booked another theatre for the same night and filled every seat.

* J. B. Booth, *Pink Parade* (1933), p.162.

Marie Lloyd wasn't, of course, the donah's only avatar. A number of singers positioned themselves along the spectrum of Cockney womanhood. One being Jenny Hill (born Elizabeth Thompson), whose unfettered energy won her the name 'The Vital Spark' and who sometimes appeared in drag as a Cockney coster, inevitably named ''Arry'. Her act had plenty of slang, which did her no good on her US tour where unappreciative audiences had to be provided with a printed glossary.

Among the other 'donahs' were Lottie (properly Charlotte Louisa) Collins, whose style is best summed up in her hit 'Ta-ra-ra-boom-dee-yay!' and in her on-stage look: a hugely-brimmed 'Gainsborough' hat* and the sort of skirt and petticoats usually associated with that naughtiest of dances 'the can-can', and Florrie Forde (Flora May Flanagan), whose best-known tunes included 'Down at the Old Bull and Bush' and the World War I staple 'Tipperary'. Forde was another splendid dresser, her tall, imposing figure bedecked with ostrich plumes, capes, trains, high heels and a good sprinkling of sequins. Plus a jewelled cane. As a modern commentator put it, Forde's delivery 'was that of a benevolent sergeant-major addressing raw recruits'.

If Lloyd was the plucky trier – accepting of bad times but always up for the possibility of good ones – her antithesis was surely Bessie Bellwood. Bellwood was full-on hen party (coined in 1879 as an all-female gathering, but only attaining its present sense in the late twentieth century): unrestrained, noisy, quite probably terrifying every passing male. Born Catherine Mahoney in 1856, she took her stage name in 1876. She was working as a rabbit-puller or skin dresser in a Bermondsey factory when she made her debut at the local hall.

* The original being that painted by the artist to adorn Georgiana, Duchess of Devonshire in 1787 and re-adopted by the contemporary Gaiety Girls.

She was, the story runs, supposed to be performing on the 'zithern', today's zither. The audience was less than receptive and the chairman, supposed to keep order, was unable to quell the hecklers. According to the indefatigable J. B. Booth, things proceeded thus:

Singling out a ringleader, a gigantic, heavy animal with the appearance of a brewery drayman, 'You, sir!' cried the little man, 'you—in the grey flannel shirt—will you allow the lady to proceed?' 'No!' bawled the brute, and the gallery shrieked its delight.

This was the last straw for the signora . . . So, slinging the zithern into the wings, she advanced to the footlights, and, arms akimbo, after calling the chairman 'an old messer,' told him 'For God's sake shut it, if that's all you can do for a living!' and proceeded to take the matter into her own hands.

Ignoring the rest of the audience as unworthy of serious attention, she went direct for the brewery drayman. He was no mean lord of language: his bright young lexicon was crammed to overflowing with recondite phrases culled from east and south, from Billingsgate to Limehouse Hole, from Petticoat Lane to Whitechapel, from eel-pie shop and penny gaff, from doss-house, tavern, court and street, and he stood up to his opponent like a man.

But after a fierce interchange of two full minutes he fell back gasping, dazed, speechless and, worst of all, he had used up his vocabulary, and could but start all over again.

Then she really began.

She started by announcing that she was going to 'wipe down the bloomin' hall with him an' make it respectable'— and she did it. His very pals sitting near him edged away, as

329

though afraid of catching something from such a mass of vileness.

Every phrase she flung at him hit an invisible bull's-eye. The last name seemed ideal—until the next one appeared and seemed the one he ought to have been christened by.

And then she gathered herself together for one supreme effort, and hurled at him a brief description of his ancestry, his present, his future, so sharp with insight, so all-embracing, that the audience shivered in the presence of the pariah.[*]

As *London Society* put it in 1896, Bellwood was 'the character singer par excellence of the halls [. . .] a lady whose great talent is backed by an amount of impudence that is, even for a Cockney, nothing less than astounding. Her ready wit never fails to stand her in good stead, and no matter what topic she may light upon her comments are always amusing and to the point. No one who has ever heard her engage in wordy warfare with her audience (a reprehensible custom to which this fair artist is unhappily too much addicted) has ever heard her come off anything but victorious.' In 1888 she threatened a libel suit against an accuser who claimed that her songs contained unladylike lyrics. It does not seem to have come to trial, a pity, since the court was thus deprived of what Ralph Nevill, in *The Man of Pleasure* (1913) termed 'Miss Bellwood's considerable powers of trenchant repartee.'

Her signature song, 'Wot cher Ria', pretty much summed her up. It was, how could it not be, as slangy as one might wish:

* J. B. Booth, *'Master' and Men* (1927), p.105ff.

I am a girl what's a-doing very well in the wegetable line
And as I'd saved a bob or two, I thought I'd cut a shine
So I goes and buys some toggery, these 'ere wery clothes you see
And with the money I had left, I thought I'd have a spree
So I goes into a Music Hall, where I'd often been afore
I don't go in the gallery, but on the bottom floor
I sits down by the chairman, and calls for a pot of stout
My pals in the gallery, spotted me, and they all commenced
    to shout.

Chorus: *What cheer Ria! Ria's on the job*
What cheer Ria, did you speculate a bob?
Oh Ria she's a toff and she looks immensikoff
And they all shouted 'What cheer Ria!'

Of course I chaffed them back again, but it worn't a bit of
    use
The poor old Chairman's baldie head, they treated with
    abuse
They threw an orange down at me, it went bang inside a pot
The beer went up like a fountain, and a toff copt all the lot
It went slap in his chevey, and it made an awful mess
But what gave me the needle was, it spoilt my blooming
    dress
I thought it was getting rather warm, so I goes towards the
    door
When a man shoves out his gammy leg, and I fell smack
    upon the floor.

Chorus: [as above]

Now the gent that keeps the Music Hall he patters to the
  bloke
Of course they blamed it all on me, but I couldn't see the
  joke
So I up'd and told the governor as how he'd shoved me down
And with his jolly old wooden leg, tore the frilling off my
  gown
But lor bless you! It worn't a bit of use, the toff was on the
  job
They said outside! and out I went, and they stuck to my bob
Of course I felt so wild, to think how I'd been taken down
Next time I'll go in the gallery with my pals, you bet a crown.

She was the darling of the era's *Sporting Times*, better known
as the 'Pink 'Un' (like the *Financial Times* it used pink stock) and
the home of such pseudonymous hacks as the Pitcher, the Shifter,
the Dwarf of Blood, Rooty-Tooty and many others. They called
her the Queen of Song and the One and Only, among many
other encomia. They hymned the joys of the Strand, especially
Romano's restaurant, when that thoroughfare was London's
gaudy carnival midway for toffs and proles alike. Bellwood grav-
itated between the two. Her lover was the indolent Kim
Mandeville, Duke of Manchester and she was not above knocking down, then thrashing a cabbie who made a dubious crack at
His Lordship's expense. The American press was less indulgent.
When in 1892 Mandeville died aged only thirty-nine, worn out
and broke, the *Seattle Post-Intelligencer* belied its nation's much-
touted egalitarianism, sneering at Bessie as 'his mistress . . . a
big, muscular, barmaid type of young woman' and implying that
it was she who ran through his fortune (though at the same time
they complained that he had lived off hers). Not that they had

any more time for 'the dissolute duke . . . the dead beat debau-chee . . . who had disgraced an honorable name by the most disgusting excesses.' However their real rancour was reserved for Mandeville's American wife. She should have known better, being an American girl; 'low-born and low-bred' Bessie, in her 'gross depravity and systematic impurity' was merely doing what she had been brought up to.*

She died in 1896, victim of her unstintingly Bohemian life-style, and the alcoholism it engendered. At the same time she was generous to the poor, giving away much of what she earned. Her estate was worth a mere £125, a pittance for someone who would have earned that and more every night. The funeral procession drove through teeming crowds from Fulham Road near her West London home to Leytonstone's catholic cemetery in the East.

London's *Pall Mall Gazette* was one of many obituaries:

She played one part — herself; and it was Bessie Bellwood playing herself that the crowd went to see. She had not a touch of pathos. No one ever saw her serious on the stage— to have done so would have been a shock to every tradition. [. . .] Music-hall fashion has advanced and it left Bessie Bellwood behind it. Mr. Albert Chevalier has made the stage coster a namby-pamby individual, seeking after something better than his native life and surroundings, and he has his hosts of imitators, male and female. Bessie Bellwood took that phase of life which suited her powers best—

THE LOW, ROWDY, FIGHTING, HAIR-TEARING GIRL of the lowest courts in the East-end, a creature all fringe and

* *Seattle Post-Intelligencer* (Washington) 28 August 1892, p.4/1.

mouth, and into her, as into all her characters, she thrust her own strong individuality. A better actress would have concealed herself in the character she portrayed, and have missed the popularity which Bessie Bellwood enjoyed. Bessie Bellwood herself—the woman we knew not only on the stage, but in what was euphemistically called her private life, her appearances in the courts, and her squabbles with her landlords and her agents—came out strongly in everything she touched.

Like many another music-hall favourite she owed nothing of her popularity to her voice. [. . .] Her songs served only as skeletons, round which, and in the middle of which, and, indeed, at both ends of which, she could interpellate her 'patter'; and in this 'patter' was her secret of success. She possessed an inexhaustible fund of slang, which flowed from her lips in an incessant stream—'back-slang,' which must have been utter mystification to many such people as now take their sisters to the West-end halls, but which any one coming into contact with East-end life could easily translate.[*]

It is hard, perhaps impossible, to track down what the larrikiness, Australia's equivalent of the donah or g'hal, had to say. The local press is full of stories that parade their horror at her language, variously branded as 'obscene', 'abusive' 'abominable', 'beastly', 'vile', 'disgusting', 'opprobrious' and whatever other synonym the writer might recall. It was clear, said a reverend, sermonising in 1881, that 'the road which leads to ruin' began 'when a girl acquired the habit of using slang and of "chaffing" young men'. Thereafter lay practical joking, and its follow-up 'lustful words'. The larrikin and

---

[*] *Pall Mall Gazette*, 25 September 1896, p.7/3.

doubtless larrikiness, 'is a proficient in double entendre, and impure himself in thought and speech, he can see purity nowhere, and therefore the most virtuous are being constantly insulted by his lustful words or acts.' The solution? Parental discipline (which like many of his type he found woefully wanting in the country) and alongside that, flogging and Sunday schools.

Reading the contemporary press – the larrikin panic began around 1870 and was still visible, if much diminished twenty years later – one's problem is discerning what exactly defined a larrikin act. The word seems to come from *larking*, i.e. playing around, but as well as targeting gangs of young people involved in that eternal pursuit of hanging around on street corners and making too much noise, the press and its parade of 'Angry of Suburbia' correspondents labelled all sorts of petty and not so petty crimes as 'larrikinism'. When it came to the larrikiness, it seemed that anything qualified a girl, from full-on rioting in the street all the way to saying 'no' to mummy and daddy. What we need is chapter and even more important verse. What we get is only indignant bloviating. In the end we can only assume that the larrikiness, like her boyfriend, used whatever slang was currently available. It bound her to the group and excluded those who were not initiates.

On the other hand, perhaps larrikiness, a cumbersome poly-syllable and probably nine-parts journalese, was too demanding. Australia could adopt the donah too. Thus a fine example of contemporary tabloid outrage from the Brisbane version of the down-market *Truth* which headlined its prurience: 'Adelaide-st. Amazons, DRUNK AND DIRTY DONAHS. Biff, Bang, Smash, and Cuss. Rorty Ructions and Lewd Language.'*

---

* *Truth* (Brisbane), 19 October 1902, p.3.

The British donah was generally beloved as a salt-of-the-earth specimen. Her antipodean cousin received a far less forgiving press. In *Truth*'s story at least she was:

> a dirty, untidy, slovenly wench, whose begrimed fingers are loaded with cheap jewellery, her greasy "poll" topped by an enormous hat of which imitation ostrich "fevers" constitute the principal ornament. Her hair usually is worn in an enormous fringe over her forehead, like the coster donah's "bang." [. . .] Her skirt generally trails on the ground behind, but is so short in front that it discloses the tops of her boots and affords glimpses of dirty petticoats. She is "loud" in manner and voice, and her vocabulary garnished with THE CHOICEST EXPLETIVES in the language. She drinks, too, and smokes.

Truth went on to describe how a young woman, 'hooked' [arrested] and sent to the Reformatory, had returned to freedom and was now bent on respectability. Unfortunately she ran across three old pals, bereft of any such pretensions and recently propping up a variety of bars. Inevitably they started abusing their old friend and when she refused to abuse them back arguments turned to fists. Much applauded by a crowd of male barrackers, the girls set to with kicking feet and hair-tearing hands, but the singleton, to general surprise, knocked down at least one opponent. This ended the fisticuffs but 'having recovered their hats the contestants resumed the slang-whanging, and the drunken girl commenced to sway and curse and blaspheme, all over the sidewalk. But though able to hold her own at a lash [a fight], the seceder from THE RANKS OF THE RORTY had no chance when it came to verbal stoush.'

Nonetheless she tried: she 'hazarded a remark anent the

drunken girl's figure, hinting that there were certain signs which told of the approaching consequences of immorality,' but her opponent was quite unworried: '"I know it, and I'm proud of it," was the retort, "it's to a soldier!" And she concluded by a reference to incestuous intercourse in which the ex-reformatory girl was a principal party.'

In the end, with the crowd definitely against them, the trio decided to 'do a bunk'. As they left 'The drunken girl addressed the mob as a lot of bludgers and one or two who spoke kindly to the harried girl were asked "What the blue blazes they meant by smoodging to a girl wot used to be — —."The drunk girl then commenced to get maudlin and started to cry. "Where's Lily?" she wailed, "poor b— Lily! She'll think I'm locked up! Let's go and find her. She's my friend." With a final look and a final curse at the object of their contempt and hatred, the trio strode away. "I'm going to look for my cobber," yelled the sot, "poor b— Lily!"'

Off they wandered, straight into the arms of a 'gentle, browse-ful "bobby".' In court the next day they 'behaved disgracefully, smiling, giggling and tittering, hanging on to dirty old drunks, winking at policemen and even trying to mash Magistrate Murray.' It didn't work: fines all round. Our heroine meanwhile, had vanished. The *Truth* wished her efforts at reformation well.

In 1921 the same paper also played host to a heated corre-spondence headlined 'Aussie Girls and British Brides'* which offered 'bouquets and brickbats for belles of both countries' and in which such Aussie girls as 'Three Aussie Tarts'and 'Diggeress' wrote in to savage 'pommie' girls ('midnight owl trollops of brazen, underfed, canary-legged microbes' … 'lazy

* *Truth* (Brisbane), 13 February 1921, p.3.

337

good-for-nothing creatures, why, I've seen better looking features in comic cuts') who had been brought back from Britain as war brides. (There was also 'An Aussie Wife's Husband' who unaccountably wrote in cod-'German' – a self-proclaimed defender of 'vorking beobles' he boasted, 'I can schwig off a quart of bier in von mit der best Aussie in der landt' and much more.) There was a good ration of slang (one English correspondent even claiming that understanding it was a major problem for her immigrant sisters): 'Not for mine, Josephine', 'slavey', 'Aussie' (Australia), 'skiting' (complaining: 'the only thing pommies are good at'), 'mag' (chatter: 'they were absent from parade when the rations of good looks were being given out, but they were in the front line [for] the mag'), and many 'poms' ('a good comparison: a pom and a Pomeranian dog'), 'pommies' and 'tarts', the latter being, in its Australian use, wholly neutral, even congratulatory.

If Lize had a real-life descendant, she was the actress Ada Lewis (1873–1925), best-known for her stardom in Ned Harrigan's 1890 musical 'Reilly & the Four Hundred'* which celebrated the triumph of a working-class Irishman over the snobs of the Four Hundred, the widely known nickname of New York's highest society, based, at least in popular myth, on the maximum number who could fit into the ballroom of the mansion owned by society doyenne Caroline Schermerhorn Astor. (In 1906 the

---

* Other than Ada Lewis' stardom, the lasting, if indirect knock-on of the musical was the creation in 1895 by R. F. Outcault of *Hogan's Alley*, his great cartoon evocation of New York slum life, which brought the 'Yellow Kid' to rotogravure life and created a new concept, from the unashamedly tabloid content of the Hearst papers in which he appeared: 'yellow journalism'. Outcault took his title from *Reilly and the Four Hundred*, in which the hit song 'Maggie Murphy's Home' began with the line 'Down in Hogan's Alley'. Outcault imagined such an alley, complete with slum kids, young toughs, a vast number of stray dogs and cats and a backdrop of merry, if implausible squalor.

democratic short-story writer O. Henry responded with a collection entitled *The Four Million*). Lewis's role was officially 'Kitty Lynch' (for all the recent arrival of Italians and Jews the Irish were still the default representatives when art demanded a quintessential New York prole) but she was better known to fans as 'Harrigan's Tough Girl'. As a contemporary paper explained, 'Her voice is only heard during a scene lasting less than ten minutes, but that short scene has undoubtedly made her the most talked-about young actress in New York.'*

Like Lize and her boyfriend Mose fifty years before, 'Kitty' was one of the audience's own. 'Dressed in an old jersey brown, pulled out of shape and too short for her long, ungainly arms, the "Tough Girl at Harrigan's" walks onto the stage exactly as the tough girl in real life walks along Hester Street [. . .] on the way to the corner saloon with the "growler" [a can used to bring home take-out beer].' The promo suggested that the actress had allegedly studied such real-life New York slum-dwellers at first hand, but the truth was that she had never left her home in San Francisco, although she had checked out the workers in one of the city's canneries. In any case, it all came together on the night, and there would be many of them: the show scored 202 performances during its first season, and 136 more in the second.

It was all about slang: 'Saay, Reilly,' she addresses the pawnbroker with whom her brother has deposited her brand-new dancing shoes, 'I wan' ter git me new spielin' shoes out o' hock. Me brother's touched me for all I got.' Like Mose's character-setting opener, 'I ain'ta goin' to run wid dat mercheen no more' that was all it took. As the paper added, 'Every one who has ever heard one of the real tough girls talk to her "feller" or try to

* *Wichita Daily Eagle* (Kansas), 18 February 1891, p.7/1.

explain things to the police justice, recognizes the fidelity of the accent at once.'

Ada Lewis worked on stage for thirty-five years, with successes such as *Her Own People* (1917), and scored a hit with the song 'The Brooklyn Bridge at Midnight is Lover's Lane', but for many she remained 'the mistress of modern slang'. In 1924 she wrote (or certainly signed) a syndicated piece on 'The Evolution of Slang'. 'Whether it's "Apple Sauce" or "The Oyster's Earrings," You Will Always Find the "Dippy Dialect" Expressive of the Fads and Foibles of Current Life" ran the strapline. And the text added, 'She has been the "dope kid," the "Bowery tough," the "matinee girl," the "dashing widow", "today's mother" [. . .] What Ada Lewis doesn't know about what people say and do and why they do it probably isn't to be known outside a college course in psychology.'

The piece itself gave Ada's opinions on the counter-language and many examples. A table, perhaps reflecting the actress' own longevity, offered three columns of 'The Jargon of the Juveniles': there were lists of seventeen terms apiece from Grandma, Mother and Daughter. Among them Grandma offered *the laugh, dude, four-flusher, quit yerkiddin', the goods* and *beat it.* For Mother there were *merry ha-ha, putting on the dog, the cheese, poor simp, o you kiddo!* and *tightwad.* Daughter, representing the cutting-edge flapper, gave *red-hot mama, flat tire, lounge lizard, petting, cat's meow* and *flapper* itself. Ada's text embellished these offerings: pretending to be too old for flapper lingo, she still gave such superlatives as *the mosquito's eyebrows, bee's knees, monkey's instep* and *caterpillar's kimono* and suggested it all began with the *cat's pyjamas.* She mentioned *finale hoppers* and *cake-eaters* and

* *Times Signal* (Zanesville, Ohio), 11 January 1924, p.33.

added her favourite 'bajenda'. It's origin, even its spelling, eluded her, but, she explained, it meant hopeless. She knew her theory too, noting that 'all slang virtually centers around the same phases or situations of life'. The only difference was chronology.

She died in 1925 – there had been a nervous breakdown and she seems never to have recovered – and Broadway's greats would follow her coffin. The slang of which she wrote has survived but she, sadly, fails to merit even a walk-on in Wikipedia.

9. The Flapper: Girl Power

She's independent, full of grace, A pleasing form, a pretty face; is often saucy, also pert, and doesn't think it wrong to flirt; knows what she wants and gets it too; receives the homage that's her due; her love is warm, her hate is deep, for she can laugh and she can weep; but she is true as true can be; her will's unchained, her soul is free; she charms the young, she jars the old, within her beats a heart of gold; she furnishes the spice of life — and makes some boob a darn good wife!

'Our Definition of the Flapper' in
The Flapper magazine vol. 1 June 1922[*]

THE IDEAL EVIDENCE satisfies one's research and requires no compromises in its analysis. In the case of slang and women that would demand its speakers and coiners be female. No ventriloquy, however sophisticated, is needed. It is arguable, perhaps even unarguable, that the flapper, that all-girl phenomenon with her all-girl vocabulary, fulfils these requirements as none ever had before.

The flapper of the 1920s, whose moment in the sun paralleled

[*] For whatever reason, while the text rhymes, it was laid out as continuous prose.

what was typically termed the 'roaring' Twenties and the 'Jazz Age', may be said to embody the first ever 'youth cult'. She had all the necessary kit: an unashamed exploitation of the generation gap (a concept, like 'youth cult' that would not enter the language for another forty years), an immediately (and to many disturbingly) identifiable uniform that was all her own, a lifestyle and a language that she had created. She both shocked and delighted that vital ingredient of every such cult: an attendant media, who gleefully pursued her, whether to celebrate or condemn. Then there was one final and wholly unprecedented fact: above all else, the flapper was *she*.

The Fast Girl

Nothing, even such a trail-cutting, even revolutionary, social movement emerges without precedent. The mid-nineteenth century had seen the emergence of the 'fast' girl, whose use of slang had been one of her identifying characteristics, but her characterisation seems to have been from the outside in and while commentators clamoured to analyse and (usually) condemn her, she did not self-identify.

The idea of *fast* in the context of lifestyle seems to appear in the very early eighteenth century. (Given its sense of movement it is the antithesis of those slightly earlier senses based on *holding fast*, i.e. stasis.*) The use is not dissimilar to slang's *flash*, but the female varieties, *flash piece* and *flash woman*, cut straight to whoring. Quoting Dryden on 'The Good Parson' – 'Of Sixty Years he seem'd; and well might last / To Sixty more, but that he

---

* The mobile and static versions of *fast* are both based on Gothic *fastan*, to keep guard; the first suggesting the vigorousness that underpins the act of guarding, the second its immobility.

liv'd too fast' – the *OED* (in an entry composed in 1895 and as yet unrevised) defines the phrase *live fast* as 'to expend quickly one's vital energy' and in a second sense, 'to live a dissipated life', quotes one of slang's contemporary favourites: Thomas Brown, a popular satirist (and allegedly the first to place blanks in proper names so as to escape threats of libel, e.g. Mr J—G—). Brown notes that by 'living very fast' a man 'had brought his nobles [i.e. 6s 8d, and thus half a mark or one-third of a pound] to nine-pence' [approximately one-ninth of the original value].That *fast* might be paired with *woman, girl* or, as the media seemed to prefer, *young lady*, was acknowledged, even if the original *OED* had only a single citation, dated 1856. 'As applied to women' it referred to those considered 'studiedly unrefined in habits and manners, disregardful of propriety or decorum'. It was still half a century premature, but it might equally well have served the flapper.

The lexicographers were running slow: the phrase and the concept of 'the fast young lady' was hard-wired into the lexicon of disapproval by the mid-nineteenth century. Hotten, defining it for his slang dictionary of 1859, showed that the term played by the usual male–female double standards: 'A *fast* man – a person who, by late hours, gaiety and continual rounds of pleasure, lives too fast, and wears himself out [. . .] a *fast* young lady is one who affects mannish habits, or makes herself conspicuous by some unfeminine accomplishment, – talks Slang, drives about in London, smokes cigarettes, is knowing in dogs, horses, &c." A year later the *Saturday Review* explains the *fast* woman as one 'who has lost her respect for men, and for whom men have lost their respect also.'[†]

---

* 'A London Antiquary', *A Dictionary of Modern Slang, Cant and Vulgar Words* (1859).
† *Saturday Review* (London),28 July 1860.

Neither definer notes class, but that was there too. Working-class women were not fast. They might be just as hedonistic as their wealthier, better-born sisters, but had the idea existed, they could not be seen, unlike the latter, as class traitors. Working-class girls, after all, weren't meant to have standards. The middle- and upper-class young lady was, and thus her betrayal of such standards – her failure to emulate her 'slow' sisters (*slow* being defined by slang as unfashionable, dull, lifeless and insipid) who did *not* smoke, did *not* drive around London (quite possibly unchaperoned), did *not* offer her expert knowledge of horseflesh or hunting packs and perhaps most important did *not* talk slang – was all the more reprehensible.

The identification of fastness with non-standard speech seems to have been worldwide. In 1871 Tom Taylor (who had talked in another script of 'The "horsey" woman of fashion, who lisps slang as easily as French'*) put on *New Men and Old Acres* and in the play characterises a rebellious young woman as 'dreadfully addicted to slang'.

In 1862, Melbourne *Punch* offered a series of 'Sketches of Society'. Among them was: 'The Fast Girl':†

> The fast girl is a 'gent' in petticoats, a connecting link between the two sexes, and exhibits some of the most unattractive qualities of both. Her voice is loud, her utterance voluble, and she has a copious vocabulary of slang at her command, upon which she makes large and frequent draughts. She has neither the modesty nor the winsomness of womanhood. She affects masculine pastimes, smokes cigarettes on the sly, and goes the pace furiously in dancing,

* T. Taylor, *A Lesson for Life* (1867).
† *Melbourne Punch*, 20 November, p.7/1.

when the centrifugal tendencies of her skirts give her the appearance of a ballet girl on the stage. At such times she is as flushed as a Bacchante, and, in the wild disorder of her spirits, might pass for one. On occasions she can tipple, and has been even known to talk incoherently and to be unsteady in her gait. She excels in 'chaff' and is proud of the accomplishment. In conversation she is loud and confident, 'stiff in opinions,' and is uneasy if she does not succeed in drawing the eyes of the whole company upon her. She knows a little of everything, and vents her observations with an entire disregard of their crudity. She has a predilection for novels of the French school and for erotic poems. She is positive in assertion and abrupt in contradiction. She cultivates a taste for sarcasm, and has no mercy on the reputation of even her dearest friends. She aims at saying smart things, and faintly resembles Lady Mary Wortley Montague, minus her wit, her ability, and her tawny linen.

If nature had made the fast girl a man, the creature would have been a fluent stump-orator or a knowing horse-jockey, or a lively Merry Andrew, or a dissipated pleasure-seeker. As it is, she possesses some of the most offensive characteristics of the gent, but none of the graces of a lady, nor the charms of a woman. She votes the more feminine heroines of Shakspere 'slow,' and speaks contemptuously of the few genuine gentlewomen to be met with in society. The gracious dignity, the sweet repose, the fortifying self-respect, the delicate courtesy, innate gentleness, modest reserve, and moral elevation of the perfect lady, she can neither comprehend nor admire – therefore she depreciates and dispraises them. If she marries from affection the chances are that she will ruin her husband by her extravagance, and persecute him with her jealousy. If she marries for a settlement, she will degenerate into a married flirt, or subside into a confirmed tippler. In any case, she is pretty sure to be both fast and loose.

The press vied to condemn her. 'Fast girls' were 'masculine hoydens—boys in petticoats, who flavor their conversation with slang, call their male friends by their abbreviated Christian names, or by their nicknames, and who are simply despicable as vulgar Amazons, or brazen flirts.'* They were 'the wildest, pertest, rudest, and most viciously impudent animals yet ever met with, their brothers having been their principle companions, they swear like hovelers of a seaport town, and are perfect adepts in the slang of the day.'† They were nothing good.

The American lexicographer Schele de Vere, whose *Americanisms* appeared in 1872, saw the problem as rooted in the foolish fashion of permitting women to say what they wanted, which license included the use of slang:

American cant and slang have some peculiarities unknown to the old World. The women even contribute to it largely, availing themselves of the national gallantry extended to their sex on all occasions, for the purpose of indulging to the utmost in unbridled license of expression, both in public and in private. There is as much truth as wit in the conundrum: Wherein do the women of the day resemble St Paul? In that they speak after the manner of men.‡

* Melbourne *Punch*, 12 December 1861.
† Melbourne *Punch*, 5 February 1863.
‡ M. Schele de Vere, *Americanisms* (1872), p.574.

Slang, as the clips suggest, was their primary sin. Taylor's pert young heroine may have justified her off-piste vocabulary and challenged her mamma's disapproval by claiming that 'men like it', but the leader-writers were far from appeased. For instance the *Sydney Mail* in 1871:

If it is necessary that any one in the family should [talk slang], let your big brother, though I would advise him not to talk 'Pigeon English' when there is an elegant systematized language that he can just as well use, but don't you do it. You have no idea how it sounds to ears unused or averse to it, to hear a young lady, when she is asked to attend some place of amusement, answer — 'Not much;' or if requested to do something she does not wish to— 'Can't see it!' Not long ago I heard a Miss, who is educated and accomplished, say in speaking of a young man, that she intended to 'go for him!' and when her sister asked her assistance at some work, she answered, 'Not for Joe!'

Now, young ladies of unexceptionable character and really good education, fall into this habit, thinking it shows smartness to answer back in slang phrases; and they soon slip flippantly from the tongue with a saucy pertinence that is not lady-like or becoming. Young men who talk in that way do not care to hear it from the lips they love or admire. It sounds much coarser then. And really, slang does not save time in use of language, as an abbreviation. No! is shorter and more decided than 'Not much.' And I am sure, Yes! is quite as easily said as 'I'll bet.' More than one promising wedding has been indefinitely postponed by such means; for however remiss young men may be themselves, they look for a better thing in the girls of their choice, and it does not help them to mend a bad habit to adopt it too.

It was axiomatic that 'the loud, confident, slang-loving, fast-living women of fashion [have] unfurnished heads and vacant hearts'.* The overriding inference: unfettered immorality: another paper savaged a well-known beauty: 'she knows as much slang as a cabman; she drinks us much as a fish . . . she gambles like Fox and Sheridan together; she wears a dress which the French police would exclude from the Jardin Mabille.'†

Yet she had her defenders. In 1860, at the height of the moral panic, the *Inquirer* of Perth, Western Australia, offered a cheeky and supposedly first-person summing-up – in verse:‡

FAST YOUNG LADIES.
Here's a stunning set of us,
Fast young ladies;
Here's a flashy set of us,
Fast young ladies;
Nowise shy or timorous,
Up to all that men discuss.
Never mind how scandalous.
Fast young ladies.
Wide-awakes our head adorn.
Fast young ladies;
Feathers in our hats are worn,
Fast young ladies;
Skirts hitched up on spreading frame.
Petticoats as bright as flame,
Dandy high-heeled boots, proclaim

---

* *Wallaroo Times and Mining Journal* (Port Wallaroo, SA), 16 November 1867.
† Melbourne *Age* 7 March 1868; the Bal or Jardin Mabille (1831–75) was an open-air dance-hall in Paris, known for its population of prostitutes, and birthplace of the polka and the can-can.
‡ *Inquirer* (Perth, Western Australia), 28 November 1860.

Fast young ladies.
Riding habits are the go,
Fast young ladies;
When we prance in Rotten Row,
Fast young ladies;
Where we're never at a loss
On the theme of 'that 'ere 'oss,'
Which, as yet, we do not cross.
Fast young ladies.
There we scan, as bold as brass,
Fast young ladies,
Other parties as they pass,
Fast young ladies;
Parties whom our parents slow.
Tell us we ought not to know;
Shouldn't we, indeed? Why so.
Fast young ladies?
On the Turf we show our face.
Fast young ladies;
Know the odds of every race,
Fast young ladies;
Talk, as sharp as any knife.
Betting slang — we read *Bell's Life*:
That's the ticket for a wife,
Fast young ladies!
We are not to be hooked in.
Fast young ladies;
I require a chap with tin,
Fast young ladies.
Love is humbug; cash the chief
Article in my belief:

All poor matches come to grief,
Fast young ladies.
Not to marry is my plan.
Fast young ladies,
Any but a wealthy man.
Fast young ladies.
Bother that romance and stuff!
She who likes it is a muff;
We are better up to snuff,
Fast young ladies.
Give me but my quiet weed,
Fast young ladies.
Bitter ale and ample feed,
Fast young ladies;
Pay my bills, porte-monnaie store.
Wardrobe stock — I ask no more.
Sentiment we vote a bore,
Fast young ladies.

But on the whole, slang was a no-no for girls. Or what passed for examples of the lexis. On 16 January 1860, writing of 'American Slang for Ladies' the Melbourne *Age* recalled:

I remember once being in company with a belle — one who had had a winter's reign in Washington. Some kind of game was in progress, when in a moment of surprise, she exclaimed 'My gracious!' [. . .] I tell you that woman fell as flatly in my estimation as if she had uttered an oath. A lady, fresh from Paris, once informed me that it would do the residents of a certain village a great deal of good to be 'stirred up with a long pole.' Let us see how you like this kind of talk: — If you wish to be an 'A No. 1' woman; you have got to 'toe the mark,' and be less 'hifalutin.' 'You may bet your head on that.' You may [. . .] 'spin street yarn' at the rate of 'ten knots an hour you may 'talk like a book;' you may dance as if you were on a regular 'break down,' you may 'turn up your nose at common folks,' and play the piano 'mighty fine' but I tell you, 'you can't come to tea.' You may be handsome, but 'you can't come in.'

You might just as well 'cave in,' first as last, and 'absquatu-late,' for 'you can't put it through,' 'any way you can fix it.' If you imagine that you may 'go it while you're young, for when you're old you can't,' 'you won't come it by a long chalk.' 'Own up' now, and 'do the straight thing,' and I'll 'set you down' as 'one of the women we read of.' If you cannot 'come up to the scratch,' why I must 'let you slide.' But if you have a 'sneaking notion' for being a 'regular brick,' there is no other way — 'not as you knows on.' If a young man should 'kind o' shine up to you,' and you should 'cotton to him,' and he should hear you say 'by the jumping Moses,' or ' by the living jing,' or 'my goodness,' or 'go it Betsy, I'll hold your bonnet' — 'you bet!'

This is an odd list and there were few that really reflected the potential of the mid-century slang vocabulary. At least half the 'American Slang' is image rather than actual slang. Sometimes the commentator – again as written in Melbourne *Punch* which journal seems to have been specially fascinated by the idea of slangy girls – managed something better. In another series, 'Women of the Time' the paper offered 'The Melbourne Barmaid' and nicknamed her 'Miss Slang'.

On your approach, [she] offers you her hand in the approved (so far as I am concerned, disapproved) manner of the class [. . .] the fair paw is not always clean; it is, alas! too often clammy, through frequent recourse to damp glass-cloths; sometimes it is sticky, owing to the viscid quality of some of the beverages, and this is a 'cordial' description of hand-shaking that I cordially hate. [. . .] After the invocation of manipulation, she inquires whether you prefer a 'nip' to a 'long drink;' shall it be 'malt' or 'soda and a dash?' Do I go in for Prunier or stick to battle-axe? She knows all the sporting youths of the town— those flashy boys who affect brass horse-shoe scarf-pins, the coat of the species, and the tight-legged trouser, the last worn to indicate that they are, or would be, legs. She talks to these precious youths in their own language, discourses of horses likely to be 'scratched,' and can tell the chances of each for the 'cup.' She alludes to meals as a 'feed,' and I think I once heard her speak of a dinner as a 'blow-out,' and a supper as a 'tightener.'

In truth the fast young lady's slang is pretty vapid. Certainly the mildest end of the lexical spectrum. The *Illustrated Police News* of 1 June 1889 noted 'awful', 'lawfully', 'nice', 'pretty', 'lovely', and 'jolly' ('Lillian' prefers 'jol' and also uses 'floored', 'old fogy', 'cram' while her comments that, 'Altogether, they are such a game! Old Bunter, with his Methodistical airs and sham piety, and Mother Bunter with her brags of her old lace and new diamonds' are ranked as 'strong expressions'). The *News* categorises them as 'young lady slang words' and rejects the lot since, however well they work in standard English, once slanged they 'suffer from the defect of being absolutely meaningless'. *The Times* added its male condescension to 'the feminine adverb "awfully"', the *Pall Mall Gazette* damned female slangsters with the faintest of praise and the *Sydney Morning Herald*, with galumphing, condescending humour, paraphrased the lot:

> Awfully is a schoolgirl's idiom, not a school boy's; and the latter only comes, to it by imitation and at second-hand. It is a hen word, the hen of our fathers' more robust expletive 'deuced' or 'devilish,' just as 'fib' is the hen of 'lie,' and 'poorly' is the hen of 'seedy.' A 'hen word' is good . . . but a schoolgirl idiom must surely be a pullet word.
>
> The real masculine of 'awfully' is a six-lettered participle, which the *Pall Mall* no more dare print unasterisked than it dare call a spade a spade in this spadonic age.* Expletives of this sort, whether strong or weak, of course prove poverty of imagination and unreadiness of speech [. . .] And for the ladies, who must devote so much time to flirtation, and to decoration of themselves, and (at Easter) the parish church, we think much allowance should he made. Let them have their 'little language,' their slang in petticoats. Shall we make it classical by publishing a lexicon of it?

In 1879 the *Burlington Free Press* of Vermont kept up the attack. 'The poorest, feeblest and most *vicious* slang [. . .] is the fashionable slang which pollutes the lips of young girls. 'Awfully jolly,' 'Immense,' 'Ain't he a tumbler?' 'He has a great deal of the dog on to-day,' 'Good form,' 'Awfully first-rate' [. . .] 'Didn't we have a stationary fling though?' meaning [. . .] a stupid evening 'Quite too awfully handsome,' 'Pitch on your hat, and let's go for a picturesque'.† It was all getting very rote.

---

* Presumably *bloody*.
† *Burlington Free Press* (Vermont), 1 August 1879, p.4/2.

The moral panic, like all such eruptions, burnt high and hard but soon guttered out. If for no other reason than from contemporary reports, its target seems to have been a class-ridden creation. Her slangy, cigarette smoking, huntin', shootin' and ridin' persona could never embrace the great unwashed. Not only that, there was an even more immediate failing that must, it was promised with undisguised relief, bring about her decline: male disapproval.

In March 1868 London's *Saturday Review* forecast her decline, and hoped for the resurgence of her sister 'the simple and genuine girl of the past, with her tender little ways and pretty bashful modesty'. The bottom line, suggested the *Review*, was that men, whatever these new-fangled girls might believe, were unimpressed. 'She thinks she is piquante and exciting . . . and will not see that though men laugh with her they do not respect her, though they flirt with her they do not marry her; she will not believe that she is not the kind of thing they want, and that she is acting against nature and her own interests when she disregards their advice and offends their taste.' It might not happen at once, acknowledged the writer, but there was time a-plenty and 'all we can do is to wait patiently until the national madness has passed, and our women have come back again to the old English ideal, once the most beautiful, the most modest, the most essentially womanly in the world.'

She did, at least in this incarnation, fade away, but she would be back, and far more threatening to an established order. Let us leave her with this piece in the *Leeds Times* of June 1895:

THE ALPHABET OF SLANG. A prize offered by the 'Gentlewoman' for the best 'Society slang alphabet' has been

won by Miss Moutray-Kead, a Herefordshire lady, with the
following:
It's 'awfully' difficult everyone knows.
A 'bally' slang alphabet thus to compose;
I feel more like 'chucking' the whole blessed show,
Being 'dotty' and 'done' at the very first go.
It's 'evens' my getting as 'edgy' as you
Will become if you do not 'funk' reading it through.
'Get out! Hook it! Hang it all!'
This is 'intense;' If I 'jack' it up now that would be 'jolly'
     dense,
Why, even a 'kid' would scarce 'kick the bucket!'
So why, for a 'lark,' should this 'lunatic! chuck it!'
I'd wager a 'monkey,' if I had the 'needful'
But the 'oof-bird' is moulting, so needs must be heedful
That some other 'pals' are now having a shy
For a Q. Will they find one? 'Query,' say I
What 'rot'! This is 'riling'; but most so to me.
Don't get 'shirty,' or lose your wool over a 'spree.'
Excuse this bad language, and just take my 'tip,'
Don't try for slang prizes betwixt cup and lip, Etcetera
To go to their 'uncle' would anyone choose
(I'm hard up, as you doubtless already 'vermoose').
The 'wherewithal, X,' minus quantity, 's wanting,
Preventing the buying from P. R. or Ponting,
Where 'yellow boys' only they'll take, they're such 'zanies.' *

* *Leeds Times*, 16 June 1895.

The Flapper

Fast young ladies notwithstanding, it is hard to claim any other embryonic forms of flapperdom. It was a movement spearheaded by young women, almost wholly represented by their increasing numbers and which in its nascent form of girl power subordinated males to disposable, interchangeable boyfriends or fathers, their authority rendered zero, serving only as escorts or bankers. Created in Britain, remade and vastly popularised in the United States, it spread, still driven by that same highly identifiable cohort, across large sections of the world. There had been noticeable groups that were mainly composed of young people, before. The various gangs of New York City, typically the Bowery B'hoys, the larrikins of working-class Sydney and other Australian cities, the market-trading costermongers of London, but in every case, girls and young women were subordinate. Adjuncts to their boyfriends and lovers, they might ape but they did not yet initiate. Certainly not in the realm of the slang that came with such groups.

But if flappers were seen as emerging almost from nowhere, or certainly in the highly publicised and increasingly stereotyped form they took in the 1920s, the word naturally has a linguistic background which one can assess. It is, however, somewhat tangled. The prevailing belief is that *flapper* comes from an eighteenth-century use of the word to mean an unfledged bird, typically a partridge or wild duck: its wings flap enthusiastically but give no traction. A secondary etymology, less common, is older still and given that the word at least emerged as slang, predictable: the seventeenth-century dialect term *flap*, meaning 'a woman or girl of light or loose character'. As the author of a glossary of *Northumberland Words* put it in 1892: 'A young giddy

357

girl [. . .] or a woman who does not settle down to her domestic duties.' There was also the Berkshire dialect *vlapper*, 'applied in joke to a girl of the bread-and-butter age'.

The term was already common enough in 1892 for the London *Evening News* of 20 August to ponder its origins. It noted the 'fledgling' theory and agreed with it, and added something of its own: 'The correspondent of *Notes and Queries* has been troubling his mind about the use of the slang word "flapper" as applied to young girls. Another correspondent points out that a "flapper" is a young wild duck which is unable to fly, hence a little duck of any description, human or otherwise. The answer seems at first sight frivolous enough, but it is probably the correct solution of this interesting problem all the same.' That opinion stands, although the word may be underpinned by standard English *flap*, to act in an emotional manner, supposedly typical of such young women. It was never noted at the time, but flapper also fitted perfectly into a long-established slang trope: the equation of women with birds. Aside from *bird* itself, such terms have included *hen, biddy, chick, chickabiddy, quail* and *pheasant*. None are actively abusive; all are somewhat condescending.

Thus the supposed roots. The usage is somewhat more contrary. The earliest slang use of the term *flapper* as applied to a girl is first recorded in Barrère & Leland's slang dictionary of 1889, where one finds '*Flippers, flappers*, very young girls trained to vice, generally for the amusement of elderly men.' In a pornographic novel of 1909, G.F. Bacchus' *Maudie*, we meet 'Her adopted niece, a little, and very typical French flapper. [. . .] Madame was educating her for the stage, equally for a life of smart prostitution [. . .] she wanted a big price for that precious virginity, but there was nothing the little darling didn't know.'

Examples are often ambiguous, and the earliest are all British: In 1909 the *Tatler* claimed that 'The first appearance of a "flapper" at a ladies' golf championship was in 1895, . . . in these two long-haired, long-legged colleens were the two most famous lady golfers the world has yet produced.' Surely no naughtiness, let alone paedophilia there. Merely the patronising *colleen* for Irish women. The *Sporting Times* (11 July 1908), its roué's eye always on 'the ladies', referred leeringly to 'the dear little flappers in the chorus' and in 1914 the usually squeaky-clean naval propagandist 'Bartimeus', in *Naval Occasions*, described how 'Little pigtailed girls with tight skirts enclosing immature figures, of a class known technically as the "Flapper," drifted by with lingering, precocious stares.' Contemporary Australia had no underage trollops, but prior to 1920 generally used flapper in the Berkshire sense, to describe a young girl, probably a teenager, who is not yet considered old enough to be part of adult society. The image was often of a girl who had not 'put up her hair', and possibly still wore pigtails. Yet this too was debatable: thus the ogling men as recorded in a Queensland newspaper of August 1901, 'Will you introduce me to those girls? That second one on the near side was simply perfection. The flapper didn't look half so bad, either.' 'May I ask which of them you call the "flapper"?' I said severely [. . .] 'Why, the little one, the half-fledged youngster.'

Australia also offered a male flapper, the inference being effeminacy, rather than the flapper's own desirable and definitely heterosexual *sheik* of later years. (Even if the *echt*-sheik, Rudolph Valentino who starred in the eponymous movie, disturbed 'real men' who found his perfect looks lacking macho.) Sydney's satirical *Truth* noted in 1913 that 'The male flapper is very prominent in Sydney just now.' Calling him a 'modern marvel' the writer was unimpressed: 'Some folks say that the haberdasher and tailor built him, and that the barber scented and perfumed him. As for perfume, the average male flapper [. . .] stinks as odorous as a patchouli-bespringled dame from questionable quarters.' His wrists go unremarked: they were presumably limp.

Quite when the meaning shifted from vice to what was seen as frivolity, however shocking and socially disruptive at the time, is hard to judge. By the late 1910s the definition, while still that of a young girl, had softened: the flapper was now a flighty, but not actively 'immoral' girl or young woman, usually middle-class, in her late teens or very early twenties, who sported short, bobbed hair, lipstick, skimpy dresses and stockings rolled deliberately below the knee (indicating her lack of the corset to which they would otherwise have been attached) and generally led a lifestyle as far as possible removed from that desired by her parents. The type would become associated with America, but its origins, it seems, were British and Chicago's *Day Book* newspaper, perhaps confusing its definitions, confessed in January 1917 that 'The flapper originated in English society a dozen years ago. She is just becoming known in the country.'

By 1922 when the flapper's fictional antithesis, Sinclair Lewis' mid-West bourgeois George F. Babbitt 'weightily pondered flappers smoking in Zenith restaurants',* the change was set in stone. She entered the movies, whether played by Colleen Moore or Clara Bow, the cartoonist John Held Jr. drew her for 'slick' magazines such as *Vanity Fair*,† and her fictional embodiments were championed above all by F. Scott Fitzgerald, whose first

---

* S. Lewis, *Babbitt* (1922; 1974), p.258.
† The illustrator Edward Gorey also went back to the 'classic' flapper when drawing a vamp in a number of his books, typically the sexually adventurous but ultimately unfortunate 'Alice' of *The Curious Sofa* (1961).

collection of short stories in 1920 was entitled *Flappers and Philosophers* and whose wife Zelda was stereotyped as the style incarnate. Fitzgerald emphasised not just her independence, but also what seemed an outrageous sexuality. 'None of the Victorian mothers,' he put it in his best-selling novel *This Side of Paradise* (1920) ' — and most of the mothers *were* Victorian — had any idea how casually *their daughters were* accustomed to be *kissed.'* Depending on one's age, the subsequent line 'any popular girl he met before eight he might possibly kiss before midnight' was either appalling or aspirational. Popularised in America she re-crossed the Atlantic. P.G. Wodehouse hymned the fictional exploits of a number of her British sisters. Never one for sex, Wodehouse preferred what he termed the flappers' *espièglerie* (playfulness): to steal from Richard Usborne's *Wodehouse at Work* (1961), the only thing a Wodehouse girl would be doing in a Wodehouse chap's bedroom would be making him an apple-pie bed.

She could be claimed for feminism and identified as a sub-group of another phenomenon of the post-World War I era, the 'New Woman', though her ambitions were less political than social. Still, earning her own money, and determining and pursuing her own desires (the more physical of which were helped by far more easily available contraception), the flapper offered at least one side of feminism. It may be hard to equate such gravity with the great army of wannabes from the sticks but she represented 'a genuinely subversive force. Willing to run the risks of their independence as well as enjoy its pleasures, there were good reasons for them to be perceived as women of a dangerous generation.'*

* J. Mackrell, *Flappers: Six Women of a Dangerous Generation* (2013), p.11.

What she was not, however, was a modern teenager. She was sometimes of the right age, though generally a little older, and she moved in a world distinct from that of conventional adults, and as we shall see, she was a great coiner of slang, but there one must halt. The word *teenage* can be found in 1921 ('in one's teens' has been recorded in 1684), but the modern concept of the teenager as representing a segregated social group is a creation of the 1940s, if not the decade that followed; it required rock and roll for the teenager proper. The flapper cannot thus be a teenager any more than could her late nineteenth-and early twentieth-century contemporaries, whether at school or college. Lists of high-school and college slang had emerged by 1910 but while flappers naturally picked up the odd term from their college-attending boyfriends, typically those meaning drunk, they still chose their own coinages. In both cases examples of the slangs would, as youth talk does, eventually filter into each other's world, and beyond that to the adults, but a distinct line can be seen between the nature of such lists and any representative lexis of flapper-talk.

What she was, undoubtedly, was part of what at least initially, was a closed world. It helped if you were rich, attractive and had access to the new and fashionable watering holes. A member of what the press, not to mention Evelyn Waugh in *Vile Bodies*, termed 'the Bright Young People'. As such she elicited the inevitable mixture of fear and fascination, and once that had worn off and the guest list had expanded to take in the entire country, commercial exploitation. The media picked her up quickly: the coverage was almost benign. The often vituperative social critic H. L. Mencken, the scourge of so much that middle America saw as admirable, gave them a very gentle ride. Writing of the emerging style in his magazine the *Smart Set* in 1915, he explained:

Observe, then . . . this American Flapper. Her skirts have reached her very trim and pretty ankles, her hair, newly coiled upon her skull, has just exposed the ravishing whiteness of her neck. [. . .] Youth is hers, and hope, and romance and —

Well, well, let us be exact: let us not say innocence. This Flapper [. . .] is far, far, far from a simpleton. An ingénue to the Gaul she is actually as devoid of ingenuousness as a newspaper reporter, a bartender, or a midwife. The age she lives in is one of knowledge. She herself is educated. She is privy to dark secrets. The world bears her no aspect of mystery. She has been taught how to take care of herself. [. . .] She is opposed to the double standard of morality and favors a law prohibiting it . . .

This Flapper has forgotten how to simper; she seldom blushes; it is impossible to shock her. [. . .] She is youth, she is hope, she is romance — she is wisdom!

These were early days: her skirts had some way to rise, and bobbed hair would leave no need for coils, but Mencken's positive take was not that different to *The Flapper's* description of the type quoted above. Not everyone agreed. In 1920, the London *Times*, debating what would come to be known, dismissively as 'the flapper vote', i.e. allowing the vote to women under thirty, railed against the 'frivolous, scantily-clad, jazzing flapper [. . .] to whom a dance, a new hat or a man with a car is of more importance than the fate of nations'. As Judith Mackrell notes[*] 'newspapers [. . .] bristled with warnings of the destabilizing effect these flappers might have on the country, as an unprecedented

[*] Mackrell op.cit. p.5.

generation of unmarried and independent women appeared to be hell-bent on having their own way.' That, given the near two million imbalance between the decimated male survivors of the War and their female compatriots meant that such women were labelled as 'surplus' in the tabloid press, did not allay any fears. On the other hand, even if sidestepped by the moralists, all these women were good for business, be it providing them with fashion or entertainment.

In 1922, back in America, when the world had reached what modernity might label 'peak flapper', the *Los Angeles Times* chose to quote one 'Bath-house John Coughlin', better known as a Chicago alderman of more than usual corruption than a reliable social commentator. 'A flapper is a youthful female, beauteous externally, blasé internally, superficially intelligent, imitative to a high degree. Her natural habitat is the ballroom, the boulevard and the fast motor car. She browses about the trough of learning, picking as her tidbits smart phrases which she glibly repeats without sensing their meanings. She comes from all walks of life and has for her main requirement nerve, a face and figure, either actually beautiful or susceptible to artistic effort.' The attack on flapper superficiality was no doubt meant to sting, but perhaps the old ward heeler recognised some of his own. His remarks as to her enjoyment of 'smart phrases' and her coming 'from all walks of life', were actually right on the ball.

Some critics might have been expected to know better. On the other hand, perhaps not. Mae West, who was hardly over the hill herself, indeed in the midst of penning some of the Jazz Age's most sexually controversial plays, turned out in this interview of 1929 not to be a fan. But then again, her style, if not the moment of her celebrity, was based thirty years in the past.

The wicked women of old days were more fascinating because there was real get-up and glamour to her. Nowadays the flappers take the edge off it for everyone else. Even if flappers aren't 'mean' they look it. They don't conceal a thing, either of their feelings or otherwise . . . Nowadays the girls all lookalike – same build, slim and sexy, short skirts, same kind of stockings, same kind of paint, same kind of hair-dress, and same kind of thoughts, if only they'd admit it. So it's just like seein' the chorus of a show go down the street. That's why I say that the dames of the old Bowery days had it all over the women of today for originality, and looks too, for that matter. Am I right?[*]

The larrikin's *donah*, the coster's *best girl* and the Bowery B'hoy's *g'hals* had undoubtedly embraced slang, conversation would have been hard without it, but it was not their own: as in their overall style, philosophy and preoccupations, it was that of their male companions; the flapper's slang, as much as her rolled stockings, her shingled hair, her cigarettes and her petting parties, underlined how much her lifestyle reflected what would in time be called the generation gap but beyond that, her gender. That slang is not all her own work – though it appears that, quite at odds with the usual generation of slang, much was indeed *her* own work rather than that of her beau – and the line between flapper slang and contemporary college usage is hard to define, and there are naturally overlaps with general usage, nonetheless a good proportion is something quite different to that of the wider world. Such talk, of which a glossary was compiled in 1922 and reprinted as 'The Flapper Dictionary' both as a short

---

[*] *Chicago Evening American*, February 1929, quoted in Louvish, *Mae West: It Ain't No Sin* (2005) p.163.

book and in a number of local newspapers, had its own themes. The flappers themselves, their boyfriends, the parties and dances they attended, the dancing and sexual activity they enjoyed (which latter appeared to stop short of intercourse, or certainly as regards descriptive slang coinages), drink, automobiles and so on. The over-thirties were barely mentioned, and if so, only with the brash dismissals of the young. Here at least Coughlin's jibes cannot be denied: it is a vocabulary that voices ephemerality and hedonism and while some seems contrived, it flourished alongside its much publicised speakers.

'The Flapper Dictionary', the contents of which were included with the first issue, in June 1922, of the *Flapper* magazine, its masthead proclaiming 'Not for Old Fogies', is an odd confection.* So too is the complementary list of 'Flapper Filogy' (a conscious mis-spelling that prefigures the far more extensive exploration of such orthographical games in the hip-hop era) that was compiled in 1927 by the *Philadelphia Evening Bulletin* and another list, under the rubric of 'Judge Junior's Dictionary' and like today's *Urban Dictionary*, compiled at least partially by readers, that came out in 1926 and 1927 in New York's *Judge* magazine. The intention, as was ever the case with specialist glossaries, was to help readers understand what they were meeting in the magazine's pages, not to mention the world at large, thus permitting 'the uninitiated' to enter the magic circle.

In retrospect and at the time, the flapper may have been claimed for feminism, but the magazine's content gives little evidence. The 'Monthly Chat' column preached that 'The Flapper stands for knickers' (knickerbockers as used for sporty activities rather than any 'naughty' reference to underwear) and

---

* Of the terms that follow those included in the *Dictionary* are preceded by an *

a story, 'Class for the Thin: Slender, Lean and Slim' was addressed to the 'chiclets'. (This may have been a reference to the popular brand of gum, but equally so, a diminutive of the centuries-old *chick*, itself shrinking *chicken* and now, if not perhaps then, seen as wholly demeaning.) The magazine's agony aunt signed her advice 'Kewpie', presumably in conscious reference to the *kewpie doll* of carnival stalls, traditionally won for young women by their boyfriends. Nor are references to the flapper's female 'sisters' within the lists of her vocabulary especially charitable. There is no sense of sorority in *fire alarm*, a divorcee or *fire bell*, a married woman, only the sense that such supposedly predatory women represented a threat. As for her own ambitions, it was every girl for herself. The *strike breaker*, taking advantage of a *flat shoe*, a lovers' tiff, 'goes with her friend's steady while there is a coolness'. (She needed to get in fast, if the couple *stepped on it*, made up, she was out of luck.) That this rendered her a *sheba*, *snake* or *flamper*, 'a flapper vamp' (*vamp* itself dates to 1915), mattered not bit; the nickname *veal*, i.e. a little cow, and one who 'sets out to vamp with malice aforethought', might have hurt.

Like the hippies of the Sixties, the flapper had no time for the over-thirties. Such oldies were *green apples* (their disapproving, jealous 'sourness'?) or *old fops*. Older women were particularly scorned: the *bent hairpin*, *covered wagon* (who was fat too), or *face stretcher* was 'an old maid who tries to look younger', while one who was seen as having given up that fight was simply a *rock of ages*, i.e. 'any woman over thirty years of age'. Her male equivalent was *Father Time*, first used in 1559 and, as the *OED* explains 'conventionally represented as an aged man carrying a scythe and frequently an hourglass; sometimes also as bald except for a single lock of hair'. Her father was a *dapper* (presumably *dad* + *flapper*), and mother a *wrinkle* (surely the ancestor of today's *wrinklies*, the old in general). Cruellest of all was *Trotzky*, an 'old lady with a moustache and chin whiskers'; the goateed Bolshevik leader himself would have been termed a **Charlie* or **whiskbroom*.

Not that such old folk could be completely ignored. There were still chaperones: the **alarm clock*, bidding flapperdom's Cinderellas to cease their fun long before they might have wished, and the **fire alarm*, dousing whatever current passions she was indulging. Actually talking to the old biddies seemed a man's job. The **crumb-gobbler* or **bun duster* 'an effete young man who attends smart tea parties and charms old ladies' was of course nothing new, an earlier age would have termed him, less than flatteringly and equally suspicious of his sexuality, a *jemmy jessamy*; the **cake eater*, 'a Piker who frequents teas and other entertainments, without ever trying to repay his social obligations', was possibly simply hungry.

Rich and Poor

Hunger was perhaps permissible, mean-ness was not. The Dictionary did not flatter the *flat wheeler*, 'a young man whose idea of entertaining a girl is to take her out for an *ankle excursion*' i.e. a walk (*ankle* as walk was another recent coinage) rather than ride, ideally in his sumptuous **cake-basket*, his limousine (and both bedecked in chrome). In fairness, he might simply be poor. He was also known as **Johnnie Walker* (a tip of the hat to another liquor brand now forbidden by Prohibition). A **slip* was a 'one-way guy': he took but failed to give back, as did the similarly despised **one-way kid*, while the **Smith Brothers* (punning on a slogan for America's then best-known brand of cough drops) were those who 'never cough up'. The *finagler* or *phenogler* played for time until a fellow-diner or drinker picks up a bill. The word borrows the verb *finagle*, originally dialect and meaning to shirk or to fail to keep a promise. In 1839 a glossary of Herefordshire words explained, 'If two men are heaving a heavy weight, and one of them pretends to be putting out his strength, though in reality leaving all the strain on the other, he is said to *feneague*.' Like the *chiseler* (more usually a cheat), the **finale hopper* was another cheapskate: as the cartoonist and word coiner TAD (T.A. Dorgan) put it, 'a finale hopper is a jobbie [a diminutive of *job*: a type rather than modern Scotland's term for a turd] who never takes a twist to a dance but who horns in on the last dance as the band is playing Home Sweet Home.' It could also be applied to a man who was somehow never there when it came to paying his share of a bill.

Money itself was always important. Among the flappers' terms were *buffos* and *boffos*, *kale*, *dough*, *berries* and *jack*. There were plenty of choices, from maybe seventy others coined in the period and of course the hundreds that predated it. If you were *broke*, then you were **on the stub* which presumably referred to the *fag-end* of one's funds, though maybe one's comfortingly bounceable cheque-book. Your only hope was a **touchdown*, a loan, which expanded on the eighteenth century's *touch*. More specific, and all the flappers' own was her take on **hush money*, coined for bribes in 1709, but in her purse, an allowance from daddy. Whether it was meant to quiet her demands or offer him a sense of cross-generational philanthropy, who knows. **Mad money*, also tweaked a known commodity. Rather than money for self-indulgent splurging, the more modern meaning, it was a stash carried by any sensible flapper out for the evening. She might need it for cab or bus if she was abandoned far from home by a boyfriend who tossed her from his car when she didn't agree to sex; the 'madness' was his anger, though some might say her foolishness for accepting the 'ride home'.

Some people had it, and flaunted it too. A *lamp-post* was a particularly ostentatious piece of jewellery, the woman who wore it, usually some plutocrat's wife or girlfriend, was a *showcase* (used for objects rather than people, since 1834) or *billboard*. *Darbs* (from *darby*, meaning money since 1688) described 'a person with money who can be relied on to pay the check', otherwise known as a *sugar daddy* or *butter-and-egg* man (coined by the nightclub hostess Texas Guinan it meant a rich dairy farmer visiting the big city from the sticks: looking for fun and usually finding exploitation; Guinan's invariable greeting, unsurprisingly, was 'Hello, sucker!'). A fortune-hunter looking for a flesh-and-blood version of the California Gold Rush, was a *forty-niner*. *Ritzy*, from the luxury hotel, was another term for wealthy, though it could mean *stuck up* and *snobbish*, and as a noun, a flapper who aped a vamp: 'black dress, jet earrings, black socks'.

Party Time

If the flapper had known modernity's *party animal* she would surely have embraced the term. Evelyn Waugh, looking back at London society from 1930 in his novel *Vile Bodies*, recalled a hyper-frenzied world of

> Masked parties, Savage parties, Victorian parties, Greek parties, Wild West parties, Russian parties, Circus parties, parties where one had to dress as somebody else, almost naked parties in St John's Wood, parties in flats and studios

and houses and ships and hotels and night clubs, in wind-
mills and swimming baths, tea parties at school where one
ate muffins and meringues and tinned crab, parties at Oxford
where one drank brown sherry and smoked Turkish cigarettes, dull dances in London and comic dances in Scotland
and disgusting dances in Paris.

Memoirist he may have been, but Waugh's fictive world was not
especially productive of slang. *Vile Bodies*, set amidst the loucher
end of the British upper classes, offers *bogus*, *tight*, *whoopee* (as a
noun and meaning a party), the abbreviation *N.B.G.* (no bloody
good) and the all-purpose suffix -*making* ('The door opened and
in came a sort of dancing Hottentot woman half-naked. It just
said, "Oh, how shy-making," and then disappeared') but little
else. This is doubtless accurate; in social terms, slang tends to rise
up, rather than trickle down.

The names and geography were naturally different across the
Atlantic, but the atmosphere, as reported in gossip columns,
high-circulation magazines and popular novels, was much the
same. The war had left a good deal of catching up.

Of all the era's flapper coinages, parties and dances topped the
list. The aim was to be invited but that never worried the determined. The era gave us the word *crash* (an abbreviation of *crash
the gate*), to come in uninvited, the *crasher* and the *crashing party*.
The young man who turned up from nowhere was a **walk-in*.
You danced to *whangdoodle*, jazz music, which was either echoic
of the sound, or back-referring to a mythical beast, lurking on
the wild frontier around the mid-nineteenth century. Whether,
given the jazz context, the 'beast' in question was black was
unspecified.

Dance-bound you *dudded up* (from the sixteenth century's

duds, clothes) in your **urban set* (a new dress) and *dolled up* in
**glorious regalia*. The whole process was known as **gandering*,
which seems to have come from French *gandin*, a dandy. It
might include a visit to the **hen coop*, the beauty parlour, though
that had already served Brits as a brothel (1821) and US women
students as a campus dormitory (1896). You abandoned your
**false ribs* (a corset), flattened your breasts with some kind of
binding and unless your flawless complexion rendered you
**waterproof*, in which case the process was un-necessary, readied
yourself for the evening's battles with a coat of **munitions*, basi-
cally powder and rouge, making sure to avoid an **overdose of
shellac*, too much of a good thing, or at least of powder: no one
wanted to be branded a **flour lover*. As for the boyfriend, the
ideal type seems to have been the **Brooksey Boy*, one who is
dressed at New York's then epitome of preppie style, Brooks
Brothers.

The dance was a *blow* (first used at Harvard in 1827), a *wrestle*
or a *struggle*, which upped the ante on the earlier *bun struggle*,
the somewhat more genteel tea party otherwise known as a *bun-
rush, bun and sandwich scuffle, muffin-struggle* or *tea-scramble*. If
it was out of town it was a *dragout* and in either case, the girl of
a couple was a *drag* (as in taken along and borrowed from the
campus). Dancing itself was *button shining* (very close, and such
cheek-to-cheek gyrations were known as **giving the knee*), **dragging a sock* or *shaking the rug*. A good dancer was a **rug shaker*, a
boy or 'a girl addicted to shimmying', a **hot foot* or *hot sock*, an
**Oliver Twist*, a *stepper*, **hopper* (boy) or **sip* (girl). A large male
was a **scandaler*, or as the glossaries put it, 'a dance floor full-
back. The interior of a dreadnaught hat, Piccadilly shoes with
open plumbing, size 13.' A **sharpshooter* didn't just dance well
but splashed his money around; a dance-mad boy was

a *floorflusher* or *sap. If he was eyeing up the refreshments over your shoulder he was a *hoof and mouth*. Their flapper equivalent was a *sloppy* or a *beazle* or *beasel*, which suggested a certain sexual precocity known as *vampishness*, and which made him a *beasel hound*. Flapper-world also coined *tomato* for an attractive girl, but the Dictionary modified her as a 'good looking girl who can dance like a blue streak, but is otherwise a perfect dumbbell'. Bad dancers included the *feet*, the *heeler*, the *cluck* (dull and stupid 'the brains of a chicken' since 1906). A boy who trod on your feet or *dogs* was a *corn shredder* or *horse prancer*; your *dog kennels*, shoes, would never be the same.

It was not mandatory. Some girls were bashful and dancing with them was known as getting the *absent treatment*. And just as the chaperon persisted, so too did the *wallflower* (coined 1819), known unsympathetically as a *cancelled stamp* or a *dud* (coined a century earlier in Scotland for a 'thowless', i.e. spiritless man). Worse still was the *dumbbell* (1858), not just a wallflower but stupid with it. Nor did everyone even want to go out. The *rug hopper, parlor hound* or *parlor leech* stuck to staying home, playing the gramophone for music. His similarly domestic partners were *ground grippers*, *gussies* (hitherto meaning a gay man), *Priscillas* or *wooden women*, none of whom wanted to go out partying. Nor did everyone want the middle-class social whirl; there were other allurements, notably the bohemian world of Greenwich Village where 'artistic' studio parties – dago red and spontaneous poetry – welcomed *slummers*, even if the word had emerged in 1887, describing a less hedonistic form of class voyeurism.

Dating/Relationships

Clothes and hairdo aside, if anything differentiated the flapper from her predecessors it was sex. The calculatedly buxom Gibson Girl of the 1900s, all whalebone, big hats and décolletage, may have fuelled male fantasy, but if she put flesh on dreams she wasn't talking (though Mae West, for whom she remained a role model, was vastly loquacious). The flapper was consciously outrageous. Or so she told the world. Contraception was more easily available, but while she was unashamedly happy to indulge in modernity's 'slap and tickle', it's hard to tell whether what the Dictionary defined as 'love-making' was what we term making love. She was seen as sexy, but there is a far stronger sense of playfulness and experimentation. So far, but no further; kitten but not yet cat. However much she wished to upset her 'Victorian' mother, that mother had still brought her up and instilled an older set of values. In Elinor Glyn's *Flirt and Flapper* dialogues of 1930 the Flapper shocks her ancestor with tales of hands-on exploration, but beyond that she can only resort to an evasive 'er . . .'. Neither great-grandmother nor readers ever discover quite what 'er . . .' may imply though the former is keen to find out. Perhaps the clue lies in the era's primary term for such enjoyments: *petting*, carried out at what Scott Fitzgerald in 1920 termed 'that great current American phenomenon, the "*petting party*"', a phenomenon that today seems somewhat structured. For instance etiquette permitted postponement. One could ask *cash or check?* which meant 'do we kiss now or later?', and if the answer was *check*, the intention was to mark some kind of sexual dance-card and get back together at a later stage. But petting, even if it reached the stage of what the Beatles so memorably termed 'finger pie', does not equate with intercourse.

You set up your date – *book-keeping* – and the first job was to *Houdini* (named for the famous escapologist) out of the parental house. Then unless either partner was a *holaholy*, a prude, and declared *the bank's closed*, which meant nothing doing, the games were on. She was a *biscuit*, a 'pettable Barlow or Beasel, a game Flapper'. He was a *snuggle-pup* or *-puppy*. If he was a smooth talker (if such time-consuming seductions were even required) he was a *big timer*, defined as 'a charmer able to convince his sweetie that a jollier thing would be to get a snack in an armchair lunch-room' or to put it another way, 'a romantic'.

They were both *smudgers* (from the older *smoocher*), *neckers*, *cuddlers* (a *cuddle-cootie* liked to do it in cars), and of course *petters*. What they did was *lollygag*, which gave *lollygagger*, 'a Bell-Polisher addicted to hallway spooning'. (A *bell polisher* was the sort of young man who turned up in the early hours, leaning on the apartment bell.) Alternatively the words were *barneymug-ging* or just *mugging*. The first seems to mix *barney* (1859), a jolly social party, and *mug*, to kiss (1821). Kisses were rated; no-one wanted a *cherry smash*, a half-hearted effort. Nothing was certain. He might be *goofy*, *stuck on* her, but that still didn't save him from the *icy mitt* (1898), and being *given the air*. She might, after all, have fallen prey to a *weasel* (1624), a 'girl stealer'. Even worse he might be *streeted*, tossed out of the party. In turn he might *toss and hike*: tell her goodbye and set off to look for some-thing better. Either way, someone was going to be *grummy*, perhaps from *grumbling* and meaning depressed. On the seem-ingly rare occasion that flapper opted for a long-term relation-ship, she was known as a *monog*; the term worked for the boy too. If they were engaged the boy was a *police dog*, presumably another put-down: he followed you around and offered (unnec-essary) protection.

Herself

Perhaps it was through her role as coiner of the lexis, that the flapper found fewer words for girls than boys. She could be a *flap*, a *barlow*, a *shifter* and although Mencken's encomium claimed otherwise, a *chicken*. The *shifter* was defined as a 'grafter', but whether that means hard worker or con-woman (both slang senses) is hard to discern. One theory has linked *Barlow* to Marie Barlow, a popular cosmetics brand of the era; slang's eternal punning would suggest a tie-in to the widely sold *Barlow knife*, because she's 'sharp'. If she was a *weed*, she was a girl who took risks, though the reason is obscure. She could be a *jane*, with its slightly noirish-overtones, though the Dictionary terms her 'a girl who meets you on the stoop'. This presumably implied the flapper's rejection of the parental grilling of her beau that represented part of the traditional dating ritual and took place in the parlour, while somewhere upstairs she primped and prettified. (It might also have used *Jane* as generic for a servant girl, forbidden to meet her boyfriends in the house.) She aimed for *meringue*, personality (presumably light and frothy) and *swanned* rather than simply walked.

Somewhat oddly, the Dictionary, published in 1922, does not mention *sheik*, for all that it has become the flapper's male antonym as far as history has decided, and gave only such derivatives as *sheiky*, *sheiked out*, and *sheik oneself up*. It came from E.H. Hull's prototype bodice-ripper *The Sheik*, published in 1919, then vastly popularised by the 1921 movie starring Rudolph Valentino, either 'Latin lover' or 'pink powder-puff' according to taste, or more usually gender. It was perhaps Valentino's ambivalent image that had the *Judge's* glossary define *sheik* not as a male flapper, but as a 'male vamp'. Perhaps *sheik* was ambivalent too;

a little over-exotic: the Dictionary, and many other sources, opted for the jocular *flipper*. It can already be found in 1905 and was common in flapperdom's heyday. As a boyfriend he was a *goof*, more usually found meaning fool and as such suggesting the flapper's cool assessment of her beaux. He could also be a *high-john* or *highboy*, a *sweetie* or *cutie* (these latter a reversal of the usual male-to-female christenings); *his blue serge*, which points once more to Brooks Brothers tailoring. *Slat*, elsewhere meaning 'rib', may or may not offer another role reversal, on slang's own use of *rib*, meaning wife. His innate disposability is reflected in *umbrella*, who could be used when convenient, folded up and tossed aside. The rainy weather that was implied presumably meant a lack of more attractive partners.

On the whole the flapper was quite disdainful of her male equivalents. The *dewdropper*, either rich or lazy, did not work, and slept all day (its origins lay on campus where it was seen as a grudging compliment but the energetic flapper would not have been impressed); the *dingle dangler* would never stop telephoning (a possible link to the eighteenth-century *dangler*, a suitor, but we shall assume that the flapper had missed a contemporary usage: the penis); the punning *mustard plaster* (coined in a British music hall song and thus a rare import) was 'an unwelcome guy who sticks around') and the *pillow case* a young man who is 'full of feathers', *feathers* abbreviating *horse-feathers* which in turn euphemised the earthier *horseshit*. The flapper was doubtless aware, and it was one of her very rare approaches to actual obscenity. The *potato* was stupid, the *monologist* a young man who hated to discuss himself and a *blushing violet* one who resisted attention. The assumption for these latter pair is somewhat heavy-handed irony. No irony was required for the *lens louse*, though it did tweak the usual use, one who monopolises the camera into one given to monopolising the conversation. A *smooth*, too smart for his own good, failed to keep his promises. Perhaps the oddest, at least chronologically, was *wally*, defined as 'a goof with patent leather hair'. Given wally's subsequent career in slang this may be assumed to be derogatory, but the possible origin, Italian *guaglio*, a boy, may give a somewhat racist clue to the focus on grooming. Finally one has the *drugstore cowboy*, and *cowboy* alone, 'a young fellow who doesn't pay much attention to girls'.

Marriage/Divorce

If their world joined those other things that could not survive the Wall Street crash of 1929 – we hear very little of flappers other than as a historical curiosity after that – it has also been suggested that by then she had grown up and surrendered to domesticity. Yet if the flapper did get married it was surely after trying all the alternatives. Her take on the institution was far from positive, in slang terms it fitted almost perfectly with the traditionally sceptic male view. He might call her his *storm and strife* (a variation on the UK's original *trouble and strife*) but 'obey' didn't seem to be part of her version of the wedding service. To be engaged was to be *insured*, which sounds like a sensible economic approach: certainly love didn't enter the calculation; but the deal soon soured and marriage itself was an *eye-opener*, i.e. a nasty surprise, the ring a *manacle* or *handcuff* (the feeling was mutual: *ball and chain* for a wife or girlfriend was coined almost simultaneously, in 1924) and a divorce was a *declaration of independence. To secure a divorce was *dropping the pilot*, echoing Tenniel's famous cartoon of Bismarck's departure from the helm of German politics, and once divorced a woman was *out on parole. She was not unconditionally free: one might, she accepted, fall for the same old snares.

Food/Drink

The flapper liked her liquor. That it had been purged from the national digestive system by the 18th amendment merely gave it extra oomph. To drink was to *lap* (which went back to 1819); throwing it back was all great fun and in the spirit of things she called it slightly jokey names such as *alky, jazz water, joy juice, giggle water, tonsil varnish, hooch* and of course good old *booze*; the era came up with a hundred-plus coinages. To be drunk was to be *feeling no pain, over the line, shnockered, cooked, laid out, embalmed, shellacked* and hundreds more, among them *half-cut* (1802), *jammed* (1844), *soaked* (1852) and *shined* (1900).

The man who supplied the goods was an *embalmer* (*embalming fluid* had meant *rotgut* whisky since the Civil War) or a *legger*. The *cellar-smeller* had started life as a prohibition agent, but for flappers he was a young man who made sure he was always around when free liquor was handed out; he was probably a *punch rustler* too, one who hung around the party's drinks table. Both were almost certainly armed with *luggage*, a hip flask. *Noodle juice*, which was tea, stood out against the alcoholic parade, but whether the *noodle* meant a fool, or whether it was the head and the liquid thus brain food, is unknown. She ate, and a restaurant, though they don't seem to have played anything like the role of speakeasies (the bar proper being in legal abeyance) was a *nosebaggery*. This drew on the late 1890s *nosebag*, a hotel or lodging-house, and the older *put on the nosebag*, which had meant to eat hurriedly, sometimes even as one worked, since around 1870.

That the flapper drank was bad enough, that she compounded it with smoking may have been even worse. For those who assessed such things, both were the unarguable badge of the loose woman. The flapper could have cared less. Much less. She enjoyed her *ciggy* (1912), handed round the pack, the *hope chest*, and punned it as a *lip stick* (*stick* for cigarette was about twenty years old). Once consumed the remains were a *dinch* or *dincher*. Those who begged cigarettes from others were *grubbbers* (it had meant a plain beggar since 1772) and a heavy smoker a *smoke-eater*. Cigarettes also lay behind the *–me* coinage as a way of asserting a demand. The locus classicus would come in the film *The Sweet Smell of Success* (1957) where the venal columnist J. J. Hunsecker confirms his absolute power over the submissive, scrabbling press agent Sidney Falco with the command, 'Match me, Sidney', i.e. light my cigarette. But the flapper had been there first.

Walk/Transport

She was a girl on the move and urged her companions, *let's blouse*, which may have come from *let's blow* and both meant time to hit the road. Ideally via limousine, but she acknowledged the *dipe ducat*, a subway ticket, the *stutter bus* which meant a truck and, presumably in smarter circles, the *stutter tub* which was a motor-boat. Failing a limo the vehicle of choice was *dimbox*, i.e. a taxicab, its ill-lit backseat doubtless useful for the inevitable petting. If all else failed one could even *ankle*.

Talk

Feathers, as noted, meant idle chat, and there was plenty of that. To talk thus was to **punch the bag* or **spill an earful* and such **low lid* (i.e. the opposite of 'high brow') chit-chat was also known as **static*, although not yet accompanied by its overtones of argument and irritation, **oatmeal mush* (the spiel of choice for a voluble *cake-eater*) and *chin music* (1821). Everyone liked a gossip, known as **prickers* or *clotheslines* (the idea of negative if fascinating information as *dirty laundry* had been around since 1863), but if gossips turned *gimlet*, a chronic bore (another flapper pun), the cry, even if was forty years old, was *pipe down!* To *Edison* was to subject to interrogation while a *bean picker* was emollient figure; patching up wobbly relationships and 'picking up spilled beans'. Boasters were *false alarms* (1902) or *wind-suckers* (which went back to the seventeenth century).

Flapper talk was liberally laced with exclamations. Some were all her own work: *for crying out loud!* (a euphemism of *for Christ's 'sake!*), **check your hat!*, **nerts!* (as in *nuts!*, nonsense!), **not so good*, **di mi!* (i.e. dear me!), **woof! woof!* for ridicule or indignation, **rhatz!*, which was the older *rats!* with added orthography and a very modern 'z', and **you slaughter me!* which had been around as 'you kill me' since 1881. There was also **I should hope to kill you!* More violence was on offer with variations on *knock* or *knocked for a row of . . . ashcans, . . . flat tires, . . . latrines, . . . Mongolian whipped cream containers, . . . Portuguese flower pots, . . . red-headed Riffians, . . . shanties, . . . shitcans, . . . silos, . . . sour apple trees, . . . stars*, and *. . . totem poles*. The imagery seemed, logically enough, to have emerged from the recent world war. Still destructive, she liked to break things down with sounded, if not actually spoken hyphens:

ab-so-lute-ly, pos-a-lute-ly and *pos-i-tive-ly. And how!* Others, coined elsewhere, included *it's the bunk!* (1893), *zowie!* (1902), *hot (diggety) dog!* (1906), *'stoo bad* and *oh yeah!* Finally there was a creation plucked from Anita Loos' *Gentlemen Prefer Blondes* of 1927, wherein the heroine Lorelei Lee, a showgirl rather than an actual flapper, noted 'When I went up yesterday to meet she and Major Falcon for luncheon, I overheard her say to Major Falcon that she really liked to become intoxicated *once in a "dirty" while.* Only she did not say intoxicated, but she really said a slang [word].'

Ms Lee's reticence seems – though the slang word was far from necessarily coarse – to have been echoed by her flapper contemporaries. If one lexical style differentiates their slang from that of the male contemporaries it is its 'cleanliness'. Or, one can never be sure, the seeming absence of recorded obscenity. She remained, in this at least, her mother's daughter. She may have replaced soap and water with paint and powder, but its threat still lingered for a 'dirty' mouth.

Good and Bad

The flapper was definitely judgmental. If she encountered offensiveness, whether in person or circumstance she fought back. Not for her the snivelling self-infantilism of 'micro-aggressions' and the cringing 'safe space'. She had an identity, she needed no accompanying politics.

Let us ponder her admiration first. *Cat's pyjamas* (or *pajamas*), along with *bee's knees* probably the era's best-known term for excellence, is so far first recorded in 1918 and credited to the cartoonist T.A. Dorgan, known as TAD and, like Oscar Wilde before him or his contemporary Dorothy Parker, credited with most of the funny lines that emerged at the time, and especially in TAD's case the slang. That said, he seems only to have used 'the cat's' and that in 1923; our current first use comes from the journal *Dialect Notes*, and no source is offered. In addition, the format may not even have begun in America. Australia's slang-dense compilation known as 'Duke Tritton's Letter' is thought to have been published in 1905. It runs, in part, 'I'm teaching Mary and all the Tin Lids in the district to Dark An' Dim, and they reckon I'm the bees knees, ants pants and nits tits all rolled into one.' However Tritton's missive may have appeared later, though still prior to 1918.

But if the flapper did not coin the phrase that she used so often, then she undoubtedly popularised it and elaborated upon its potential. Among its variations, then and later, are: the *cat's meow* and *cat's particulars*, the *frog's eyebrows, goat's whiskers, duck's quack, bee's knees, kitten's ankles, monkey's eyebrows, bullock's bollocks, cuckoo's chin, duck's nuts, elephant's (fallen) arches, elephant's manicure, gnat's elbow, nit's tits, owl's bowels, snail's ankles, hips* or *toenails, turkey's elbow*, and *turtle's neck*. As the lexicographer Tom Dalzell, in his book on teen slang, *Flappers to Rappers*, explains, 'whatever the origin [of the phrase] the same enthusiastic praise garnered by cat's pajamas was conjured by the combination of practically any animal and any part of its anatomy.' He then lists some forty-two terms.

Two other words, even if coined at other hands, were much loved. One was *lallapaloosa* (first recorded in 1881 and variously spelt as lalapalooza, lalapazaza, lalaplunko, lalapoloosa, lalla, llallapalooza, lallapaluza, lallypaloozer, lolapaloosa, lolapalooza, lollapaloosa, lollapalooza, lollypalooza, lollypaloozer, wollapalooza). It was defined as something or someone outstandingly good, stylish or pleasing of its kind. The other being *copasectic*. If lallapaloosa had problems with its spelling, then copasetic was not to be outdone, with: copa, copasetic, copasetty, copesette(e), copissettic, copus, kopacetic, kopasetic, kopasetee, kopasette. It has yet to find an unimpeachable origin. Among the suggestions are the Chinook jargon *copasenee*, everything is satisfactory, especially as first found on the waterways of Washington state. Others include: (i) the painfully contrived phrase 'the cop is on the settee', i.e. the cop is not paying attention, which elided into copacetic and was supposedly used as such by US hoodlums; (ii) a word presumed to be Italian but otherwise unknown; (iii) French *coupersetique*, from *couper*, to strike; thus striking or worth a strike; (iv) the Yiddish phrase *hakolb'seder*, all is in order or, earlier, *kolb'tzedek*, all with justice. We are perhaps best advised to dismiss the lot and accept the dictionary's dour, but safe declaration 'etymology unknown'.

On the whole the flapper's approval was directed at boys (which makes a change from her generally sceptical, even jaundiced eye). The good-looker could be *tight* or *airtight*, his style could be *klippy*, i.e. neat, and his clothing *ducky* (first applied to a moustache in 1851 Australia). Other positives included *the berries* (1908), *keen* (1899), *nifty* (1865), *swanky* (1846), *swell* (1812), *tasty* (1788) and *the real McCoy*, which evolved in the early twentieth century. Perhaps the most interesting is *unreal*, a term that would not reappear until the 1960s, and then used by Australian surfies.

As for negatives, they too hit out at items and individuals. The great cover-all was the mysterious (to us) **seetie*, 'anybody a flapper hates'. Its etymology defeats modern research but might this be a rare example of flapper obscenity, taking *seetie* as 'C.T.' and thus, in the widest sense, 'cockteaser', coined quite recently in 1890?

Much was nonsense; *blooey* (1910), *fluky* (1910), *apple-sauce* (1884) and which perhaps comes from an old minstrel show joke, based on the problem of dividing eleven apples equally among twelve people and horses: the answer, one makes apple-sauce. There was *baloney* (1885), *banana oil* (1925), *bunk* (1893), *blah* or *blaah* (1918) and *hokum* (1908). There was *dumb*, which applied to people as well as objects, ideas or places, *punk* (1904) and a *lob*, which originally described a useless racehorse but for flapperdom meant a waste of time.

For individuals the greatest crime seems to have been stupidity. One might be a *dumb dora* (another alleged TAD-ism), a *bozark* (from *bozo*, a fool), an *egg* (1917), a *dumb-bell* (1858), or a *dumkuff*, from the German *dummkopf* and found as the literal *dumb-head* in 1887. An *oilcan* was 'an imposter', not necessarily stupid, even ingratiating (*oil* had long implied verbosity), but lacking real social grace. And lack of brains segued into lack of social skills, making one a *wurp* (perhaps from *twerp*), a *boiler factory*, a *dud* (1825), a *gobby*, usually meaning over-talkative, was defined as a 'Dumbell who has no style, no pep, no nothing'. Those who thought too much of themselves were *high hatty* (which came from contemporary vaudeville where a topper, symbolic of prestige and wealth, was known as a high hat), *grungy*, envious and perhaps from *grudge*, and *upstage* (1901). After that an *airedale*, a 'homely man' and which seems to render the long-established *dog* more specific, almost kind.

Finally came the outside world, the realm of the nay-sayer and the censorious. *They*, represented those in authority or power, the Establishment. The pronoun, as the Dictionary added, was 'used by Flappers with tone of disgust to denote the older generation'. They provided the *crepe hangers*, the *killjoys* (1776), the *pills* (1830), the *wet blankets* (1810) and the *slapper* who presumably slapped down one's enjoyments. The outside world went further: beyond the city. Being, at least at her birth, an urban creature, the flapper had little time for the peasant. Not enough time even to coin any new descriptions; the country folk, stupid and dull by default, were *bush hounds, brush apes* (1913), *apple knockers* (1913), *hicks, hay-shakers* and *country jakes*. They were beyond her pale. They were not her problem.

A Word of Her Own?

Do not trust the dictionary, especially when, as for too much of our knowledge of flapper-speak, that lexicon must fall back on no more than three random glossaries, culled from and perhaps created for the newspapers and magazines that featured them. If they are relatively consistent, then one senses simple plagiarism. The core list appeared in *The Flapper*, was immediately disseminated through America's network of small-town papers, and pretty much remained the authorised version. We are lost for the vital information: who assembled the lists, who or what (books, magazines, movies?) were their sources, was there any fieldwork? And beyond that, one step nearer the 'truth', who coined the words in question?

Setting aside the terms they adopted, and looking at those for which the Dictionary is a first, and sometimes only example, flapper slang is perceptibly different to its mainstream equivalents. And by mainstream, it should be acknowledged that term refers to that bulk of slang that had been largely and traditionally coined by men. Groups of women had coined their own lexis, typically prostitutes, but flappers are the first to do so as 'civilians'. Its pre-occupations are not all unique – the mainstream also notes physical attractiveness or lack of it, drinking and drunken-ness and of course wealth and poverty – but some are. It is often a matter of a new emphasis, a different point of view. That, for once, of a woman. Parties and dancing play a far smaller role in general slang; men are assessed there, but usually in terms of their own self-images and the cold light – veering between cynicism and pity – that flappers could cast on them is the reverse of the way the male mainstream dealt with such calculations. Marriage is the usual bad joke but in this case the laugh is on the groom and not the bride.

Flapper slang acknowledged sex, as we have noted, but only, it would appear, sex within limits: the physical exploration of petting, with its emphasis on kissing, but, as far as her language went at least, stopping short of intercourse. The harsh, unbridled sexism of male slang is wholly absent. Indeed, the aggression that underpins so much of male-generated slang is not for the flapper. In parallel, her slang seems to suggest a different class background. Male slang is gutter-upwards; flapper, that is female slang, seems far more middle class. This may be an assumption too far, but the flapper certainly lived a life some way beyond the usual slang-coining proles. She might not be a Zelda Sayre, but neither was she Stephen Crane's fictional Maggie, 'a Girl of the Streets'.

Literature and Beyond

If the Flapper's Dictionary seems now, and perhaps did so even then, somewhat contrived – did any flesh-and-blood young woman, however keen to establish her credentials, really use that many of its terms? – one can look elsewhere for what flappers actually said. The first port of call tends to be Scott Fitzgerald, forever linked to the type, even credited with their creation, but it may be a bum steer. Neither his Flappers nor Philosophers, by which he generously characterises the earnestly self-important young men who surrounded and pursued them, whether in full-scale novels such as *This Side of Paradise* ('A Novel about Flappers, Written for Philosophers') or its successor *The Beautiful and Damned* seem especially slangy. After all the latter appeared in 1922 when Zelda Fitzgerald, in the way of all those who ride the peak of a trend, was declaring the whole thing dead – and thus shutting the door on the great mass who were still queuing to jump onto the slowing but far from stationery bandwagon. But Fitzgerald had caught a wave and would dedicate much of his diminishing career to staying afloat. And Fitzgerald, in any case, was a man. His ability to delineate the flapper did not imply unalloyed approval. The flapper, in her early days a spoiled rich girl with time and cash to spare, both fascinated him and regularly broke his heart. The struggle of middle-class mid-Western-ers, such as himself, to woo such girls fills his early stories: and it was by no means successful, and if he was fascinated by the flap-per, he also found her problematic.

Elinor Glyn's *The Flirt and the Flapper* (1930), a series of concocted dialogues between a notional Flapper and her nine-teenth-century great-grandmother, the Flirt, barely overlaps with the Flapper Dictionary. A single term: *soaked*, drunk, links the two. She is better paired with Fitzgerald, although again the dozen similarities – among them *ants in my pants*, *fall for* and *stewed* (another synonym for drunk) – are hardly plentiful. Glyn was no flapper, born in 1864 she was far too old, but she had form. In 1927 she published a novel, *It*. The word was a slang veteran, having served as a euphemism for sexual intercourse and the genitals of both sexes for several centuries. In her hands, still essentially euphemistic, it meant sex appeal. She was not the coiner; that honour, somewhat paradoxically, goes to Rudyard Kipling who in his short story 'Mrs Bathurst' (1904) had opined, 'Tisn't beauty, so to speak, nor good talk necessarily. It's just It. Some women'll stay in a man's memory if they once walk down a street.' However there might have been a link: according to Kipling's biographer Andrew Lycett it was possible that he had picked up the idea from his acquaintance Lord Milner, a one-time pursuer of Glyn's hand. Whatever the source, Glyn's novel popularised the word, which would, soon afterwards, expand to describe the *It-Girl*, originally movie star Clara Bow, but more recently used to describe any (briefly) fashionable young woman, usually best-known for her supposed sexual exploits. Glyn already had her own 'it', especially after another, earlier novel, *Three Weeks* (1907) a tale of decadence and debauchery, in which a European vamp (the flapper's wicked, sexualised cousin, as it were) seduces and deliberately lets herself be impregnated by a naïve product of Eton and Oxford. The use of a tiger-skin rug as the scene of their (unstated but inescapably obvious) copula-tions gave rise to the jocular verse;

Would you like to sin
With Elinor Glyn
On a tiger skin?
Or would you prefer
To err with her
On some other fur?

The Flirt and Flapper appear relatively late: not only had Zelda Fitzgerald disclaimed flappers but so too had most of those who had once bobbed and rolled so enthusiastically. Nonetheless the short book, which offers ninety-nine slang words and phrases, gives a good look at a very recent lexis. All come from the Flapper, with useful, if faux-naïve questions placed in the Flirt's mouth so as to allow for explanation.

To cite those for which Glyn can so far claim a first use, they are: *ants in one's pants*, to be in a state of nerves or agitation; *arteried up*, emotionally excited or confused; *big idea*, a love object; *cream in one's coffee*, praise for the 'perfect' person, usually a lover; *flat tyre* or *highbrow*, a kill-joy or puritan; *light-head*, a simpleton; *put it over on*, to outwit; *warm someone up*, to pass on (confidential) information. Other terms, already in use, include *batty about*, obsessed with, *back number*, one for whom one no longer feels affection, *debbie*, a debutante (shared with Fitzgerald), *dim bulb*, a fool, *dope* and *lowdown*, inside information, *fast worker*, one who is sexually forward (thus in 1918 the teenage Zelda Sayre, temporarily rebuffing a newly met Fitzgerald who had asked to see her after a dance: 'I never make late dates with fast workers'), *heavy*, one's current boyfriend (Glyn and Fitzgerald also use the synonymous *crush*, applicable to either gender), *helluva*, i.e. the intensifier 'hell of a', *raspberry*, a dismissal, *scream*, an admirable individual, *snow*, cocaine, and *whoopee*, which the Flapper explains as 'when you feel you could beat the band, and are not sure if it's your own sweetie you're with or your best girl friend's — and you don't care a damn which!'

For the mass, those who had perhaps seen the Flapper Dictionary in their local paper, there was of course the movies. The industry realised the profitable charms of the sexy, but ultimately light-hearted flapper. Naturally, they showcased the sex (plus lashings of ciggies, cocktails and jazz), with titles such as *The Wild Party* (1929), *Flaming Youth* (1923), *Our Dancing Daughters* (1928) and *The Plastic Age* (1926). *Dancing Mothers*

(1926) – staid old mum loses her family to 'jazzmania' – was a sop to the wrinkles. The genre made stars of two comediennes; Clara Bow and Colleen Moore. The moralisers, the flappers' crepe hangers, saw only corruption and demanded censorship. They were especially exercised by the slang. The industry's own self-regulator, the MPPDA, tried to head off the killjoys. Reading the script for a Clara Bow vehicle, *The Fleet's In* (1928), an executive noted possible problems with a dozen 'colorful' sub-titles. Local censors would never accept lines such as 'We gotta greet 'em, grab 'em, goal 'em and go!' (*goal* was apparently the culprit and perhaps reminded bluenoses of the synonymous *score*), 'look hot and keep cool', the presumed professional slur in 'most of them are osteopaths – operating without a license' (although the image was more likely that of roaming hands), and the derisive 'that stretches my girdle' (though surely no real flapper would wear one?). In the event these slipped through, as did the double-entendre title included in *Wine of Youth* in a scene in which a boy offers a girl a glass, albeit labelled 'ginger ale', and having drunk, she collapses onto his conveniently placed pillow. The title read; 'A little evening class in home jazzing' and the flapper, if not her mother, presumably appreciated that *jazzing* might refer to a very different form of 'dance'.

Back in print, but low on the cultural scale came a variety of pulp magazines, named for the cheap wood-pulp paper on which they were printed. They lacked in every sense the veneer of the sort of magazines that might offer Scott Fitzgerald, but they knew a selling topic and duly promoted their flapper heroines both on their covers and in their texts. Appearing in 'snappy' or 'peppy' titles (synonyms for slightly sexy) they were pictured as strong, independent figures, challenging social givens and pushing modernity. They promoted physical fitness and proposed a

moral system that eschewed the old-school strictures of mono-
theistic, and far from feminist religion. They were by definition
lowbrow but as *The Oxford Critical and Cultural History of
Modernist Magazines* suggests, titles like *Flapper's Experience* (the
successor to the *Flapper*) and *Home Brew* (a direct nudge at the
need to bypass Prohibition's ban on breweries) were 'dedicated
to the challenging of old world conventions'. As such they
carried a 'DIY, underground feel about them, sort of Prohibition-
inspired "little magazines".' Slang played a lesser role than in the
contemporary 'hard-boiled dick' pulps, where it was an essential
element of the macho, noir appeal, but the stories featured flappers, and the language was always there. Like the movies, they
had a nationwide reach: what better way, quite literally, to spread
the word.

Then there were cartoons, notably pioneering woman cartoonist Ethel Hays' *Flapper Fanny*, a single image plus semi-aphoris-
tic wisecrack ('At six she wants a candy store, at 16 a box of
sweets, at 26 a "sweet papa".' Or, accompanying a picture of a
half-clad girl putting on stockings, 'Silk is the least important
thing that goes into hosiery.') Born in 1892 (she would live till
1989) Hays was a perfect age. She knew of what she wrote and
drew, and 'Fanny', launched in 1925, was appearing in five
hundred papers within twelve months. It was all rather risqué,
almost cosmopolitan by provincial standards, but ultimately
safe. Just like the flapper herself. Fanny was soon imitated, notably by Irma Benjamin (writer) and Harry Weinert's (artist) *Rolls
Rosie*. Rosie, whose fashions were even more obviously 'flapper'
than Fanny's, also offered one-liners, with an accent on the jokes
rather than the cracker-barrel philosophy. Far less successful
than Fanny, she did offer one speciality, like the flappers she was
drawn to represent, she had an obsession with automobiles

(hence the *roll*, more likely as in travel than in the luxury marque). Every cartoon either pictured one or at least mentioned cars in the text. Most famous of all was Max Fleischer's *Betty Boop*, launched in 1930 as a caricature of the singer Helen Kane, known as the 'Boop-Boop-a-Doop Girl' (in 1932 Kane would sue for the imposture: she lost). She began life as a flapper, a full-on Jazz Baby, with short skirt, plunging neckline, garter, shimmying hips, naughtily winking eyes and an overriding sexuality that ensured that despite her existence as an animated cartoon, her main fans were adults. But the Hollywood Production Code, stultifying a generation's movies, ensured that Betty's allure was much diluted. Her image today is associated with the Depression rather than the Jazz Age, and like the UK's Jane, whose daily strip (literal as well as pictorial) allegedly inspired British troops throughout the Second World War, Betty served as a cheering antidote to the Depression's miseries.

Then suddenly, almost as soon and abruptly as she had appeared, the flapper was gone. The Crash did for her cash flow, or rather her father's or boyfriend's, and the playgrounds to spend it in closed down. The Thirties were a dour decade, subject to endless financial problems and culminating in a devastating, global war. She had materialised, emboldened by the previous world war's temporary role reversals, flourished for a season before her butterfly existence, as some would term it, died. She had grown up, she may well, as the *Flapper* itself had suggested back in 1922, have chosen marriage over solo performance, even if the husband was no more than a 'boob'. Like the inevitable and wholly artificial 'moral' ending of the 1924 movie *The Perfect Flapper*, she had become 'the perfect wife' and for all her seeming excess, turned out just like another movie title of 1927, to be *Naughty But Nice*. To what extent she left a social legacy is hard

10. Riotous Girls

THE TEENAGER, AS a concept rather than an individual who is making their way through a decade of various progressions – emotional, physical, sociological – that takes in the years from thirteen to nineteen, is barely a century old. The earliest examples offered by the *OED* (as revised in June 2018) have *teenager* in 1913 and *teenage* a year earlier. The earliest examples, the dictionary suggests, seem to have been used 'particularly in connection with churches'. The concept of branding this particular period of adolescence is much earlier. In 1747 David Garrick, stealing from the French play *La Parisienne* (1691) by Florent Carton Dancourt, created as an afterpiece (following a more important performance, in the case of its first night, *Macbeth*) the farce *Miss in her Teens, or The Medley of Lovers*. It featured a heroine 'Miss Biddy' (played by 'Mrs Ward'*) and her efforts to play off a series of suitors in order to find Mr Right. Garrick played 'Mr Fribble', using a slang term that meant a sexually inadequate, probably effeminate male. In 1818 a book appeared entitled *Advice to the teens; or, Practical helps towards the formation of one's own character*. The modern teenager, however, was born in the 1940s, though she at least was initially known as a

* This was probably Sarah Ward, wife of the actor John, but reference books (relying mainly on programmes or posters) almost always omit an actress' given name.

bobbysoxer, and pledged her adoration to 'crooners' such as Frank Sinatra. Rock 'n' roll put the seal on the sociology, and while the influence of popular music on that same age-group appears in an infinity of variations today, it has yet to relinquish its importance during those crucial years.

The idea that teenage girls and boys might forge a language – which by their and its marginal nature would be categorised as slang – that was dictated by their age and pursuits, and that that language might play a central role in dividing them from their parents (the term 'generation gap' is currently dated to 1955 – though its use that year in a syndicated US strip cartoon suggests it was already well-known), came with the territory. But the idea that the genders might move on to creating different, if complementary lexes is comparatively recent. There had been, as noted in chapter 1, an attempt to differentiate the slang talk of male and female high school students in 1903, but research had moved away to look at college lingo, and that – at least as seen in the various glossaries that were produced – does not seem to have considered the idea of gender divisions.

Sometimes, however, they stated themselves. If, for instance, one looks at such stories as *Tom Brown's Schooldays*, set at a British public school or, at the very end of teenage, at *The Adventures of Mr Verdant Green*, set in Oxford and both published in 1857, one finds a good deal of site-specific slang. The problem, of course, is that neither of these institutions admitted girls. Nor do they appear in the rash of public school stories that followed towards the end of the century, whether produced by such as Talbot Baines Read (for the serious end of things) or P.G. Wodehouse (for the deflatory).

However, there was an important exception. The work of Angela Brazil began appearing in 1906 with *The Fortunes of*

Philippa. She had created some titles for children but this was the first of the books that made her famous: a series of stories set in girls' public schools. There would be forty-nine titles before she died in 1947. Brazil was hardly alone – the ultra-prolific Enid Blyton inevitably jumped onto the boarding school bandwagon – but where Blyton kowtowed to morality, a Brazil girl was much more fun.[*] As Katharine Hughes suggested in the *Guardian*,[†] 'Brazil's books glory in this new complicity, showing loud, boisterous teenagers forming themselves into self-policing groups, untroubled by the distant rumble of prefects and teachers. The girls of St Cyprian's, St Ronan's and St Chad's jump out of windows, play pranks, go awol on cliff tops and tie things to weather vanes. From here it is but a short jump to the dystopian fantasy of the St Trinian's series, Ronald Searle's accounts of posh-girl thuggery.'

Hughes also recounts the moment, in 1936, when the then headmistress of St Paul's Girls School in London 'declared in assembly that she was minded to gather all of Miss Brazil's books and burn them. It wasn't the repetitive plotlines and sketchy characterisations that offended her, nor even the vague possibility that St Paul's might have loosely figured in one of Brazil's books; it was the terrible language: "Rouse up, you old bluebottle, can't you"; "Right you are, O Queen! It's a blossomy idea!" "Miss Jones is a stunt, as jinky as you like", and, the one that got everyone especially riled, "Twiggez-vous?"'

Not everyone agreed: reviewing Gillian Freeman's study of

---

[*] A revamped version of Blyton's *Mallory Towers* series was announced in 2018. Promoting the current obeisance to 'diversity', one may assume that morality, however disguised, will still be central.
[†] K. Hughes, 'Angela Brazil: dorm feasts and red-hot pashes', *Guardian*, 14 February 2015.

Brazil for *The Spectator* in 1976[*] Brigid Brophy suggested that while neither characterisation nor plots were remotely exceptional, it was Brazil's use of slang that won her so devoted and persistent a following. Some of the livelier girls seem not that far removed from 'fast girls' in embryo, or perhaps flappers-to-be. Scapegrace younger sisters of Wodehouse's Bobbie Wickham or Waugh's Agatha Runcible? Meanwhile was not The Mystic Seven, created for *The Madcap of the School* (1917) the first and best evocation of what Blyton would water down for her own royalty statements.

The slang is of course vastly dated. *A Fourth Form Friendship* (1912) offers *grind* (hard work), *jolly* and *ripping* (excellent), *the pater* (one's father), *swot* (to work hard) and *turn off the waterworks* (stop crying). There is also *nigger*, though in some tiny mitigation the term is not directly racist but refers to minstrels (whites blacked up for entertainment purposes; it had been thus used since 1840). *A Madcap of the School* (1917) has the minstrels once more, also known as *darkies*, *coons*, *Sambos* and *Dinahs*; such hugely popular shows were to be found worldwide but even a century later the terms are very hard to overlook. Other terms include *rag* (to tease), *splendiferous*, *top-hole* and *topping* (first-rate), *nuts on* (enthusiastic), the affirmative *rather!*, *jaw-wag* (a lecture), *jinky* (found both as amusing and as nervous, problematic), *this child* (oneself), *chubby* (delightful), *stuff* (mistreat), *blighter* (a distasteful individual), and a couple of words that reflect the real-life backdrop: *Zepp* (a Zeppelin airship, currently bombing UK cities) and *stunt* (an all-purpose word for 'activity' in the trenches). Brazil also adjures a character: 'Don't on any account shock the neighbourhood by an unseemly exhibition of

* B. Brophy in *The Spectator*, 26 June 1976.

vulgar slang!' but one senses a tongue well in cheek. A year later came *A Patriotic Schoolgirl* (the war raged on and the cover boasted a union flag). The slang included *jubilate!* (be happy), *blub* (to weep), *knock off* (create at speed), *piggy* (unpleasant), *fast* (overly sophisticated), *katawampus* (ill-behaved), *blossomy* (very good) and *gruesome* (the opposite); *bluebottle* (an insult), *ostrich* (to bury one's head whether literally or figuratively), *cock-a-doodle* (to gloat) and *blow-out* (a feast 'so far as the rationing order would allow'). The on-going war added the exclamation 'strafe it all!'* and the militant slogan 'Save a bun and do the Hun!' None of it of course was remotely sexual; there was absolutely no mention of menstruation and that soon to be popular warning of a visible petticoat, 'Charlie's dead'† was some time in the future.

One can position a Brazil girl as a proto-flapper and a St Trinian's girl's larky great-aunt, but that's as far as it goes in the context of the teenage girls to come. She stayed strictly in genre. Setting aside and moving on beyond flappers (see chapter 10), whom I have chosen to see as candidates for being the 'first youth cult', the idea of a succession of youth movements, which deliberately take on a counter-cultural role – however temporarily in most cases – that challenges those prescribed by the adult world, is a post-World War II phenomenon.‡ There had doubtless been fleeting examples of those who might, today, qualify as

---

* 'Strafe it all. It's a grizzly nuisance. I should like to slay myself' (*A Patriotic Schoolgirl* p.73).
† The phrase defeats etymology; first recorded in 1942 (in America) it seems to have peaked in the 1950s. Popular etymology links it to Royalist ladies dipping their petticoats in the blood of the executed Charles I (or less gruesome, simply wearing them to show), but why the 300-year gap before it came on stream?
‡ There had been criminal girl gangs – typically south London's Forty Elephants – but the importance of these was the crime – primarily shoplifting and thus seen as typically 'female' villainy – rather than the gender of the criminal. Teenage certainly had nothing to do with it.

'teen idols' – Lord Byron, Goethe's fictional Young Werther, a growing number of movie stars such as Rudolf Valentino – but their fans were not restricted to the young (though the last was usually a female taste). Nor, prior to the Fifties, did the teens-to-be create what might be termed 'cults' or 'movements'. Likewise feminism, of which the version that emerged in the mid-1960s was so important, was already acknowledged to be 'the second wave' of a movement that was already much older. It could and did look back to its late eighteenth-century pioneers, and even, as noted in chapter 5, might be seen in the creation of the *querelle des dames*. Youth may have been attracted to the movement but youth were not its leaders.

Whether one chooses to start with the mainly middle-class beats or, at the meaner end of town, the various urban gangs (see chapter 7), girls were there from day one, but if they were not separate, nor were they equal. (The beats, of course, embraced homosexuality; if the gangs did, they were at pains not to admit it.) In the latter world they acted as subordinates in those areas of gang life to which they were permitted access. They might fight rival 'debs' but while they might also carry weapons – being less likely to face a policeman's frisking hands – they were very unlikely to use them. They were also providers of sex, sometimes one-to-one, sometimes, typically in initiatory ceremonies based on taking on multiple partners, in the most literal sense of 'gang-banging'. As for language, they shared that of their boyfriends. There is no sense of independent coinage. The late Sixties launched the predominantly middle-class hippies: there was not the slightest need to be 'patched up' with a gang's logo; just tie-dyed and stoned. Evocations of 'my lady', that Sixties recreation of a pre-Raphaelite Guinevere, all wimple and flowing velvet, a dab hand at rolling joints and throwing the I Ching, were only flesh deep. Few longhaired freaks would have found anything amiss in the celebrated *Rolling Stone* piece which had such a *cat* requesting his *chick*, 'put on the [Grateful] Dead, get on the bed, and spread.'

It can be argued that the sort of slang that accumulated around the early-model Beatles was popularised if not coined by their teen girl fans. Back from their Hamburg Bacchanalia and repositioned by Brian Epstein as a boy band – the collarless Cardin jackets and winkle-picker boots, the 'Beatle-cut' hair, the love songs challenging the rock 'n' roll classics – they were considered the girls' choice (the 'white negro' Rolling Stones faithfully recycling blues standards, offering 'Mockney' accents rather than new slang and appealing to the lads). The slang itself can be found in early issues of *Mersey Beat*, the Liverpool-based pop paper. Most of it is breathlessly, fan-driven positive:

Fab, *ginchy*, *gear* and *swinging* all stood for excellent; *skizzy* was crazy – but in a good way, as was *w(h)acky* which could also be a noun, *whack*, and meant a person; *do your nut* to go crazy, presumably with pleasure; *cool cat* was an admirable individual; *rave*, to extol. If an all-purpose negative was required, then that was *grotty* (from grotesque). The nation learned a *Scouser* was a Liverpudlian (though perhaps not its origin: the sailor's dish *lobscous*). There were also the nick-names for the four stars: 'The Fabs', 'The Mop-tops', but these were surely journalese.

Little, however, was that original, any more than the hippie terms that followed on, which usually came, whether their users knew it or not, from the slang of 1930s African-America. Again, there was no gender division.

Music undoubtedly lay behind the popularisation of a slang vocabulary that was not simply associated with but blatantly named for a subset of young women: the 'Valspeak' created around 1982 by the 'Valley Girls' (soon clipped to 'Vals') of southern California's San Fernando Valley. The music in question was what was essentially a novelty song written by Frank Zappa and 'narrated' by his then fourteen-year-old daughter Moon Unit. The song, which ran down a good proportion of the basic Valley vocabulary, gave Zappa *père* his first (and only) Top Forty hit. It also gave this unarguably female idiolect a wide, if short-lived fame. Films such as *Fast Times at Ridgemont High* (1982) showcased the speech, and the Sherman Oaks Galleria (name-checked on the song and the closing of which was head-lined by CNN Interactive on 15 April 1999, 'Like, Totally the End of One's Mall Era') became a totemic piece of geography.

A Valpseak dictionary of the era offered:

As if – lit. 'as if' except it does not use a subject; expresses disbelief.

Bitchin'– adj. slang for excellent; first-rate. Though a deriva-tive of 'bitch', bitchin' is not considered profane.

Whatever! – short for 'whatever you say'; sarcastic comeback.

Barf me out! – 'So disgusting it makes me want to vomit.'

Fer shur – lit. 'For sure.'

Betch – literally 'Bitch.'

Totally – 'I agree' or 'completely.'

Grody to the max! – 'As gross as he/she/it can be.'

Like, oh my God – can be used many ways; expresses shock (OMG for short).

I'm suuure! or I'm so sure – 'I'm absolutely positive,' but usually used sarcastically.

Tre – A synonym for 'very' (derived from French 'très').

Trippendicular! – It can mean either 'awesome' or a drug high.

Betty – An attractive woman.

So – Very; used too often and said with too much emphasis.
'He's so not cute!'
Baldwin – An attractive man.
Seriously – Frequent interjection of approval.
Gag me with a spoon! – expression of disgust.
Zlint – 'excellent', derived from the phonetic spelling of the
classifieds abbreviation 'Xlnt'.

The Zappas' lyrics used some of this and added a few extras: *tubular, awesome, no biggie, bu-fu* (gay, from *butt-fucker*), *gross*, and the verb *bag*, typically in 'go bag your face' which suggested that so disgusting was the object cited, that only hiding it beneath a bag would efface its horror.* Like most of Frank Zappa's work, there was a deep vein of irony; the song had no illusions of what it was up to:

'Whatsa matter with the way I talk? (*chorus*: Valley Girl) / I am a VAL, I know (*chorus*: Valley Girl).'

Not every term was original – *bitchin'* and *tubular*, for instance, were veteran surfer-talk and *grody*, a local variation of the Beatles' grotty – but the combinations and perhaps equally important the intonation were new. What the Vals did was known to linguists as 'high rising terminal intonation', otherwise known as 'uptalk'. Its effect is to render every statement, the meaning of which is no more than a simple declarative, a question. If very little of the lexis has survived, then uptalk undoubtedly has, and is branded by its critics, as symbolic of much that is 'wrong' with female speech.

---

* Valspeak, male department, also claimed *double-bagger*, an exceptionally unattractive girl and either based on the need to place not just one but two bags over her before having sex or the need for each participant to be covered with a bag; an extreme version was *double-bag and stumper*, in which as well as the masking, the male declared that he would rather have his limbs amputated than have sex with this female.

The reality, as ever, is otherwise. Vals did not originate 'uptalk', though they undoubtedly spread it. Terry Southern found it at Ole Miss (the University of Tennessee) in a 1963 piece on baton-twirlers.* Aside from America, linguists have discerned it in South Africa and the Falkland Islands, and particularly in Australia, from where – the assumption being via a number of popular soap operas that were exported in the 1980s – it spread to the UK. While it is undoubtedly associated with female speech, it has also spread to men, among them ex-US President George W. Bush.

The link to female speech patterns remains. Robin Lakoff noted it in her book *Language and Woman's Place* (2004) where she saw it, along with tag questions (terminating an otherwise declarative sentence with 'don't you think?' and similar artificial 'questions'), as a woman's way of using what at least seemed to be an interrogative to avoid clashes with those – i.e. men – who at least presumed their own views to be what counted. As she put it:

> These sentence types provide a means whereby a speaker can avoid committing himself [*sic*], and thereby avoid coming into conflict with the addressee. The problem is that, by so doing, a speaker may also give the impression of not being really sure of himself [*sic*], of looking to the addressee for confirmation, even of having no views of his own. This last criticism is, of course, one often leveled at women.

---

* T. Southern, 'Twirling at Ole Miss', *Esquire*, February 1963. '"Yessuh, I *do*," she agreed, [. . .] continuing to speak in that oddly rising inflection peculiar to girls of the South, making parts of a reply sound like a question: "Why, back home near Macon . . . Macon, Georgia? At Robert E. Lee High? . . . we've got these outfits with *tassels!* And a little red-and-gold skirt? . . . that, you know, sort of *flares out?*"'

And, she wonders, 'how much of it reflects a use of language that has been imposed on women from their earliest years'.* Such structure is what, she notes, creates the sense of women's speech being more 'polite' than is men's. Subsequent research suggests more positive uses, for instance the inference that the speaker is first confirming that the person to whom she speaks is keeping up, and that she, the speaker, has not actually come to the end of what she has to communicate.

All of which went to prove what has become a matter of faith: while young women may not originate a large amount of slang's content, they are the mistresses of its form.

Punk, which boasted a number of all-girl bands, seemed to have sidestepped slang in its lyrics. Fifteen years later came the Riot Grrrl movement, positioned as a form of revolutionary feminism that was best known to a wider world through the quasi-punk band Bikini Kill. The band lyrics and the texts of a variety of 'zines laid out their beliefs, typically in the movement Manifesto, published in 1991, but if there was slang – as seen in some songs – it was purely coincidental. As Kathleen Hanna, the movement's best-known figurehead, put it in the Manifesto, 'I believe with my wholeheartmindbody that girls constitute a revolutionary soul force that can, and will change the world for real.' One might have expected slang from such a movement, but if it even entered the picture, it was more likely than not seen as over-allied with boys.

For teen girls talking slang one had to go to the movies: titles included *Fast Times at Ridgemont High* (1982), *Heathers* (1989), *Clueless* (1995) and *Mean Girls* (2004). *Clueless*, which took the plot of Jane Austen's *Emma* and moved it from England's early

---

* R. Lakoff, *Language and Woman's Place* (2004), p.49.

nineteenth-century west country to California's late twentieth-century west coast and like *Ridgemont High* was directed by Amy Heckerling, came very much out of the Valley Girl world. Its star Alicia Silverstone ('Cher Horowitz') was pure Val, and the slang (which Heckerling researched in situ) included *betty, do someone a prop, random, Val* itself and the dismissive duo: *as if* and *whatever. Mean Girls*, coming later, had some novelties, though as ever in slang, the imagery was much as ever. The snotty 'mean girls' of the title were the *plastics, grody* had become *grotsky, bitch* was now *byotch* (WASP cousin to rap's *bee-atch*), and *fetch*, attractive, had supposedly been imported from the UK (its origin appears to be in *fetch*, recorded in 1888, meaning a success, i.e. that which 'fetched' one's admiration).*

In and out of the movies teen girls were omni-present and there's no way of name-checking every instance. One best-seller was the Australian writer Kathy Lette's *Puberty Blues*, written with Gabrielle Carey in 1979. Set around the Sydney surf scene, it follows a pair of wannabe 'surfie chicks' fighting, not always very successfully, against the innate sexism of the scene. Teens loved it, adults were inevitably 'shocked' by the frequent sex scenes and, though written without the slightest sympathy, the appearance of heroin. The book was slang-heavy and showed the extent to which Australia was maintaining its own corner of the lexis. Some was mainstream Oz: *arvo*, afternoon, *bludge*, to cadge, *bubbler*, a water fountain, *dob in*, to inform on, *rack off!* go away!, *packing shit*, frightened, *slack-arsed*, lazy, *root*, to have sex or one who did so. Some was teen- or surf-specific: *tit off*, to caress a girl's breasts, *nelly*, semen, *hip-nippers*, bikini panties,

---

* It is *fetch* that is used to display the wilfulness of slang when faced by a conscious import: the character Gretchen Wieners tries continually to promote it as a trendy neologism. No-one else bites.

scungies, men's briefs, worn under swimming trunks, *doll* or *spunk*, an attractive male (thus *spunky*, good-looking), *pash*, love-making short of intercourse, *wrapped*, obsessed by, *go slops*, to be the last man in gang-sex, *stoked*, elated and *perf!* excellent!

Australia is also responsible for the creation of Ja'mie [pron. 'J'may'] King – 'Australia's favourite beyatch' – a wealthy private schoolgirl whose adventures are charted in a series of TV comedy mockumentaries – *We Can Be Heroes* (2005), *Summer Heights High* (2007), and *Ja'mie: Private School Girl* (2013) – by male comedian Chris Lilley, who portrays her on screen. Ja'mie's intonations are very Val, and Lilley claims that he created the part by interviewing real-life equivalents, though he has stated that it's not a show for teen girls who would surely dismiss it as something 'an older guy' thought up.

Ja'mie's vocabulary duly blends young Australia with Valspeak.* Terms include *bogan* (Australia's version of white trash or chav), *box gap* (i.e. the thigh gap, ideally three inches between one's thighs when standing), *care factor* (the extent one cares about a given subject or individual – this is rarely high), *crack onto* (to flirt), *go off* (to lose control), *goss* (gossip), *hot as* (excellent, e.g. of a garment), *ILY* (I love you), *pash*, *povo* (impoverished, working-class), *random* (strange, eccentric) and the inevitable *OMG!* The term of terms – and the only one that has been created by Lilley himself – is *quiche*, defined as 'incredibly attractive, sexy. A step above hot.' The show has reached America and the former teen movie star Lindsay Lohan apparently tags her Instagram pix *#soquiche*.

Eight thousand miles to the north-west comes *The Sopranos* (1998), by the Scottish writer Alan Warner, with its tale of the

---

* Terms from http://www.vulture.com/2013/11/handy-guide-to-jamies-jamiezing-vocabulary.html

more tearaway members of a convent choir on their trip to a performance in the big city. Written by a man, it might be dismissed as ventriloquy but with this book and its predecessor *Morvern Callar* (1995), Warner won a reputation for his ability to recreate himself as an avatar for the way his young female protagonists think and talk. Carole Jones* has written of the skills of his 'literary cross-dressing' and his intent to 'escape the dominant masculinism' even if others, playing the 'cultural appropriation' card, see him as no more than a 'colonialist' of female experience. For Warner it's simple: he enjoys writing about young female characters because of their energy and honesty and while he admits to the possibility of falling for an over-romantic take, he sees them as refreshingly resistant to cynicism.

The Sopranos might have readers arguing with that last opinion. The girls, hell bent on fun and far more interesting in 'copping off' with visiting sailors than winning the competition, are hardly wide-eyed innocents. Not for nothing is the club they're aiming for named 'The Mantrap'. There is much consumption of alcohol and talk of drugs; sex is a constant (and one of them reveals that she's pregnant).

Sex provides the bulk of examples: *fanny*, vagina, *beastie*, penis, *shag*, to have sex (though *shag* is also used as tell off, scold), *cop off with*, *spunk*, semen, *bonk* and *spunker*, an attractive male (thus *bonkable*), *pubes*, pubic hair, *flunky*, a condom, *hand job*, to masturbate a boy, *hit on*, to chat up, *nuddy mag*, pornography, a *snog*, necking, *horny*, sexually excited and *screw*, to have sex.

Drink and drugs give *pissed*, *mortal* and *chronic*, extremely drunk, *mashed*, high on *blow* or *loco weed*, i.e. cannabis, *skin up*, to

* C. Jones, *Disappearing Men: Gender Disorientation in Scottish Fiction 1979-1999* (2009), pp.161–162.

make a joint, *roach*, a cardboard filter, *fire up*, to light some form of cigarette, *magic mushie*, psilocybin. Last of the major sub-groups is insult: *grungy*, *mental*, a *loon*, a *swot* or *pencil-pusher*, a *mink*, an *asswipe*, a *twat-fuck*, a *bass*, a *bogger*, a *dosser*, a *grot*, a *wanker* and a *turn-off.* None are exceptionally fresh, but we must trust the author. This is very likely how 'his' girls would talk.

11. Some Creators

Before attempting any specifics, one thing should be made clear: I make no pretence at including every woman who, in whatever creative medium, has used some words of slang. This might, once, have been possible (it was once possible of men too, so rare were such occurrences) but those days are long gone and a little spicing with the counter-language is so regular as to be invisible. The tabloids remain bashful, loading their texts with 'what about the kiddies' asterisks, which only serve to underline the censored terms, but when the *Times* runs a headline, albeit quoting, that declares 'When you get your arse handed to you, you learn',[*] so do we.

Slang is used by a wide range of writers, sometimes the least likely, even canonical.

The playwright (and sometime spy) Aphra Behn, who fought her creative corner with such as the Earl of Rochester and other libertines of the Restoration court, offers more than one hundred slang terms but they are mainly placed in male mouths. She is big on swaggering oaths: *afsheartlinkins! 'slife! 'sheart! rot! 'sbobs! 'sdeath! zoz! piss! odsbobs! ifecks! damme! catso!* (which as a slang noun means penis) *adod!* and *zounds!* There are whores: *bona*

---

* Times online, 27 October 2018.

roba, pullet, quean, convenient, jilt, the punning *wagtail* and *frigate* and the plain and simple *whore.* There is *foutre,* to fuck, and *fountain of love, commodity, altar of hymen, road* and *you know what* to represent the vagina while the penis is the *knick-knack, pistol* and *pestle.* Her lexis is not wholly sexual, there are such fools as *cabbage-head, jack-hold-my-staff* and *noddle,* but her plots depend on sexual and other dalliance and the words must suit.

There is also, for instance from act III of *The Rover,* the possibility of an elaborate burst of double entendre:

Will. Hark ye, where didst thou purchase that rich Canary we drank to-day? Tell me, that I may adore the Spigot, and sacrifice to the Butt: the Juice was divine, into which I must dip my Rosary, and then bless all things that I would have bold or fortunate.

Belv. Well, Sir, let's go take a Bottle, and hear the Story of your Success.

Fred. Would not *French* Wine do better?

And another, here, from *Sir Patient Fancy* (1678):

Knowell. Come, come, Ladies, we lose fleeting time, upon my Honour, we do; for, Madam, as I said, I have brought the Fiddles, and design to sacrifice the intire Evening to your Ladyship's Diversion.

Sir Credulous. Incomparable Lady, that was well thought on; Zoz, I long to be jigging.

Sir Patient. Fiddles, good Lord! why, what am I come to?—Madam, I take it, Sir *Patient Fancy's* Lady is not a proper Person to make one at immodest Revellings, and profane Masqueradings.

Where *fiddle* may be another form of *instrument*, i.e. a penis, and *jigging* one of the many forms of 'dance' that euphemised intercourse. And the following line warns, 'we ought not to offend a Brother that is weak, and consequently, a Sister.'

Like Behn, her contemporary and slightly younger rival Susannah Centlivre (a Whig to Behn's Tory) played the role of ventriloquist, dancing her male puppets (usually a pair of young men – one a shy virgin, the other more than a bit of a lad – pursuing the same young woman) around the stage. And like her there was much macho exclamation: *adod! agad! egad! faugh! gad! gemini! hang! lud! murder! my stars! oons! piss! wounds! zooks! zounds! 'sblood! 'sdeath!* In addition *ads* and *ods*, both meaning God and available for a variety of compounds, e.g. *odsfish! odsbud! odhsheart! odslife! odso! ods precious!* plus *the deuce!* the dismissive *pox take* ... and *a fig for* ... and finally *damn* and *damned*.

There were whores: the *baggage*, the *frigate*, the *heifer*, the *lady about-town*; all were *draggle-tailed* (the image of their garments – and their morals – dragging through the gutter). Attractive girls were *charmers* or *gimcracks* (with a possible play on *crack*, the vagina) and powerful women exerted a *petticoat government*. An indeterminate man was a *body* or a *jack*; a cheeky one a *sauce-box*, a tough one a *strapper*; an old one an *old boy* and a high Church clergyman a *high boy* or *high flyer*. Insults included the *cuff* (a surly old man), the *muckworm* (any unpleasant individual) and a trio of misers (*Jew*, *gripes* and *skinflint*). There was the usual ration of fools (*blockhead*, *gudgeon*) and peasants (*clodhopper*, *country put*) and they were *thick-skulled* and *clod-pated*. There was much gambling which gave *chuse*, *cog* and *bob* (all meaning to cheat); to *shake one's elbow* was to throw the dice, which if loaded were *doctors*; one might *nick* (win) if one didn't succumb to *ambs-ace* (bad luck). Failing dice there were the *devil's books* (playing cards). As for sex *man* and *tumble* meant to have intercourse, the *harbour of hope* was the vagina and *horns*, as ever, implied cuckoldry. A few random terms included the *leathern conveniency* (a coach), a *mittimus* (a dismissal), *twinklers* (the eyes), *see through a millstone* (to be especially perspicacious), *humming ale* (strong beer), an *Irish cry* (crocodile tears), *bardash* (a gay man) and *addition* (cosmetics).

Skipping forward, there are a few words in Jane Austen: *all to pieces* (bankrupt), *buzz* (chatter), *do for* (to ruin), *make ducks and drakes* (i.e. a mess), *fagged out* (exhausted), *hop* (a dance), *knowing* (fashionable), *rough it* (to live without comforts), *screw out of* (defraud), *scrubby* (vulgar), *set-out* (a table full of food), *sponge* (to be a parasite), *stick* (a dullard), *take-in* (a hoax), *touch up* (to jog someone's memory) and *warm* (suggestive). Not being a Janeite I was surprised to find these. Elizabeth Cleghorn Stevenson ('Mrs Gaskell'), at least in *Sylvia's Lovers* (1863), offers *lazyboots, moonlight flitting, give someone the bucket* (to jilt), *widow-bewitched* (a 'grass widow') and a couple more. Seven of Mary Ann Evans' ('George Eliot') titles produce a total of nearly sixty terms, including *geck* (a fool), *elbow grease, moony* (amorous), *plummy* (excellent), *not care a toss, pill* (anything unpleasant), *comb someone's hair* (to reprimand), *maw-worm* (a hypocrite), *prick-eared* (a term of abuse), *nincompoop, phiz* (the face), *pocket pistol* (a flask) and *nutcrackers* (false teeth). None of these represent the more squalid zones of slang, at times they dance along the border with colloquialism, but slang they remain.

Such literary *grandes dames* may be noted, quoted but, for these purposes, must also be dismissed. One word, even twenty, is not enough to render an individual a candidate for mention. I have doubtless overlooked some qualifiers, I have tried but have not succeeded in avoiding infelicitous choices, I can only offer a few representative figures from forty years of research and a bibliography of 10,000+ titles and hope that I have checked out at least a good selection of those who qualify.

Slang has various uses, among them the affirmation of a group, usually localised, but sometimes national. The work of Stella Maria Sarah Miles Franklin, writing as 'Miles Franklin', uses a substantial slang lexis in its stories of mid-nineteenth-century Australia. Notably in the novelised autobiography *My Brilliant Career*,* published in 1901 and set in the preceding decade, and the century-spanning family saga *All That Swagger*, published in 1936. Franklin offers around three hundred slang words and phrases. Many are in general use and used as widely in the UK street as in the Australian bush, but there is a solid core of Antipodean coinages. Like the Sydney *Bulletin*, launched in the 1880s and at its fiercely nationalistic peak when *My Brilliant Career* was published, Franklin seems to have identified emergent Australian identity with the nation's language, using English, but in new and inventive ways and often in the form of slang. It was perhaps not coincidental that the novel was backed by the poet and short-story writer Henry Lawson, one of the *Bulletin's* stalwarts and who wrote a preface to the first edition.

Of her Australian lexis we find *binghi* and *gin* (a Native Australian man and woman), *blob*, *woop-woop*, *mopoke* and *wombat* (all fools), *dingo* (a cheat, scoundrel, traitor or coward)

---

* A sequel *My Career Goes Bung* (a phrase meaning to die or fail, and first recorded in the *Bulletin* in October 1880) appeared in 1946; written in 1902–04 and revised in 1935 it was both a feminist tract and a thinly-disguised and less than flattering *roman à clef* featuring such eminences as the vastly popular poet A. B. 'Banjo' Paterson.

and *gabbletrap* (a silly chatterer). A *cow* (an objectionable thing or horrendous situation), *no chap* (second rate, presumably a variant on Anglo-Indian *no chop*), *shicer* (something worthless, originally a worked-out mine and original German's *sheisse*, shitty), *nark* (a bad temper or grudge), *have a derry on* (to be prejudiced against and punning on the lyrical refrain 'derry down' and slang's *down*), *full of* or *full up* (thoroughly displeased by, 'fed up with'), *perform* (to make a fuss, swear or get angry) and *jack up* (to refuse or resist). In the positive sphere one finds *straight goer* (an honest person), *good iron* (something admirable or trustworthy), *straight wire* (the honest truth) and *dinky-di* (first-rate). *Happy as Larry* suggests great satisfaction, and is generally attributed to the Australian boxer Larry Foley but has a possible source in Irish *learaire*, a lounger, an idler. Other terms include *Hay, Hell and Booligal*, a mythical place that is beyond all the bounds of civilisation and devoid of any proper comforts,* and the verb to *hat*, to live alone in remote area (perhaps from Alice's *mad hatter*); *bullock* (to perform heavy manual labour), *duff* (to steal livestock and thus *duffer*, a thief), *Chow* (a Chinese person), *bail up* (to trap or corner; used as an exclamation it was the bushrangers' homegrown equivalent to 'stand and deliver!'), *swag* (the pack carried by an itinerant or vagrant), *sly-grog* (a shop selling illicit liquor), *smoodge* (to ingratiate oneself), *mick off* (to leave), *cubby* (a small room), *slush-lamp* (a fat lamp, i.e. a wick placed in a dish of fat), *waddy* (a cudgel) and the exclamations *love . . .* or *stone the crows!*

---

* Booligal is a real place, situated within the Riverina area of New South Wales and known for its isolation and a variety of natural disasters including the rabbit plague of 1890; Hell has been identified with One Tree, on the stock route between Booligal and Hay, another small town; the phrase comes from an 1896 poem by Banjo Paterson (in part): 'We'd have to stop!' With bated breath / We prayed that both in life and death / Our fate in other lines might fall: / 'Oh, send us to our just reward / In Hay or Hell, but, gracious Lord, / Deliver us from Booligal!'

Another of Australia's pseudonymous woman writers was Ethel Florence Lindesay Richardson, who wrote as Henry Handel Richardson (1870–1946). Less prolific than Franklin, she too used the nation's homegrown slang to emphasise the national aspect of such works as *The Getting of Wisdom* (1910), which is based on her own days at boarding school, and the historical novel *Australia Felix* (1917).

If Franklin has the slush-lamp, Richardson offers the *Ballarat lantern* (a candle stuck in the neck of a bottle, the bottom of which has been knocked off); oaths include *by the bones of Davy Jones!* and there are reference to a *bullpuncher* (a bullock driver), a *tulip* (an attractive girl), *mopoke* (a fool), *nobbler* (a small measure of alcohol), *tucker* (food), *the logs* (a local gaol). She has *dished up* (exhausted), and *dollymop*, used in England for a promiscuous girl, but here as non-female insult: 'The Dolly mops! The skunks! The bushrangers! — Oh, damn 'em, damn 'em!'

Homegrown Australian slang lexicography began in 1882 with the *Sydney Slang Dictionary* (the *Australian Slang Dictionary* appeared in 1895). In 1916, as something of a sidebar, appeared *The Australian Comic Dictionary of Words and Phrases*. The cover claimed one 'Turner O. Lingo' as the author: the truth led to the feminist, suffragist, anti-conscriptionist, left-wing activist and author of novels, stories and poems, Mary Eliza Fullerton (1868–1946).

Born on a farm in the Gippsland (Victoria) bush, Fullerton quit the country and by the 1890s was in Melbourne, immersed in a wide range of socially progressive causes and pursuing a parallel career as a writer, sometimes under the pseudonym 'Alpenstock'. Her first collection of verses appeared as *Moods and Melodies* in 1908 and a childhood reminiscence, *Bark House*

Days in 1921. She wrote three novels under her own name – *Two Women* (1923), *The People of the Timber Belt* (1925) and *A Juno of the Bush* (1930) – plus two more under male pseudonyms. She was a friend of Miles Franklin and they sustained a twenty-year correspondence. In 1922 she moved to Britain and lived there with her companion and patron Mabel Singleton in Maresfield, Sussex until her death.

The Comic Dictionary presented a mix of standard and slang headwords with their consciously amusing, even aphoristic 'definitions' echoing the American Ambrose Bierce's *Devil's Dictionary* of a decade earlier. The introduction underlined its homegrown credentials: 'The endeavour has been to make this dictionary especially Australian in character.' The primary form is the pun and while some definitions – for instance that of *shickered* – do stand up, for the majority one would be best advised to prioritise the 'comic' over the 'dictionary.

Entries mixed standard English and slang. Typical entries ran:

'Cocky' —Name for the farmer when his wheat has brought him anything over six and six per bushel. Sometimes he is only a 'little cocky,' at other times 'pretty cocky;' all depends on the price.

Cobber — Cob, a nag with a cropped tail. Cobber, one who is never a nagger or whose tale ever requires to be cropped.

Debble-Debble — the ab-original golly-wog.

'It Isn't Cricket' — what you have to keep telling your old lady relative when you take her to a football match.

Ropable — what the man is when the animal isn't.

Shickered — liquored.

Tinned Dog — bushman's pate de fois gras.

Wallaby (on the) — refers to the custom that prevails in Australia of travelling on a wallaby; a favourite pastime with persons who cannot afford a horse.

Yarra Banker— usually a man who stands on a soap box telling the great unwashed how 'dirty' the rich man is.

The flow has not dried. The Melbourne journalist Katherine Susannah Prichard (1883–1969) wrote a number of novels with a heavy slang presence, notably *Coonardoo* (1929), *Haxby's Circus* (1930), *Winged Seeds* (1950) and *Working Bullocks* (1926). Prichard, who would go on to become a co-founder of the Australian Communist party, broke into fiction when in 1915 she won a writing prize of £250 for her first novel, *Pioneers*. In its celebratory report the *Launceston Examiner** obviously saw her as the ideal 'lady writer': she was

a creditable and earnest pen worker, a philanthropist, a humanitarian, a reader of strange men, and a helper of lame dogs of every nationality over every possible kind of domestic stile. In a swathing of brownness, demure-eyed, and tender, she seeks out the little, unwashed city children, and finds in them an excuse for her shrinking bank balance. In the mothers of the generations of little unwashed babies she gets a hearing for her marvellous philosophy. The spirit to 'buck up—because it is more reasonable and easier than being overthrown—is the teaching she supplies. That every woman, as well as man, should be a free-breathing, thinking, self-asserting soul is a creed that helps her to help the down-trodden ones.

* *Examiner* (Launceston, Tasmania), 3 April 1915, p.2/5.

In 1982, Nancy Keesing, a former speech-writer for prime minister Paul Keating and well-established 'words person', published *Lily on the Dustbin*, a mix of narrative and lexicography which focused on 'The Slang of Australian Women and Families'. The title itself is slang, a harsher version of the age-old *wallflower*, and means a girl who has been stood up, or, perhaps and, is badly over-dressed. The book was sourced from a wide range of correspondents, drawn in by Keesing's appeal on her radio show. What she compiled was a wide range of domestic slang, a.k.a. 'sheilaspeak' or 'family speak', a vocabulary that in her opinion was rarely acknowledged by lexicographers. Domestic suggests a gentler world than that delineated by 'male' or mainstream slang. If Keesing's correspondents were offering genuine material, it also seems to opt for the metaphor and the phrase: 'he's tight as a mouse's ear' (very mean), 'slow as a wet washday', 'runs like a heavy goat', 'a hand like a foot and a foot-like a hand and a face like a honey-doodle', 'kiddlywinks knee-high to a grasshopper', 'hair like a birch broom in a fit', 'wouldn't it rot your socks'. To what extent these qualify as what is usually considered 'slang' may be debatable. Linguistic domesticity is perhaps characterised by what can be seen as a variation of hoary old saws, issued by the family's matriarch. Nor are all her entries 'sheila-specific'. 'Mad as a meat ax', 'on for young and old', 'I could eat the bum out of an elephant' and 'rushing around like a one-armed fiddler with the itch' are wholly ungendered.

Most interesting are what, at the time of the book's writing, were her seeming discoveries. Among them *after dinner mint* (a woman who is willing to swap sex for material favours but not cash), *free traders* ('knee-length calico pants trimmed with lace but, instead of a front and back seam, [they] were open from the front waist to the back waist, and fastened around the waist by long tapes. It meant you could use the toilet without pulling your pants down'), *hubcap biter* (a woman who chooses the men she goes after on the basis of their cars), *mow the lawn* (to shave one's legs), *mohair knickers* (extremely dense female pubic hair), *Mediterranean back* or *gut-ache* (a supposedly fake illness or incapacity, used to justify malingering, apparently by Italians, Greeks, Yugoslavs and others seen as lazier than 'white' Australians), *spackle-filler* (cosmetics, from a compound used by builders), to *feel like sixpennorth of God help us* (to feel miserable, and thus a weakling) and *skippy* (a white child, from the TV series *Skippy, the Bush Kangaroo*; the word is one of the few examples of racism directed at rather than by the dominant culture).

More group affirmation comes from America's Zora Neale Hurston whose literary output ranges from memoirs of her own work as an anthropologist, *Mules and Men* (1935), such novels as *Jonah's Gourd Vine* (1934) and *Their Eyes Were Watching God* (1937) and a wide range of essays focusing on African American life and folklore. Her works are permeated with slang, over five hundred terms; in 1942 she created a piece of pure ventriloquy, *A Story in Harlem Slang*, in which she abandoned her usual back-country, Southern world for the big city heart of black America, and offered, with attendant glossary, a lengthy dialogue between two Harlem sports. The density of terms runs in the age-old tradition of the animated glossaries created by a number of writers seeking after street authenticity, in this case the hip lexis was most likely 'borrowed' from recent 'jive' dictionaries assembled by such as the bandleader Cab Calloway, but the effect is undiminished.

Hurston was responsible for bringing nearly two hundred slang terms to print for the first time (among them *breath-and-britches*, self-promoting, a variant on *all mouth and trousers*, *gum-beater*, a chatterer, *jackleg*, an itinerant preacher, *puzzlegut*, a large stomach, *rusty-dusty*, the buttocks, *shoo-shoo*, to whisper, *tiddy-umpty*, completely), but it is possibly in the non-fiction *Mules and Men* (1935), where she was transcribing rather than fictionalising, that her lexis is most interesting.

Among the slang terms that the book offers are *astorperious* (arrogant, based on the doyenne of New York society, Mrs Astor), *Aunt Hagar's children* (blacks, from *Hagar* the Egyptian, wife of Abraham and mother of Ishmael), *bee-luther-hatchee*, *ginny gall*, *west hell* and *zar* (all meaning a 'far away place'), *book-ity-book* (to run off, echoic of the sound of shoes slapping on the ground), *bookoo* (talk loudly, from French *beaucoup*, a lot), *eat acorns* (to suffer humiliation), *fade* (to respond, from poker imagery), *fast alec* (a speedy person), *fat around the heart* (cowardly), *frail eel* (a pretty woman), *froe* (a plantation-era pocket knife), *git-fiddle* (a guitar), *goozle* (the throat), *gospel bird* (a chicken, from the tradition of treating itinerant preachers to a chicken dinner), *high brown* (mixed race; the *Story in Harlem Slang* offers a full colour palette: *high yaller*, *yaller*, *high brown*, *vaseline brown*, *seal brown*, *low brown* and *dark brown*).

Kaiser baby (of a woman, to leave home and return married to a successful, wealthy – and usually white – husband*), *little britches* (the point of three in craps dice), *make someone's love come down* (come to orgasm), *long house* (a brothel), *don't pay no rabbit* (pay no more attention than one would a rabbit jumping a fence), *put on roll* (fight), *shake baby* (a dress that is tight across

---

* The 'real' *Kaiser baby* was the first realistic baby doll, manufactured by the German firm of Kammer & Reinhardt. It was supposed to be modelled on one of kaiser Wilhelm II's six sons. Given that such 'babies' were invariably male, it is hard to see quite how the slang term emerged, though the new bride was presumably her husband's 'baby doll'.

the hips and has a short, full skirt), *shake one's shirt* (to make an effort, to 'get stuck in'), *skillet blonde* (a very dark-skinned person), *spread one's jenk* (to celebrate, to have sex, perhaps from *high jinks*), *stump knocker* (travelling amateur preacher) and *toe party* (a party game whereby all the women present line up behind a sheet with nothing visible but their toes. The men then take turns to choose their preferred toes and pair off accordingly).

The delights of what the critic Sam Leith has termed 'the weaponization of cultural sanctimony' are irresistible to the Mrs Grundies (actual gender no bar to membership) who hope to rule the modern world.[*]

Those whose existence pivots on the extent to which they can proclaim themselves offended, and in so doing interfere in the existence of those around them, are less interested in a logical critique than in a critique pure and simple. Thus the birth of a new form of literary entertainment, the novel, was at least part-responsible, like most novelty, for the inspiration of moral disapproval. The checkmark, as so often in matters moral, was the supposed effect on women, especially the young. It was either too sensational for young women or too sentimental for any but young women. Either way it lacked gravitas and thus respectability.

Slang does not do sentiment, but it is dominated by various expressions of sensation. For this, in the context of literature, or at least fiction (literature's more popular relation), one must wait – other than as regards the subset known as 'Gothic' – until the mid-nineteenth century. The term sensation novel

---

[*] Sam Leith 'Call yourelf well-read?' *unherd.com* 2 May 2019.

(and its necessary accomplice the sensation novelist) appeared in the 1850s and the first recorded examples of either term so far are both American. It was, as defined by the *OED*, 'a novel written to provoke a strong emotional response in the reader, featuring material which is lurid, shocking, or thrilling.' It was the younger cousin to its immediate predecessor, the 'Newgate novel', which focused one hundred percent on crime (Newgate being Britain's most notorious prison, and until they retreated behind closed doors in 1868 site of the most sensational public hangings), and it was assumed took its audience from men. It was a cut, if a thin one, above the equally popular, but far cheaper, penny dreadful, a form of cheap, lurid story that did exactly what was proclaimed on the packaging. The canonical Newgate novels, by authors such as Harrison Ainsworth and Edward Bulwer Lytton,* generally concentrated on the quasi-fictional exploits of popular villains, such as the highwayman Dick Turpin and the robber and multiple prison escapee Jack Sheppard, but in one case, Lytton's *Eugene Aram* (1832) focused on a notorious killer who, despite also having committed his crime many years earlier, had not been overlaid with the patina of public affection. This book above all led the outcry against such tales. The Newgate genre was that of the 'ripping yarn' of such late-century boys favourites as Rider Haggard or G.A. Henty, but in one way at least it also prefigured modernity: such tales did not merely place villains at the heart of the plot and thus make them anti-heroes, but like *romans* and *films noir*, in accepting moral ambiguities the author refused to take on the black and white dichotomy of 'goodies' and 'baddies'.

* Some would suggest (though not its author who protested vehemently against the charge), that *Oliver Twist* qualified as a volume of the same micro-library.

Whether 'Newgate' or 'sensation', the emotions that were indulged were far from wholesome or earnest, that grim, repressive duo that, at least as professed in public, so constrained so much of Victorian life, and given the adjectives that its description favoured, it was a natural home for slang. Lytton and Ainsworth each gave readers around 350 terms, though unlike Dickens' use of such language in *Oliver Twist*, one could see the joins, and both had very obviously dipped into the most recent slang dictionary.[*]

The sensation novel was similarly aimed foursquare at twitching the senses, but in this case the writers and the audience were female.

Mary Elizabeth Braddon (1835–1915), known as M.E. Braddon or Mrs Braddon (though she was in fact Mrs Maxwell), was among the queens, if not, other than her contemporary Rhoda Broughton, the queen of the genre. Her life as often remarked, was in itself fit for a plot. Quitting respectable schooling for life as a jobbing teenage actress on the provincial stage when her single mother (her charming but dissolute father – 'no-one's enemy but his own' – long disappeared) was hard put for cash, moving on from that thanks to the generosity of a mysterious benefactor (a rich, older Yorkshire gent) that allowed her to write, honing her craft via immersion in the best-selling but lowly esteemed world of penny dreadfuls, abandoning the patron and his hopes of marriage when she met and married Mr Right (albeit already bigamously married and with his original wife locked up in an asylum) who had appeared in the form of a publisher, scoring a huge hit with her fifth novel *Lady Audley's*

---

* Most likely the sporting journalist Pierce Egan's 1823 revision of Francis Grose's *Classical Dictionary of the Vulgar Tongue* (1785). This was long outdated, but served very well for eighteenth-century tales.

Secret (1862) and . . . never looking back. There would be eighty novels in all, many of them 'sensations' but Braddon, like a prototype Simenon or Graham Greene, mixed those tales with more serious fictions.

Everyone who was anyone admired her: Dickens (whose style she was not above mimicking), Thackeray, Charles Reade, Willkie Collins (whose *Woman in White* was bracketed with the 'sensations') and later R.L. Stevenson, Tennyson, George Moore, Henry James, Ford Madox Ford and Arnold Bennett: all the Victorian and Edwardian heavies. There were also theatricals such as Squire Bancroft and painters including W.G. Frith. These at least were the men. Her intimates were often women, but as for her professional peers, she seems to have assessed rather than socialised with them. France's Georges Sand was 'spooney when virtuous and unnecessarily immoral at other times', Fanny Burney was rejected as a childhood 'bugbear',* Charlotte Brontë rated as 'the only *genius* the weaker sex can point to in literature' (though her friend Lytton credited Braddon with a genius of her own) and George Eliot was 'somewhat passionless' though acknowledged as 'a fine mind cultured to the highest point'. They were probably unmoved; Mrs Braddon, with her vast popular audience, was doubtless seen, at very best, as a 'guilty pleasure'.

Serialising her work in a variety of magazines, notably the *Temple Bar* (owned by her husband John Maxwell), she came to know the raffish, competitive world of British bohemia's journalistic branch, notably the larger-than-life George Augustus Sala, one of Dickens' leading acolytes. As editor of her own magazine, the *Belgravia*, she took her place in what was still

---

* Burney used her own micro-lexis of slang in *Evelina* (1778): *flummer*, to flatter, *buck*, a rake, *take-in*, a con trick, *trim*, to scold, *Frog*, a Frenchman and half a dozen others.

physically as well as figuratively Fleet Street. She was an especial friend of Edward Bulwer-Lytton, arguably her equivalent in the world of Newgate melodramas. If Braddon, in *Vixen* (1879), would come up with the Wildean declaration, still a perfect definition of Victorian social pretension, 'It is worse than a crime, Violet, it is an impropriety', then it was her friend, forty years earlier in *Paul Clifford*, who had given readers the immortal 'It was a dark and stormy night; the rain fell in torrents, except at occasional intervals, when it was checked by a violent gust of wind which swept up the streets (for it is in London that our scene lies), rattling along the housetops, and fiercely agitating the scanty flame of the lamps that struggled against the darkness.'

All of which name-dropping underlines Mrs Braddon's social acceptability, but casts little light on her real importance. Reading her works well over a century on, she comes across as a remarkable social commentator. The barbs are lightly camouflaged – she needed in the end to sell and the reading public always wanted comfort, even as she titillated their sensations with those popular staples: bigamy, murder and arson – but they are there. There is a fine irony pervading her asides, and her direct descriptions. Joining the theatre as a sixteen-year-old suddenly forced to face life stripped of its comfortable assumptions doubtless dragged her into more challenging realities than might have been encountered had she trodden the path ordained by her birth: respectability, marriage and motherhood. In the event, whether in penny dreadfuls, sensations or in more seriously intended work, she wields a fine-honed and deep-cutting razor.

She also had a sense of humour, always at a premium amidst the proclaimed earnestness of the high Victorians. In *The Doctor's Wife* (1864), her Englished, i.e. severely bowdlerised, remake of

Flaubert's 'immoral' *Madame Bovary*, she introduced the hack writer Sigismund Smith (who 'enjoyed an immense popularity among the classes who like their literature as they like their tobacco – strong'), who should have been a Byronic hero but was in fact the mildest-mannered of young scribes, 'with perennial ink smudges upon his face'. Through Smith she teased herself, typically in 'his' professional credo: 'The best thing you can do, if you haven't got ideas of your own, is to steal other people's ideas in an impartial manner.'

The humour could be pleasingly gruesome. Writing to the journalist Edmond Yates in 1863, she proposed 'a splendid novel' that could be written 'on a protracted search for the missing members of a murdered man, dividing the tale not into *books*, but *bits*! BIT THE FIRST: the leg in the grey stocking found at Deptford. BIT THE SECOND: The white and the onyx ring with half an initial letter (unknown) and crest, skull with a coronet, found in an Alpine *crevasse*!'

At the same time Braddon could be startlingly radical. Everybody's arse, as Lenny Bruce would one day put it, was up for grabs. She took apart the canting self-satisfaction of the evangelicals, dismissed upper-class snobbery and the vacuity of 'empty, drawing-room life', and noted county gentry who love money but hate what she euphemised as 'the money-lender'.* In *Rough Justice* (1898) she offers a self-promoting professional philanthropist, demanding the abolition of 'everything that makes up the old fashioned people's idea of England and to create a new England, without an established Church, or a

---

* Braddon's own take on 'money-lenders' was a good deal more nuanced than, say, that of Dickens or the outright and stereotyping anti-semitism of many canonical authors. Tracing their appearances in her work specialists have noted that her portrayal of Jews is a valuable mirror of real life, in which the position of Anglo-Jewry both changed and improved as the century passed.

House of Peers or a great capitalist and possibly without a beer-shop along ten miles of dusty road'. He is, perhaps inevitably, her murderer.

As for sex, a Victorian bugbear far greater than any of her problems with Miss Burney, she refused to kowtow to propriety. Her own experiences in the theatre may have helped, and she learned from the realism of Émile Zola, whose novels (even in much-gelded translations) were so terrifying to Britons that their publisher would end up in prison. In *Phantom Fortune* (1883), a book where Zola's influence is notable, the heroine Lesbia's chaperone describes a French play, *La Demi-monde*, as 'rather strong meat for babes' but Braddon's fiction sees that off fast: 'Why should a young lady be forbidden to see a fine play because there are some hard and bitter truths in it? Lesbia sees Madame d'Ange and all her sisterhood in the Park and about London every day of her life.* Why should she not see them on the stage, and hear their history, and understand how cruel their fate is, and learn to pity them if she can? I really think this play is a lesson in Christian charity.'

As suggested by her biographer Robert Lee Wolff (*Sensational Victorian*, 1979) she achieved a far-from-simple double-appeal. On the one hand she gave her middle-class, church-ridden audiences what they wanted: a 'happy' ending in which those they had condemned as 'bad' were duly punished and those they fêted as 'good' received their condign reward. On the other, cutting an eye in the direction of her more sophisticated readers, and suggests Wolff, to posterity, she shared the joke: Victorian morality, so beloved of a thousand canting hypocrites (in vestments, gaiters or otherwise), was a sham. Real life was a good

---

* London's *grandes horizontales* rode openly in Rotten Row, a fashionable ride in Hyde Park.

deal more interesting and a good way from cultural provincial-ism's black and white.

To what extent her readers were aware of it, many, often crit-ics, failed to see the joke. Between what was suspected (possibly rightly) to have been the author's own rackety private life (setting aside those years on stage and all that they implied), the blood-and-thunder penny dreadfuls that represent her literary juve-nilia, and her willingness (in which she was far from alone) to skate a little close to unabashed plagiarism when it came to 'adapting' a variety of French originals, she made an easy target. The attacks, whether literary or *ad feminam*, hurt. Fortunately she had friends, best of all George Augustus Sala.

Writing in her magazine *Belgravia* on 'The Cant of Modern Criticism' in November 1867 he saw off the carping whingers. Noting that English literature was far from the wholesome, cleanly edifice they claimed, and dismissing their attacks on Braddon as 'unjust, mischievous and disingenuous', he dismissed that earlier age of voluntary self-infantilism: 'We men and women . . . want novels about That which Is . . . We don't want pap or spoon-meat or milk-and-water or curds-and-whey or Robb's biscuits,* or boiled whiting, or cold boiled beef without salt. We want meat; and this is a strong age, and we can digest it.'

The critics would not disappear, but for the most part they would shut up. Mrs Braddon, meanwhile, continued to write.

That Mrs Braddon permitted slang an entry into her books is hardly surprising. Slang too prefers 'That which Is' and is unim-pressed by what Michael Sadleir termed 'a smug insistence on maidenly virtue, manly continence, and general irreproachable

---

* A staple of contemporary infant feeding; they were supposedly easily digestible by the very young.

domesticity [that] was hopelessly at odds with . . . actuality'.*
She had no especial interest in recording the register, simply
using it for its usual role of authenticity in one social sphere or
another. Nonetheless she does seem to have been the first to put
a few terms into print. *Baby* (a man, e.g. 'this baby'), *barnacle* (a
parasite), to *chuck* (to end an affair), *jolly* (a thrill or pleasure), to
jump on (to attack, whether literal or figurative), *lardy-dardy*
(affected), *muddle* (to make oneself drunk), *off one's nut* (very
eccentric, insane), *rattle* (to hit), *rat-trap* (a shabby or ramshackle
building), *roof* (the head), *smash* (a heavy blow), *muchly* (as in
'thank you muchly', predecessor to 'ta . . .') and she seems to be
the first to record *the thick* (in this case asylum coffee, but used
of any drink with a dense consistency, e.g. porter, tea or coffee).

Of the eighty novels, the slangiest seems to have been *The
Trail of the Serpent* (1860, originally *Three Times Dead*) sporting
a suitably lurid plot that depended on violence, bigamy and a
visit to the locked ward. It has also, one candidate among a
number, been cited as the first British detective novel (featuring
as it does the need of its hero to prove his innocence of murder).
On the other hand it predates her creation of an actual detective,
Faunce, who debuted in the much later *Rough Justice* (1898).

The Trail again gives us nothing special, but it is home to a
steady flow. As well as baby, a man can be a *cove* and the indeterminate *thingamy*, he can be a *knowing card*, a *downy one* or a *rum
'un* (sophisticated), a *bad lot* (villain) and a *nice lot* (an epitome,
not always positive). A *barnacle* is a parasite, i.e. someone 'hard
to shake off' and a *bird* a prisoner who may have lurked in *Alsatia*
(albeit even if sited in provincial, fictional 'Slopperton' rather
than London where the real thing, an officially licensed criminal

---

* M. Sadleir, 'Mary Elizabeth Braddon', *Things Past* (1944), p.88.

sanctuary, had once been found, but still 'a refuge for crime and destitution') but has been *blown* (betrayed), and being unable to *walk his chalks, cut and run, bolt* or *tumble up* (all to move speedily away) is now arrested for *boning* (theft) and incarcerated in the *stone jug*.

Drink plays the inevitable role: *dry* (in need of a drink), *blind* (drunk) and the *blue devils* (delirium tremens) with their knock-on effect, insanity, typified as a *loose slate in the roof, garret, upper storey, knowledge-box* or *nut*. So too does money, a *bob* (a shilling) and a *tanner* (sixpence) and conversation, *palaver, jaw, chaff* and to *cut up*. Other terms in *The Trail* include the exclamations *egad!* and *lord love you!, scrag* (to hang), *cat* (a spiteful, malicious woman), *in chancery* (trapped), *blow a clou*d (smoke a pipe or cigar), *fall in with* (associate with), *Brother Jonathan* (an American), *keep one's pecker up* (to stay cheerful), *bunch of fives* (a fist), *rattle* (to hit) and *smasher* (a hard hitter).

Of other slang that turns up elsewhere in her work, some of the more interesting were a couple from the theatre: *gorger* (the manager) and *ben* (a benefit night). Others include *this bangs Banagher* (stating a superlative), *bow-wow* (a lover who 'yaps'), *counter-jumper* (an arriviste), *big drink* (the Atlantic), *drum* (a party) and the punning extension *kettledrum* a tea party, where the tea was *catlap, old hunks* (a miser), *dog's nose* (a drink that mixes gin and beer warmed), *couple-beggar* (a clergyman), *jockey* (to trick), *lubberly* (unsophisticated, rural), *bosh* (to tease), *hempen necklace* (the hangman's noose), the *marrowbone stage* (walking), *chummage* (a payment made to one's cellmates by a new arrival in a prison) and a glance to America with *catawampously* and *absquatulated*.

Sensation – whether in the form of fiction or 'fact' – was known in the States. Sufficiently well to be decried by one writer as 'the parent, of, at least, one-third of the sin of the day. Directly or indirectly it is dragging down the pure, the innocent, the beautiful, and the brave into the slime, the degradation and the corruption of the lowest haunts of infamy."* However its predominant creators seem to have been men. It flourished in mid-century and its driving argument was that the city was of itself sensational and could be exploited as such. There were Asa Green's *A Glance at New York* (1837), G.G. Foster's *New York in Slices* (1849) and *New York by Gas-Light* (1856); James D. Mccabe's *New York by Sunlight and Gaslight* (1862), *The Secrets of the Great City* (1868) and *Lights and Shadows of New York Life* (1872). Edward Z. Judson introduced *The G'hals of New York* in 1850 and the 'Members of the New York Press' added *The Night Side of New York* in 1866. All these were on the traditional titillation-cum-morality pattern, and larded themselves with 'authentic' slang to make sure their readers appreciated their insider expertise. Less worried about morality were the authors of sensationalist fiction whose yellow-backed works – the long-form version of the equally ribald penny papers – poured from the new Hoe cylinder presses, introduced in 1832.

Of these authors two stand out: George Lippard the pioneer and George Thompson the exploiter. Lippard's *The Quaker City; or, The Monks of Monk Hall: A Romance of Philadelphia Life, Mystery, and Crime*, set the pattern for subsequent fictionalised exposés of the city's evils. His tale of upper-class depravity and excess was first serialised then published as a novel in 1845 and ran to twenty-seven editions. Lippard continued the genre, showcasing the social injustices of urban life in *The Empire City* (1849), *Memoirs of a Preacher* (1849), and *New York: Its Upper*

---

* A. V. Petit, quoted in Barton & Huston (eds), *Transatlantic Sensations* (2016), p.10.

Ten and Lower Million (1853). George Thompson, writing in
the 1850s, took things even further, mixing thinly veiled pornography (with constant references to nymphomania, paedophilia,
incest, gay sex, miscegenation and group sex), true-crime stories
and a fascination with the bizarre in best-selling titles such as
*Venus in Boston; City Crimes; New York Life; The Gay Girls of New
York;* and *The Mysteries of Bond-Street*. Based among the upper
classes, Lippard's work resisted slang; George Thompson's books
were shot through with it.

Women were offered other things. Or rather grabbed them
with both hands. Journalism, hitherto a male preserve outside
the predictable concerns of the 'women's section', was invaded
by the 'stunt girl', a young, purportedly respectable woman who
thrust herself, at her editor's behest and always undercover, into
a variety of challenging environments. This was not what many
advocates of 'female respectability' felt should happen. In the
first place much of the work went on late at night, in the second,
the 'girl reporter' might have to venture into unsuitable places,
finally, working with men meant that she had to act like a man:
journalism was 'not an occupation which tends to the development of feminine graces'.*

None of which stood in the way of the 'stunt girls'. The exem-
plar was Nellie Bly. In 1887, despite a succession of knockbacks
from male editors, Bly suggested a new take to the man at the
New York World. She would travel to Europe and come back in
steerage class, i.e. surrounded by those huddled masses who,
quitting their 'old countries' for whatever reason, were queuing
to gain a foothold on the golden streets of the New World. This
pitch was rejected too – she was too young, too inexperienced;

---

* Quoted in *Victorian Periodicals Review* vol. XXV (1992), p.109/2.

the expenses would be too high – but the *World* had a counter-suggestion: why didn't Ms Bly fake it as a loony and get herself locked up inside the notoriously wretched, filthy wards of the insane asylum on Blackwell's Island. What followed was her series with its blunt title 'Ten Days in a Madhouse', recounting the adventures of one 'Nellie Brown' from committal to release. A vast success, it spawned follow-ups such as 'The Girls Who Make Boxes: Nellie Bly tells How It Feels to be a White Slave' (in a non-sexual sense – the sexual trafficking sense had emerged around 1870 – though her report made it clear that managerial groping long predated #metoo), 'Visiting the Dispensaries: Nelly [*sic*] Bly Narrowly Escapes Having Her Tonsils Amputated' (and again seems to have fended off a male's straying hands), 'Nellie Bly in Pullman: She Visits the Homes of Poverty in the "Model Workingman's Town"'. It also made room for Bly's rivals: Ada Patterson 'the Nellie Bly of the West'; 'Annie Laurie' (real name Winifred Black) or, 'Nell Nelson' (actually Nell Cusack) who had, among other topics, her own brand of 'white slaves': the makers of cigarettes. Unfortunately, projecting their image of 'middle-class white girl in possible sexual peril amidst the ravening proles', they eschewed the language of those they encountered. The white slaves provide no slang, nor do the inmates of the Island.

The stunt girls did not cross the Atlantic nor were they recreated by British newspapers. High-minded lady slummers, 'missionaries' both literal and figurative, did descend on the poverty-stricken East End, but they wished to preach, not listen, and certainly wrote no works of interest. There is, however, an exception: the Anglo-Indian journalist Olive Christian Malvery (born in Lahore in 1871) who arrived in the UK in 1900 and in 1904 parlayed her part-time career as a short-story writer into a series for *Pearsons* magazine. Malvery was to disguise herself in a variety of roles, each representing a badly-paid occupation: street singer, street peddler, factory girl, shop girl, costermonger, waitress and barmaid. The series was titled 'The Heart of All Things' and was republished as a book, *The Soul Market*, in 1907. The book made enough for Malvery to build two shelters for London's homeless women. She characterised her text as 'the first book that roused the public to shame and sympathy' and would claim that it had inspired 'a great many missions . . . founded by people who were stirred by that book'. She invited one thousand working girls to her wedding (to an American diplomat) and appointed two costermonger girls from Hoxton, still one of London's poorest areas with its gentrification a good century in the future, to be her bridesmaids.

The Soul Market is slangy, although the lexis is that of the girls and women she met, rather than her own which remains the standard English of the over-viewing narrator. They represent the Cockney slang of the era. Neither 'male' nor 'female', it is the language spoken by London's East End working class.

It will not be surprising that her primary group of terms devolved upon crime. A *head* was a thief, as she claimed, as were a *bent* and a *hock*, yet there remain some questions about the latter pair. As recorded by Malvery, 'I learned much of the habits of our neighbours. Of course many things that she told me would be utterly impossible to relate, and can only here be hinted at. From her I learned that most of the men in the house were "hocks" or "dead bents,"as she called common thieves.' The problem being that all other examples of *bent* and *hock* when describing an individual make it clear that both terms mean 'a homosexual'. Either Malvery had the wool pulled over her eyes, or she preferred to pull it over those of her readers. We still don't know.

Other criminal terms included *box-lifting* (robbing a till), *toby-lifting* (luggage stealing at railway stations), *mugging a red* (stealing a gold watch), *pinching a leather* (stealing a wallet), *working the boards* (practising the three-card trick) and *flying a kite* (passing a bad cheque). She included to *pole* (to steal), *do a burst* (to rob by a break-in) and *weed* (to steal money, usually from some form of 'kitty'). To *hold up*, *ramp* or *bounce* all meant to cheat and a *tale-pitcher* was a 'story teller', i.e. a confidence trickster; they would all pursue *mugs* (suckers). Other villains included the *blacksmith* (a forger) and *smasher* (who passed counterfeit money) and the *shicer* (a racecourse swindler). To *chive* was to stab and a *stretch* a year in prison. The law was represented by the *flat* (from *flatfoot*) and the *rozzer* (from Romani *roozlo*) and the *split* (a detective, from *split*, to betray).

After villainy, street entertainers and beggars. The former, all singers, might be *buskers*, *chanters* and *griddlers* (or *needy grid-dlers*). These produced the verbs *busk* and *chant*; they might be accompanied on the *dominoes*, a piano. A popular pose was that of the *grizzler* (a beggar who pretends blindness or physical disa-bility). After the show the entertainer passed round the hat, known as *nobbing*, and hoped for plenty of *oof* (money) for the *lead* (the collection). If that failed then there was the *big house* or *spike* (both the workhouse; the former better known as a prison in America, the latter apparently from its lack of comfort), where inmates were known as *casuals* (from casual pauper). If there was some money to spare, then there was the *kiphouse* (a cheap lodg-ing house).

Food and drink could both be *muck* (such food being presum-ably near-inedible), but one might obtain *mud* (pea soup), *thick* (coffee), a *wally* (a pickled cucumber), *hokey-pokey* (ice-cream as sold in street*) and a *two-eyed steak* (a herring). Drink came from the *carsey* (public house, from Italian *casa*, a house) and too much made you *bug-proof* (in a drunken stupor, i.e. so drunk that you no longer felt the bed bugs biting).

Other terms included *look slippy!* (hurry up!), *hop it!* (go away!), *all my eye* (a dismissive phrase and usually coupled with 'and Betty Martin' – neither version has permitted a concrete etymology), *fever cart* (an ambulance), *knocked out* (physically run down), *pennyhop* (a cheap dance), *oner* (a remarkable individual), *penny shocker* (a cheap 'sensation' magazine, usually known as a *pennydreadful*), a *bummaree* (a fish porter, specifically at Billingsgate market) and *the water* (the river Thames).

Back in the States we are no better served by the stunt girls' contemporaries: the 'sob sisters'. These, not to be confused with the agony aunts,[†] rose to fame during the much-followed trial in January 1907 of celebrity architect and serial womaniser Stanford White, murdered by the millionaire Harry Kendall Thaw after Thaw took exception to White's relationship with his wife, Evelyn Nesbit. The murder took place during the première of the satisfyingly named *Mam'zelle Champagne* at Madison Square Garden. As the song 'I Could love a Million Girls' filled the auditorium, the psychotically jealous Thaw, shouting 'You've ruined my life!', shot White dead. Ms Nesbit was young and beautiful, 'a lily broken on a stalk' as one of the sisters would

---

* Such ices were sold by Italians, sometimes doubling as organ-grinders, at one penny or a halfpenny each, but despite the popular belief, it does not come from Italian *o chepoco!* 'o how little!'; more likely is a link to another use of hokey-pokey, meaning trickery i.e. the passing off of cheap versions of superior products.

† The role existed from at least the 1930s, though the teasing job-title emerged in the 1950s and Nathaniel West's *Miss Lonelyhearts*, published in 1933, suggests origins a decade earlier. The original *agony column* arrived in the mid-nineteenth century, it was that section of a newspaper dedicated to special advertisements, particularly those for missing relatives or friends, and thus filled with personal agony.

describe her; she was inevitably the focus of the trial. She delivered her frank testimony seemingly unaffected by any need to play the innocent and recounted tales of a mirrored room and a red velvet swing and the debauchery that took place therein (that said, the then sixteen-year-old Nesbit explained that she had, of course, fainted before succumbing to White's wicked embrace: M.E. Braddon, one suspects, would have loved it).*

The press, spearheaded by the sensationalist Hearst papers which labelled it (enthusiastically if perhaps prematurely) 'the trial of the century', realised that their usual gang of male crime reporters – hard-drinking, hard-smoking, pretty much devoid of empathy with either plaintiff or defendant – were not up to the job. Instead they set their women reporters – more used to weddings or fashion shows and isolated in what was known to the newsroom as the 'hen coop' – on the case. Nicknamed the 'sob sisters' aka the 'pity patrol', the best-known was probably 'Dorothy Dix' (Elizabeth Gilmer), they duly milked the tale, driving up daily sales with a mix of mawkish sentimentality, and melodramatic titillation (hard on the hints, more restrained on the detail). All of which elicited heightened language; the crime may have been sordid (those who heard the testimony, it was suggested, might forever carry a 'permanent polluting stamp'†), but there was no need for the language to suggest the lower depths.

If we want to find slang in American journalism and with female by-lines, it is necessary to move on a decade or two. To a

---

* She also gave the court accounts of dog whips and drug-dripping syringes; the judge attempted to ban women spectators, women spectators were unimpressed and crowded in anyway; after the trial she was picked up by vaudeville, earning $80,000 for her appearances on stage.
† *N.Y. Evening World*, 22 February 1907, quoted in Jean Marie Lutes *Front Page Girls* (2006), p.83.

group of women, who with a fine sense of punning, have been named the 'Mob Sisters', the credit for which must go to Beth Fantaskey Kaszuba, whose PhD thesis on 'women reporting on crime in Prohibition-era Chicago' (2013) coined and incorporated the name.

Ms Kaszuba chose five female journalists, all working for the 1920s *Chicago Tribune* who were deputed to report on gangland when the 'Roaring Twenties' were at their height. They were:

Genevieve Forbes Herrick, whose byline was a fixture on the paper's front page throughout the Roaring Twenties;

Maurine Watkins, who drew upon her work as a crime reporter to write the enduring social satire Chicago;

Kathleen McLaughlin, a confidante of mobsters whose crime reportage in Chicago earned her a coveted spot in *The New York Times*'s once exclusively male newsroom;

Leola Allard, who covered Chicago's juvenile and domestic courts, reporting on crimes ranging from spousal abuse to kidnapping;

Maureen McKernan, whose clear-thinking, no-nonsense coverage of crime for the *Tribune* begins to move closer to the modern ideal of objective, factual reporting.

All, she suggests, shared the 'three characteristics that defined the mob sister style: use of sarcastic humor; a pervasive cynicism; and the employment of popular, sometimes coarse, slang'.

This slang came naturally with the territory: reporting on Twenties gangland turned papers like the *Tribune* into adjuncts of the burgeoning world of pulp magazines and their women writers into prototype Hildy Johnsons (created in 1928 by Ben Hecht and Charles Brackett as a man in their movie *The Front*

Page, but in the 1940 movie *His Girl Friday* a feisty hackette portrayed by Rosalind Russell). The 'girl reporters' (to use their own possibly self-conscious coinage) interviewed the male gangsters (and their families, taking in weddings and other social occasions) and descended enthusiastically on the imprisoned female occupants of what was termed Murderesses' Row. All seemed to be perfectly aware of the necessary pose, and all came over as pleasingly hard-boiled. Much of the slang came between an interview's quote marks, but the writers employed it too. Thus in a Forbes Herrick interview of June 1926 her subject, an alleged cop-killer, explained how 'You birds caught me napping . . . I didn't mean to kill the dick but he had a gun and I had to plug him' while a year earlier, kicking off a piece telling how Chicago's Cardinal Mundelein had refused to permit a burial service for gangster Spike O'Donnell, she wrote 'He doesn't carry a gat or pack a mean wallop with his fists but a middle aged man, alone and quietly, yesterday defied the O'Donnell Brothers, there are eight of them and they are mighty.'

A typical Forbes Herrick piece put her readers right next to the action:

'Say, lady,' shouted the sergeant over the wire when I finally got him, 'you know the dame you wuz just chinnin' with? Well, she done it.'

'Done what?' I queried stupidly. For the moment I had quite forgot that an ugly murder with a packet of poison had probably been 'done.'

'She bumped her old man off . . . She's just confessed . . .'

Sophie's in jail. Her trial's coming along . . . And if there is a Polish equivalent for the phrase 'nine o'clock lady,' I'm sure Sophie will use it the first time she gets a chance on the witness stand.[*]

Elsewhere she threw in *slugs* for bullets, *leggers*, *rats* (traitors), and a reference to the rough area known as *the back of the yards* [i.e. the holding pens of the city's stockyards]. Her colleague McLaughlin peppered her accounts with terms such as *chic young gun widow*, *alky dealer*, *moonshine* and *moonshine joints*, *booze sellers* and *synthetic booze*, *the bridewell, on the spot* and *taken for a ride.*

The era was especially fruitful in female killers and the 'mob sisters' lapped them up. Maurine Watkins covered the trial of alleged murderess and triple-divorcee Belva Gaertner. Faking it or for real, Gaertner seemed blithely unworried. She laughed as she told Watkins:

> 'Gin and guns – either one is bad enough, but together they can get you in a dickens of a mess, don't they. Now, if I hadn't had a gun, or if Walter hadn't had the gin — . Of course, it's too bad for Walter's wife, but husbands always cause women trouble . . . Now that coroner's jury that held me for murder,' she said, 'That was bum. They were narrow minded old birds – bet they never heard a jazz band in their lives'.' [†]

In what might be a foretaste of today's 'fake news' and

---

[*] G. Forbes Herrick, 'Nine O'Clock Ladies', *Chicago Daily Tribune*, 1 May 1927, J4; 'nine o'clock lady' was a Herrick coinage referring to the good-time girls who invariably claimed to lead a blameless lifestyle, eschewing excess and getting to bed by 'nine o'clock every night'.
[†] 'No Sweetheart Worth Killing – Mrs. Gaertner', *Chicago Daily Tribune*, 14 March 1924, p.17.

'clickbait', Ms Kaszuba notes a newspaper reader of 1925 declaring 'O, I never read the papers for facts, just for thrills.'" Gaertner, like seemingly any attractive woman, was acquitted ('gallant Cook County', teased the mob sisters, mocking the local authorities, and as they regularly pointed out, things were not quite so promising for plain girls); she died in her bed in 1965. Meanwhile Maurine Watkins had quit the *Tribune* and parlayed the Gaertner story and that of another murder suspect Beulah Annan (again attractive, again acquitted), into a play: *Chicago*. Originally and ironically titled *Brave Little Woman*, it opened in 1927 (Gaertner was at the first night of a solid Broadway run that lasted for 172 in all) and was filmed and revamped as a vastly successful 1975 musical (filmed in 2002). The Gaertner character, relatively minor, was 'Velma' (later 'Velma Kelly'); Annan (notorious for watching the boyfriend she had just shot bleed out for two hours as she serenaded the cooling body with repeat plays ofthe foxtrot 'Hula Lou') was showcased as 'Roxie Hart . . . the prettiest woman ever charged with murder in Chicago.'

According to Genevieve G. McBride and Stephen R. Byers[†] if there was a real-life model for fiction's Hildy Johnson (female version), then it was Ione Quinby. Quinby, with her trademark cloche hat invariably pulled down over her fashionably bobbed hair (she claimed it gave her confidence), plus a penchant for flapper-style short skirts, covered Chicago news for the city's *Evening Post*. She did stunts: the first involved applying for psychotherapy. Turned down because she didn't seem to have

[*] G. Forbes Herrick, 'Married Men in Demand as Stokes Jurors', *Chicago Daily Tribune*, 5 February 1925, p.1.
[†] MacBride & Byers, 'On the Front Page in the "Jazz Age": Journalist Ione Quinby, Chicago's Ageless "GirlReporter"', *Jrnl. Illinois State Historical Soc.* vol. 106 (Spring 2013), pp.91–128.

any problems, she only achieved the analysis when the male photographer the paper had sent along assured the shrink that she was indeed sufficiently off beam: there was the hat thing plus an apparent obsession with where her desk was placed in an otherwise male newsroom. (Quinby consistently refused to be relegated to any form of 'hen coop'.) Another stunt took her to the circus where she appeared in full costume atop an elephant. But her story turned out to be not so much the 'stunt' but that of the women animal trainers and other circus females. She did her stints as a mob sister (covering mob weddings and funerals, major trials and interviewing Al Capone himself) and like her peers wrote up the 1924 trial of rich boys Nathan Leopold and Richard Loeb (aged respectively nineteen and eighteen), charged with killing fellow junior plutocrat, fourteen-year-old Bobby Franks. She liked a good gangland widow and wrote them up, no doubt, as they would have liked: When Mrs 'Big Tim' Murphy (given name Margaret, known as Flo) returned from church 'to find her husband's body sprawled lifeless on the floor' (Tim having answered the door to the wrong visitor, most likely hitman Murray 'The Camel' Humphreys) 'she threw herself down upon him and cried, "Oh, Tim, darling, why didn't they take me too? But then I must live to avenge you."' After noting a marriage that had been 'blissfully happy' for seventeen years, Quinby added 'Except for the little interlude when Tim spent a year or two [for which read seven] at Fort Leavenworth, their home was a haven of peace and quiet.' In the event Flo decided to pass on revenge; she wiped her tears and in time remarried John 'Dingbat' O'Berta, one of Big Tim's pals.

When required, Quinby could play the sob sister, but the overall verdict was what she did was take risks. Equally important was her news policy: when she wrote about women, murderesses or otherwise, what qualified them as 'stories' was that what they did was news. They could be politicians, movie stars, business-women, visiting foreign royalty: for Quinby the angle was always that they were women.

The execution of killer Ruth Snyder pushed all her buttons. Light on slang, but unrestrained when it came to the lurid image, her piece was more mob than sob:

> They had assembled to see a woman killed, and centuries of man's chivalry to women seemed to rise up at that moment in a desperate urge to save the woman now crouched before them . . . [Ruth Snyder] whimpered again as she gazed straight toward them. The silence! . . . A crunching sound as the grim executioner rammed down a lever! A sinister, crackling whine, and a sputtering noise . . . Fascinated, unable to move, the twenty-four men were like creatures in some diabolical nightmare . . . As they watched, blue darts of electricity emerged from Ruth's body in sinister spurts like small pale devils dancing about . . . Then came a weird silence that strained at their ears and bore down upon their minds as if weighted by sash weights . . . Seconds crawling slowly like wounded soldiers dragging themselves back to the trenches . . . Finally the guards reassembled about the chair, picked up Ruth's inert body, and wheeled it out of the room.[*]

On the other hand when a teenage mother was jailed and was parted from her daughter, 'Tootsie', it was Quinby who semi-adopted the child, bringing her to the jail to see mom (the child

[*] Quoted in MacBride & Byers op. cit.

444

thought she was in hospital and the matrons gave her milk and cookies).

At risk of jumping far ahead, one can make a case for one other stunt girl, this time British, in the shape of Nell Dunn, whose *Up the Junction* appeared in 1963. The book, its title a coarse double entendre (the 'junction' being both that of the Clapham railway station and of the female thighs), drew on its upper-class author's experience of what might unkindly be termed slumming amongst the south London working class. No newspaper sent her off to plumb the lower depths, but the short stories that made it up came from what she experienced when in 1959 she moved from smart Chelsea to far from gentrified Battersea and worked for a while in a sweet factory. The book was nominally fiction but for its middle-class readers it was also sociology by default. A second 'sarf Lunnun' title, *Poor Cow*, arrived in 1967. The novel (subsequently made into a film by Ken Loach) follows Joy, a single mother whose boyfriend is sent down for twelve years after a bungled robbery. Joy struggles on, living with her aunt, working in a pub and on occasion on the streets.

The two books yield just over a hundred slang terms. (Her interview book, *Talking to Women* (1965) is far less fruitful; her interviewees, often successful contemporaries, seem to have been far more restrained in their conversations though there are a couple of fucks for the dedicated searcher.) The topics are as one might expect: sex, crime (and criminals), various sorts of people, various terms of affection and abuse, language that can be loosely linked as 'problems' and intoxication. This last effectively means drink; drugs, for all that the dates put us slap-bang in the midst of 'swinging London' are almost invisible. 'Swinging', if one excludes the rock 'n' roll stars, the snappers and models, the art school whizkids, the up-and-coming young thesps and the rest of the cool elite, remained a very middle-class pursuit. Battersea or Clapham were places one left on the way to better things. Thus while drink yields such tried-and-tested staples as *well away*, *pissed* and *paralytic*, drugs give only *blocked*, intoxicated with some kind of pill, and *weed*, marijuana.

Nor, however much one might yet again wish otherwise, do her embryonic 'dolly-birds' come up with women-only slang. The two candidates: to *fall* (i.e. pregnant and known here as *up the spout*, a situation that follows the injudicious rejection of a *French letter*) and *the change* (the menopause) are hardly new coinages, both dating to the late nineteenth century.

Sex on the other hand does deliver, even if the terms are rarely modern inventions. To have sex can be to *have a bit of the other* or to *chop it off* (the 'chopping' presumably playing on a *slice of a cut loaf*, one of slang's many synonyms for intercourse); to *carry on with* or *go with* is to have an affair; there are *dirty old men*, and *glamour girls*, *tarts* (girlfriends), *floosies* and *slags* (available but not commercial) and *brasses* (prostitutes) who are *on the game*. Actual genitals are rare: there is the *willie*, the penis and *grandmother*, for vagina – both suggest the nursery rather than what Dunn records as the *knocking shop*. Other sex terms include *snog* (both noun and verb), *touch up*, *drag* (female impersonation), the blithe stereotyping of *jungle juice* (black sexuality) and *knackers*, usually the *balls*, i.e. testicles but here in the figurative sense of courage).

Crime, and its usual concomitant prison, have their own share. A *job* a is a crime, to *nick*, to arrest, to *do for* to charge with committing one and to *do* to send to prison where one serves a *stretch*. To *put away* also means imprison but the walls can be those of psychiatric institution. *Screw* can mean a swindle but also a warder and as a verb to burglarise (all rely on the earlier *screw*, a key). Other terms include *plant* (to 'frame up'), *toot* (rhyming slang for loot and thus any form of money), *ringed* (of a car, altered for some criminal purpose), *jemmy* (a crowbar) and *dear John* (a girlfriend's letter, sent to a man inside and breaking off the relationship). 'Problematic' terms include *ballsed up*, *crappy*, *fucked*, *poxy*, *rotten* and *up the spout*. There is to *fuck someone up* (to cause them problems), *skint* (bankrupt), *get the sack* (to lose one's job) and to *do oneself in* (to commit suicide). Finally, people. The *big noise* is important, the *toff* an aristocrat, the *beauty* an admirable individual, the *stirrer* a trouble-maker; terms of affection include *old cock*, *old fruit*, *old dear*, *sweetie* and *duck*. *Old crab*, *old bag*, *fatty*, *gink*, *dopey* all suggest distaste. *Blighter* and *fucker* mean simply 'person' though the implication is probably negative.

There are plenty more – *hokey-pokey* (ice-cream, a survivor from the 1890s), *arse-upwards* (upside down), *crack it* (succeed), *piss oneself* (i.e. with laughter), *posh up* (improve, e.g. a building), *chin* (to hit) and so on – but the tone should be obvious. This is slang of its time and place. No more than one might expect. No more than one should want.

If as a man your lack of class or wealth precluded your capture of that playboy's dream the Gibson Girl – she of slender waist positioned between a notable bust and curvaceous butt, her figure topped by a swanlike neck, youthful features, a bouffant chignon and an overall look that was alluring but never lewd – then the less exclusive chorus girl was your alternative of choice. She provided the majority of late nineteenth-century American males with their primary sex symbol. Found on the stages of Broadway and out in the sticks, the members of what were known as the *merry-merry* delighted their admirers in the *bald-headed row* (the often ageing patrons of the front row stalls who leered hopefully up at the flashing legs before them).* It was unsurprising that she also found herself in print.

The first attempt seems to have been in 1903, when Roy McCardell published the *Conversations of a Chorus Girl*, followed up in 1904 with *The Show Girl and Her Friends*. His creation used a thin sprinkling of slang: *hand someone the frozen mitt* (to dismiss or reject), *jay town* (a small provincial town), *mug* (to make faces), *buzzwagon* (an automobile), *pea and thimble* (the shell-game), *dinge* (a black person), *zizzy* (crazy), *on the dink* (failing, malfunctioning), *pipe* (to look at), *shell-back* (a conservative), *the nuts* and *the gazizz* (the fashion), *kike* (Jew), *dead one* (a useless individual), *dopey* (a fool), *chaser* (a womaniser) and *newsie* (a newsboy).

Far more substantial was *The Sorrows of a Show Girl* (1908) by Kenneth McGaffey. 'Sorrows', readers soon realised, were less regrets as to one's own life but to the state of the world, and a succession of chapters recounted how our heroine, Sabrina, dealt with a variety of such problems. Chapter titles included: 'Sabrina Denounces the Male Sex as Being All Alike, and Threatens to Take the Veil' and 'After Investigating the Country Atmosphere Carefully, Sabrina Says the Only Healthful Ozone is Out of a Champagne Bottle.'

In what he termed the 'Explanation' McGaffey sets her scene:

In the following chapters some of Sabrina's remarks are likely

---

* There were of course British equivalents (the *Gaiety Girl*, named for the theatre where they appeared, and the *Stage-Door Johnnies* who lusted after her), much fêted in the 'sporting' press of the era. Yet while they played the same on-stage role, often moving on to successful acting careers, and like their US cousins might go on to make advantageous marriages, they don't seem to have been ventriloquised into print.

to cause the reader to elevate his eyebrows in suspicion as to her true character.

In order to set myself right with both the public and the vast army of Sabrinas that add youth and beauty to our stage, and brilliancy and gaiety to our well known cafes, I wish to say that she is all that she should be. She is a young lady who, no matter how old she may be, does not look it. She is always well dressed, perhaps a little in advance of the fashion, but invariably in good taste. Among strangers or in public places her conduct is all that could be desired, while with those of her own set she becomes more familiar and may occasionally lapse into slang.

Thereafter, and other than a brief framing sentence or two, each chapter was narrated by its heroine. A few examples ran thus:

To go back sometime, there was a certain skirt that I used to room with in Chicago when we were both broke, but one night she went out with a bunch of siss-boom-ah! boys and came home with a large and juicy snoot full and spent the early morning hours in leaning out of the window of the apartment and whistling through her fingers to the milkmen, as well as staging a disrobing number in the middle of the room with the curtains up to such an extent that the inhabitants of the outlying districts had to wait sometime for their morning milk.

This, naturally grated on my refined sensibilities, so the next morning while she was yet beating the hay, I packed my little suitcase and took it on the run away from there, leaving her, you might say, on the pan. I went into the pony ballet of a La Salle Theatre show—can you see me as a pony?—and

I heard that she was advancing Art with a stock burlesque in South Chicago. That evening she was among those present at the aforementioned social function. And while we kissed and embraced each other with the affection of long lost sisters, still I could detect above the odor of cocktails an underlying current of soreness. So we clinched, but I took particular pains to see that we went clean in the breakaway.

Well, I got to toddle along. The Ladies' Auxiliary to the Anvil Chorus is going to hold a meeting in Alla Sweenie's apartments. Was you ever one of them? Well, when those dames get on the job and are grouped it makes Elinor Glyn's opinion of the Pilgrim Mothers seem like words of praise. So long.

Then I delivered my philippic as follows: "If you spangled-eyed dubs think you are going to shake me down for any more change you had better drop in your penny and get next to yourselves. Nix, not. I've already coughed up more than the rest of the entire population, and you are not going to lance me for any more just because I've got a bundle. You're good people, you've got big feet, and I would like to see you run fast. Now beat it. I'm going to blow the burg on the next caboose, and while I don't wish you any bad luck I hope the town hall burns down. Now take it on the run or I will give you all a good scolding and send you to bed." And the funny thing about it is, they slid. I tell the folks that my light is hid under a bushel in Emporia, grab the bus, and here I am and nothing short of an explosion will make me leave. Put this on your 'call board, the only good thing about these hick hamlets is they remind you of New York because they are so different. So long. Don't fall down the elevator shaft.

Translation: *skirt*, a girl, *siss-boom-ah boys!*, collegians (from their formalised cheering), *snoot full*, state of drunkenness, *beat the hay*, to sleep, *take it on the run*, to leave, *pony*, a chorus-girl, *anvil chorus*, negative critics (they 'knock' a performer), *dub*, a sucker, *shake down*, to extort, *change*, money, *get next to*, understand, *nix*, no, *lance*, extort, *bundle*, a large amount (of money), *beat it*, go away, *blow*, leave, *burg*, town, *caboose*, railway train, *slide*, to leave, *hick*, rural. 'Clinching' and 'clean in the breakaway' take their image from the boxing ring.

The best-known example of a literary showgirl was probably Anita Loos' *Gentlemen Prefer Blondes: The Intimate* [later editions had *Illuminating*] *Diary of a Professional Lady* (1925) which was supposedly sparked when Loos saw the celebrated critic and essayist H.L. Mencken reduced to mush in the presence of a pneumatic blonde. (A less popular sequel, *But Gentlemen Marry Brunettes* appeared in 1927.) The tales were voiced by one 'Lorelei Lee' (her given name presumably an extra dig at the opera-loving Mencken, of German stock himself and a lover of that nation's operas) but rather than using slang it was all about tone. Lorelei's self-description 'A Girl Like I' (it would become the title of Loos' biography in 1963) set the scene (and the *Time* magazine reviewer called it 'Moronese'). Lorelei is also impressively aphoristic: 'You can say what you want about the Germans being full of "kunst" [art], but what they are really full of is delicatessen' and 'Kissing your hand may make you feel very very good but a diamond and safire bracelet lasts forever'.

The showgirl in a wider sense – the movie star – can be found in *West Broadway* (1921), by the prolific Nina Wilcox Putnam. Author of five hundred short stories, a thousand magazine shorts and much else, including the story that Hollywood made into the Boris Karloff vehicle *The Mummy* (1932), Putnam, naturally, threw in a few full-length books. This one purports to be the story of Maria La Tour (originally Mary Gilligan) and her first reluctant and then revelatory road trip from 'civilised' New York to the 'jay town' that is Hollywood. Being raised on Avenue A – 'and raised is right. I raised myself from there to Broadway and Riverside Drive and you know it!' she's properly slangy. Though her hundred-plus examples give nothing special – *spill* (talk), *chew the rag* (gossip*), double-O* (stare), *knock* (criticise), *lamp* (to observe), *spinach* (facial hair) and so on. She also gives us the *pneumonia blouse*, a transparent blouse of muslin and lace with next to no collar and thus, for some puritan contemporaries, a shockingly low neckline, and coins *pneumonia car*, an open-topped variety. Other 'first uses' in the book include *bird* (an eccentric), *cootie* (usually a bug but here a term of abuse), *frisk oneself* (to discard or do without), *greasy vest* (like *greasy spoon*, a cheap, dirty restaurant, but here focused on the waiter's coat rather than the eater's utensils), *jazzed up* (augmented, embellished), *mourner's bench* (the seats in a theatrical agent's outer office where hopeful performers wait for jobs), the *Quaker City* (Philadelphia, PA) and a self-referential use of *sister*. The slang grows less obtrusive as she hits the fly-over states, but in the era's boosterism of things provincial, she is ever-keener to confess that there's more to life than Broadway.

Showgirls, working or 'resting', also make their appearances, along with many other 'theatricals', in the work of Helen Green van Campen, whose short stories appeared in the popular New York press in the first fifteen years of the twentieth century. A hit at the time, her stories are effectively invisible today, like those of a number of her male peers – e.g. C.L. Cullen and *Tales of the Ex-Tanks*, i.e. alcoholics, or 'Hugh McHugh' (George Vere

Hobart) and his best-selling tales of the Wodehousian New Yorker 'John Henry' – whose slang-sodden works, once so vastly successful that the half-title of each successive work printed the current six-figure sales of its predecessors, have wholly disappeared from anywhere other than second-hand book dealers.

Over time she went by four names: Helen Tabor. Helen Green. Helen van Campen. Helen Cotter. One for childhood turning teenage, two acknowledging at least fifty percent of her four husbands (two divorced, two dead), a last one that accompanied busy widowhood. Van Campen seems to have been the name that lasted, though early fans still met her as Green. Born in 1880 to Louisiana bluebloods with the obligatory plantation, which meant that while there was money, there were its perks and she enjoyed pre-teen travels on a Gilded Age Grand Tour: Europe, the Middle East (Luxor) and Russia (St Petersburg). In 1893 the family money ran out: another victim of that year's 'Great Panic' on the stock market and the depression that followed. Ms Tabor was unfazed; she turned her attentions to horseflesh and for the next few years bred and raced steeplechasers; this led to more travels, this time alongside her bloodstock, across the States, down to Brazil and back to Europe. In 1897 she looked north, to the Klondike Gold Rush in Alaska, a world more usually associated with men, and in literary terms with Jack London, though the miners needed sex and could obtain the heterosexual variety via a number of 'dance halls' (home of the 'dollar a dance') and a hierarchy of brothels down to the so-called 'cigar store' (a homegrown version of London's earlier, but similarly louche 'cigar divan'). There the 'good-time girls' included a trio of Wilsons – 'Dutch Kate' (who went straight and may have become a nurse), Cad and Ella, an African-American woman whose murder, seemingly for her $2000 stash, was never solved – Rose Blumkin, 'The Gypsy Queen', 'French' Marie Larose, Georgia Lee, Dora Wells, whose brothel was named 'The San Francisco Laundry' and Edith Neile, aka 'The Oregon Mare'.

Mrs Green played things straight: she based herself in Nome, a shorefront tent city that stretched 30 miles, and which claimed itself the world's largest gold-pan. It was said that the lucky, even the barely competent could pick the precious metal off the sand. She visited Alaska three times, but she doesn't seem to have left town rich.

She appeared in New York in 1905. A new town launched a new career: writing. Her journalism and short stories focused on the legitimate version of 'working girls' – gossiping while they switched plugs and put through calls on hotel switch-boards and toiling behind the counters of department stores – and on the world of vaudeville and its lowlife professionals. Published in the *N.Y. Telegraph* the vaudeville stories appear in a couple of collections: *At the Actors' Boarding House* (1906) and *The Maison de Shine* (1908). Ethel Barrymore, of the theatrical family, predicted imminent fame for the author. In 1909, a third volume, no bananas, top or other, this time but featuring *Mr Jackson*, Green's version of the well-heeled rogue-with-a-heart-of-gold. At some stage, maybe 1905, she married Burt Green, a vaudeville pianist, who clued her into the world he knew and these early pieces appear under his surname. New York palled, or maybe it was the marriage: in 1910 they divorced and he moved on to a career that would partner him up with such as Oscar Hammerstein II; she returned to Alaska.

By now she had married again: husband number two was Frank Rumsey Van Campen, chief mining engineer for the Alaska Syndicate's Beatson Copper Mine, then the biggest in the state. The New York gossip hacks claimed him as one of their own: a writer; they also saw the literary couple as purchasers of a gold mine and sympathised with the new bride, sweeping snow off the front porch and pining for 'the reeking hop houses' of Chinatown and the 'gilded cafes' of Times Square. In 1915, P.G. Wodehouse, writing in *Vanity Fair* on 'The habit of picking on New York' cites 'Mrs. Helen van Campen (Helen Green, of blessed gifts and memories) is the latest writer to commit mayhem on our unoffending city.' Her theory, he claims, being that 'the population of New York are a set of effete worms', while in Alaska, which she prefers 'and does not care who knows it, every man is a Galahad and every woman is like the heroine of a three-volume novel'.

The couple lived on LaTouche Island in Prince William Sound. Mrs van Campen rode horses and wrote (working in a small cabin which the miners build for her out in the bay), still looking locally for her copy, which now meant stories with an Alaskan theme. Nonetheless she had not wholly abandoned New York: in 1913 she wrote 'Life on Broadway', nine sketches for *McClure's*, a popular slick, eight of them featuring what the critic Susan Harris Smith has termed 'social-climbing, gold-digging, fast-talking slang-slinging hustlers': Flossie, the opera-tor, Elmer the front lobby coat-boy and Evangeline, their show-girl pal. Their speech is a mixture of current slang, everyday working-class New York speech and a heavy larding of mis-applied pretension. Nearer home there was 'Corsets in Alaska' and 'What Miners Read', a puff job for a literary mag. She would always write: in 1946, her contribution 'I'll See You in Alaska', published in that year's state Guide, took the form of a Q & A:

QUERY: 'I'm crazy to go to Alaska Just divorced (he was

n.g. {no good}) and considered glamorous (won a beauty
contest) and where are all those MEN?'

H van C: 'Interior, sis. More fems on the coast. You'll get a
man.'

The marriage did not last: in 1918 Mr van Campen quit the
mine and in 1919 Mrs van Campen quit her husband. His
successor arrived the next year: this was George Cotter, a contrac-
tor and big game hunter and the two of them moved across the
bay to Seward. Her writing prospered as did her life. To quote
her entry in the Alaska Mining Hall of Fame, 'She traveled
throughout the Alaska Territory by boat, railroad and dogsled
and on horseback. She looked at reindeer herds near Teller,
visited with hard rock miners at Nebesna Gold Mine, hunted
moose on the Kenai Peninsula, and visited placer miners in the
Chisana district. For nearly two years, Helen operated a small
placer gold mine on Cooper Creek, near Seward on the Kenai
Peninsula.' She took photos, mainly of indigenous peoples, and
would click away for the rest of her life. There are photos of her
too: on horseback, toting a rifle, decked out in 'Wild West'
buckskins and fringes.

Ever mobile, the couple moved to Argentina (George had a
mining gig) in 1921, then back to Texas (for another job: oil) in
1924. He died that year, out on the road. From around 1915
she'd been writing Hollywood scripts and commuted between
there and Alaska – Seward and later Fairbanks, where she moved
in 1939. During the war she worked as director of personnel
services at the U.S. Army Air Force Base at Ladd Field in
Fairbanks. At some stage there was a fourth marriage: to Edwin
C. Hill, a CBS radio star who put out 'The Human Side of the
News'. She doesn't seem to have taken his name.

She died in April 1960. She remains a major figure in Canada, memorialised in a scholarship aimed to help young journalists.

The works of Helen Green van Campen offer six hundred slang terms of which she could claim to have put 165 in print for the first time (and which make her a major user of the counter-language). Among them she brings us *shroud and boiler*, a dress suit, including its 'boiled' shirt (a better-known equivalent was the Wodehousian *soup and fish*), *dead bird*, a hopeless case or situation, *off one's dip*, crazy, *brace game*, a crooked gambling game and thus any form of fraud, and to *put on the fritz*, to spoil, to render out of order, to put a stop to, which term probably originates in the spluttering of a faulty wire or connection, though it may have been popularised by Fritz, a German, and the hostility to such generated by World War I propaganda. Then there is *get hunk* with, to get even with, which used standard American *hunk* (originally from Dutch *hunk*, meaning 'home' in a children's game), in a safe or good position or condition and which may thus be linked to *hunky-dory*. Van Campen also pioneered *fix someone's clock*, to take revenge upon, to get even with or to foil an antagonist's plans (modernity prefers that the clock should be *cleaned*). Her use of *Joe Hep*, which extends the slightly older *hep* (which she also launched into print), suggests the possibilities of the lexicographer David Maurer's supposed (and generally rejected) etymology for hep: that Joe was real, ran a Chicago bar (perhaps, we might fantasise, even adjacent to that tended by slang's other mythological *booze-hoister* and administrator of knock-out potions Mickey Finn) and dispensed 'the real thing' when it came to inside dope. Perhaps but the best guess for hep is a variation on *hip*, and hip came from opium's on the hip, the position the smoker took and suggests an early identification of drugs and cool.

Other terms, already known before she added them to her roster, included *tough sledding, I'm from Missouri (you'll have to show me), moll buzzer, on the water wagon, give someone the eye, also-ran, monkey business, legit, souse, shoot the con, put the bee on, watch my smoke, a roll that would choke a mule, four-flushing, johnny-at-the-rat-hole, twenty-three skidoo* and much besides. All mainstream slang; nothing criminal.

No-one would suggest that Mrs Green was the first to use slang. Even that of New Yorkers who being metropolitans were the pioneers of the form in the USA. But she is undoubtedly one of the best of a rash of late nineteenth century/early twentieth century purveyors of non-criminal slang, and whose stories, often at least partially humorous, started their life in the contemporary tabloid press. And what singles her out from such as George Ade, a mid-Westerner whose *Fables in Slang* (and much beside) would make millions from the register, was that her slang words integrate into her text without the slightest pause. A typical Ade fable is bespattered with almost Germanic capitalisation, and each capital betokens another example of the counter-language. Green's slang flows as and where required. Whether, as some suggest, Burt passed on what he knew, is unproven: Helen seems quite capable of hunting it down alone. As regards the stories, the source of her slang is irrelevant. What matters is the way that she uses it: its appearances are matter-of-fact, wholly natural.

Never more so in the one area that I would suggest she does pioneer: the drug scene. At least beyond the usual irresistible sensationalism of its coverage. Again, she wasn't the first to note the city's drug consumption: first opium, and more recently such injectable and sniffable narcotics as morphine and then heroin (cocaine seemed to have side-stepped her vaudevillians).

The overriding scenario, usually as filtered through the more sensational newspapers, was very much of the 'shock! horror! . . . I made my excuses and left' style. One either had a mis-transcribed and mis-labelled taxonomy of the *outfit* required for opium smoking, the inevitable, supposedly reprehensible admixture of white girls and yellow men, and the horrors, invariably much deserved, of withdrawal. But nothing more. Drugs, and their stereotypically *Celestial, slant-eyed* purveyors, were a Bad Thing.

Green offers a dozen terms, perhaps not many, but as many as any peer would have known. And she offers them straight. 'One night I'm a layin' on the hip, smokin' up a few' says a boarder at the Maison de Shine. That's her take: no more, no less, it's what, if you so desire, you do. Other examples of drug slang include *dope* and *smoke* (both opium; large-scale cannabis use had yet to materialise in New York), *morph*, morphine and *white stuff*, which stood for both heroin and morphine and *bunk*, weak or counterfeit drugs; a *shell*, a measure of opium; *hit the stem*, to smoke opium, *fix up* or *take a shot*, to inject oneself and thus the *gun* or hypodermic syringe; *yen*, the desire for narcotics, *against*, addicted, *gag* and *habit*, both meaning regular use, and *winging*, withdrawing (a seeming precursor but definite antonym of the widely used and positive *flying*); and the *hop joint*, opium's equivalent of a shooting gallery.

In terms of her writing and like the vaudeville she once hymned, Green, with or without the Van Campen is largely invisible. She has a presence in Canada but it is for her achievements beyond New York's demi-monde. But this is hardly unique for those whose work is based on the counter-language: slang, as ever, is not a good career move. With the exception of Damon Runyon, he who parlayed sports reporting onto

Broadway and thence to his 'Guys and Dolls', most of Green's early contemporaries have faded. Even Ade, for whom a town in Indiana, a football stadium (at Purdue University) and a World War II Liberty ship were all named. The great slang-wielding gossip writers – O.O. McIntyre, Walter Winchell – might never have been. If Helen Green has joined their lost Valhalla, so be it. Slang will not forget.

We should not quit the printed page without a nod to a product which, while still hugely popular, has long since colonised other media. Literary sex is traditionally divided into two: erotica, which is approved, and pornography, which is not. In movie terms erotica's lens is smeared with vaseline, pornography demands a gynaecological close-up. Erotica, runs the rule, is seen as a feminised construct, written by women for women and fastidiously sidestepping slang's self-indulgent vulgarities. If a straight man tackles the same topics, then what we have is porn, and porn embraces slang. Its language, a broad synonymy but essentially limited to variations on what Anthony Burgess christened 'the old in and out' and those fleshy giblets with which we perform it, is a reliable showcase for the register. Never more so than in printed porn's golden age, the Seventies, when America's dirty book factories churned out a seemingly endless succession of 'one-hand titles' for sale in the nation's local variations on New York's once lubricious 42nd Street.

Of course that book-clutching single hand – the other was more actively employed – was male. Yet a glance at the crammed shelves of what slang termed 'stroke books' shows a good showing of female authors. Very unreliable narrators in every sense, of course. In the end, who, outside the publishers, can tell whether Victoria Parker (*Incest Schoolgirls*, *The Cousins Eat Out*, *No Cherry*

Cheerleader) or Kathy Andrews (*A Mother without Panties, Getting Behind Mother, Stepmother in Ropes*) were really women. But then again, were such as Nick Eastwood (*Hot Licked Librarian, Eager Beaver Aunt, Babysitter in Heat*), Ted Leonard (*Feeding the File Clerk, Daughter's Loving Pet*) or even the punningly named Dick Gozinya (*Daddy's Girl*) in fact men. But did it matter? The 'creators', explained a contemporary piece, signed in every morning, chose themselves a template (incest/rape/bestiality or whatever) and knocked out the necessary 30,000 words. (Romance giants Mills and Boon and Harlequin also offered templates, albeit with variant plots.) The target may have been male, the creator surely suffered no such restrictions.

It is presumably just as impossible to gender the current successors of such outfits as the Liverpool Library Press and Companion Books: those amateur but enthusiastic contributors to the various on-line porn sites that still prefer words to pictures. *Literotica.com* and *asstr.org* and their many emulators churn out tales in a production line that would have impressed the old professionals. But who is exactly who? Like the rest of the internet, the rule is pseudonymity.

Creativity is no longer a matter of the printed word. Slang has always found a powerful voice via popular entertainment, whether it be on stage, screen or in song lyrics. We have looked at Britain's music halls, but if the 'coster' singers touched on the vulgar, they still remained within 'decent' limits. Not so the blues singers of post-World War I America. Some of the coarsest, slangiest lines on record were sung by female blues singers around 1930.

The blues, defined by the *OED* as 'A melody of a mournful and haunting character, originating among the African

Americans of the southern U.S.' is first recorded as a term in 1912, in the title of W.C. Handy's 'Memphis Blues'. It was an extended use of the slang term *blue*, depressed, which had been used since the late seventeenth century. Initially merchandised as 'race records' the music was performed by black artists and sold to the black audience. The blues offered a different take on life to the black music of the nineteenth century, which, in the form of spirituals, focused on religion or its tropes. The blues singers, the best-known of whom, at least in the century's early decades or so, were women, such as Ma Rainey (Gertrude Pridgett) and Bessie Smith, and they were talking about life very definitely in the here and now.

As its etymology indicated, that life was hard and painful, its unhappiness often engendered by failed relationships; fantasies of the hereafter with its delayed rewards, so central to African-American spirtuals, did not enter the picture. As for punishments, they were already available on earth. The blues, again as opposed to spirituals, had no problem in including slang.

As Stephen Calt writes in his dictionary of blues language *Barrelhouse Words*, 'Blues songs were not written compositions in the customary Tin Pan Alley manner, involving literary or poetic diction on at least a rudimentary level. As declaimed by the singer-guitarists and singer-pianists [. . .] the blues lyric was a snippet of vernacular speech set to song [. . .] Recorded blues of the period are so saturated in slang and assorted colloquialisms as to create a peculiar dialect that is only half-intelligible to present-day listeners.'* Blues singers used the language of the barrelhouse, the low-down black nightspots where one could drink, gamble and hire prostitutes. The word meant the place

---

* S. Calt, *Barrelhouse Words* (2009), pp. xi, xiii.

and what one did there and it was a world that inspired W. C. Handy's 'Mr Crump Blues' (1912) in which he declared 'Mister Crump won't 'low no easy riders here. / I don't care what he don't 'low, / I'm going barrelhouse anyhow.'

The early blues were raw, both in emotion and vocabulary. Handy, looking for a wider commercialisation, complained of 'a flock of lowdown dirty blues'* but he was unable to stem the flow. Audiences seemed to relish the sexual references, the singers were happy to provide them. They could be unmediated, but often they resorted to double entendre.

Such thinly disguised smut might be discerned in nineteenth-century minstrelsy – for instance such classic songs as 'Long Tail Blue' and 'Coal Black Rose', where Sambo alludes to being "tiff as a poker' and Rose replies' 'Cum in Sambo, don't 'tand dare shakin,/ De fire is a burnin, and de hoe cake a bakin" – but the blues singers took it to another level. Nor need the entendre be remotely double. Louise Bogan (born Lucille Anderson in 1897 and presumably taking the name of a well-known contemporary white poet purely by coincidence) left absolutely nothing to the imagination in 'Shave 'Em Dry' (1920s):

> I got nipples on my titties, big as the end of my thumb,
> I got somethin' between my legs'll make a dead man come,
> Oh daddy, baby won't you shave 'em dry?

while a later verse declares

> Now your nuts hang down like a damn bell sapper,
> And your dick stands up like a steeple,

* Quoted in Calt op. cit. p.xiv.

Your goddam ass-hole stands open like a church door,
And the crabs walks in like people.

Few singers, male or female, could follow that, though Bo Carter (Armenter 'Bo' Chatmon) did what he could, even if he did feel it best to mask his sexual references in somewhat obvious double entendre. His song titles included 'Pin In Your Cushion' (1931), 'The Ins and Outs of my Girl', 'Let Me Roll Your Lemon' (1935) and 'Banana in Your Fruit Basket' (1931).

Other Bogan songs hymned streetwalkers – 'Tricks [i.e. customers] Ain't Walking No More' – and cocaine – 'Baking Powder Blues.'

What was known as the dirty blues was open to both genders. Lil Johnson brought such songs as 'Press My Button (Ring My Bell)' (1932: 'Come on baby, let's have some fun / Just put your hot dog in my bun'), 'You'll Never Miss Your Jelly Until Your Jelly Roller Is Gone' (1929: 'If you don't like my sweet potato, what made you dig so deep? / In my potato field three, four times a week'), ' My Stove is in Good Condition' (1936), 'Meat Balls' (1937) and 'If It Don't Fit (Don't Force It) (1937: 'Now it may stretch, it may not tear at all / But you'll never pack that big mule up in my stall'). Bessie Smith sang 'Need a Little Sugar in My Bowl' (1929; further requests from the song included 'a little hot dog on my roll,' and 'a little steam-heat on my floor') and Dinah Washington praised that 'Big Long Slidin' Thing' (1954: the 'slidin' thing' was, of course, a trombone and other instruments simply didn't cut it: 'He brought his amplifier / And he hitched it in my plug / He planked it, and he plunked it / But it just wasn't good enough'). Finally Julia Lee's repertoire included the phallic worship of 'Gotta Gimme Whatcha Got' (1946), 'King Size Papa' (1948: 'Everything that I need he carries in his king size pack') and 'My Man Stands Out' (1950: 'Down at the beach when we walk by / The other girls give him the eye / 'cause my man stands out').

Bogan was also happy to wear the mask of double entendre. She hymned the *baking powder man*, a braggart who like a cake had been 'blown up', *barbecue*, the vagina, i.e. 'hot meat', *boogie alley*, another term for vagina, where *boogie* meant sex, and a couple of phrases for intercourse: *grind one's coffee* and *get one's ashes hauled*, where *ashes* was a variation on *ass*. She also told of the *B.D. Woman*, who 'ain't gonna need no men', and she was the first, at least as written down, to use *b.d.* standing for *bull-dyke* (or *bull dagger*); her young *femme*, was what Bogan called a *juve*, i.e. juvenile.

B.D. women, they all done learnt their plan
They can lay their jive just like a natural man
B.D. women, B.D. women, you know they sure is rough
They all drink up plenty whiskey and they sure will strut
  their stuff

She used *clap*, gonorrhoea, *cock*, the African-American and white Southern term for the vagina, from *coquille*, a cockle-shell; *cold in hand*, impoverished, *fuck* ('So I fucked all night and all the night before, baby / And I feel just like I want to fuck some more'*) and *fuck it*, *get one's habits on*, to be intoxicated by narcotics, *jump-steady*, alcohol, *roller*, a hard worker, *suck* for oral sex of both varieties ('If you suck my pussy, baby, I'll suck your dick'†), *tommy*, a girl (the term had originally meant a lesbian), possibly a prostitute and *trick*, her client.

* 'Shave 'Em Dry' (1935).
† 'Till the Cows Come Home' (1935).

The blues might deal with travelling (specific towns were often named), violence, partying, work and prison (some singers included the names of real-life prison wardens and guards in their songs). But many were about sex, and specifically sexual intercourse. For the last one finds *action*, to *jam*, to *ring someone's bell*, to *ball the jack* (which is also used to mean move fast), to *grind* and thus *coffee grinder*, a lover, to *jazz*, to *rock* (*and roll*), and to *squeeze someone's lemon*, immortalised in Robert Johnson's 'Travelling Riverside Blues' (1937). In 'Empty Bed Blues Part 1' (1928) Bessie Smith talked about cunnilingus: 'He's a deep-sea diver / with a stroke that can't go wrong, / He can touch bottom, and his wind holds out so long.' The penis was a *biscuit*, thus the female lover is a *biscuit roller*, the *stick of candy*, the *hambone* (which doubled as a vagina); semen is *jelly*, *baking powder*, *medicine* and *sugar*. The vagina the *coal bin*, the *jelly* and most popularly *jelly-roll*, (otherwise a doughnut, both sweet and offering a *hole*), the *sweet potato* and the *potato field*; *cock*, in the Southern sense, is found. The female buttocks were *ya-yas*. Adultery was a regular theme: the lover was a *back-door* or *outside man* (or *woman*) or a *triflin'* man; to cheat was to *dog* or *mess around* (which could also mean dance), to *tip*, to *steamroller*; an ex-lover was a *used-to-be*.

Sex wasn't, however, everything – many lyrics had other subjects and offered other slang words. Examples include *arnchy* (one who puts on airs), *have a ball*, *boog* or *bring down* (to annoy or depress), *burner* (a pistol), *cold in hand* (impoverished), *cop your broom* (to leave), *easman* (i.e. a kept man whose life is 'easy'), *eight rock* (one whose complexion is notably black), *fatmouth*, *loco*, *get off* or *raise sand* (to enjoy oneself), *gimmies* (a bad mood), *high-stepper* and *high-stepping*, *red-hot* as in 'red-hot mama', *knock a jug* (to drink), *jump salty* (to become aggressive), *Jim* (as a term of address), *burn leather* (to dance energetically), *market* (a prison), *mojo*, *monkey man* (a weak-willed man), *Mose* (generic for a black man), *piccolo* (a jukebox), *play for a chump*, *rat* (a straight-haired wig), *run one's mouth*, *the square* (honest), *strut one's stuff*, *stuff* (narcotics), *sugar* (money), *Stavin Chain* (a womaniser or wanderer) and *turn one's damper down* (to calm oneself).

Under which identity one situates Gladys Bentley, a black woman of colour, openly lesbian and a singer of the blues, is down to taste. Sometimes known as 'the Brown Bomber' (deliberately or otherwise copying the nickname more usually associated with the hyper-masculine world heavyweight champ Joe Louis), her own focus seemed to be on her sexuality. She had, she claimed in 1952, begun identifying as a male in her childhood and near the end of her life described herself as having 'inhabited that half-shadow no-man's land which exist between the boundaries of the two sexes'.

The modern gay historian Eric Garber has written that she 'earned her living – as an openly black lesbian – for decades. She had insisted on being herself during a time when others hid their difference. And she had increased public awareness about sexual variations and spoken for many who could not speak for themselves.'*

As singer she was one of the features of Harlem's best-known gay speakeasy, Harry Hansberry's Clam House at 146 W. 133rd St, a stretch of tarmac and sidewalks between 5th and 7th avenues better known as 'Jungle Alley'.† Here she took popular favourites and revised them, with her own indulgently obscene

---

* In *Outlook* vol. 1 1988 p.61/2.
† The street was the focus of interwar black jazz and a magnet for white cultural 'tourists'; a less stereotyping name was 'Swing Street' which would also be used of a new jazz mecca, 52th street, after World War II.

lyrics. No-one was taking down what must have been spontaneous riffing, but J.D. Doyle, of the online Queer Music Heritage,
found one example.[*]

The song 'Alice Blue Gown' was a hit for Judy Garland in the
1919 Broadway show *Irene*. A verse ran:

> A new manner of fashion I'd found,
> And the world seemed to smile all around.
> 'Til it wilted, I wore it,
> I'll always adore it,
> My sweet little Alice blue gown!

Ms Bentley had variations on that glutinous theme:

> And he said, 'Dearie, please turn around'
> And he shoved that big thing up my brown
> He tore it. I bored it. Lord, how I adored it.
> My sweet little Alice Blue Gown.

Witty? Maybe not. Transgressive? Damn straight!

There were other songs, with lyrics that required no elabora-
tion. 'Big Gorilla Man' (1929) tells of 'That big gorilla, a woman
killa, and I ought to know, / he mistreats me, knocks and beats
me, still I love him so, / 'cause he's got that something that I
need so bad.' In 'Red Beans and Rice' (1929) Bentley has found
herself an involuntary vegetarian: her man is playing away, and
his 'meat' has left with him.

Ms Doyle adds that:

---

[*] https://www.queermusicheritage.com/feb2013s.html accessed 19 November 2018.

In the Harlem nightclubs she was wildly popular, with both blacks and whites, and especially with the Harlem Renaissance literary crowd. Langston Hughes called her 'an amazing exhibition of musical energy.' Another club customer wrote to poet Countee Cullen, 'When Gladys sings St. James Infirmary, it makes you weep your heart out.' Bentley was the inspiration for characters in several books of the time, including a gay novel by Blair Niles called 'Strange Brother.' Carl Van Vechten, one of the homosexual literati, described someone obviously like her in his book 'Parties.' He wrote about his character, 'when she pounds the piano the dawn comes up like thunder. She rocks the box, and tosses it ... and jumps it through hoops.' She was definitely a larger than life figure.

Another Bentley venue was the Ubangi Club (previously Connie's Inn). Here, dressed as ever in full evening dress (white-tie-and-tails and a white silk topper) she worked with a chorus line of 'eight liberally painted male sepians with effeminate voices and gestures.' Or one newspaper put it 'Jungleys Bentley and her "pansie" entertainment.'

Around 1940 she moved to the west coast, basing herself at Mona's 440, San Francisco's top lesbian nighterie.* The nudge-nudging songs continued, typically 'Gladys Isn't Gratis Anymore,' 'Lock and Key' and 'Jailbait.'

But as Eric Garber added, 'The United States cold war society could not tolerate a strong, uncompromising, Afro-American bulldagger'. As the country's Fifties-style moral panic, McCarthyism, shut down American freedoms, Bentley claimed

---

* The club was sold around 1955 and renamed Ann's 440 (from its new owner Ann Dee); it kept its lesbian wait-staff and its lesbian clientele but was happy to welcome mainstream entertainers, among them Johnny Mathis and a young Lenny Bruce.

to have renounced the lesbian life; she dressed straight, and rechristened herself as 'Fatso' Bentley. Writing under the headline 'I Am a Woman Again' she claimed to the readers of *Ebony* that after course of hormone injections she had returned to heterosexuality and was even married. Like all alleged converts she piled on the *mea culpas* as regarded her youthful 'sins'. She died in 1960; there was supposedly an autobiography 'If This be Sin' which sounds as if the convert had regressed. It wasn't published and we shall never know for sure.

Bentley was hardly alone in enjoying relationships with other women. Ma Rainey was perhaps less openly devoted to her girlfriends, but she too sang about such relationships, typically in *Prove it on Me Blues* (1928).

> I went out last night, had a great big fight
> Everything seemed to go wrong
> When I looked up, to my surprise
> The gal I was with was gone
>
> Folks say I'm crooked
> I don't know where she took it
> I want the whole world to know
>
> I went out last night with a crowd of my friends
> They must've been women, 'cause I don't like no men
> It's true I wear a collar and a tie,
> I like to watch the women as they pass by
>
> They say I do it, ain't nobody caught me
> They sure gotta prove it on me

Rainey's *Bo-Weevil Blues* (1923) is perhaps another 'coming-out' song.

> I don't want no man
> To put no sugar in my tea,
> I don't want no man,
> To put no sugar in my tea,
> Some of them are so evil,
> I'm 'fraid they might poison me.
> I went downtown
> and bought me a hat
> I brought it back home,
> I put it on the shelf
> Looked at my bed,
> I'm getting tired of sleeping by myself.

As well as the typical blues image of 'sugar in my tea', it might be noted, though there is no way of proving a conscious connection, that *hat* in the slang of the time meant variously the vagina, a prostitute and sexual intercourse.

Bessie Smith, the lover of a married woman, also used lyrics to out herself:

> When you see two women walking hand in hand,
> Just look 'em over and try to understand:
> They'll go to those parties – have the lights down low –
> Only those parties where women can go.
> You think I'm lying just ask Tacky Ann.
> They took many a broad from many a man.[*]

* Rainey sang it but the song was written in 1931 by George Hannah, an out gay bluesman; he entitled it 'The Boy in the Boat' (slang for the clitoris).

In any case, if showbiz rumour was true, the openly bisexual Smith didn't have much 'out' to come. As the story went, she was overheard one night on tour telling her lover Lillian Simpson, 'The hell with you, bitch. I got twelve women on this show and I can have one every night if I want it.'

If the UK had the music hall, then the US had its own version of 'variety': vaudeville.* It offered a show that mixed a wide variety of acts – listed in wikipedia as 'popular and classical musicians, singers, dancers, comedians, trained animals, magicians, ventriloquists, strongmen, female and male impersonators, acrobats, illustrated songs, jugglers, one-act plays or scenes from plays, athletes, lecturing celebrities, minstrels, and movies'[†]. Many of America's mid-twentieth-century popular stars began their professional lives on its stage. As theatres rushed to convert to cinemas many went on to the movies and triumphed yet again. Vaudeville did not. Born around 1880 it was gone by the early 1930s.

It could cut things pretty fine – like music hall there was a solid leavening of double entendre from those stars who used it – but 'vaud' was never so louche (or downright obscene) as the theatrical family's black sheep, burlesque, essentially the home of striptease, and showcasing a parade of what H.L. Mencken termed ecdysiasts[‡] sandwiched between comedians who, generally bereft of genuine wit, worked unashamedly 'blue'. It was

---

* The name boasts rival etymologies. As stated in the *OED* (1916): 'French *vaudeville*, earlier *vau* (plural *vaux*) *de ville*, *vau de vire*, and in full *chanson du Vau de Vire* a song of the valley of Vire (in Calvados, Normandy). The name is said to have been first given to songs composed by Olivier Basselin, a fuller of Vire in the 15th cent[ury].'

† https://en.wikipedia.org/wiki/Vaudeville accessed 21 November 2018.

‡ Minted from the Greek *ecdysis*, molting and first attached to the celebrated stripper Georgia Sothern who had asked the great essayist/critic for a 'new and more palatable' term for her occupation.

representative of the mindset and tastes of its mainly working-class audiences (often recent immigrants from Europe). Racial stereotypes were a given; the Marx Brothers for instance offered a Jew (Groucho), an Italian (Chico) and an Irishman (Harpo). There was a WASP (Zeppo) but the others were the top bananas.

As in music hall there were as many female stars as men. Perhaps the greatest, both then and later, would be Mae West, but before her came 'the girl who made vaudeville famous', Eva Tanguay (1879–1947). Scoring her first hit in 1901, by 1910 – 'the biggest attraction in vaudeville bar none' as her rival Sophie Tucker put it – she was earning $3,500 a week –$80,000-plus today – and when in 1924 she launched a list of new songs, the attendant publicity ballyhooed 'The Dynamic Force of Vaudeville, Resistless as the Torrential Tide That Tosses Madly Over the Teeming Cataract of Niagara [. . .] As Easy to Check the Rush of Waters Over the Falls as the Oncoming Multitudes of Pleasure Seekers to the Theatres Where the World's Most Popular Comedienne Appears.' In truth Tanguay was past her prime (and vaudeville too) but for a while she was untouchable. Like West she traded on her independence, her quite literal 'woman's liberation'.

Everything came back to sex. The style of dance, the costumes (what there was of them) the song titles. But Tanguay, like her disciple Mae West, was no passive fantasy: she made the rules. If she exploited her body then it was on her own terms. She was combative, self-interested, irrepressible, immodest. Seventy years on and she'd have been a punk. Now she was simply one of a kind. None of which seemed to alienate her audiences who queued round the block. And all of which made her a problem for such magnates as B.F. Keith, along with his partner Edward Albee, the dominant force in vaudeville. On the one hand Keith and his peers promoted their form of theatre as family entertainment – a clean, wholesome environment with its jugglers and animal acts, its country-wide chain of theatres known as the 'Sunday School Circuit' and the antithesis of shameless, working-class burlesque. On the other, while he cosied up to America's clamouring, censorious puritans, usually self-appointed, often allied to some version of religion, he remained a businessman. Eva Tanguay – racy, suggestive, overt – made sure the bottom line remained black. Blind eyes were turned.* Whatever its claims for 'cleanliness', vaudeville, after all, was the era's primary showcase for the sexualised female body. For all the moralistic mouthing, audiences could still enjoy Charmion, whose strip revealed 'fearful and wonderful lingerie', Princess Raja, whose own wriggle outdid that of her attendant snake, and swimming champ Annette Kellerman, whose skills justified an onstage appearance in her bathing costume, her figure carefully accentuated by Edward Albee's well-lit arrangement of revelatory mirrors. In 1908 there was the Salome craze, featuring various young women giving their own version of the 'Dance of the Seven Veils'. If one wanted a composite and ideal female performer it was probably 'Marie' of the team O'Rourke and Marie, set down by a reviewer as 'a young woman of lively spirits and exuberant personality who can undress on a slack wire and sing a song at the same time.'[†]

Tanguay fitted the bill, and moved beyond it. She made it all very clear – even if employing a necessary wink – in her songs: 'It's All Been Done Before But Not the Way I Do It', 'I Want

---

* This was Keith's way: the 'Sunday School Circuit' was also happy to host 'Art Studies', i.e. barely draped, if motionless females posed on stage, and such tableaux as 'The Bridegroom's Reverie', featuring a cigar-smoking young man watching as a succession of pretty girls 'in provocative attire' stepped through a picture frame.
† *N.Y. Dramatic Mirror*, 17 August 1907, p.11.

Someone to Go Wild With Me', 'Go As Far As You Like, Kid', and 'That's Why They Call Me Tabasco' (doubtless both 'hot' and 'saucy'). Above all there was what would become her theme song: 'I Don't Care', premiered in the Ziegfeld Follies of 1909. It gave her nickname, 'The I Don't Care Girl', and the lyrics ran in part:

They say I'm crazy, got no sense,
But I don't care,
They may or may not mean offense,
But I don't care,
You see I'm sort of independent,
Of a clever race descendent,
My star is on the ascendant,
That's why I don't care.

I don't care, I don't care
What they may think of me
I'm happy go lucky
Men say that I'm plucky
I'm happy and carefree
I don't care, I don't care
If I should get the mean and stony stare
And no one can faze me
By calling me crazy
'Cause I don't care.

A note on the sheet music prescribed: 'Sung with increasing volume and rowdiness.'

Tanguay would come to despise 'that wretched song' but like a catch-phrase, it was all part of the brand. Other nicknames included 'The Evangelist of Joy,' 'The Electric Hoyden', 'The Queen of Perpetual Motion', 'The Queen of Vivacity', 'The Modern Mystery', and the inevitable 'Miss Tabasco'. It was all press agent baloney, but Tanguay did her best to live up to her billing. The online magazine *Slate* looked back on her act in 2009:

> The effect was heightened by Tanguay's outré appearance and performance style. She had a pudgy face and reddish-blond hair that stretched upward in a snarled pile. (She sometimes dumped bottles of champagne over her head onstage.) She was of average height and a bit lumpy, but athletic; she squeezed herself into gaudy costumes that flaunted her buxom figure and powerfully muscled legs. She delivered her songs while executing dervishlike dances, complete with limb-flailing, leg kicks, breast-shaking, and violent tosses of the head; often, she seemed to be simulating orgasm. Tanguay suffered severe cramps from her performances—backstage, she instructed prop directors to unknot her calves by beating them with barrel staves. She told reporters that her goal was 'to move so fast and whirl so madly that no one would be able to see my bare legs.' Then there was Tanguay's voice. She sang in a slurred screech punctuated by yaps and cackles, ricocheting seemingly at random between her upper and lower registers.[*]

If some stars boasted of their refusal to carry money, Tanguay went the other way: her billfold, it was claimed, carried nothing smaller

---

[*] http://www.slate.com/articles/arts/music_box/2009/12/vanishing_act.html

than $1000 bills.* Her costumes were sensational. A thirty-minute act might include up to ten changes of dress, each one as over-the-top magnificent a confection as the last. Best-known was the '$40 dress', made of 4,000 one-cent coins and created in honour of the newly issued 'Lincoln' penny. It weighed 45 pounds. There was the Marseillese dress, in which she sang the French national anthem dressed in a few tricoleur flags. Tanguay was naturally keen to offer her take on the Salome craze of 1908: she came up with a dance of the seven veils which was maximum dance and minimum veils. Her costume, she claimed, was limited to a pair of pearls.

If there were no actual scandals in her life, she was always happy to create one, picking fights with fellow stars and those critics who dared give an unfavourable review. Her transgressive style extended to her affairs. There was her lover and fellow star, the black comedian George Walker, and her much-publicised engagement (one assumes unconsummated) to the then cele-brated cross-dresser and female impersonator Julian Eltinge. In case anyone might be mistaken, she dressed as a man (top-hat and tails) and he as a woman throughout the relationship. Tanguay naturally doubled down on the publicity with a song, 'That Wouldn't Make a Hit with Me':

When you marry some old guy
Who hasn't the decency to die,
Or you marry some old pill
Who you can neither cure nor kill
That wouldn't make a hit with me

---

* Her fortune was estimated at $2 million; it vanished in the Crash of 1929. She eked out what little she could salvage for the rest of her life and died, impoverished, in 1947. Still she was not yet forgotten: five hundred people – fans, fellow vaudeville veterans – attended the funeral and the L. A. *Examiner* headlined the event 'S.R.O.' showbiz for 'standing room only'.

It was, of course, a hit.

Her fans were legion. Among them Aleister Crowley, currently (albeit by his own reckoning) 'The Wickedest Man in the World'. He saw her in 1912 and claimed her as the perfect specimen of 'The American genius', who 'is, above all things, FREE; with all the advantages and disadvantages that that implies'. Tanguay was an epitome, 'starry chaste in her colossal corruption'. As for her performance, it

> is like the hashish dream of a hermit who is possessed of the devil. She cannot sing, as others sing; or dance, as others dance. She simply keeps on vibrating, both limbs and vocal chords without rhythm, tone, melody, or purpose . . . I feel as if I were poisoned by strychnine, so far as my body goes; I jerk, I writhe, I twist, I find no ease . . . She is perpetual irritation without possibility of satisfaction, an Avatar of sex-insomnia. Solitude of the Soul, the Worm that dieth not; ah, me! She is the Vulture of Prometheus, and she is the Music of Mitylene . . . I could kill myself at this moment for the wild love of her.*

In her time Tanguay was a one-off, but she was also a dry-run for a successor. She was the inspiration – 'without doubt the primary role model' according to West's biographer Simon Louvish† – and for a while over-arching rival of the woman who would take her place in vaudeville and thereafter parlay that level of success into something of a whole different scale.

Mae West, born Mary Jane West around 1893 (though

---

* A. Crowley, 'Drama be Damned! An Appreciation of Eva Tanguay', *The International* (New York), April 1918, pp.127–128.
† Louvish op. cit. p.17.

publicity always claimed 1900) was variously a vaudevillian, novelist, playwright, singer, movie star, gay icon and self-proclaimed feminist pioneer. In vaudeville, on Broadway and in time in Hollywood and thence around the world, West was also doing her best to challenge the censor and using slang to help her cause. With a career that rendered her synonymous with the 'naughty' double entendre, and being elevated as one of those, alongside Wilde and Dorothy Parker, to whom quotes were attributed whether or not she was the genuine originator, West became one of the great exploiters of language and slang, naturally, played an important role.

Tanguay, as suggested, was her immediate inspiration, but there were others: France's superstar singer-actress Gaby Deslys, another with a penchant for elaborate form-fitting gowns and lavish jewellery, the New York nightclub hostess Texas Guinan with her catchphrase 'Hello, sucker!', the British music hall male impersonators Vesta Tilley and Vesta Victoria and even Tanguay's 'non-husband' Julian Eltinge. In the end she was a consciously created brand: the blonde hair, the elaborate costumes – more like something from the Nineties than her own era, with a 'Gibson Girl' figure to match – the unfettered sexuality and the language. She was, it was said, a somewhat diminuendo figure away from the lights, but 'Mae West' was not Mae West, let alone Mary Jane.

In her many interviews she acknowledged the 'man-eater' image, adorning it with all her well-honed one-liners. Intellectuals, looking back, saw her as the 'intersection of power and sexuality'; critics, both kind and less so, saw a combination of raunchy dialogue, over-the-top costumes and in-your-face personality as the epitome of the working-class woman on the make. A difficult figure, in other words, but an inescapable one.

Aside from what became a lifelong crusade against 'narrow minded censors and silly taboos' West herself saw herself – tongue apparently far from cheek – as an educator and expounded the theory in her piece 'Sex in the Theatre' published in the New York theatre magazine *The Parade* in 1929.[*]

> For years I have been devoting my career in the theater to the education of the masses to certain sex truths. My last four plays [. . .] have all dealt with major, vital sex problems.
>
> In my play 'Sex' I presented the picture of a girl whose great beauty and economic poverty forced her into bad ways . . . 'Sex' has its educational value because it shows the life and psychology of a prostitute and also has its morals. Many people who saw it learned a lesson.
>
> In my play 'Pleasure Man' I showed the true picture of a man who was weak and who forgot the wise law of moderation – who was oversexed. The man came to no good in the end and many young men learned a lesson from the play. A great majority of our young men are oversexed or repressed, which is the same thing because it is unnatural.
>
> I admit that in my play 'Drag' I was a little bit premature. The public is still too childlike to face like grownups the problem of homo-sexuality. How few are the people who even know what the words means? Because of the universal ignorance I wrote 'Drag' with the intention of taking it to all the theaters in the country to teach the people.

Her career of course left Broadway for Hollywood, and she did not relinquish her love for slang, but the depredations of

[*] *The Parade*, p.12.

Hollywood's censor the Hays Office, embodiment of that mind-sapping campaign by Catholic blue-pencillers to impose their superstitions on a creative world seen as dangerously dominated by Jewish businessmen, hit her too. Her plays won no friends among the tiny-minded, but on the whole the Broadway scripts she created as 'Jane Mast' survived to a far greater extent as she wrote them than would the lines she spoke in scripts such as those of the play *Diamond Lil* (1928) and the movie that was based on its story, *She Done Him Wrong* (1933).

Like many writers before and after her, West used slang as a source of tangible authenticity. Whores talked like whores, villains like villains, cops like cops and gay men, at least to an extent, like gay men. This was not to position the showbusiness goddess as some kind of part-time lexicographer. She sought and found as she needed, and used her trophies as necessary. Simon Louvish offers an insight into her technique:

> Mae's use of slang, like her collection of quips, was built up as much by picking words and phrases from written sources as any oral memory of underworld phrases. One clipping in her personal archive, dating from April 1929 [. . .] gives a clue to her ongoing magpie tendencies: an article by one Colonel Givens, ex-Chicago reporter, in the Saturday Evening Post sets out the different words used by rooks [. . .] old English terms such as 'cadge . . . patter, filch, moonshine, booze', or the prison argot: 'death house, hot seat . . . slug, blackjack, heat, rod, gat' et cetera.[*]

Slang plays a large part in the plays. It has a role from the

* Louvish op. cit. pp.156–157.

earliest, *The Albatross* (1924), which opens with three pimps chatting. Their talk is all counter-language, and offers *B-girl* (a prostitute working a bar), *chisel* (to cheat), *dough* (money), *squawk* (inform), *roll* (to rob a client), *wise* (criminally astute), *business* (prostitution), *dump* and *hole* (an unpleasant place), *this baby* (oneself), *dame, wise crack, give someone the air* (to dismiss), *folding money, racket, highbrow, go straight, heavy sugar daddy* (a gullible rich man) and *bunch* (a gang). Whether she picked up the lexis first-hand or whether, like so many others, she plucked it from the gangland interviews offered by the tabloid press, was of no importance. That she interwove slang into her work from day one was what mattered.

Sex, the first 'educational' play, followed in 1926. One can see what was coming from the first ten characters to be listed in the programme: 'Margy LaMont – A prostitute, Rocky Waldron – A pimp, Manly – A thug, Curley – A pimp, Dawson – A corrupt officer of the law, Agnes – A prostitute and best friend of Margy LaMont, Red – A prostitute, Flossie – A prostitute, Jones – A client.'

The play was a huge hit, running for 375 performances and bringing in some 325,000 customers. On a good night it could pull down around $16,500, which challenged the take at many 'legitimate' box offices. What brought its problems was that West refused to punish her heroine – if one must portray a prostitute, then this was (and often remains) her mandatory fate – and used her script to savage middle-class hypocrisy. In short, *Sex* told audiences: if commercial sex must be seen as 'bad' then this was not women's fault but men's. This was not what suburban America, out for a few proxy thrills on the Big Apple's wild side but always keen to have their prejudices confirmed, wanted to hear. The *Variety* reviewer 'Con' (Jack Conway, always a fan even if his boss 'Sime' Silverman was consistently negative when it came to West's writing) called the play his 'three-star special'; and Mae 'the Babe Ruth of the Stage "Prosties"', urging audiences to 'bring along your sweat shirt. You'll need it.' But the positive review added, 'Mae's conception of Margie La Mont will sentence her to the scarlet sisterhood for life.'

The New York Police Department obviously agreed, and confusing fiction with fact, raided the show on the grounds that it violated public decency. As 'Con' implied, Mae/Margie might as well have been a real-life hooker. The play had been running for eight months and maybe the law had finally decided that since enough of their own, plus a selection of judges, lawyers and DAs had by now found the time to see it, it could at last be shut down. In addition there were rumours that among its angels was Owney Madden, the British-born gangster now cutting his swathe through New York.* It was also down to timing; the alleged problem of 'dirt plays' was obsessing the authorities, urged on, as ever, by the puritan chorus. West and the company were charged with obscenity. The verdict: West was fined $500 and jailed for ten days in the workhouse on Welfare Island (now Roosevelt Island). She cleaned floors but the warders, acknowledging her celebrity, were generally pleasant. The publicity, as ever, did her nothing but good. The script offered the usual share of slang – among it *all to pieces*, *attaboy*, *don't make me laugh*, *freight* (the bill), *goat* (i.e. scapegoat) and *charity* (a woman who 'gives it away') – but nothing exceptional.

If *Sex* aimed to take a more liberal look at prostitution, West's

---

* Whether, as rumoured, the pair had an affair remains unproven (there is one photo of them side by side). But Madden, who with partner George Fox 'Big Frenchy' de Mange, was owner of Harlem's main nighterie The Cotton Club, knew show business and Mae West certainly liked tough guys.

follow-up, *The Drag* (1927) turned to another of her interests: the gay scene. Its message was embodied in one character's declaration: 'How was I to know it was wrong when it seemed perfectly natural to me.' The climactic scene was a drag ball for which West employed forty real-life gay men, including 'truck driver types'. It was another hit, reportedly earning its creator thirty thousand dollars on its opening night, but if the public proved broad-minded, the critics did not, uniformly decrying so open a portrayal of homosexuality. The show, according to one, was 'A "homosexual" comedy drama, exploiting sixty – count 'em, sixty – of those strange individuals that pathologists call the "third sex".'* The final curtain came down after a mere two weeks, another victim of the campaign against 'dirt'. *The Drag* was not the only gay play that year. *The Captive*, based on a French original (*La Prisonnière* by Édouard Bourdet) and focusing on lesbianism, ran for 160 performances before it too was hauled off by the authorities for its own obscenity prosecution. West was unsympathetic and made no effort to support her equivalent as defendant, the actress Helen Menken (Humphrey Bogart's first wife): her sexual teaching did not extend to that kind of woman, whose tastes she found 'unnatural'.

The Drag obviously offered a brief slang lexis. In strictly gay terms there was *drag* itself, i.e. man–woman cross-dressing, *queen*, *bitch* and *moll* (both effeminate males), *rag* (a wig) and *trade* (a gay male whore's male client).

Two busts down and West refused to give in. In 1928 she offered audiences *Pleasure Man*, essentially a heterosexual

---

* The *third sex* was a new invention, first recorded for homosexuals in 1896 (though there had been joking uses to mean clergymen prior to that); it also flourished briefly during World War I as a description of women who, usually unemployed, took over 'male' jobs.

reworking of *The Drag*, although she kept the last act's drag ball. This time the cops didn't even wait for their play-loving members to visit. The bust came after the première on 1 October and West and her fifty-five-strong cast were hauled off to the hoosegow and charged with indecency. They were out with permission to play a (revised) matinee the next day but that was busted as well, with the police pulling the plugs in the middle of the show and the cast, still powdered and dragged up for the ball, were piled into a queue of Black Marias. There was time, however, for one of the queens to deliver a speech on police oppression. The press talked of a mayoral campaign to 'purify Broadway' in a Presidential election year.

It would be two years before the play arrived in court. Meanwhile the critics had their say. It was generally negative. And while the new play had an ostensibly heterosexual plot, *Variety* – where Jack Conway stood out as a constant supporter – had *Pleasure Man* down as 'the queerest show you've ever seen. All the Queens are in it.' Still, he urged, offering his own double-entendre, 'Oh my dear, you must throw on a shawl and run over to the Biltmore [Theatre]' for a ticket, adding 'you must see it to appreciate the strides we girls are making.' Elsewhere there were mentions of 'Harlem bacchanales', 'filth' and 'foul exhibitionism'.

If the plot was straight, the scenes set among a group of chorus boys enjoying an after-work get-together made it clear the West was still not compromising. It's all very *Carry On*:

FIRST BOY: I hear you're working in a millinery shop.
SECOND BOY: Yes, I trim rough sailors.
THIRD BOY: My, what a low-cut gown you've got!
FOURTH BOY: Why, Beaulah, a woman with a back like mine can be as low as she wants to be.

FIRST BOY: I hear you're studying to be an opera singer.

THIRD BOY: Oh, yes, and I know so many songs.

FIRST BOY: You must have a large repertoire.

THIRD BOY: Must I have that too?

FOURTH BOY: Oh, look, I can almost do the split.

SECOND BOY: Be careful, dearie, you'll wear out your welcome.

Or, as the prosecution put it, this was 'sex, degeneracy, and sex perversion'. The trial, notes Louvish, 'was riddled with homophobia, chastising the "degenerates" that they saw on the stage, and asking if their manners of female impersonation carried on off stage. The jury failed to reach a decision and the charges were dismissed.' West, who had not been among the actors, did not have to give evidence; she was still fined $60,000.

The script was among her slangiest. There were more gay terms: *lavender* and *queer*, *cream puff* and *queenie* and the camp suggestion 'stick to your knitting'. Other terms included *boudoir bandicoot* (a variation on the era's *lounge lizard*) and *drugstore cowboy*, *baloney*, *bimbo*, *false alarm* (a braggart), *dirt* (information, usually scurrilous), *mess* (an ineffectual individual), *giggle-water*, *pushover*, *pipe* (anything easy), *pull a fast one*, *get one's hips up* (*on one's shoulders*) (to get upset), *keep your trap shut*.

There were other plays. Even 'Con' couldn't save *The Wicked Age* (1927) and while Louvish calls it the 'sassiest' of her play-scripts *Variety* dismissed it as 'tripe'. Mae plays Babe Carson, a girl in her late teens (offstage she was actually thirty-four) who goes 'from flapper tantrums to the darker shores of a cocaine habit'[*] and, on the upside, minor stardom. The play managed a three-week run but didn't even need the police to force an early

---

[*] Louvish op.cit. p.141.

finish. Still, West offered her usual philosophy. When her stage grandfather condemns her 'immodesty' as 'filthy, low – a wicked – bad', 'Babe' ripostes: 'I want to be bad – I'm sick and tired of trying to live the life you want me to live – I don't want to be good – I want to be rotten – I want to be filthy low – vile – call it anything you please – but God I want to live my own life.' Hollywood's future teen rebels Marlon Brando and James Dean couldn't have put it better.

There was also a novel, *Babe Gordon*, published in 1930. It featured yet another soiled dove and focused on what might have been predicted by those who had been following Mae's socio-cultural 'classes': race relations. (The book was renamed *The Constant Sinner* after a publicity competition judged by the gossip columnist Walter Winchell; the play based on its plot took the same name.)

There is no evidence of West as a fan of pulp magazines and the hard-boiled, proto-noir fiction that the 'detective pulps' promoted. Still, Babe definitely had the right stuff. The book began:

Babe Gordon leaned against the crumbling red brick wall of the Marathon Athletic Club in Harlem . . . and pulled at a cigarette . . . Babe scanned the humans with an eye to business. Babe was eighteen and a prizefighter's tart, picking up her living on their hard-earned winnings. Her acquaintances numbered trollops, murderers, bootleggers and gambling-den keepers. Two well-modelled bare legs were crossed at the ankles; her waist pressed to the wall rose to voluptuous breasts that almost protruded from the negligible neck of her black dress. Babe waited for Cokey Jenny.

As for the slang, it was as one would expect. West may have picked it up from her researches, but as ever it fitted the bill:

> *airedale* (an ugly man), *bust* and *lemon* (a failure), *chassis*, *chef* (to prepare opium for smoking), *choke* (to stop an action), *chop suey* (Chinese), *circus* (a live sex show), *connection* (a drug wholesaler), *cube* (a block of morphine), *dinge* (a person of colour), *double-X* (an act of betrayal), *fix-up* (a narcotic injection), *policy king* (a 'numbers' racketeer), *leg worker* and *steer* (a tout), *parking* (necking in a parked car), *pink* and *pinktoe* (a white person), *put the knock on* (to disparage), *reek* (obscene speech), *shuck* (to tease), *socker* (a boxer), *spaghetti bender* (Italian), *trick house* (a brothel), *turn on the waterworks* (to cry), *two-cent* (second-rate) and *wallop* (a blow).

West, with her vaudeville antecedents and worldwide movie stardom was ultimately a one-off. Yet there were descendants, and not merely what the tabs might term 'busty blondes with a good line of gab'. West's love of sex-based double entendres would come to typify other women, less stars than herself but still highly successful in their moment.

The Sixties and Seventies were the moment of the 'party record'. Star of the men's corner was the African-American entertainer Rudy Ray Moore (1927–2008), who took the name Dolemite from the famously hard (nudge-nudge) mineral and his style from the traditional prison 'toasts' (unfettered, grossly obscene rhyming tales of the world of pimps, players and hos, passed down as oral fantasies from con to con). A selection of Moore's album titles – *Eat Out More Often*, *This Pussy Belongs To Me*, *Sweet Peeter Jeeter* and *The Dirty Dozens* (a form of ritualised insults, usually involving slurs against a rival's mother and delivered as a quasi-competition between two players) – makes his hugely popular *shtick* wholly clear.

What Moore could do for the boys, a group of women did for the girls. Some, such as Hattie Noel were black, but the core – among them Pearl Williams, Rusty Warren, Bea Bea Benson and Belle Barth – were Jewish, though 'nice Jewish girls' need not apply. These 'unkosher comediennes', as Sarah Blacher Cohen calls them in *Jewish Wry*, the collection of essays she edited in 1987, were working-class women, tough-talking, earthy *balaboostas** straight out of the old country, who sprinkled their smut with Yiddish and offered an up-front rejection of the 'whitebread' American strictures that were the price of the assimilation that so many of their *landsmen* (whether men or women) craved.[†]

Largely invisible today (excepting occasional snippets online) they were enormously successful. They earned top dollar and played Carnegie Hall, Caesar's Palace and fashionable nightclubs like El Morocco; their records sold in the millions. Belle Barth (born Belle Salzman), self-titled 'Doyenne of the Dirty Ditty', racked up two million units of albums called *I Don't Mean to be Vulgar, But It's Profitable* (1961) and *If I Embarrass You, Tell Your Friends* (1960) which latter sold 400,000 despite being banned from record store displays. She was indeed dirty, scatological even. The Barth version of 'Home on the Range' embellished 'Show me a home where the buffalo roam . . .' with 'I'll show you a home full of *pishartz*' [i.e. urine]. Adolescent wit at best,

---

* Not, despite the assonance, from the derogatory *ball-buster*, however regularly used of women, but the Hebrew *ba'alathabayit*, the master of the house (such a woman of course rendered male by proxy).
† Ms Cohen sees such female comedians as, by religious standards, having literally 'foul mouths'; their humour was irrelevant: simply by standing on a stage and talking they profaned everything sacred that had been adduced to a 'kosher' Jewish woman.

but in 1960, definitely non-standard; and she regularly pushed the envelope much further than that.

As Cohen says, Barth's humour was far more raw than any male contemporary. Lenny Bruce, another christened Jew and hounded as a 'sick' comedian, was restrained in comparison, but his primary sin, obscene polysyllables aside, was mocking the political status quo plus of course his drug use and an affection for jazz, which meant blacks. Bruce mocked men for their sexual insecurity. Barth, one more fat girl armoured by her perceived ugliness, savaged men by teasing women. To quote Ms Cohen again, 'Barth states "the most difficult thing for a woman to do on the first night of her second marriage is to holler it hurts" and for the new husband "to tie his feet to the bed so he doesn't fall in and drown".'[*] All you needed was the emphatic rim-shot and you were in the grubbiest depths of burlesque.

Their origins, if not directly with West, lay with her contemporary and one-time rival Sophie Tucker (born Sofia Kalish and like the 'party' performers, Jewish), who might have begun her vaudeville career sporting blackface and a grotesque 'southern' accent – seen as too fat and unattractive to sing as a white girl, she was billed as the 'Manipulator of Coon Melodies' – but hit stardom when she went back to her own basics and moved onto hardcore schmaltz with such titles as 'My Yiddishe Momma'.[†] Her nickname, 'Last of the Red Hot Mommas' (no-one has ever identified the first), allegedly referenced her appetite, rivalling that of Mae West, for sex. It also called up that period between blackface and *yiddishkeit* where her act approached nearest to

---

[*] Cohen op. cit. p.113.
[†] Despite the Williams-Barth double-act, that stereotype, as Jeremy Dauber notes in his 'serious history' of *Jewish Comedy* (2017) was the one that these raunchy mistresses of the double entendres left well alone.

burlesque. Cohen quotes her fellow star Eddie Cantor: 'She sings words we used to write on the sidewalks of New York.'[*] Or perhaps implied them. A typical couplet from 'Mistah Siegel, you Better Make it Legal' ran 'My mamma told me yesterday I'm gaining weight / It's not from something I ate'. A few lines on, talking of her unborn child, she masks it in Yiddish. Not a foetus but a 'kiegel', a noodle pudding. Her heroines seemed to have a problem with contraception: 'You promised to give me the mink in July,' she sang in 'When am I Getting the Mink, Mr Fink?', 'It's three months overdue and so am I.' In the end, as Ms Cohen notes, Tucker played 'the feisty lady [who] knows her own worth and will not be short-changed by men.'[†] As another song title put it: 'I'm Living Alone and I Like It.'

According to one album sleeve, Tucker, on meeting Pearl Williams, had told her 'You're me at your age, only better.' Williams' titles suggest a mix of folksy American Judaism and smut: *Bagels and Lox*, and *Battle of the Mothers* (with Belle Barth) mixed with *Pearl Williams Goes All the Way, She's Doin' What Comes Naturally! A Trip Around the World Is Not a Cruise* (1961) and the 'best of' compilation, *Party Snatches*. Williams' own take was simple and unabashed: 'I get broads come in here, they sit in front of me and they stare at me. Everything I do, they stare at me. Then they walk out saying, "She's so dirrr-ty!" If they're so refined how come they understand what I'm saying?'

Typical Williams lines were 'Definition of indecent: if it's long enough, hard enough and in far enough, it's in decent . . . Definition of a cotton picker: a girl who loses the string on her Tampax . . . Hear about the broad who walks into the hardware store to buy a hinge? The clerk says, "Madam, would you like a

---

* Cohen op. cit. p.107.
† Cohen op. cit. p.109.

screw for this hinge?" She says, "No, but I'll blow ya for the toaster" ... Two broads are passing a beauty parlor and one turns to the other and says "Gee, I think I smell hair burning". And the other says "Maybe we're walking a little too fast".' Old jokes, probably worn thin in burlesque, but not usually retailed by a woman. She kept things up off script. Faced by a heckler who shouted at the undeniably zaftig performer, 'Pull your dress down!' Williams hit back: 'Pull my dress down? To where? Which part of me do you want to see first? I got an awful lot here, honey. Take a good look. You could never handle this, boy. You need eight guys: four to put you on, four to take you off. A night with me and you'll disappear for a month, ya dope, ya. And how's he gonna find this thing, there's so many wrinkles around it! I'll have to urinate to give you a clue!' There was, of course, no honour among minority thieves. 'Hear about the fag who was brushing his teeth one morning and his gums began to bleed. "Thank God," he says, "safe for another thirty days."'

The press, which covered them and were happy to run the ads for their shows, handled them with care: reviews might be kind, but smirking 'health warnings' were mandatory. All the comediennes were billed as 'explosive', no paper printed any of their spiel, merely words like 'risqué' and 'saucy'. The 'explosive blond bombshell 'Bea Bea Benson, 'rated XXX' – 'she's a horny honey and pretty damn funny' – made just two albums: *Let It All Hang Out* and *Open and Enter*. If one paused a moment, the speech bubble that displayed the title of the first took the shape of an impressively well-hung penis and testes; that of the second offered a caricatured, lingerie-clad Benson waving a large key and making it clear that it would open the padlock adorning her genital area. Many routines seemed to focus on rape: 'Gee but it's great after rapin' your date, draggin' the body back home' . . . 'The gal who didn't know she'd been raped till her cheque bounced' . . . 'Poon tang cocktail – very refreshing no matter *whose* joint you get it in.' The Sixties: a definitely other world.

An online biography names Rusty Warren 'queen of the party records'.* Born Ilene Goldman in 1939 she started in classical music training but after a summer in a piano lounge fell hard for show business. Directly influenced by Sophie Tucker, whose bluer material was passed around via 'underground' recordings, she set off in the same direction – though unlike Tucker or her own contemporaries, she made no attempt at a Jewish persona – and in 1959 issued her first record: *Songs for Sinners*. The title of its standout track, 'Knockers Up!' (urging her fellow-women to discard their inhibitions and express their sexuality – the method seemingly based on free-swinging breasts and a good decade before the 'libbers' supposedly advocated burning one's bra) was recycled to name the follow-up album release a year later. When this became a huge hit (publicity-free, it was all word-of-mouth; one million copies sold), and featured on the charts for thirty-six months, Warren was made and albums such as *Sin-Sational* and *Rusty Warren Bounces Back* followed. In hindsight she would be nicknamed the 'mother of the sexual revolution'. A little hyperbolic, but as she put it, she was saying the previously unsaid: 'It was improper for a woman to speak the way I did. Hell, I admitted to the entire world that we women liked sex . . . We weren't even telling the ones we were doing it with that we liked it.'

Times changed. What worked in 1960 was more than a little embarrassing five years later. This, for instance, was the

* Jason Ankeny at https://www.allmusic.com/artist/rusty-warren-mn0000806900/biography

performance of another of Warren's mammary-focused cries for female freedom, 'Bounce Your Boobies: a patriotic song' (complete with *piano* military cadence) released in 1961.

> You know girls, it's great to live in a democracy today, where freedom is everywhere. But girls, we often take this freedom for granted: freedom of speech, freedom of thought, and freedom of action. But you know gals, just because a bunch of men signed that Declaration Of Independence in 1776, doesn't mean that freedom was for men alone. Oh no, you take Tom Jefferson, Ben Franklin, John Hancock – there's a helluva guy for you right there! All these men had wives. They probably had a few broads on the side too. These women wanted freedom just as much as their men did. But gals, I wonder, do we? I think it's time that we women thought about it a bit. Hell, I think it's time we did something about it. So come on, fellow females of the 20th century! Be glad that you're an American! Proclaim your freedom! Stand at attention! Pledge Allegiance! And . . .

> Bounce your boobies, get into the swing.
> Bounce your boobies, the swing is everything.
> Makes no difference if they're big or small,
> As long as you – ooh! –give 'em your all.

> Bounce your boobies.
> Come on, honey, bounce 'em up and down.
> Bounce your boobies.
> Come on, bounce your boobies, honey. Come on.

Loosen the bra that binds you!
Take it off if you feel like it!
Come on, bounce your boobies.
Here we go. Doesn't that feel good?
Bounce your boobies.

You know girls, men aren't the only people in the world
today that have something to give, but it sure looks like it
sometimes. Just look around you – men stick out all over
the place. Big fat cigars. Big fat stomachs. And just where
they should stick out – phhbtt! – where *is* it?!

Yes, girls, we know what we've got, and we know what they're
worth. So come on, gals, let's get into the swing of things.
Give your boobies some freedom! All together now!

Bounce your boobies, let 'em rock 'n' roll.
Nudge your knockers, keep 'em hot and so.
Just admit it, gals, it sure feels great
To feel them swingin', ooh, titilate!

As ever, it's all down to context.

Hip-hop, latterly rap, emerged in the late 1970s and has come to
dominate popular music on a worldwide level. It too can be seen
as beginning as party music – performances taking place in
private houses rather than clubs and then full-scale venues.
Women were involved from the start, among them Salt-N-Pepa,
Lady of Rage, Roxanne Shanté, The Real Roxanne, Sparky D
and Missy Elliott. Over the last thirty years stars have included
Foxy Brown, Lil Kim, Rah Digga, Da Brat, Queen Latifah,

Lauryn Hill, MC Lyte, Sister Souljah, and current goddesses Nicki Minaj and Cardi B.

If their lyrics use slang, then it is no more nor less than their male peers. The bulk of the contemporary slang lexis is available, it is pointless to select one over another. If slang, once so secretive and so disdained has moved into the mainstream, then it is the rise of rap that has propelled it. Some knowledge is required for even a basic understanding. Subsets – London's drill music, which seems to be a male-only territory, or the local variation coming out of 'the Dirty South', i.e. Houston, TX – remain less immediately accessible, but slang being slang, the established synonymy is still generating the predictable stereotypes. One could assemble a vocabulary from cherry-picking the lyrics of all the artists mentioned above. Instead, and proof that if slang may no longer be as secret as it once proclaimed, the form still maintains a daunting challenge to an unversed 'translator', here is an example of the 2018 state of the art from the first verse of the out lesbian rapper Young M.A.'s 'I Get the Bag' (which had notched up over 21.6 million hits at date of access).

All this is what we doin'
I gotta get cocky on this one
I gotta get a little *bocky* on this one

You get the *bag* and fumble it, I get the bag and flip it and
    tumble it [a bag of drug money]
Car came with a slut in it, then I made the bitch cum in it
Double cuppin' it, no *lean* just the red punch with the rum in
    it
Silky on, fresh white tee with the Constructs on, thuggin' it

The block *hot* so I'm *tuckin'* it, *Glizzy* came with a drum in
it

Treat my *Nina* like my old hoe, start actin' up and I'm
dumpin' it

I don't really play the scenes like AD, I'm *in the cut* with it

Louis bag with the hunnids in it quarter million in it had to
stuff it in it

Wake and bake in the oven with it, if it ain't skunkin I ain't
fucking with it

White Cars with the black rims, but the inside *peanut butter*
with it

Still *gutter* with it, still Red Colors with it, still blood for my
brother with it

Benz truck put my mother in it, these checks keep on
repeating

Bank account got a stutter in it, bitch nigga I'm eating

Treat the pussy like a *plumber* nigga, put my *plunger* in it she
screaming

Kickin hoes out the hotel like a punter with it, they schemin'

Not stupid or a sucker nigga, hoes wanna come up I *peep* it

Young nigga from the concrete, now I'm seeing palm trees

Tryna get a double R on my car keys and on the car seats

bocky: the practice of members of the Bloods, whose colour
is red, to replace initial 'c' with a 'b' as a sign of gang
loyalty

double-cuppin': two styrofoam cups – one inside the other –
filled with *drank or purp*, a codeine-based cough mixture

lean: an alternative name for drank

silky: a form of bandana wrapped around the head

hot: dangerous, i.e. from police or rival gang activity

Glizzy: a Glock semi-automatic pistol

tucking: concealing, in this case the bag

nina: a 9mm handgun

in the cut: present

Louis: i.e. the luxury brand Louis Vuitton

wake and bake: marijuana

peanut butter: brown leather automobile upholstery

gutter: a synonym for 'street', i.e. 'real life' as led by gang-bangers, drug dealers

plunger: Young M.A. being a lesbian she has no penis and the plumber/plunger imagery suggests using a strap-on dildo during woman-to-woman sex

peep: to check out, to assess

concrete: the city, again synonymous with 'street'

double R: the initials of Rolls Royce

The problem is that as the use of slang becomes less esoteric, then that use becomes more widely spread and while it is ever easier to track it down, there are proportionately fewer creators for whom slang is the rationale of what they write.

12. On the Job

'Dixon is sure to remind us of that. I was thinking that, if we wanted any help in the house while he is here, we could perhaps get Mary Higgins. She is very slack of work, and is a good girl, and would take pains to do her best, I am sure, and would sleep at home, and need never come upstairs, so as to know who is in the house.'

'As you please. As Dixon pleases. But, Margaret, don't get to use these horrid Milton words. "Slack of work:" it is a provincialism. What will your aunt Shaw say, if she hears you use it on her return?'

'Oh, mamma! don't try and make a bugbear of aunt Shaw' said Margaret, laughing. 'Edith picked up all sorts of military slang from Captain Lennox, and aunt Shaw never took any notice of it.'

'But yours is factory slang.'

'And if I live in a factory town, I must speak factory language when I want it. Why, mamma, I could astonish you with a great many words you never heard in your life. I don't believe you know what a knobstick is.'

Mrs Gaskell *North and South* (1855)

DESPITE WHAT MAMMA terms its 'vulgar sound', not to mention a definite potential for coarseness, *knobstick* in a factory context means a strike-breaker, a scab.[*] And Mrs Gaskell was another major nineteenth-century female author who threw into her work a variety of slang.

Knobstick aside, there is *bishop* (to let something burn), *clem* (to be hungry), *cousin betty* (a foolish woman), *give someone the bucket* (to jilt or reject as a lover), *go off* (to take place), *lazyboots* (a lazy person), *moonlight flitting* (running off to avoid paying the rent), the adverb *sore* (utterly), *sport* (to read an author for amusement rather than instruction), *squiffy* (tipsy), *weedy* (spineless, weak) and *widow-bewitched* (woman whose husband is temporarily absent). As ever, some have survived and others, again including knobstick, have not.

North and South deals in part with factory life, and while Mrs Gaskell doesn't offer any other in-house language, there is no doubt that factories and other work environments have their own language. One might term it occupational slang, otherwise categorised as jargon.[†] It often deals with circumstances, people and things that can only be found in a specific context. In a hospital it might deal with names for various instruments, for instance nicknames for syringes, catheters and those of specific drugs, in the military the jargon would refer to the names of weapons or vehicles or perhaps specific places, whether within a barracks or on a battlefield. Place-names can also be found in much campus or school slang. In all occupations there will be names for given people, or more likely their job titles. It is

---

* The *OED* offers no etymology and nor can I, other than wonder if the term suggests a strike-breaker's hardness of head, or perhaps a pun on *stick*, to stay in place.
† From French *jargon*, the 'twittering of birds'. This is not the obfuscatory jargon of self-preserving authoritarian mendacity, but a local slang generated and used by a specific job.

widespread: there is probably as much jargon as there are occupations to cultivate it.

Jargon, while rubbing up close to slang, is still not slang as such. However a degree of in-job slang is generated, short-cuts that like all slang facilitate conversation and understanding between associated groups and at the same exclude the uninitiated. This will naturally refer to circumstances that do not exist outside the job, but the words and phrases are likely to be more general, and less focused. In occupations that tend to be dominated by a female workforce, one may assume that the language is created by those women.

As ever there is the problem of evidence. Or lack of it. We can assume the presence of on-the-job slang but we rarely find it listed. The revised *OED* currently finds the first instance of *shopgirl* in 1752 (there is then a gap until 1824 and further citations are from America). What it doesn't offer is the sort of things she said. This isn't just a problem of lexicography. Émile Zola's *Au Bonheur des Dames* ('The Ladies' Paradise' 1883) takes place almost entirely within what was then a new phenomenon, the department store (his model being Le Bon Marché*). It teems with shopgirls, but we are never allowed to eavesdrop on their chat. One of slang's few direct references to the occupation comes in the definition of the mid-nineteenth-century *dollymop*, a servant or shopgirl (often a milliner) turned part-time prostitute, who sells her body to supplement her otherwise meagre income.† We have the same problem with *factory girls*, who appear in 1816 initially 'as a term of

---

* Literally 'the good market' it is now French for 'cheap'.
† Her French equivalent was the *grisette*, another shopgirl turned amateur whore when necessity called. A statue, commemorating this working-class heroine, stands near the place de la Republique in Paris.

degradation' and applying to a very young girl employed in an adult job.

The journal *American Speech* (founded in 1925) at one time specialised in amassing and publishing 'local' glossaries, but they tended to focus on heavily male institutions: colleges, the military, sports. And as we have seen, when a researcher did turn to an area of life in which women might predominate, e.g. Maurer and his comments on prostitution, it was proclaimed that there really wasn't much to discuss. The journal pioneered the study of college vocabularies, but these were undifferentiated so far as gender was concerned nor did subsequent lists make any effort to split girls from boys. By 1985 the journal had offered sixty-two lists of terms for a wide range of topics, from architecture to wrestling and including such taxonomies as those of barbershop quartets, truck-driving, jazz, law, medicine, moonshining, chess, death, and a variety of sports, but gender (other than coincidentally, e.g. in certain studies regarding homosexuality) does not feature among them. In 1939 W.J. Burke of the New York Public Library used the library's holdings to create a booklet, *The Literature of Slang*. It devotes a dozen pages to 'Occupational' language (cowboys, glassblowers, lumberjacks, oystermen, etc.) but again, none have division by gender (and there no 'women's jobs'), any more than do the trade jargons collected by the contemporary Federal Writers' Project.

We have a few fleeting examples to tease us. The US short story writer O. Henry, whose collection *The Four Million* deliberately mocked the 'four hundred' i.e. New York's aristocratic elite, gives us a number of working girls, but they are not exceptionally slangy. *The Fairmount Girls*, a series by Etta Anthony Barker & Maud Tarsey, notes that the local factory girls define themselves by use of slang, arguing 'Dollars to donuts it is!'

'Betcher life it ain't'. But slang's status is obviously not high: the Girls themselves – middle-class schoolgirls – have set up a slang box with five cent fines for every time they use it. Another series, *The Girls of Central High on Lake Luna* by Gertrude W. Morrison ('My! what frightful whiskers.' 'He looks just like a pirate.') has such stereotypes as the (all too likely) Irish 'hired girl'. Like her stereotypes everywhere she knew her linguistic place: 'Sure and I was a bogtrotter when I landed, and we did kape the pig in the kitchen.' Still, she's not the Italian organ grinder and his monkey: '"Which is the 'monk'?" demanded Lance, in a whisper.'

Slang isn't much for clothes – there are words for hats, but most seem to be male, and if there is a little rhyming slang for 'dress' (*more or less, mustard-and-cress, watercress*) then skirts and blouses miss the cut. Nor, other than *lippy*, lipstick, is there cosmetics. What there is, however, is hairstyles. Again these are often male, but for once girls, who were presumably the ones to use the terminology, get a look-in. And there have been:

aggerawator (a well-greased lock of hair twisted and pointing either at the corner of an eye or at an ear)

beavertail (a style in which middle-class women wore their hair in a net, which then fell onto their shoulders)

bee-gum (a woman piles her hair on the top of her head)

beehive (it resembles a hive from excessive back-combing)

biscuit (the hair is done up in a small knot, usually favoured by elderly women with thinning hair; the word is a pun on standard English *biscuit*, a 'small bun')

burn (a permanent wave)

Croydon facelift (the hair is pulled back tightly from the face, supposedly giving the effect of a facelift; stereotyped as beloved of working-class young women) *door-knocker* (two plaits bunched on top of the head)

doormat (a short hairstyle once popular in Australia)

flop (the hair is worn low over the brow)

idiot fringe (the hair is hair combed down, fringe-wise, over the forehead)

love curls (the hair is cut short and worn low over the forehead)

Newgate knocker (two broad plaits behind looped up and tied with a ribbon; a parallel male version featured a lock of hair shaped like the figure 6 and twisted from the temple back towards the ear)

Piccadilly fringe (the hair is cut short into a fringe and curled over the forehead)

We need, however, something more substantial. It existed, but we must revisit that land of larrikinesses, Australia. The world of the cardboard box and allied stationery manufacturers, known as 'Spats' Fac'try' and created by the Australian writer Edward Dyson, flourished in a fictional Melbourne either side of 1910. Initially published in the weekly Sydney *Bulletin*, the tales were soon offered as books. *Fact'ry 'Ands* appeared in 1906, *Benno and Some of the Push* in 1911 and *Spats' Fact'ry* (largely reprints) in 1922. Dyson wrote in the densest of Australian slang. His characters were often male – from Spats the boss down to Billy the Boy – but the fact'ry workforce was mainly female. Dyson called them 'Spats' Beauties', and named a selection: Kitty Coudray, Annie Mack, Sis Twentyman, Spotty Cobbit, The Fat Girl, Bell Olliver, 'Porline' the Man-Eater, The Spadger, and others. The nature of their work is pasting together a variety of pre-cut boxes.

The majority of the girls worked at square boards on trestles. There was a heap of paste in the centre of each board, and the piece-workers stood to their task, pasting and folding at the terraced stacks of stationery with the dexterity of machines, bare-armed, bare-necked, in slovenly gowns caked with dirt-colored dough, their tousled hair powdered with the fibre of the paper.[*]

The factory comprises various 'flats' (open lofts dedicated to specific manufacturing processes) but that's about as near Dyson approaches to jargon. What he prefers is slang and the fact'ry stories are good for well over 250 examples. The Beauties, always up for giving somewhat better than they receive, are as fluent as the next bloke. 'Girls of a kind commonly given to rebellious and frivolous practices,' they were nothing if not outspoken: 'Spats' girls did not usually whisper; their ordinary conversation was shrill and over-bearing, and there were at least eighty of them, young and old .'[†] When they do, it is not admired: 'I'll give yeh whisperin' an' tisperin',' cried Annie. 'I'll tear the eyes out of yer monkey face, you pig's sister. What 're you, to go whisperin' about people? What 're you, more'n a half Chow? [a Chinese person rather than the dog] [. . .] I'll do yeh, though! I'll do yeh!' . . . 'See,' cried Annie, 'see, you dirty stop-out.'[‡]

Another Beauty, Martha Pilcher, was once an 'artist', appearing on the variety stage weighing 24 stone 4 lbs and there displayed to the copper-clutching masses as 'The Fat Girl'. Now, paste-pot in hand, she is down to a mere 12 stone.

[*] E. Dyson, *Fact'ry 'Ands* (1906), p.16.
[†] Dyson op. cit. p.15.
[‡] Dyson op. cit. pp.23–24.

She showed many photographs of her prodigious former self, dressed in a scant and scaly bathing-dress, standing by a painted sea; she had an old exercise book in which were pasted clippings from the up-country papers referring to her enormous disproportions in terms of wondering eulogy; she had also the proud privilege of free entree to the waxworks.

Though fallen from her high estate, Martha did not despair. She still had hopes of regaining her old magnitude, and strove for it by judicious dieting and careful attention to a set of rules for the guidance of skinny people, which were published in a medical almanac. She weighed herself about three times a week, and her spirits varied in accordance with the tally of the slot-machine; rising with an increase, falling with an appreciable loss.

Her foreman, Feathers, asks what went wrong:

Martha looked round cautiously, and then whispered, ''Twas love!'

'Oh, catch me!'

'Yes,' persisted Martha, 'I was mug [fool] enough t' go 'n' fall in love, 'n' it brought me down to this.' She opened her arms, inviting attention to her fragile figure. 'He was dark 'n' tall, with long, black 'air 'n' piercin' dark eyes. Pale he was, 'n' 'andsome. Perfessor Pedro was a hartist, too, readin' palms 'n' tellin' fortunes, 'n' ownin' a trick dog with his tail growin' out between his ears. He would smooge [chat up] to me when the boss wasn't about, 'n' he said we could run a grand little show on our lonesome. Well, I got fair struck mad on him, 'n' began t' dwindle away from that minit. I lost a stone in less'n a fortnit. I near over-ate meself t' death, tryin' t' stop

the drift. 'Twasn't no use, 'n' the Perfessor, seem' me goin' t'
waste, done a guy [ran off]; 'n' that finished me. I come a
reg'lar slump after that, 'n' now where am I.'

'You're right in the ash-barrel, Sissy.'

Martha groaned. 'But no more love fer me. The bloke that
comes canoodlin' here gets that in his feed-bag!' [face] She
flourished her paste-tub fiercely. 'Love! Love! I'd sooner get
the bloomin' bubonic.'*

The Fat Girl reappears in another story, in *Benno and Some of the
Push*, where she encounters the newest Beauty, 'the Fickle Dolly
Hopgood'. By their tone we might presume that Martha has
regained those missing pounds.

'Yow, there, Tilly! Scratchin' a livin' 'ere, are yeh?' [Dolly]
cried shrilly, shaking her crib basket at a distant paster. The
ex-professional fat girl caught her eye. Miss Pilcher was
wearing a superior expression. Ginge raised her hand, and
wagged playful fingers at Martha. 'Buck up, puds,' she said,
'you're all right. They're payin' quids a bar'l fer your sort at
Stonkie Watson's.' Watson's was the soap-boiling establishment that gave rank to a river-side suburb. The fat girl
resented the insinuation with a loathly sneer, and Ginge
passed by in triumph.

The atmosphere is nothing if not lively. The Beauties tease each
other: 'Garn, le' go me leg!' retorted Miss Twentyman saucily . . .
'Gar'n scratch!' retorted the young lady . . . You tok t' me, she
screamed, you 'r fat ole Pig's Whiskers downstairs, 'r any iv yer

* Dyson op. cit. p.54.

rats. Do it! Do it! Tork t' me, monkey face, 'n' I'll — "And see off foolish admirers: '"Cheeky boy," said Miss Gleeson. "Get goin' 'r I'll hit y' in the squint." She threatened him pleasantly with her brush.'† Such young men do not impress: '"They's scrougers [mediocrities] what think they's jist the lolly [fascinating] in a red tie," piped Minnie, "but they ain't respectible if yer arsk me."'‡

Heaven help the Beauty who does permit an admirer to advance:

In the course of a week Mr. Duff came twenty times to the factory flat and he never left without exchanging a little airy badinage with Miss Gleeson. On each succeeding occasion the conversation was a little more familiar, and Connie moistened her lips, giggled ingenuously, and, glancing up through her hair, said again and again: 'Oh, Mr. Duff, you are a one!' [. . .]

Harrerbeller Harte's little burlesques of the meetings convulsed the factory. 'Popsey-wopsey mustn't play with the wicked gentleman,' cautioned Harrerbeller. 'Wicked gentleman steal mummy's ickle sweetie away, and then bub cry her pretty blue eyes out, she will. Popsey's a teeny weeny sillikin; nice gentleman eat her all up!' In concluding, Harrerbeller aped a cow-like coquetry, and squealed with affected rapture: 'Oh, Mr. Duff, you are a one!' And then the Beauties gave the chorus: 'Oh, Mr. Duff, you are a one!' But Connie was not distressed by this by-play. She merely giggled, and wriggled, and rolled her blue eyes, and said, mincingly, with her

---

* Dyson op. cit. pp.128–129.
† Dyson op. cit. p.181.
‡ Dyson op. cit. p.160.

most ladylike air: 'Stop it off, y' lot iv wasters. I wouldn't 'ave him on me mind.'*

Perhaps the most productive occupation is nursing, a female-dominated profession filled with in-house language. The lexis that follows has been culled from a number of websites, and I am duly grateful to all those who have contributed to them.† It is said that the stress of the job drives staff into others' arms (and thereafter beds or some equivalent) there to play real-life 'doctors and nurses' but it also creates the blackest of humour. It is to be assumed that patients are blithely unaware of what they and their conditions are called. It is some way from TV's once hit show 'Angels'. More like slang's own term for the nursing staff: *needle pushers*.

These are only a selection. To what extent they are used outside specific hospitals – from which the lists have been collected – is unknown. It is unlikely that every nurse (and perhaps junior doctor) uses every one, but they give a good idea of what the care-taking staff really think of those who have been thrown on their mercy. (Fortunately thoughts and deeds are substantially distanced.)

Adult humane society – dropping grandma off at the Emergency Room before a holiday trip.
Attorney induced symptomology – symptoms that present when a lawsuit is involved.

---

* Dyson op. cit. p.189.
† https://thehappyhospitalist.blogspot.co.uk/2011/05/medical-slang-vocabulary-in-icu.html
https://www.nursebuff.com/medical-slang/
https://www.rd.com/health/healthcare/medical-jargon/
http://scrubsmag.com/top-47-slang-terms-for-nurses/
https://www.nursespost.com/20-funny-slang-terms-used-nurses/
http://www.onlyanurse.com/nursingtopics/nursingslang

Bingo – a patient with a very long list of medical conditions and needs.

Boyfriends – charming old men that are a pleasure to care for.

Celestial discharge – death.

Code brown – involuntary defecation.

Crispy critter – a patient with severe burns.

Digging for worms – trying to find a vein.

Dyscopia – the inability to cope.

Eternal care unit – patients who have died and are currently in the morgue.

Frequent flyer – people who frequently come to the Emergency Room or hospital.

Horrendoplasty – a long and difficult operation on a morbidly obese patient.

Jack in the box – a patient who can't stand or walk yet insists on trying.

Jesus bus – about to die and thus is 'hailing the Jesus Bus'.

Lantern test – to shine a pen light in a patient's mouth and see their eyes light up (i.e. they have no brain).

Monkey box – the female genitalia region.

Negative wallet biopsy – when a patient is transferred to a cheaper, less intensive hospital after discovering he/she has no health insurance.

One-point restraint – the insertion of a catheter into the bladder. The 'restraint' element comes with such a catheter: once it is inserted the patient will have limited mobility.

Peek and shriek – for a surgeon to open the abdomen, see something horrible and close immediately.

Pumpkin positive – the notion that a patient's brain is so small that shining a penlight into her mouth will result in her empty head glowing like a Halloween pumpkin.

Shotgun approach – ordering every test known to man on a patient when the diagnosis is unknown.

Turf – to transfer the patient to another service, usually associated with dumping a patient.

Train wreck – a patient who has every drip known to man going and every piece of equipment on too.

Treat and street – get them out of the Emergency Room.

Velcro – family that never leaves a patient's room.

Wallet biopsy – refers to what community hospitals do to patients before shipping them to expensive tertiary care.

Doctors:

Baby catcher – an obstetrician.

Blood sucker – phlebotomist.

Bone cracker – an orthopaedic surgeon.

Butts and guts – gastroenterologist.

Cock docs – urologists.

Code princess – a doctor acting up and in need of administrative attitude adjustment.

Cut first, diagnose second – a surgeon.

Freud squad – a psychiatrist.

Gas Passer – an anaesthesiologist.

Knuckle dragger – orthopaedic surgeon.

Other torture – occupational therapist.

Pecker checker – a urologist.

Roto rooter – gastroenterologist.

Slasher – a surgeon.

Snot doc – pulmonologist.

Stream team – a urologist.

Vampire – phlebotomist.

Nurses:

Doctart – female nurses who have a thing for doctors.
Noctor – a recently trained nurse acting like a doctor.
Nurseoblasts – student nurses.
Nurslings – student nurses.

Acronyms:

ADASTW – arrived dead and stayed that way. [Baltimore emergency room nurse]
AGMI – ain't gonna make it.
ALS – absolute loss of sanity (crazy patient).
AMFYOYO – alright motherfucker, you're on your own.
BFB – big fuckin' baby; not talking about kids either.
BFH – brat from Hell.
BFMC – baby's fine mama's crazy.
BONITA – big ol' needle in the ass.
BUNDY – but unfortunately not dead yet.
CLL – chronic low life.
COPD – chronic old persons disease.
CRS – can't remember shit.
DIB – dead in bed.
DIC – death is coming.
EDGATWTTTF – elevator doesn't go all the way to the top floor.
FLK – funny looking kid.
FMPS – 'Fluff my pillow' syndrome. A demanding patient that acts sicker than they really are.
GDA – gonna die anyway.
GFPO – good for parts only.
GOMER – get out of my emergency room; thus

GOMERGRAM – ordering all tests in the ER because the patient can't say what the problem is.

HIBGIA – had it before got it again.

LGFD – looks good from doorway.

LOLITS – little old lady in tennis shoes.

MIDI – myocardial infarction during intercourse.

NARS – not a rocket scientist.

NFN – normal for Norfolk.

OBS – obvious bull shit.

OMGWTFBBQ – bad car accident victim.

PBTB – pine box to bedside (death is imminent).

PPPP – piss poor parental protoplasm.

SWI – something wrong inside.

TMFB – too many fucking birthdays (for the really old folks who just won't die, no matter what).

UFO – unidentified frozen object (homeless winter death).

VSGP – very shallow gene pool.

WAPOSS – whiny ass piece of shit syndrome.

If rhyming slang, a British invention, is (mistakenly) taken to be emblematic of slang's entirety (it is in fact a merely 3,000 often ephemeral terms out of around 135,000) then there are those who see its role as echoed in America by the language of the short-order diner and the waitresses who work there delivering the food. The diner has long passed its peak and so too has the slang it cooked up, but we must assume that a good proportion of what has been termed 'hash-house lingo' came from the minds and mouths of what that lingo termed variously a *beanery queen*, *biscuit shooter*, *cookie-pusher*, *grub-slinger*, *hash-juggler* or *-slinger*, *knife-thrower*, *dish slinger* and *soup jockey*. In other words, a waitress.

O. Henry rhapsodised her in 'An Adjustment of Nature' (1906)*

[T]he chief thing at Cypher's [café] was Milly. Milly was a waitress . . . She belonged, largely, to waiting, as Minerva did to the art of scrapping, or Venus to the science of serious flirtation. Pedestalled and in bronze she might have stood with the noblest of her heroic sisters as 'Liver-and-Bacon Enlivening the World' . . . You expected to see her colossal figure loom through that reeking blue cloud of smoke from frying fat just as you expect the Palisades to appear through a drifting Hudson River fog. There amid the steam of vegetables and the vapours of acres of 'ham and,'† the crash of crockery, the clatter of steel, the screaming of 'short orders,' the cries of the hungering and all the horrid tumult of feeding man, surrounded by swarms of the buzzing winged beasts bequeathed us by Pharaoh, Milly steered her magnificent way like some great liner cleaving among the canoes of howling savages.

Such a 'Goddess of Grub' surely justified a unique vocabulary. 'Her voice rang like a great silver bell' but sadly readers are offered no examples. We can nonetheless dream.

Unlike rhyming slang, one of the bases of which is the clipping off of the rhyming section, *hash-house Greek* (*Greek* being an all-purpose synonym for 'incomprehensible language') tends

---

* O. Henry, 'An Adjustment of Nature' in *The Four Million* (1906), p.89.
† The absent term being 'eggs'; *and* . . . with nothing further specified, is a regular in short-order commands, e.g. *coffee-and*, where the doughnuts (the cheapest meal on offer) was unspoken. Used adjectivally, and beyond any food emporium, one has *coffee-and*, anything seen as cheap, minimal, second-rate, e.g. a tiny theatrical role, or *coffee and habit*, a small-time addiction to narcotics.

to render its descriptions more rather than less cumbersome. The celebrated *Adam and Eve on a raft and wreck 'em* is surely more demanding of a speaker than a simple rendition of its meaning, scrambled eggs on toast. Given how often this can be the case, it has been suggested that irrespective of time consumed in delivering the words involved, the use of such language is an intrinsic part of a necessary performance that underpinned the diner's service. Calling steak 'slaughter in the pan' or, in a less racially conscious era, a small chocolate soda a 'midget from Harlem' supposedly added a more exotic tone to what was in fact a wholly quotidian experience. The language, it seems, was considered as another aspect of the modernist aesthetic – chrome, neon, curves, sans serif fonts – that were found in the design of many diners.

Most of these terms are taken Jack Smiley's *Hash House Lingo* (1941) which listed some 1,500 examples from the many newspaper pieces which wrote up the phenomenon in the late nineteenth century and subsequent decades. We have to wonder to what extent some of these – with such an imbalance between slanged and simple – were ever actually used in place:

> *stare that cow in the face*: a corned (UK salt) beef sandwich
> *Boston labor and Chicago capital*: pork and beans
> *fairy on the iron*: boiled chicken
> *with the shoes on*: take away/to go
> *ancient order of Hibernia*: a potato
> *clean up the kitchen* (also *sweep up the kitchen*): [the (alleged) use of all or any leftovers] an order for hash or a hamburger [a non-culinary use refers to ani- or cunnilingus]

There is no doubt that some of the material, this time very much in the tradition of the best rhyming slang, offers an intrinsic humour:

> *Joe with cow and sand*: a cup of coffee with milk and sugar [all three nouns were already well-known in slang]
> *Sheeny funeral*: pork chops [*Sheeny*: a (supposedly kosher) Jew]
> *whiskers*: mutton chops
> *Saturday nights*: beans [either beans' notorious effect on the wind or the pop-pop of a *Saturday night special* during a gunfight]

and there is a certain charm in the permutations that come with *two*, that is two fried eggs:

> *two looking at you* (also *two looking up*): two fried eggs 'sunny-side up'
> *two with their eyes closed*: two fried eggs turned over in the pan
> *two with their eyes open*: two eggs fried on one side only

Two in a bowl, however, was a plate of oyster stew.

Some are of course incomprehensible. The words are simple enough but the connection to the food thus indicated much less so:

> *twist it, choke it, and make it squeal*: an order for an egg malted milk
> *mealy bustle*: potato

The modern restaurant is perhaps less productive, but a job-specific vocabular does exist. The website *restaurantlaughs.com* has compiled a short list. Among its terms are:[*]

Sticker Shock (aka *Swing and a Miss*): This is a term to describe a first-time guest who sits down, looks at the prices, and immediately leaves. This is common at high-end restaurants in tourist heavy areas.

Deuced to Death: Having your tables seated with parties of two all evening. This generally leaves many open chairs in your section and limits your income.

Fly By: Walking by a table specifically to check out one of the people sitting there. This is often at the urging of a co-worker.

Crop Dust (aka *Fart and Dart*): Passing by a table and passing gas as a passive aggressive way of agitating them.

Sharking: When a server seats guests at the door in their section rather than following the rotation. This is a severe infraction of server etiquette.

Round Tripping: This describes a server bringing food to a guest, generally in a different server's section, only to find that they are not ready for the food.

One Time (aka *Nickel and Dime*): When a server is asked for something by a guest and when they return they are met with another request. This can happen in an endless cycle.

Irregulars: A guest who frequents the restaurant and requests a certain server who is not thrilled to see the guest. This is usually out of fear of stalker-ish tendencies.

---

[*] http://www.restaurantlaughs.com/restaurant-terms-from-the-side-station/2011/12/16/

Meanwhile back in the kitchen, describing the pressure of work and the knock-on effect on service, steals happily from mainstream: such problems leave the cooking staff *in the shit*.

If in slang as a whole women tend to represent object and not subject, then the military services, repositories and generators of so much slang themselves, undoubtedly follow this rule. A glance at the slang dictionary offered online by ARRSE (the Army Rumour Service, self-described as 'the unofficial voice of the British Army') brings:

> *Dorris*: 'a female member of the Royal Air Force'; prior to 1980 these were also described as Penguins, since like the bird, aircraftswomen were 'all flap and no fly'.
>
> *Daz challenge*: 'when a pad's* wife places a box of washing powder in her window when the husband is away hoping she will get finger blasted by 5–10 drunk squaddies'†
>
> *Lizard*: 'A individual who screws up in the most idiotic way, or just used for idiot. Also a female, especially a promiscuous one.'
>
> *1664 Girl*: 'A term used to describe a girl who on approach from behind seems like a young venus but on looking at the front is an old crusty medusa! 16 from the back 64 from the front!! Also known as a *Golden Deceiver*.'

This is hardly a comprehensive list; no matter: it gives the tone.

---

* 'PAD married quarters; also term used for any married soldier in quarters PAD RAT a married soldiers daughter who had had sexual intercourse with half the garrison PADS WIFE a woman usually in the 20-25 stone weight category who will perform sexual acts on other soldiers while her husband is away on exercise or operations.'

† The washing powder can alternatively be *Omo*, which adds the 'translation' Old Man Out/Overseas or On My Own.

It has been suggested that the 'feminisation' of the military may change this, but the services, geared to breaking down the new recruit and remaking them on a soldierly template, may instead choose to militarise their female members. It may be that, in the case of the cadences chanted by marching US soldiers, some of the most nationalist have been quietly abandoned (or simply unrecorded by watchers). The all-important military 'hooah' is undiminished.* The frigidity of 'Eskimo pussy' (as hymned by the all-male square-bashers in *Full Metal Jacket*, 1987) may have been set to one side (and gender alternatives in the modern ranks presumably reject such assumptions) and there is no female equivalent amongst girl troops of 'This is my rifle / This my gun / This is for fighting / This for fun' since the clitoris, for all its slang synonyms, does not include weaponry among them, but there are female drill instructors, and cadences that reference women. The first purports to have a female 'narrator':

'I'm the Mack Daddys Girl'†
I'm not the mack I'm the mack daddy's girl
I rock the Mack the mackdaddys world
I took the mack daddy on a lil trip
I taught the mack daddy how to pimp
If you ask what I got in return
I got the Mack dadd'ys lil baby girls
If you ask us what keeps us so tight
It's cause we're fit to fight day and night
He's airborne and so am I

* Cadences from www.armystudyguide.com/content/cadence/
† In slang *mack daddy* is a pimp; here the reference is presumably to MAC, Military Airlift Command, now Air Mobility Command of USAF.

And someday our babies will fly
Jump right out and count to four
Hit the ground runnin', beggin' for more.
Cause we're A-I-R-B-O-R-N-E
All the way
Everyday

The rest can be sung by either gender, but all unite in presenting the 'army girl', 'G.I. Jane' or even 'airborne Barbie' as both desirable (you should be so lucky) and as rough and tough as any male:

'Army Girl'
Never talk to an army girl,
She'll find ways to make you hurl.
Watch your mouth and watch your hands,
She knows more ways to kill a man.
Watch your neck and watch your ears,
She will bring you down to tears.
If you try to hit on her,
She will have you to make a fur.
You don't mess with an army chick,
She will break you with a stick.
If you take her on a date,
You have found your perfect mate.

'G.I. Jane'
There's this Army girl named G.I. Jane,
Her favorite phrase is no pain, no gain.
When she gets to Iraq she's gonna say,
'Hey Saddam, get outta my way!'

She's rough, tough, and hardcore,
She'll beat you down, till you can't take more!
She busts onto the scene with her M-16,
She's a lean, mean fightin' machine!
She's proud to defend our flag,
She never lets her troops' heads sag.
And when she gets home, she'll be a hero,
The chance of her retiring is next to zero!
If you look on the battlefield, you may sight her,
Cause she's one damn, hell of a fighter!

'Airborne Barbie'
Airborne barbie rollin down the strip
With a pink parachute and some red lipstick
How she got here I don't know
With her high heels on, baby's ready to roll
Stand up buckle up, shuffle to the door
Don't mess with her, or you'll hit the floor
What makes her motivated, what makes her true
She says she fights for the red, white and blue
Where is she from, who does she know
I saw her jump the CO [commanding officer]
Look out son, I'd watch your back
Good luck getting her in your rack [bunk]

The women of Britain's Royal Air Force (originally WAAFs, then WRAFs) generated a small lexis. Among the words recorded have been:

Airmen's comforts – WAAF and WRAF personnel
Black outs – WAAF knickers, navy blue winter-weights

Bluebird – the 'bluebird of happiness', which she could give to male troops

Hen house – WAAF or WRAF quarters see also *Waafery*

Ladybird – WAAF officer

Lumpy jumpers – WAAF or airwoman; originally from difference in profile of issue 'woolly pully' when worn by female personnel

Mother hen, Mother superior or *Queen bee* – senior WAAF or WRAF officer

Nunnery – the WAAF and WRAF quarters

Passion killers – regulation underwear

Twilights – WAAF underwear, light coloured summer-weights

Waafery – WAAF or WRAF quarters[*]

---

[*] List at http://www.rafaberporth.org.uk/page25.html

13. Lesbians

Tonight we gonna have a ball
down to the old Bulldaggers' Hall
You tell old Razor-cuttin' Annie to tell her fast-fuckin' mammy,
that all three can come in for a quarter
What we gonna do romp and tromp till midnight
fuck and fight till daylight

'The Bulldaggers' Ball' in B. Jackson,
Get Your Ass in the Water (1974)

IT IS SURELY not unreasonable, given the tropes that underpin slang's use and creation – marginality and secrecy, inward observation of the group, the need for an intra-group code that denotes membership at the same time as it sets up barriers for the uninitiated – to hope, even assume that if there was anywhere that would encourage woman-generated slang it would be the lesbian community.

Lesbians, runs the celebrated tale, were not included in Victorian anti-homosexual legislation because Queen Victoria refused to acknowledge the possibility of their existence. A separate lesbian slang, it is generally pronounced, is equally implausible: while gay men have a wide vocabulary, recorded since the 1910s, lesbian speech generally defeats the researchers.

As is slang's way, its vocabulary treats lesbians, as well as bisexuals and others who stand outside heterosexuality, as objects. There are over two hundred slang terms meaning 'lesbian' but virtually all come through male eyes. Yet there is a lesbian lexis, albeit largely resistant to discovery. It is to be found in closed institutions, e.g. prisons where terms include *gay for the stay*: taking on a woman-to-woman relationship to palliate one's sentence and a female equivalent of the male prison's *jailhouse turnout*; *purple whale*, a home-made dildo using maxi-pads wrapped round a toothbrush and covered in a purple medical glove, and *ag*, short for *aggressive* and thus one who takes a 'masculine' role.

As it is necessary to do when considering the relationship of slang to gay men, it is worth a slight pause to ascertain how slang treats their female equivalents. The answer brings no surprises. If women as a group – even those who are supposedly the objects of male devotion – get rough treatment from the counter-language, then so too does the lesbian, she who in male prescription 'just needs a good seeing to' to bring her to her heterosexual senses (unless or should that be especially if she has togged up in pornography's predictable lingerie so as to indulge in a bit of 'hot all-girl-action' for the cameras; but such girls, ordered up for male delight, may be more professional – and less homosexual – than the dreamer wants to believe.)

Like the earliest terms for gay men, the first point of call was the classics, most obviously the use of *Sappho*, adopted directly from the name Sappho (c.600 BCE), the poetess of the island of Lesbos (although it would take slang-coiners several centuries to pick up on the potential of the latter). There is the *she-centaur*, a development of the mythical creature 'with the head, trunk, and arms of a man, joined to the body and legs of a horse' (*OED*). In this context it is a pun, spelt out by Charles Cotton in *Erotopolis* (1684) who talks of 'She-Centaurs shall they be [. . .] for in these places it is, the young Shepherdesses first learn the Art of Horsemanship and Horse-play, first riding one another.' Logically the only other term reverses male practice where gay men get female names (*nancy, molly*) and adopts a male name, *Tommy*, for all-girl use, and circuitously suggests in 'A Sapphic Epistle' (1773) that 'Miss Sappho [. . .] was the first Tommy the world has upon record.'*

There follows a gap, at least as recorded, and not until *bull-dyke* is recorded in 1892 does slang pick up the thread once more. Maybe Victoria's blind eye extended to cover her subjects too. But Her Majesty notwithstanding there were lesbians and they used language and some was probably not standard and it is possible that such nineteenth-century slang that did exist remained very much on the level of personal coinage. For instance the diaries of Anne Lister (1789–1840), some twenty-three coded volumes over thirty-four years, reveal that her term for sex was *kisses* or *grubbling*, and that for her partner's vagina *queer.*† The first pair are euphemisms, with *grubbling* coming from *grabbling*, feeling with the hands, searching about. *Queer*, while unused in this sense by slang, seems, whether Ms Lister appreciated it or not, to fit easily into those *qu*— terms (*quim, queynte*, etc) that themselves euphemise *cunt*.

Pornography has always made space for lesbian stories, whether observed or as supposed memoir-confessions. The nineteenth century is no exception, often using a girls' school

* Other than its adoption of a common male name, there is no proven etymology for this sense of the word.
† K. Lister, 'The woman who had a lesbian church wedding in 1834 . . .' in inews.uk 12 Feb. 2019; Anne Lister 'dressed entirely in black, enjoyed firing pistols at supper, and was known as "Gentleman Jack" by the tenants she ruled over with an iron fist.'

– flagellation almost invariably offered on the curriculum – as a backdrop. Thus *School Life in Paris – A Series of Letters from Blanche, aged seventeen, who has just been sent to a Paris finishing School, to her cousin Ethel, in England, with whom she had formerly been at School* (published by the Erotica Biblion Society – a subscription-only imprint of 'dirty books' – in 1899). Blanche is soon enrolled in the 'Lesbian Club' (although there is plenty of heterosexual coupling for those whose fantasies required it). Here the primary action is via a graded collection of dildoes (the 'baby' through to the 'giant'), thus supporting the usual male dictum that all these girls need is the much-mythologised 'good seeing-to'.

The book has no author, but it is more than likely man-made. Its language, while placed in girlish mouths (even though 'we always pretend not to know the naughtiest words'), parades porn's predictable staples: *cunt, cunnie, pussie, hot* (sexy), *prick, balls, poke* (as noun and verb), *dolly* (for penis, as in 'Dolly was sick when I played with it' – the burden of a very old joke), *tool, instrument, cock, masher, come, gamerouge* (usually *gamahuche*, to give oral sex), *frigging* and *ride a St George* (the woman on top).

When things do recommence, as is slang's way, the bulk of the terminology reflects its stereotypes of lesbian sexuality. That and a couple of words – *lesbian* and *dyke* – and their variations. Thus *lesbian* gives *les/lez, liz, lezzie, lezzer/lesser, lesbo/lezbo* and the slightly more creative *les-be-friends, les girls* and *leslie-anne*. Slang's primary term remains *dike/dyke*, even if its etymology is still unresolved. There is a possible link to US slang *dyked down*, used of a man and meaning dressed up, which at least covers those women who have dressed as men. Another theory opts for a gradual corruption of the standard English *hermaphrodite* to *morphodike* and beyond that to *morphodyke* and thereafter dyke/dike, and after that coupling with the masculine generic *bull* to give *bull-dyke* and the variations offered below. The problem with this, as noted at length by the slang collector Richard Spears in 1985[*] is 1. that we have no records of hermaphrodite or its variations as meaning lesbian and 2. that the first recorded use of bull-dyke (1892) substantially predates that of simple dyke (1930), which makes the latter an abbreviation, rather than the basis of a compound. There are more outlandish theories, e.g. linking the standard English *dyke*, a channel, to the vulva and moving from there to theories about 'male cunts'. These are better dismissed.

Using the bull-dyke pattern slang has come up with *bodaggle, boydyke, bull, bull-dagger,* and *B.D., bull-bitch, boldyke, bull-dicker, bulldyker* and a variety of specifics such as *baby dyke, diesel dyke, dinky-dyke, drag dyke, granola dyke, leather dyke,* and *van dyke.* The sole spark of wit is reserved for *Dutch girl.* Dyke is seen as linked to masculinity (the equivalent of *butch*) and that generates a number of terms that echo traditional male imagery: *top sergeant, battle cruiser, diesel, enforcer, gal officer, hard daddy, he-bitch* and *he-she, jasper, poppa* and *truck driver. Amazon,* and perhaps *apache,* promotes the 'woman warrior' image.

But just as many male gay terms focus on what slang sees as the quotidian imperatives of male-to-male sex, i.e. fellatio and sodomy, so are lesbians almost invariably associated with all-girl cunnilingus. Whatever other pleasures two women can offer each other in the absence of men it is this that jerks slang's chain. Perhaps the fact that many of the terms also apply to heterosexual men make them more acceptable. They include *bush-licker,*

[*] R. Spears, 'On the Etymology of Dike', *American Speech* 60:4 (Winter 1985), pp.318–327.

box-biter, slot-licker, carpet-chewer, carpet muncher, rug-muncher, cat-lapper, chuff-muncher, clam-diver, clam-smacker, clit-hopper, cunt-eater, cunt-lapper, cunt-sucker, cunt-muncher, crack snacker, fanny nosher, gap-lapper, lover under the lap, muffer, muff-muncher and *muff-diver*. Despite this fixation one of the first ever terms for lesbian intercourse, the *game of flats*, from *flatcock*, a woman (i.e the 'flat' vagina vs the 'bumpy' male genitalia) suggested face-to-face genital rubbing rather than face-to-groin consumption.

Of the rest, and slang has amassed getting on for 250 terms in all, one may assess a few of the less obvious. Rhyming slang (on dyke) gives *Raleigh bike, three-wheel trike* and thus *three-wheeler*. The theatrical-cum-gay jargon Polari reverses its usual *omee-palone*, a 'man-woman' and used for a gay man, to give *polone-omee/polone-homi*, a 'woman man'. A *chemise-lifter* plays on the mainstream slang *shirt-lifter*, a male homosexual. The *tennis fan* is a euphemism that is presumably meaningless outside those who already appreciate the 'translation'. Finally a term that stands as antithesis of the glamorous *lipstick lesbian* of fantasy: a *woman in comfortable shoes*.

Yet slang created and spoken by lesbians is far more prob-lematic. In purely lexicographical terms it is a frustrating search. Mainstream slang dictionaries draw on what little they can find and the same small lexis is repeated. Even purpose-built dictionaries have little to offer. Gershon Legman's appen-dix ('The Language of Homosexuality: An American Glossary') to G.W. Henry's *Sex Variants* (1941) has fourteen 'lesbian' terms out of a thousand; the great 'gay slang' lexicon, Bruce Rodgers' *Queen's Vernacular* (1971) attributes barely 4 per cent of its terms (69/1939) to lesbian usage. A search through a 'lesbian classic' such as Radclyffe Hall's *Well of Loneliness*

(1928) may turn up twenty slang terms, but none relate to sexuality, even if there is the possible conscious double-nudge of labelling a female character 'a queer fish' (though that term – devoid of sexual implication – had been recorded since 1772). In *The Scarlet Pansy* (1932) by the pseudonymous 'Robert Scully' (i.e. the ex-pat gay writer Robert McAlmon who ran with the American branch of the Parisian avant-garde), the reader follows Fay Étrange (from Kunstville 'in the lower Pennsylvania hills'), Henry Voyeur and Percy Chichi as they make their way around gay America. As well as *auntie, fairy, fruit, gay, go down* (fellate), *Miss* (used in combination as a nickname for a gay man), *queen, queer, sissy* and *tearoom* (a public lavatory popular for casual sex and assignations, the US equivalent of the UK *cottage*), we also encounter *butch, bull* and *bull-dyker, femme* and *mantee*. In what the cognoscenti were fully aware was a *roman à clef*, taking in most of McAlmon's friends, we also meet 'Marjorie Bull-Dike', ' "Clittie" Thorndike', and a number of other lesbians (including portraits of Alice B. Toklas and Gertrude Stein) with such surnames as Fuchs, Godown and Kuntz. Not to mention 'Bobby Dike' a 'collar and tie woman', and the high-living family of Beach-Bütsches. Hemingway is allegedly in there somewhere, but these were apparently a nod to Sylvia Beach, publisher of *Ulysses* and owner of the progressive bookshop Shakespeare and Co., and her companion Adrienne Monnier.

Still, for all his flamboyance and a plot that brought in every variety of homosexual life and placed them on the most fluid of sexual roundabouts, Scully/McAlmon remained a man. He may well have picked up valid contemporary 'lesbian' language from those he knew, and put it between hard covers, but even he must join the ventriloquists. Finally, however unimpeachable his gay credentials, is most of this still not the language used *of* lesbians rather than *by* them?

Finding sources has remained a challenge. Greg Jacobs, in an assessment of the literature of gay and lesbian language,[*] was unimpressed: 'Not one single study focuses primarily on lesbian words. Most of the studies completely ignore lesbians. Some early studies even use the term homosexual to refer exclusively to men as if it were an entirely male phenomenon. Those studies that did address lesbian issues did so sparingly, almost as an aside. Can this apparent lack of lesbian words be interpreted to indicate that lesbians share more in common with heterosexuals than with gay men? Or is it an unfortunate commentary on the status of lesbians in general, or within academia in particular?'

We are forced once more to address the basic questions: where is lesbian slang, and if not, why not? The first person to opine seems to have been Legman. Writing in 1941 he offered a two-pronged answer: a 'tradition of gentlemanly restraint among lesbians stifles the flamboyance and conversational cynicism in sexual matters that slang coinage requires' and suggested that '[l]esbian attachments are sufficiently feminine to be more often emotional than simply sexual'.[†] In this case there would be no need for a wide-ranging sexual vocabulary. Quite how that jibed with the emotional excesses (however artificial) of 'queen culture' among some gay men, was not addressed.

A more modern analyst, the feminist linguist Julia Penelope has seen the answer in more political terms. Lesbians don't favour slang because slang doesn't favour lesbians. Taking on board the

---

[*] G. Jacobs, 'Lesbian & Gay Male Language Use: A Critical Review of the Literature', *American Speech*, 71:1 (Spring, 1996), p.57.
[†] Quoted in D. Kulick, 'Gay and Lesbian Slang', *Annual Review of Anthropology*, Vol. 29 (2000), p.249.

belief that slang is a male construct, and that all males – gay or straight – are de facto misogynists, why should a woman wish to borrow their lexis, however rebellious and counter-cultural. The idea that lesbians might wish to develop a slang that reflected their own position did not enter the picture.

In 1970 she circulated a questionnaire as part of a piece (written as Julia P. Stanley) aimed at categorising 'Homosexual Slang'.* What she saw were two slang vocabularies; the core (which might be shared in part by heterosexuals) and the fringe (which existed for communication within the homosexual group). As regarded lesbian 'fringe' slang, the results were nugatory – just five words: two were the very well-known *dyke* and *bulldike*, two, *fluff* and *twist*, were for 'feminine' lesbians, the equivalent of a straight boy's girlfriend, and one was a supposedly humorous male put-down: *dump truck*: a car full of lesbians. Lesbian-to-lesbian use of such terms was far more nuanced than that of the wider world, but that did not ultimately influence the big picture. Given that she believed that it was the fringe vocabulary, which reflected 'the most innovation and the greatest restriction [i.e. defining boundary] to homosexual activities' that was the true 'homosexual slang', the absence of a lesbian version was problematic. 'To [accept that theory] however, would make it necessary either to say that lesbians do not belong to the homosexual subculture or to define two separate groups. Neither alternative is attractive.' She advocated 'further research with these problems in mind'.

As an example of that research came in her suggestion, writing in 1979 in tandem with Susan J. Wolfe, that lesbians 'have been socially and historically invisible . . . and isolated from each other

* J. P. Stanley, 'Homosexual Slang', *American Speech*, 45: 1/2 (Spring-Summer, 1970), p.47.

as a consequence, and have never had a cohesive community in which a Lesbian aesthetic [and presumably lexis] could have developed."* The authors have also suggested that what is known as 'gay slang' (using Rodgers as her source-book) is little more than slang's usual anti-woman putdowns. They, among other feminists, also criticise such habits as using 'she' for another gay male, labelling or addressing such men as 'Miss', the self-referential use of 'Your Mother' and the adoption of women's given names as generics for gay men, e.g. *molly*, perhaps the first such and noted in 1693, *nancy*, *mary-ann* and so on. This may be qualified as reading the past through the eyes of the present, but such were the foothills of what would become identity politics.

Boots of Leather, Slippers of Gold, by Elizabeth Lapovsky Kennedy and Madeleine D. Davis, an oral history of working-class lesbian life in Buffalo, NY from the 1930s to 1960s, and based on interviews with some forty-five women ('narrators'), was first published in 1993. The second biggest city in the state, still dominated by heavy industry (shipbuilding and steel) in the era of which these interviewees spoke, Buffalo was as far as one could get from what little else has been recorded of lesbian life in the mid-twentieth century. The patrons of its lesbian bars lived lives that were the antithesis of, say, the Nathalie Barney circle's chic get-togethers in some recherché *boîte* on the Left Bank, or the isolated pair of ladies – one somewhat tweedy, occasionally be-suited, the other opting for floaty, flower-printed tea-gowns – living quietly together in some Agatha Christie village. This is not the world of Parisian bohemia, louche London parties or Miss Marple's neighbours, but of tough bars, physical fights and bowling leagues.

The interviewees, all working-class women, and both black and

* J. Penelope & S. J. Wolfe, '*Sexist* slang and the gay community: Are you one, too?' (Women's Studies program, University of Michigan 1979), p.12.

white (though not Hispanic) speak in the language that would be expected. There is a good deal of slang – *no-no* (impossibility), *necking* and *petting*, *crush* (amatory obsession), *fuck up* (to blunder), *rough up* (to assault), *boobs* (breasts), *box* (the vagina), *balls* (as courage), *hang-up* (neurosis), *shit* (to fool), *trip* (an eccentric), *hit on* (to approach sexually), *have it* (to have sex), *go off* (to reach orgasm), *smooch* (a kiss), *doll* (a pretty girl), *broad* (a woman), *squeal* (to betray), *carry a torch* (mourn a lost relationship), *shithouse* and a good deal more. This is all mainstream. If these examples seem to focus on sex/relationships, then that was the framework in which many of the interviews were carried out. None are especially 'lesbian' and none are attributed to a single gender.

There are also a number of terms that are usually found in a gay or heterosexual context but are here repurposed for lesbian use: *bull session* (usually involving a group of males, but here an all-female discussion), *funny* (sexually 'deviant', usually aimed at gay men); *drag* (usually men dressed as women but here reversed, although a reference to *drag queens* presumably does refer to male impersonators in female dress), *sixty-nine* (simultaneous mouth-genital sex; mainly found in heterosexual use, but here of lesbian lovers); *daisy chain/threesome* (again repurposing what is usually associated with heterosexual sex: '[A friend] wanted me to go to this daisy chain gang [. . .] I was not interested. I have never been at all intrigued by multiple sex or sex orgies or groups'). The *closet* and the phrases *coming out* and *out* (*of the closet*) also seem to have been borrowed from male homosexual use (although, despite lack of recorded instances, they may have always been used by both men and women.*) Finally the

* Slang's first examples appear in 1961 and these interviews deal with earlier decades, though they were actually recorded in 1980s, thus the possibility of using modern slang to describe older events.

self-description of lesbians as *homo* or *queer*: the authors suggest that in both cases what is being borrowed is not so much two of the best-known (and at that period derogatory rather than reappropriated) terms for gay men, but the image of social stigma that accompanies them: we too, say the lesbian users, occupy exactly the same position in the eyes of 'straight' society. *Bulldagger* is also noted, 'used by hostile straights as an insult'.

The remaining terms can be seen as coming from a genuine lesbian lexis.

The general self-description was *gay/gay girl/gay kid*, though the sense is that this would not have been used outside the lesbian world. ('[There] was plenty of gay people at that time, but [. . .] they kept it in the closet'; some people, not all, would use the term 'gay girls,' or 'gay kids' to refer to either butch or fem, or both). Gay, in any homosexual sense, is first recorded in 1922, though it does not really enter mass use until the late 1960s (propelled beyond homosexual life by the counter-culture).

As explained by many interviewees, lesbians of the time had a strict division: one was either *butch* (masculine) or *fem(me)* (feminine). Butch, which enjoyed such synonyms as *diesel* (*dyke*) and *truck driver*, offered the adjective *butchy* ('tattoos on her arms, she really looked rugged . . . rough') and several subgroups. The *lavender butch* ('butch but femmy') suggested that her masculinity was tinged with a degree of femininity; *femmy* is explained by an interviewee who recalls: 'I wanted a girlfriend, a girlfriend that was more, like, femmy [. . .] That was what really turned me on was bleached blondes, and of course makeup and real femmy clothes, y'know, dresses and high heels.'

There was also the *stone butch*. As explained in 1998 in the online *Rebecca's Dictionary of Queer Slang* 'The term comes from

African American slang, in which "stone" means "very." It has come to have other meanings as well. A butch can be sexually stone, as in, not being able to permit herself to be touched on the genitals for sex; emotionally stone, meaning that she has locked away her emotions and has trouble acknowledging or expressing them; or physically stone, having trouble being touched at all. A stone butch is usually some combination of all of these.' Kennedy and Davies explain that 'We confronted Stormy, who referred to herself as an "untouchable," with the opinion of another narrator, who maintained that stone butches has never really existed, she replied, "No, that's not true I'm an untouchable. I've tried to have my lover make love to me, but I just couldn't stand it.") Meanwhile in the African-American community *stud broad* and 'stud and her lady' were common terms.*

If one fell betwixt and between, there was the term *ki-ki* (perhaps from *chichi*), which played the same part for gay men: one was homosexual but undecided as to whether one wished to be overtly 'masculine' or 'feminine'. As one interviewee put it, 'Yeah, they called them neither-nor, ki-ki . . . double role playing' and suggested that the pose was not so much the result of indecision, but rather of leaving oneself open to whichever sexual experience one might choose from a given encounter. Not everyone was so fluid. Faced with a femme partner who suggested that they might take the sexual initiative, and spend time pleasuring their butch companion, the stone butch used the dismissive phrase 'I don't take the sheet'. In other words, I'm the only sexual aggressor in this relationship. The idea of 'taking the sheet'

* In Colin MacInnes' *Absolute Beginners* (1959) the lesbian Big Jill addresses the anonymous narrator as 'stud', presumably transferring her own slang to a flesh-and-blood (and heterosexual) male.

presumably suggesting that the partner who is being pleasured is the one lying underneath and thus directly on the bedsheets. As a butch put it, 'You know what I mean "don't take the sheet," don't you? That mean a stud make up to a fem all the time, a fem did not make up with a stud.' *Make up* being another version of *come on*.

Although heterosexual (and male) generated slang almost invariably equates lesbians with cunnilingus, the interviews suggest that the primary interactions were face-to-face frottage, the rubbing together of the partners' genitals, mimicking heterosexual 'missionary position' intercourse. The seventeenth century's *game of flats* had things right. This was known variously as *banging*, *friction* and *dyking*. It was, as one woman put it, 'just like a man would do to a woman, except for there's no intercourse [. . .] you don't feel the penis inside you.'

Unlike male homosexuals, whose sexual vocabulary runs to thousands of terms, the lesbians of the pre-gay liberation era seem to have had very few. Soixante-neuf was as much a matter of embarrassed giggling as it was of 'girl-on-girl action'. One interviewee recalls actually getting a picture drawn to help explain what she would be supposed to do. Kennedy and Davies suggest that the lack of terminology came from a wider reticence; women simply didn't wish to discuss sexual intimacies, or not outside the bedroom. And add that the whole butch pose consciously precluded much talk. Short hair, leather jacket, T-shirt, boots . . . one was already coming on like the monosyllabic hard man of stereotype, and he had little to say.

They also note that the era's lesbians were as lacking in sexual sophistication as many others of their time, straight or gay. A bottle of mouthwash in a friend's bathroom 'meant' that she must practice cunnilingus and as such that in turn 'meant' that she was 'dirty'. Men, being penis-centred and refusing to believe that women could do without the male organ, even (or perhaps especially) in the physical absence of its owner, burdened all lesbian intercourse with dildos and other phallic 'toys'. The truth would have disappointed them. But as one woman put it: if women wanted a fake penis she might as well get the real thing. And if so, so much for lesbianism.

As noted above, closed institutions do much to foster slang, in this context a woman's prison. In 1967 Sara Harris, who had already worked as co-author to John M. Murtagh's study of New York City prostitution – *Cast the First Stone* – in 1958, published her own study: *Hellhole: The Shocking Story of the Inmates and Life in the New York City House of Detention for Women*. The prison, replacing the old Jefferson Market jail in which, among others, Mae West had been briefly incarcerated when in 1927 censors brought obscenity charges against her play *Sex*, lasted from 1932 to 1971. It was a well-known Greenwich Village institution, especially for the crowds – family members, lovers, pimps – who gathered outside to carry on noisy conversations with the inmates who were able to lean out of the eleven-storey cellblock and talk. Among many celebrity inmates were Dorothy Day, Ethel Rosenberg, Valerie Solanas and Angela Davies. It was also notorious for its appalling conditions, but for the majority of prisoners – often working women or habitual drunks, and many of them poor and African-American – these were largely taken as one of the prices that accompanied their lifestyle. This acquiescence changed when in 1965 a young feminist protestor, Andrea Dworkin, was arrested for her role in a demonstration against the war in Vietnam. Subjected on arrival to the usual savagery of the prison's medical staff, she was so injured in the application of a speculum that she was rendered sterile. The testimony she gave to a Senate grand jury and the campaign she and others launched to showcase such brutality led, at least in part, to the closure of the House of Detention in 1971.

Harris' own experience – we have no personal biographical details – began during her four months' residency at the prison in 1957, helping with Murtagh's researches. She returned to research *Hellhole* and the text essentially comprises a series of case histories. Of these the 'stars' are Molly McGuire, at seventy-four a veteran of the 'the bloody oul' Sixth Ward', otherwise known as the downtown Five Points area that was the nineteenth-century city's crime central, and twenty-seven-year-old Rusty Bricker. Only the very naive could miss the implication of Harris's portrait: 'Every time you see Rusty she just got a haircut. Her mannish-cut red hair is constantly slicked down as tight as she can get it, and she smells of barbershop perfume. She wears new, resplendently bright (orange-brown with traces of yellow) men's shoes, blue jeans but men's jeans that button in front, a sickeningly green sweatshirt, and a thick, shaggy army jacket dyed brown in a vain attempt at matching the color of the highly shined shoes. Yet she's a handsome woman, and would be even handsomer as a man, even though she's drunk, reeking drunk, most of the time you see her. And she's a mean alcoholic.'

In any case, Rusty is quite open: her kick is intimidating gay officers – to be one is to know one – and threatening to out their sexuality if they give her grief; it's 'one way I become king of my floor in whatever jail I'm in. That is one way. And I am always the king, always the leader, in jail and out.' She's given men a try, but decided against them: 'I had been out with guys a little bit so I knew the score on both sides. I didn't want to be possessed. I didn't want them domineering me. I wanted to be the domineerer.'

The remainder of the book focuses on Rusty and the predominantly lesbian world of the prison. Naturally this leads to a great deal of slang. Some of this relates to whores: *bat* or *owl* (usually nightworkers), *cat, gook, shitkicker* and *fleabag* (down on her luck and probably diseased) for prostitute; *hustle, shitkick, kick the street* for the job, and *freebie* (a no-charge fuck) and *Frenchy* (fellatio) for its services. The remainder reflects lesbian life.

Among the lesbian 'fringe' terms she introduces, drawing on a variety of conversations, are those listed. These are not always reserved to lesbian use only – some overflow into the male gay world, some beyond that into mainstream slang. I have marked those that do seem to exist specifically within this particular world with an *.

ass: sexual intercourse
baby: woman-to-woman address
bulldyke
circus: sex show
party: an orgy
daddy-o: a lover, in the prison world a female
*dog or *guttersnipe*: an inmate who turns temporarily to homosexuality; like the *jailhouse turnout*, seen as ultimately untrustworthy and thus the negative imagery
*drag: male dress as worn by lesbians
duck's ass: the popular male haircut and 'the greatest single affection among the "stud broads"'; such haircuts were forbidden and inmates smashed lightbulbs to obtain ersatz 'razors' with which to cut each other's hair
*femme: a feminine lesbian, a partner or girlfriend
**give up the work to someone*: of a lesbian, to take the active role in sexual intercourse

j.t./jailhouse turnout: one who turns to homosexuality for
    period of incarceration
king: a masculine lesbian
les
love up: to caress
mac it: to wear men's clothing, from, presumably *mack*, a
    pimp
meat rack: a city's primary gay pick-up centre, in this case
    Washington Square Park; the Park and other meat racks
    get substantial mention in John Rechy's 1964 novel of US
    gay life, *City of Night*
mom: a passive partner in a lesbian relationship
play: to be involved in an affair outside one's primary
    relationship
racket: the world of homosexual relationships
square or *straight*: heterosexual
stud broad: masculine lesbian
suck: to perform cunnilingus
swinging: sexually active

The Internet seems, as in so much else, to be making a difference. It is, perhaps, because for once those who have the option to
amass this language are part of those who use it, rather than lexicography's traditional coterie of old and certainly not lesbian men.
The appearance online of a variety of lesbian slang lists may also
be a generational thing. If one's sexuality is far more out than has
been the case, why not one's vocabulary. That said, Julia Penelope
may still be right: her arguments against the need for lesbian slang
are not without justice. And Deborah Cameron, another feminist
linguist, has suggested that however much of such material is
ostensibly online, there are still only a couple of primary sources.

Searching for 'lesbian slang' does indeed generate many hits, and as is always the way with search engines, a relative minority deliver the goods. But the lexis is there, and I have assembled a list based on the most productive websites.* I have generally chosen to maintain the online definitions as written though where headwords appear in a number of websites, with slightly altered metadata, these have sometimes been combined. I have removed those terms which have already been listed above (most of which have already been picked up in print dictionaries).

Like so much on the Internet (especially when it comes to slang), one is hard put to ascertain quite what proportion of this glossary is widely used, what is localised and what was simply thought up to bulk out the list.† What is more interesting is the overriding character of the terms. In the first place, that popular stereotype is completely absent: while there are a variety of sexual references, none deals with cunnilingus. Stimulation with fingers is far more common. There is also far more attention – following Julia Penelope's comments on the in-group's use of dyke or bull-dyke as part of the 'fringe vocabulary' – of the gradations or styles of lesbian life. The lists are often collaborative efforts – I have excluded the regular 'thanks to . . .' or 'submitted by . . .'

* http://www.theotherteam.com/common-lesbian-slang-and-terminology/
https://www.autostraddle.com/20-lesbian-slang-terms-youve-never-heard-before-129728/
http://www.titaniasoho.com/news/lesbianwords
Lesbian Lingo Meanings: By E. J. Rosetta
The Dyketionary
http://themostcake.co.uk/love-life/gay-slang-vol-1-lesbian-toilet-party/
† A random online search came up with the following: *vulva hands* comes up only in the context of a £65 gold pendant that represents them; *stirring the bean curd* and *pillow princess* are among several terms that appear, but only in other glossaries; *manesia* occurs only with a male subject, referring to one who forgets everything he's ever promised a woman; *faux mo* (from *fauxmosexual*) is similar and identifies a man who protests to being gay and dresses and acts accordingly but does so only to attract girls who like gay men. Finally a *Jack and Jill party* is defined as 'an event designed to help raise funds for a betrothed couple's impending nuptials.'

credits. The lists are also far more personalised – in other words humourous – than traditional lexicography can permit itself. However this may represent the medium and the age and, as regards language, 'amateur status' of those involved.

andro/androgynous: a 'unisex' lesbian (neither butch or femme, i.e. neither masculine nor feminine in appearance or behaviour).

baby dyke: a young, newbie lesbian predominately under the age of 25.

bambi-sexuality: physical interaction centred more about touching, kissing, and caressing than around genital sexuality.

beard: a 'beard' is a person of the opposite sex who marries or dates a closeted lesbian or gay person to cover up their homosexuality.

bicurious: a typically straight girl who is somewhat intrigued by the idea of hooking up with another girl. she is 'curious' about her sexuality and interested in exploring relationships with girls.

bumper-to-bumper: vagina-to-vagina. generally used in reference to two lesbians engaging in sex, or dancing, etc. occasionally used in referring to gay men or heterosexual couples.

butch: a masculine lesbian often opting for a more masculine approach to style.

Cantonese groin: a dildo. The term appears in a medieval novel, describing a plant used in China for this purpose.

celebudyke: 'a lesbian who is famous or near-famous for doing almost nothing. Ingrid Casares, who is known primarily because she has dated her way through the lesbian elite, is a prime example. on a local level can refer to a dyke on the scene, whether activist or club hopper, who everybody knows.'

chapstick (*lesbian*): a tomboy lesbian who doesn't quite fit the stud or femme description; usually in between the two extremes; the opposite of a lipstick lesbian, otherwise known as a soft butch; a lesbian who wears chapstick (a transparent lip balm) rather than lipstick.

cliterfearance: the lesbian version of *cock-blocking* (also known as a 'beaver-dam').

comadres: 'in Chicano/Chicana communities of the American southwest, two unmarried women who live together in a close relationship, as in Boston marriage or romantic friendship.'

crone: derogatory term for old, witchlike woman, reclaimed by 1970s feminists as proud names for older lesbians.

daddle: to engage in lesbian sex, in a face-to-face position.

desperation number: a sex partner found just before closing time at the bar.

dez: desire.

Firstly, you must understand that there are 3 states of dez.

1) predez (when you are young and innocent and never been desperate for anyone before . . . good time). 2) dez (when you are are soooo into someone you start acting in a freak like nature. Midnight drunk calls leaving hundreds of tragic messages, stalking, building shrines in their honour. 3) post/anti dez. You are finally over it and never ever want to be such a loon ever again. Your heart is sealed . . . until dez comes back around

dishonorable discharge: to masturbate at home after unsuccessfully going out in search of a sex partner.

drag king: a drag king is a woman who dresses to look like a man, usually for performance; drag kings are often lesbian, but not always.

dyke tyke: 'men, sometimes gay, sometimes straight, who perpetually hang out with lesbian friends, and aspire to lesbianism as a higher consciousness.'

dykealike/doppelbanger: dating a woman who looks just like you/morphs into another version of you.

dyke-o-nomics: the way lesbians interact, work, and exist.

dykon: a lesbian icon, usually a celebrity such as Ellen Degeneres.

fairy lady: 'in the mid-1990s, a lesbian bottom.'

faux mo: straight girls who act/look/seem interested in being queer, but are as straight as they come. bummer.

femme: a feminine lesbian.

FLA: Future Lesbians of America (also known as 'baby dykes').

frig: 'in lesbian sex, to finger fuck or stroke a woman's genitals.' [the word, meaning to masturbate oneself or another, is first recorded in 1598]

fruit fly: a woman who is friends with a gay [i.e. a *fruit*] or bisexual man but who does not have an interest in seducing them like many fag hags do.

funch: a quick sexual encounter performed at lunchtime.

fusion: 'in lesbian love relationships, an intense intimacy between the two partners that causes them to be over-involved in each other; the result is that the differences between the two seem to be lessened, and each partner's ability to maintain and independent identity is weakened. Often blamed for lesbian bed death, or loss of sexual desire. also called merging.'

galimony: 'descriptive term for what is owed to the "divorced" partner of a rich/famous lesbian, generally in the act of suing for same. Coined when Billie Jean King and her former lover became the test case.'

gaybie: a child either adopted by a homosexual couple, a child conceived by a lesbian couple through artificial insemination, or a child carried by a surrogate for a homosexual couple.

gaydar: an intuitive ability to determine whether another person is gay or not. Gaydar relies heavily on social mannerisms and behaviors. The word derives from a combination of gay + radar.

gaysian: an Asian lesbian.

genderqueer: means you don't limit your gender identity to the typical man/woman archetype. For instance, maybe you feel like you're both man and woman, or maybe you feel like you're neither. Either way, it's all good.

gillette blade: a bisexual woman (they 'cut both ways').

girlsloth: 'a lesbian slacker'.

glamour butch: a butch lesbian that like to dress in fine suits and tuxedos.

glamour dyke: 'a lesbian for whom fashion, elegance and glamour are important aspects of personal style and expression.'

gold-star: describing a lesbian who has never had sexual intercourse with a male; being a gold-star lesbian is an excellent method of birth control.

granola lesbian: a lesbian who is usually vagetar . . . sorry vegetarian or vegan and who is either new age or neopagan; thought to be at one with mother nature and rumoured to like a good pair of birkenstocks.

granola-dyke: a lesbian of the birkenstocks-wearing, tofu-eating, folk music-loving, 'earthy crunchy' hippie variety. Often seen with an acoustic guitar.

hasbian: a term used for a woman who previously identified as a lesbian but now dates men.

het-lagged: 'how a gay person feels after having spent the holidays with their hetero extended family, hetero friends from way back, and generally hetero small town, on the other side of the continent.'

hetty: heterosexual.

hold a bowling ball: to sexually stimulate another woman by rubbing the thumb and forefinger, simultaneously, on her clitoris and anus.

hundred footer: a lesbian one can notice from 100 ft. away.

jack and jill party: 'in the late 1980s, a circle jerk (group masturbation party; from slang *jack off* [men] + *jill off* [women]) that welcomed gay men and lesbians, who occasionally had sex with one another.'

jam: 'mid-century slang for straight people.'

janey: vagina.

johnson bar: a dildo [earlier use = a penis; both refer to a reverse bar of an early locomotive].

kiki: 1940s slang for a lesbian comfortable with either a passive or aggressive partner. [possibly linked to *chi-chi*, gay]

kissing fish: lesbians [from slang *fish*, a woman]

lensbian: a woman who engages in lesbian behavior overtly solely for the camera usage: while some believe Lohan had genuine feelings for Samantha, most of the American public insist that Lindsey is nothing more than a lensbian.

lesbian bed death: invented by sex researcher Pepper Schwartz to describe the supposedly inevitable diminishment of sexual passion (and activity) in a long term lesbian relationship.

lesbian thought police: 'extreme political correctness, based on the idea that there is one certain way that all lesbians should think. A lesbian who feels guilt about her s/m sexual fantasies, for example, might joke that she is going to be hunted down by the lesbian thought police.'

lesbro: a non-creepy straight guy who really just wants to hang with the dykes.

lipstick/lipstick lesbian: a lipstick lesbian is a woman who loves other women, but also loves her clothes and makeup and shoes. she tends to dress on the femmy side; the lipstick lesbian is considered the most girly breed of bi/gay woman.

lipstick mafia: group of (generally femme) lesbians who either 1) work to recruit new lesbians into the lesbian community or 2) form a close-knit protective circle around members of their group of friends.

l.p.: (lesbian potential): used in 'spot the gay' scenarios in public places, i.e. 'she's got high lp'.

LUG (lesbian until graduation): the dorm roommate experimenter who stops lesbian encounters after college.

luke: the coital fluid in a woman.

luppies: 'lesbian yuppies.'

LURD (lesbian until release date): a female inmate who, due to the lack of men in prison, resort to lesbianism.

make scissors of someone: to masturbate a woman by simultaneously rubbing her clitoris with the thumb and her anus with the forefinger.

manesia: a term bisexual women use when they fall for a guy and then change their mind when he whips it out. Like amnesia . . . but with men. i.e. 'I got manesia and then remembered I like tits too much.'

missionary work: an attempt by a gay man or lesbian to seduce a straight person of the same sex.

molly dyke: the more passive woman in a lesbian relationship or liaison.

noodle: a curious straight woman: straight until she is wet. Also, spaghetti.

pancake: 'among African-American lesbians in the 1950s, a butch who allowed herself to be flipped (from "top" to "bottom").'

pants: butch.

pillow princess/pillow queen: a lesbian who is more than willing to receive oral sex from a woman, but not at all willing to perform oral sex on another woman.

platinum-star: describing a lesbian who has not even kissed a male.

poppa: an underage lesbian.

primary lesbian: 'a woman who experiences her lesbianism as innate or biologically determined, rather than as chosen or elected.'

pumps: femme [*anglice*: high heels]

running-shoe lesbian: 'lesbians, usually over thirty-five, who wear jogging shoes with everything (also called a *yuppie dyke*).'

scissoring: the smooshing together of lady parts, keeping your legs apart in the shape of a pair of half opened scissors; mainly fictional and most probably invented by porn.

sergeant: 'in the mid-1990s, a butch lesbian.'

slacks: a lesbian; the term is now considered obsolete.

soft butch: a lesbian whose appearance tends to be on the butch side but is softer and more feminine in nature; can also be used to refer to a lesbian that is in between 'butch' and 'femme', but usually closer to the butch side.

sport fishing: when a straight girl flirts with a lesbian with no intention of following through, testing whether or not she can get a lesbian want her; called sport fishing because no one eats any fish.

stem: a lesbian who identifies somewhere between 'stud' and 'femme.'

stirring the bean curd: 'English translation of a Chinese term for the lesbian sexual act of finger-fucking.'

strum queen: a lesbian that likes to masturbate in front of other lesbians.

stud: a lesbian who exhibits dominate behaviour. Tends to be butch; what some ill-informed individuals would refer to as 'the man'.

switch: a lesbian (or otherwise) who acts as both a submissive and a dominant, switching back and forth between the two; predominantly used in sexual terms.

tit king: a lesbian attracted to women with large breasts.

toaster oven: a toaster-oven is a marker of a gay woman's sexual experience with a straight woman: as in, if you turn a straight girl, you get a toaster-oven.*

top: the more dominant woman of a sexual relationship, who often prefers to give pleasure.

* 'The term, as so many gay things do, comes from *Ellen*, that seminal offering from the inimitable Ellen Degeneres. In the "Puppy" episode . . . in which Ms. Degeneres came out . . . A friend of hers named Susan reveals that she's like, a lesbian, innit. Ellen, still pretending to be a woman of the heterosexual persuasion . . . accuses Susan of trying to "recruit" her to the homosexual army. Susan sarcastically says that she'd have to call national headquarters and inform them of her failure to, in fact, recruit, Ellen, and states that, had she been successful, she would have been rewarded with a toaster oven.'

tourist: a straight person in a gay bar. someone 'seeing the sights' without actually wanting to . . . you know . . . buy any souvenirs . . .

U-haul: to move in with another lesbian woman after only dating or barely knowing the woman usage: the problem with kathleen and nina was they moved too fast; they totally u-hauled after a week of knowing each other. Thus *U-haul lesbian*: a lesbian who tends to move in fairly quickly with those she dates.

vulva hands: 'a gesture used in lesbian gatherings during the 1980s, probably originating in the women's peace camp at Greenham common in England and continuing at the Seneca women's peace encampment in upstate New York, and indicating the strength of lesbian sexuality. The two forefingers and thumbs were placed together to form a triangle, and then the hands were held over the head in the air; some lesbian jewelry still employs the image of vulva hands.'

zap/zap action: 'a form of direct action intended to be loud, quick and showy, to capture media attention.'

Conclusion

Slang has a job. It provides – subject to certain long-established stereotypes and topics – a means of saying what in standard language for one reason or another – typically secrecy or good manners – is considered unsayable. Nothing in that sentence establishes the least restriction as regards gender. This is not to deny that in nearly forty years of excavating sources for a succession of slang dictionaries, I have to accept that there have proved to be more of those focused on or written by men than by women. (Or any other gender, though as I have said, slang is deeply traditionalist and is more than satisfied with the usual duopoly.) How I would wish that this were not so, and that I could plunge my hand into some form of lexical lucky dip and pull out a whole confection of women-created material that has hitherto escaped discovery. There is doubtless some – recent advances in looking at women's contributions to history may track them down – and there is doubtless some undiscovered men's work too, but I would suggest that in the main those of us who research slang's past have explored most basements and thrown open most attic doors.

Whether readers will agree with me I cannot say, but my own feeling, at the end of this book, is that I see slang more than ever as an equal-opportunity employee. There are no restrictions,

certainly no VIP room: slang is open to all. Yes, there is ventriloquy but I have tried to show that this goes in more than one
direction. And sometimes, even if a man has prepared the
preliminary sketch (as, for instance, a song-writer), it is the
woman (as performer) who has completed the picture, brought
the colour and the subtle definition and rendered the outline
three-dimensional. There have certainly been social constraints
– almost invariably artificial and of no actual value – that have
persuaded some women that slang was an area of language that
they should avoid. If these constraints have gradually been
eroded and even tossed aside, then I see that as all to the good
and I would hope that today's women agree. The arguments that
sought to restrain the 'new woman' in all her many guises are as
absurd today as they were when some man or fellow-travelling
woman thought them up.

What I cannot do, nor will my researches give me ingress to
such information, is find what does not seem to be there, nor
will I rewrite the past through sensibilities that are driven by the
true beliefs (no doubt as ephemeral as any) of the present.
Counter-factuals are fun, but ultimately irrelevant. Of course
my research may be inadequate and I may have missed vital
material. I say again: bring it on.

Write about what you know, runs the instruction, usually in
the context of fiction, but it works for non-fiction too. The
difference, I would suggest, is that the writer of non-fiction must
make the effort to broaden that knowledge. This, of course, is
called research. Looking at women's relationship to slang, a topic
that as far as I know has not yet been analysed, research has
taken me to many new places. But there are dead ends, and
certain beliefs have foundered on such facts as I have found. If
this research has at times proved frustrating, and made all too

clear why this is a topic that has not hitherto been addressed, then so be it.

Nor, in my rooting around the waterfront, have I been able to follow every wynd and ginnel. The use of slang is wide-ranging: as I found when composing my dictionary, one cannot look at everything, and must focus more practically on those sources where the rewards are greatest. I have no doubt, for instance, that the burgeoning world of young adult novels or of romance (often historical, often self-made and regularly more adventure-some as regards gender pairings than has hitherto been the case) have examples of slang. It is not to belittle either that I have not attempted to read this vast outpouring (and as for much histori-cal fiction, there is no point: the slang use, however accurate, is inevitably artificial).

When pondering and then pitching this book I realised quickly that it had never been attempted before. The reason may be that it was a leap too far, a study in piling up bricks in the absence of even a single straw. I would like to believe otherwise. If it proves a first, minuscule step in assessing a sub-set of language, then all to the good. Ladies and gents, roll up! Don't let me stand in your way.

Acknowledgements

G IVEN THE CENTRALITY of my slang researches to this book, I should begin by thanking, not for the first time, everyone who has been involved in that research since the *Green's Dictionary of Slang* project began in 1993. Times have changed, the book has been online since 2016 and aside from myself, the sole survivor is my partner Susie Ford, almost certainly the most skilful researcher of slang citations ever.

The genesis of this book came around 3 a.m. in a Caribbean bar in Oxford and a conversation with Sarah Iversen and Michael Adams.

For the specific purposes of this book I would also like to note certain names:

Michael Adams
Zoe Apostolides
Deborah Cameron
Judith Flanders
Nick Groom
Sarah Hoem Iversen
Katharine Connor Martin
Anthony Rhys

plus Kate Lister, who has been kind enough to take time off from her own work (both academic and as the curator of the Twitter account *@whoresofyore*) to write a Foreword.

That I owe much to Lisa Moylett, my agent, is of course a given.

At Robinson, my publisher Duncan Proudfoot, Amanda Keats, Una McGovern, Hannah Witchell and the rest of the team.

Index